Chapters.

AF470977

7 10 11 12 20 23 25 28.

Chap 6

THE NATIONALIZED INDUSTRIES
SINCE 1960
A Book of Readings

EDITED BY

LEONARD TIVEY

Senior Lecturer in Public Administration
University of Birmingham

for the

ROYAL INSTITUTE OF PUBLIC ADMINISTRATION

LONDON · GEORGE ALLEN & UNWIN LTD

RUSKIN HOUSE MUSEUM STREET

First published in 1973

ISBN 0 04 338054 9 hardback
0 04 338055 7 paperback

Printed in Great Britain
in 10 point Plantin type
by Alden & Mowbray Ltd
at the Alden Press, Oxford

PREFACE

The aim of this volume is to provide a selection of readings that illustrate and explain the development of nationalized industries in Britain between 1960 and 1970. Its main intention is to follow a previous collection edited by Professor A. H. Hanson and published in 1963. The selection covers a broadly similar range of topics, and maintains the same non-technical level of discourse.

However, this collection must fall short of its predecessor for two reasons. In the first place the tragic death of Professor Hanson in 1971 has deprived the present editor of his advice and guidance in shaping the collection. His helpful encouragement at the inception of the volume has made the deprivation at later stages all the more noticeable and harder to sustain.

Secondly, a rapid rise in the costs of book production has compelled a drastic reduction in the length of this volume. This has necessitated the removal of many useful items originally planned for inclusion, and the curtailment of others. In this process the aim has been to keep a balance in the range of subject-matter, but material on particular industries has perhaps suffered more than other sections. There has been some editing within the various items, but it is hoped that sufficient body has been retained to keep the readings readable. In the introductions to the various chapters, there are references to sources not reprinted, and these at least provide some sort of guidance to items which it has not been possible to include.

The period covered here is, of course, much shorter than in Professor Hanson's volume. Nevertheless, the amount of usable mate ial has been very great. In particular, there are now a great many 'official' publications on the nationalized industries. A high proportion of the extracts come from such publications, a tendency accentuated by the curtailment of the length of the volume. This stress reflects, however, a genuine change in the state of writing on this subject, and is not merely the result of editorial preference. Indeed, greater attention to particular industries would have led to more material not only from the reports of the

Select Committee but also from those of the National Board for Prices and Incomes.

This volume could not have been compiled without a great deal of help and advice. In particular I am grateful to Mr D. N. Chester and Professor W. A. Robson for general guidance on some critical problems; to Mr Richard Pryke for numerous suggestions; and to Professor David Murray and the members of nationalized industries team at the Open University for appraisal and support. I would also like to thank Dr E. F. Schumacher, formerly economic adviser to the National Coal Board, for his advice; and numerous public relations officers in the nationalized industries for advice and for large quantities of relevant material. It was impossible to use the bulk of this material in any case, and the curtailment of the volume has reduced it still further. Mr Raymond Nottage and Mr Ivor Shelley of the Royal Institute of Public Administration have provided guidance and much practical help. I am also most grateful to Miss Marjorie Davies, secretary to the Department of Political Science, University of Birmingham, for meticulous typing and patient photocopying; and to Miss Gill Lucas for research help.

For the result and all its inadequacies, both in the final selection of the readings and the accompanying material, the responsibility is mine.

LEONARD TIVEY

Department of Political Science
University of Birmingham
February 1972

CONTENTS

CHAPTER I

BRITISH NATIONALIZATION IN THE 1960s

The 1960s were years of constructive development for the British nationalized industries, in spite of critical problems in the economy as a whole. The development was manifested not only in the performance of most of the industries, but also in the fashioning of techniques of control and accountability, and in some evolution of structure and organization.

THE POSITION IN 1960

The situation at the beginning of the 1960s may be sketched as a beginning. By then the general outline of nationalization in Britain had become familiar, and seemed to have achieved some political stability. The role of public enterprise in the British economy was largely, but not entirely, concentrated in the basic industries of power and transport. Nationally owned industry is not, of course, by any means the whole of the public sector of the economy – this includes the central administration, local authorities, and the armed forces. Nor is nationally owned industry the whole of public enterprise, for this must include many activities of local authorities. Furthermore, not all nationally owned industries are in the form of public corporations, for there is some government shareholding – for example in Cable and Wireless Ltd, in Short Brothers and Harland, and now in Rolls-Royce (1971) Ltd.

Nevertheless, in spite of these exceptions and clarifications, there is no doubt that the great industrial public corporations hold the centre of the stage, and it is with them that this volume is almost entirely concerned.

Briefly, in 1960 the fuel and power industries were very largely nationalized, the petroleum industry and the merchanting of coal being exceptions. The National Coal Board controlled the whole of its industry, with some ancillary interests and some brickmaking capacity. Electricity was by 1960 controlled by a structure of bodies: the Electricity Council with supervisory duties; the Central Electricity Generating

Board; and twelve Area Electricity Boards concerned with distribution. In Scotland there were two separate electricity corporations, the North of Scotland Hydro-Electricity Board and the South Scotland Electricity Board. In 1954 a new public corporation, the United Kingdom Atomic Energy Authority, was set up, concerned with research and development including that of nuclear generating stations. The gas industry had a federal structure, the Gas Council co-ordinating the Area Gas Boards, which covered the whole of Great Britain.

In 1960 the British Transport Commission was still in control of the various parts of inland transport, though by the Transport Act of 1962 it was broken up. Thereafter the British Railways Board with strong regional organization dealt only with railways, and the British Waterways Board and the British Transport Docks Board were set up, together with a Transport Holding Company described in chapter II. London Transport also became separate.

The other industrial corporations in 1960 were the two airlines, British European Airways and the British Overseas Airways Corporation.

These industries were beset with critical problems – of falling demand in some cases, of mounting demand in others, often of changing technology. There were, however, more general problems, connected with the status and functioning of the public corporation, and with the proper definition of the role of the industries in the economy – in other words, problems of accountability, control, and objectives. The most signal contribution of the 1950s to this situation was the establishment, by the House of Commons, of the Select Committee on Nationalized Industries in 1956. There are sufficient excerpts from the reports of this committee in this volume to give some idea of its work: but in reports and in the evidence for them the material of the SCNI has provided a wealth of information which can only be glimpsed in this volume. The existence of SCNI did much to improve general public and parliamentary understanding of the industries, and its early reports were important in that they emphasized the need for improvements in other matters – in particular, for clarification of the methods of control and of economic objectives.

There had been some initiative in these matters, it is true, in the Herbert report of 1956 on electricity supply (Cmd. 9672), which had declared that the industry should not undertake anything 'other than a purely economic course unless so instructed by the Minister'. But without further guidance, about for instance proper rates of return on capital, it was not clear what the 'purely economic' interests of an industry were. Further elucidation, and the determination of certain issues by the government, was necessary: and this began with the White

Paper *Financial and Economic Obligations of the Nationalized Industries* (Cmnd. 1337) in 1961. This was noted in Professor Hanson's volume, and it is briefly repeated in this one. It marked the culmination of the first phase of the problem: later developments are recorded in this volume.

MAJOR DEVELOPMENTS 1960–70

There was one major extension of nationalization in the usual sense in the decade: the renationalization of steel. In the period 1948–53 there had been a major party-political controversy over the first attempt to nationalize the industry. The Labour Party had continued with its intention to nationalize, and though there were critical divisions on the issue in the House of Commons in the period 1964–66, when the government had only a tiny majority, the necessary legislation was passed in 1967.

What happened to the existing industries in this decade?

In the fuel and power corporations there was not much structural change. The National Coal Board simplified its organization in 1967, and the Gas Council acquired new powers in 1965. But there was great technical and industrial change. The coal industry contracted dramatically, from an output of 194 million tons in 1960 to 147 million tons in 1970, while vastly improving its mechanization and its productivity. Its manpower policies during this contraction must be counted as one of its major successes. The electricity industry expanded from an output capacity of 27,000 megawatts in 1960 to 47,000 megawatts in 1970, while patiently establishing a new status agreement for its staff. The gas industry underwent two production revolutions: first, from coal-burning to oil-burning plant and imported methane; and second, to natural gas from under the North Sea. The atomic energy industry continued its search for economic nuclear generation of electricity.

In the communication and transport sector, on the other hand, the period was one of wide structural change. The Post Office was transformed from a government department to a public corporation in 1969; and London Transport was transferred from the auspices of the Ministry of Transport to those of the Greater London Council in January 1970. The other transport industries were twice restructured, following an earlier restructuring in the mid-1950s. After 1955 the railways were proceeding with a programme of modernization, involving electrification and diesel traction. The chronic deficits of the railways, however, brought the reshaping policies of Dr Richard Beeching in the early 1960s; and this was accompanied by the division of other transport concerns already mentioned. The Labour government undertook its own new policy-making, later in the decade, resulting in a set of White Papers and the great Transport Act of 1968. This meant new corporations in the shape of the Passenger Transport Executives in conurbations, of the National Bus Company, the Scottish Transport Group and the National Freight Corporation.

In air transport a new body, the British Airports Authority, took over international airports in 1966. It rapidly became concerned with the development of a third London airport. The ensuing controversies led to the appointment of the Roskill Commission, which reported in favour of a site at Cublington (1971); nevertheless, the government chose Foulness. The airlines themselves had times of financial difficulty, but kept well abreast of international standards in their industry. Their future was reviewed at the end of the decade in the Edwards report on *British Air Transport in the Seventies* (Cmnd. 4018, 1969).

THE TREND OF THE DECADE

It is in the question of government control of the corporations, however, rather than in their structure, that the most marked trend of the decade can be seen. The central theme, dealt with particularly in chapters 3 and 5, has been the rationalization of control and performance by economic criteria. In general, the decade could be characterized for the nationalized industries as the era of the economists. What began as plain assertion with the Herbert report on electricity in 1956 became sophisticated calculation by 1967. This work goes on: economists have applied themselves to the problems, and they have propounded answers. In contrast, there has been little political or administrative study of the industries. They have become unpopular subjects.

The consequences of this 'economization' have been in many ways admirable: there has been clarification and a new efficiency. It has however brought a conceptual change which is sometimes unnoticed and often underrated. It has now become normal to look upon the nationalized industry as a large firm which is publicly owned; and this is not quite the same thing as being a special part of the machinery of government. This revised outlook has been reflected in practice. The British Steel Corporation did not take over the whole industry; and it included elements not strictly in the steel industry. Other industries were encouraged by the Labour government (but not its Conservative successor) to undertake sidelines as it suited them. There was furthermore a growing interest in 'mixed enterprise' and in the use of the company form – for instance, by the Transport Holding Company, and later by the National Freight Corporation and the National Bus Company. Not that there was any acute loss of faith in the public corporation; indeed, the creation of the Airports Authority and the Post Office Corporation seemed to show renewed confidence. But there was a new flexibility of approach, and this was more amenable to the idea of the nationalized 'industry' being in fact a large firm, rather than an administrative sector of the economy.

Whether the shift in concept is altogether satisfactory cannot be decided here. It can perhaps be argued that the concentration on economic criteria of performance has sometimes obscured the political and administrative purposes of control.

THE POLITICAL BACKGROUND

Professor Hanson's volume began with readings from the period when there was scarcely any nationalization of industry. The concept of the public corporation was then little formed, and the creation of the corporations by legislation in the period 1945–50 in fact consolidated the institutional form. The contents of that volume show therefore something new being fashioned out of deep political controversy. In the decade covered by this volume, there is some expansion of nationalization – most obviously into the steel industry – and some restructuring. The political background, however, was not irrelevant to the emphasis on functional efficiency and on economic concepts.

It is an oversimplification however to present controversy about nationalization as a crude political issue, with the Labour Party in favour and the Conservative Party against. The currents of opinion within the parties, and outside them, have been too complex, and too fluctuating, for any such generalization. Yet it remains true that, on balance and taking one thing with another, the attitudes of the Labour party tend to be benign and those of most Conservatives suspicious.

At the beginning of the 1960s the Labour party was divided by a fierce dispute about fundamental party doctrine. The leader of the party, Hugh Gaitskell, and others wished to modify the principle set out in the party constitution, which referred to 'the common ownership of the means of production, distribution and exchange'. The attempt to remove this pronouncement was unsuccessful; but in retrospect it can be seen that a more pragmatic outlook had emerged. In the Labour party programmes of the 1960s there was still a sympathy for public enterprise, but it is seen as a means to improved economic growth and technological progress. This adjustment of attitude was a formative influence on the policies towards nationalization of the Labour government from 1964.

The Conservative party, in office in the 1950s, had completed most of intended denationalization – its programme at the 1964 general election proposed merely to denationalize remaining parts of the steel industry, mainly Richard Thomas and Baldwins. In the early 1960s, the Conservative government was in process of readjusting its economic policies and searching for institutionalized methods of economic planning. It was obviously necessary for the nationalized industries to play a major part in this work. The Conservatives seemed inclined to accept a *status quo* situation as far as the general structure of the industries went: the main alterations were in transport.

After 1964 the government was provided by the Labour party. It therefore had the opportunity to put its new pragmatism into effect. There was in fact some new nationalization in this period, and the Labour party's long insistence on renationalization of steel was used by its critics as evidence of dogmatism. In turn it accused its opponents of doctrinaire hostility to public ownership, stressed the weakness of the existing arrangements in steel, and concerned itself with a variety of measures in other industries both public and private. There is no denying that the Labour government was highly interventionist in its industrial philosophy. It began with an attempt at a National Plan and made sustained efforts to achieve an incomes policy. It encouraged industrial progress through Economic Development Committees, and tried to influence regional development by investment grants. It set up a public corporation, the Industrial Reorganization Corporation, in 1966 which had substantial funds available to assist the merger or establishment of industrial firms, and it promoted the Industrial Expansion Act of 1968 which gave the government power to acquire enterprises, or shares in enterprises, by agreement without further legislation. All these ventures stressed the government's concern with industrial operations and with the direct promotion of its efficiency.

This general approach – intervention in the cause of efficiency – was apparent in the policies towards nationalized industries; and the pragmatic expansion, the structural flexibility and economic rationalization can be seen to be in line with this outlook. This in turn can be seen as the product of the revisionist shift in principles and the technological emphasis given to Labour party policies in the early 1960s.

THE SELECTION OF READINGS

The nature of nationalized-industry concern is reflected in another way in the choice of contents in this volume. A very high proportion of the material comes from 'official' sources of one sort or another. Some of this is from the government, much from the Select Committee, some from the corporations themselves. It does, however, indicate that much of the development in ideas had been effectively harnessed to the problems, through institutional channels. There is a good deal of work by academic economists which is not reflected here, because it is of a specialized nature.[1] Nevertheless, both material stemming from political controversy and material of an academic nature on administrative aspects is sparse, compared with that available for Professor Hanson's volume.

The focus of this collection must be fact of nationalization, and this means that the items chosen cannot fully illustrate the economic and other problems of the various industries. Not all the material is generalized, of course: a good deal does relate to particular industries. But the reader must be well aware that for full examination of fuel policy, or transport policy, other sources will be necessary. The aim here is to use such material as vitally concerned British nationalized industries in the period.

The extracts in chapter II give indications of the new and revised structures that were set up in the period. In chapter III the key issues of economic criteria of performance are explained, and in chapter IV the economies and the policies of particular industries are described. Chapter V presents the arguments of the decade about accountability and control, and in chapter VI important material about the organization of some of the industries is extracted. The final chapter takes the reader to the frontiers of the industries – in employee relations and in customer relations.

In the extracts and the accompanying footnotes there are many references to material that has not been reprinted here. In general, these references have been retained as a matter of policy. They provide means of direct recourse from the readings to the original sources, and they often indicate where statements are based on other authorities.

[1] See, for example, R. Turvey (ed.), *Public Enterprise – selected readings*, Penguin, 1968.

CHAPTER II

NEW STRUCTURES

The great creative period in British nationalization was of course the late 1940s, but the 1960s provided a period of secondary growth. As explained in chapter I the political temper of the period was very different from that of the 1940s, and the spread of public enterprise was cautious and pragmatic: and this meant a more flexible approach to structural arrangements.

Signs of this new approach can be detected before the arrival of the 1964 Labour government. The Conservative government's Transport Act of 1962 replaced the British Transport Commission with a more fragmented structure. One of the elements in this was the Transport Holding Company, a body reminiscent of the Italian system of public enterprise if not actually copied therefrom.[1] The Conservative government was also concerned with policy for British airports and proposals for an independent body were made in a White Paper *Civil Aerodromes and Air Navigational Services* (Cmnd. 1457) of August 1961. The result of this policy was establishment of the British Airports Authority as a public corporation, which took over the main national airports, at Heathrow, Gatwick, Stansted and Prestwick in April 1966.

There can be no doubt, however, that the principal new structure of the period was nationalized steel, in the shape of the British Steel Corporation, created by the Iron and Steel Act of 1967. There is only space in this volume to give the Labour government's White Paper on *Steel Nationalization* (Cmnd. 2651). There was, however, extensive debate about the state of the industry. It is a fair assumption that without some ideological preference on the part of the Labour government there would have been no public ownership; nevertheless there was widespread acceptance that some reform and large-scale reorganization was necessary.[2] In that sense, the nationalization of steel can still be

---

[1] See J. J. Richardson, 'The Transport Holding Company and the Transport White Paper', *Public Administration*, vol. 45, Autumn 1967.

[2] For the debate, see Richard Pryke, *Why Steel*, Fabian Society, 1965, and the Federation of British Industries, *British Industry and the Proposal to Nationalise*

regarded as a continuation of the type of nationalization that occurred in the coal, gas, and electricity industries in the 1940s, where a Labour party case for socialization was accompanied, at least, by some need for rationalization.

The public corporation set up by the Act was mainly of the classical type, but there were one or two new features of interest. There was no attempt to take the whole of the steel industry into public ownership: only the fourteen largest firms were concerned, and therefore an appreciable privately-owned sector still remains in the industry. However, these firms were taken over as going concerns, and their ancillary activities were included. Some civil engineering and wire manufacture was therefore part of the Corporation at the outset, and the possibility of further diversification was envisaged (paras. 28 and 29). Soon after the establishment of the Corporation an experiment in employee representation on various boards within was begun; and this is discussed in chapter VII.

Transport had already been reconstructed by the Act of 1962, but new developments were put in hand by the Labour government. Many of the policies involved are relevant to chapter IV. The structural programme, out of which emerged the four Passenger Transport Executives in conurbations (Tyneside, the West Midlands, Selnec, and Merseyside), the National Bus Company, and the Scottish Transport Group is explained in an extract from the government's White Paper of 1967. The Transport Executives were supervised to begin with by Passenger Transport Authorities, but in the 1970s proposals for local government reform envisaged large metropolitan authorities which could undertake this role. A White Paper on the *Transport of Freight* (Cmnd. 3470) described the role of another public corporation, the National Freight Corporation, to manage goods transport by road and rail, and an extract from this is included. It should be added that part of this reorganization in transport was the transfer of London Transport, one of the earliest public corporations, from the ambit of the Ministry of Transport to that of the Greater London Council.

One of the most interesting structural changes of the decade was the creation of a new Post Office Corporation. This was the final stage in an evolution that had begun in the 1930s. The gradual adoption of new organization and new accounting methods had been accompanied by vast changes in telecommunications, and in the 1960s a Giro payment

Steel, 1965. For the industrial background, see Iron and Steel Board, *Development in the Iron and Steel Industry*, special reports 1961 and 1964; and British Iron and Steel Federation, *The Steel Industry: the stage 1 report*, 1966 (the Benson report).

system was added to Post Office services. The changes foreshadowed in the excerpt from the White Paper printed here were embodied in the Post Office Act of 1969 and the new Corporation came into operation on 1 October 1969.

The other notable statutory change of the period consisted of additional powers granted to the Gas Council in the Gas Act of 1965, not the subject of an extract here. This gave the national Gas Council powers of co-ordination, and of manufacture, acquisition and supply of gas which it had not had before; added up to three members to the Gas Council; and made provision for underground storage of gas.

It has been emphasized in chapter 1 that the period was one of flexibility and experimentation. Some examples may be mentioned. The Industrial Reorganization Corporation was a public corporation, but it can scarcely be called a nationalized industry. The nature of the IRC may be better understood by reference to the White Paper of 1966 (Cmnd. 2889) and to its annual reports. It aimed to encourage mergers and changes in industrial structure by advice, persuasion, and perhaps by temporary financial involvement. In particular, it should be distinguished from the operations under the Industrial Expansion Act of 1968. The purpose of this legislation was to facilitate government shareholding by agreement and here measures of public ownership clearly were contemplated, as described in Cmnd. 3509 of January 1968. The IRC had a busy career, being involved in several notable mergers. The industrial expansion legislation brought fewer results. Both measures were repealed by the Conservative government in 1971. The Labour government also interested itself in the power of public sector purchasing, but its main contribution *Public Purchasing and Industrial Efficiency* (Cmnd. 3291, 1967) was concerned with the central government, not with the nationalized industries.

It would not be out of place to record here some proposals of the period about nationalization that did not result in action. In 1965 the Plowden committee reported on its *Inquiry into the Aircraft Industry* (Cmnd. 2853), and the majority recommended government shareholding in the British Aircraft Corporation and in Hawker Siddeley, as 'the basis for a suitable partnership between public and private capital in the circumstances peculiar to this industry'. But other policies were followed. The most substantial move which failed in the end to bring about public ownership was in the ports. The report of a Labour party study group in June 1966 recommended public ownership of the ports by a National Ports Authority, with regional authorities as the sole employers; these bodies would include workers' representatives. A fully-fledged scheme appeared in the White Paper *The Reorganization of the Ports* (Cmnd. 3903, 1969). This proposed a National Ports Authority to take over ten existing port authorities and the British Transport Docks Board. The Labour government fell, however, before the plan was enacted. A further report of relevance is of course that of the Edwards committee on *British Air Transport in the Seventies* (Cmnd. 4018, May 1969), of which a brief excerpt is printed. This had much influence, particularly on the establishment of an independent 'second-force' airline, and proposals arising from it, including the establishment of a Civil Aviation Authority, were announced in the House of Commons by the Conservative government on 24 November 1970. Again, there was considerable controversy in the second half of the decade about the structure of the nuclear power industry. This can be followed in two reports of the Select Committee on Science and Technology (H.C. 381–XVII of session 1966–67 and H.C. 401 of session 1968–69), a statement by the Minister of Technology in the House of Commons on 17 July 1968, and a Bill debated in the House of Lords on 14 and 23 April 1970. The Bill was not enacted before the general election and the fall of the Labour government. Two other Bills were also lost: one to re-organize the gas industry, and one concerned with the electricity industry. In 1972, the Conservative government brought forward new plans for the establishment of a British Gas Corporation.

Four major readings are included; on steel, public transport, freight, and the Post Office. A fifth item summarizes the views of the Edwards committee on the ownership of civil airlines.

1. STEEL NATIONALIZED[1]

III. DEFECTS OF THE PRESENT SYSTEM

10. The government do not believe that the system of private ownership in the main part of the steel industry, combined with the present form of public supervision, or indeed any workable version of such supervision, can be reconciled with the national interest and with the proper functioning of private enterprise itself. There are three reasons for this. First, the steel industry has a dynamic and positive role to play in sustaining a satisfactory rate of general economic development and the balanced distribution of such development between regions. The powers of the Iron and Steel Board are, however, essentially negative. They can, within limits, prevent action which is contrary to the public interest; they cannot insist on positive developments which are in the interest of the nation but which, for commercial reasons,

[1] From White Paper, *Steel Nationalization*, April 1965, Cmnd. 2651, paras. 10-39. Reprinted with permission of the Controller of Her Majesty's Stationery Office.

individual companies may be unwilling to undertake. Conflict between the requirements of private enterprise, with its responsibilities to its shareholders, and the requirements of the public interest, has arisen in the past and is, in the nature of things, likely to recur in the future so long as the industry is in private hands. Thus, there were differences of view about the timing and location of the provision in recent years of the new strip mill capacity in South Wales and Scotland; and a settlement of these problems was achieved only with government intervention and the injection of public funds on a large scale. While adequate capacity has now been created to cover requirements for some years ahead, new decisions will have to be taken in that period. It is, in the government's view, wrong to allow a situation to persist in which effective plans to meet these vital needs should continue to be dependent on the initiative of private interests; and in which State control over the industry results in the granting of substantial, and perhaps exclusive, privileges to particular private concerns.

11. Second, difficulties have arisen over the financing of expansion programmes. Over the past 10 to 15 years public money totalling over £400 million in aggregate has been provided to the steel companies. With technological progress and the growth in the size and complexity of units, the cost of major projects in the steel industry is high and increasing. A single new large integrated works may cost £150 million – substantially more than the cost of a nuclear power station. There are difficulties in raising private funds for projects of this sort, which take many years to complete and which, when completed, have to go through a long commissioning period before they can earn a return on capital sufficient to attract private enterprise. These difficulties are increased when, as happened in the case of the strip mill expansion programme, the national interest requires provision of additional capacity to be made on a larger scale and rather earlier than could be justified on a strict commercial view. The government think that if the industry continues in private ownership, the need for further public assistance is likely to recur over the years, or alternatively, that prices will tend to be fixed at an unnecessarily high level in order to provide the necessary finance.

12. Third, despite the provision in the Iron and Steel Act, 1953, requiring the Iron and Steel Board to promote the efficient, economic and adequate supply *under competitive conditions* of iron and steel products, the system was operated in such a way that there has been very little competition on price between British steel companies selling in this country. This tendency towards arrangements of a monopoly type is not confined to this country; the capital-intensive nature of the industry and the effects upon it of cyclical fluctuations in demand, are

well known. The industry in the United Kingdom entered into arrangements to ensure that members generally observed as actual selling prices the maximum prices fixed by the Iron and Steel Board under the Iron and Steel Act, 1953, and sought to defend this as justifiable before the Restrictive Practices Court. One of these arrangements was the subject of an enquiry by the Court which, in its judgment on 22 June 1964, found that it 'must be declared contrary to the public interest'. Since then, that agreement and others of the same type in the industry have been abandoned, but it does not follow that effective and widespread price competition will emerge. Because of the size of its units and the nature of its market, the steel industry here, as in other countries, is likely to tend towards common pricing through price leadership. In the government's view, these monopoly characteristics in this basic industry point to the need for public ownership under which price policy would be determined and prices fixed with regard only to the public interest.

IV. THE GOVERNMENT'S PROPOSALS

Objectives of the New Arrangements

13.   The government's proposals are designed not merely to remedy the manifest weaknesses inherent in the arrangements introduced in 1953 but also to secure further advantages as follows:

(a) Investment and capacity

The present negative control by the Iron and Steel Board over projects initiated by the individual companies will be replaced by central planning of investment programmes under which new projects will be initiated in accordance with a national programme designed to ensure that adequate new capacity is provided and that major new units of plant are located in accordance with the national interest. Under such a programme, it will be possible to strike the right economic balance between continuing to use obsolescent plant and incurring capital expenditure to replace it, and to ensure that effect is given to the conclusions of such analysis.

(b) Production and marketing

Central planning of production and marketing over the main part of the industry will make it possible to concentrate production in the most advantageous fashion in the national interest and to eliminate uneconomic practices such as unnecessary crosshauls. The development of new management techniques, including the central use of computers, makes it possible to plan production and marketing centrally in some detail; full advantage can only be taken of these techniques by using them to secure the best pattern of production and marketing for the main part of the industry as a whole and not merely for the individual companies. This will improve the industry's service to consumers generally.

(c) Exports

Expansion of exports of iron and steel as such becomes increasingly difficult as more countries develop their own steel industries. The Iron and Steel Board and the British Iron and Steel Federation foresee no increase in such exports between 1964 and 1970. The improvement in its competitive efficiency under nationalization will assist the British steel industry to meet these difficulties and, even more important, will contribute to the exports of the engineering and other steel-using industries. Common ownership of the main units of the steel industry should further help the export drive by making possible a better organisation of iron and steel exports by concentrating them on works best placed to meet overseas requirements; and under nationalization the need to develop exports will be taken fully into account in decisions on the siting of new works.

14. Central planning of the positive kind described in sub-paragraphs (a), (b) and (c) above and a far-reaching rationalization of the structure of the industry require common ownership of the main producing units, thus permitting the finances of the main part of the industry to be dealt with as a whole. Common ownership should also make it possible to improve the central services, particularly in the fields of raw materials and research, which the industry has already developed within the limits set by the existence of a large number of companies in separate ownership.

15. It is essential in the interests of the British economy that the improvement in the efficiency of the iron and steel industry which can be obtained from the common ownership of its main units should be secured as quickly as possible. It is unlikely that common ownership could be brought about by private mergers. In any event, there would be obvious and very strong objections to private ownership of a unit of such overwhelming power and importance in the economy. In the government's view, a nationalization of the main part of the iron and steel industry is the only appropriate means of securing quickly the benefits of common ownership. Nationalization will also provide new opportunities for increasing co-operation between management and the trade unions so as to improve the use of manpower and increase productivity, and to resolve in a fair manner the human problems to which structural and technological changes will inevitably give rise.

The Scope and Method of Nationalization

16. The government are satisfied that the essential objectives of nationalization can be secured without bringing into public ownership all the 260 limited liability companies in the industry. The industry is dominated by a small number of very large groups, each of which produced more than 475,000 tons of crude steel in the 12 months July 1963 to June 1964. One of these groups, Richard Thomas & Baldwins Ltd, is already publicly owned. The government think that the right course is to take over these groups in their entirety as going concerns except certain very large mixed groups whose main interests are clearly outside iron and steel. In the latter cases, only the subsidiaries concerned primarily with steel production will be nationalized.

17. Nationalization will be effected by the vesting in a National Steel Corporation of all the shares and securities[1] of the following 14 companies, which alone comply with the criteria in the preceding paragraph:

Colvilles Ltd
Consett Iron Co. Ltd
Dorman, Long & Co., Ltd
English Steel Corporation Ltd
GKN Steel Co. Ltd
John Summers & Sons Ltd
The Lancashire Steel Corporation Ltd
The Park Gate Iron and Steel Co., Ltd
Richard Thomas & Baldwins Ltd
Round Oak Steel Works Ltd
South Durham Steel and Iron Co. Ltd
The Steel Company of Wales Ltd
Stewarts and Lloyds, Ltd
The United Steel Companies Ltd

18. These 14 companies own or control the 22 integrated works[2] and 42 other iron and steel works. They employ on their iron and steel activities about 220,000 men and women – about 70 per cent of the

---

[1] Excluding (a) securities forming part of the loan capital of a company which can be redeemed at par at less than one year's notice and (b) securities created by a company as collateral security for a loan to that company. The latter will be cancelled as from the vesting day.

[2] The figures in this paragraph include the subsidiaries of the 14 major companies and companies in which the 14 major companies collectively have a majority interest. One of the 22 integrated works is owned by the Skinningrove Iron Co. Ltd, which is itself owned by Iron and Steel Investments Ltd – a consortium 90 per cent of the shares of which are held by nine of the companies which will be nationalized.

total manpower of the iron and steel industry. Details of their production and capacity are given in Annex A. They account for over 90 per cent of the production of iron ore, pig iron, crude carbon steel, heavy steel products, sheet and tin plate. They occupy a strong position in the production of most of the other main steel products. They control about 60 per cent of known reserves of iron ore in the United Kingdom.[1]

19. Four of the 14 companies are subsidiaries of holding companies of large mixed groups. They are the English Steel Corporation Ltd, which is a subsidiary of Vickers Ltd; GKN Steel Co. Ltd, which is a subsidiary of Guest, Keen & Nettlefolds Ltd; and The Park Gate Iron and Steel Co., Ltd and Round Oak Steel Works Ltd, which are subsidiaries of Tube Investments Ltd. The government have given much thought to whether the national interest would best be served by retaining vertical integration between these companies and their parent groups or by securing horizontal integration between them and the main part of the steel industry. They have decided that the balance of advantage lies with the nationalization of the companies in these groups, specified in paragraph 17. These four steel companies had an output of 3.4 million tons of crude steel in the 12 months July 1963 to June 1964 and have a potential output of 4.4 million tons in 1965. Their exclusion from nationalization would seriously prejudice the possibility of national planning of production and marketing and would make it more difficult to rationalize the structure of the industry. The government will, however, expect the National Steel Corporation to conduct their affairs with due regard to the existing close links between the steel-producing units and other units of Vickers, Guest, Keen & Nettlefolds and Tube Investments; and these concerns, like other consumers of steel, can expect to benefit from the improvements in efficiency which should result from common ownership of the main part of the industry.

20. Two of the 14 companies – Dorman, Long & Co., Ltd and The Lancashire Steel Corporation Ltd – are holding companies for groups which have important interests outside the iron and steel field, particularly in structural engineering, bridge building and wire manufacture. The position of these groups is, however, different from that of the Vickers, Guest, Keen & Nettlefolds and Tube Investments groups because their main interests are clearly in iron and steel activities; and they should, therefore, be nationalized as a whole.

Vesting Date

21. Vesting date will be the day after 36 weeks have passed from

---

[1] One per cent of known reserves is controlled by independent iron ore producers. The remainder is outside the control of the iron and steel industries.

Royal Assent to the nationalization measure, or an earlier day fixed by order of the Minister of Power.

Compensation

22. On nationalization the government will provide compensation for the holders of securities of the companies mentioned in paragraph 17 above other than Richard Thomas & Baldwins, which is already in public ownership. For the securities which have been quoted in the Stock Exchange Daily Official List, the government consider that an average of the quotations over an appropriate period, reflecting as they do the stock market's view of both commercial and political prospects, offers the fairest basis of valuation for this purpose. The period which the government have selected is October 1959 to October 1964, both months inclusive, which includes not only the turns of the trade cycle and the corresponding variations in utilization of capacity, but may also be presumed to cover fairly the movements of opinion about the prospects of renationalization. Prices and yields during this period will therefore have reflected these factors. Since, however, some securities have made a better showing towards the end of this period, the six months' period May to October 1964 will be taken if it gives a higher valuation. The value of unquoted securities will be for settlement between the Minister and the stockholders' representative on the basis of what the value of the securities would have been if they had been quoted. If agreement cannot be reached between the Minister and the stockholders' representatives about the valuation of either quoted or unquoted securities, the question will be settled by arbitration. The method of valuing quoted securities is more precisely explained in Annex B. Compensation will be satisfied by the issue of such amount of government Stock as, in the opinion of the Treasury, is at the date of issue equal to the valuation of the securities. For purposes of the capital gains tax the transaction will be treated as an involuntary realization and no tax charge or loss allowance will arise until and unless the new stock is sold.

Safeguarding Provisions

23. The nationalization measure will contain provisions to guard against the dissipation of the property and assets of the companies to be nationalized and their subsidiary companies in the period until vesting day. Annex C contains a summary of these provisions which will apply in some cases to transactions entered into after 30 April 1965, and in others to transactions entered into after 4 November 1964 – the date of the announcement by the First Secretary of State that the government

intended to take into public ownership the main part of the iron and steel industry.

24. The day-to-day operations of the industry and the implementation of its programmes of capital expenditure have been continuing normally. This is clearly required in the national interest and in the interest of the industry itself. Although the safeguarding provisions are necessary, they should not hamper the normal operations of the companies. Actions taken in good faith and in the normal course of business are unlikely to be challenged under these provisions; and the Minister of Power is ready to discuss with the directors concerned any transactions of an unusual character.

Organization of the Nationalized Industry

25. The National Steel Company will consist of a chairman and from 10 to 16 other members appointed by the Minister of Power. The Corporation will initially be in the position of a holding company in relation to the nationalized companies. However, as sole shareholder, they will in practice be able to exercise all necessary central control over the organisation as well as the policy of the nationalized companies. They will be able to secure the regrouping of assets among the existing companies or the replacement of the existing companies by a completely new company structure or the setting up of a unitary organization under which the underlying assets would be directly owned by the Corporation which would wind up the companies and set up their own administrative substructure.

26. One of the main tasks of the Corporation will be to combine necessary and desirable centralization of the main policy decisions with the maintenance of vitality and a sense of responsibility in the subordinate units. This problem is common to all large organizations whether in the public or private sector of the economy. In this connection, special attention will have to be given to the substructure of organization below the Corporation. The government think it would be wrong to lay down a rigid substructure in legislative provisions which would be inflexible for the future and which would have to be framed before the Corporation have had an opportunity to offer their advice on the appropriate organization. The nationalization measure will, therefore, not contain a detailed scheme of organization for the nationalized industry; but it will require the Corporation to undertake an immediate review of the organization for carrying on the activities under their ultimate control and to submit a report to the Minister within 12 months of vesting day (or a longer period allowed by the Minister). The Corporation will also be required to submit further reports whenever they think it necessary or the Minister asks them to do so. The Minister will have

the power to give the Corporation specific directions on organization; and he will, of course, be answerable to Parliament for the use he makes of this power.

Powers of the Nationalized Industry

27.   While a company structure is retained, the powers of the nationalized companies will in general be those in their memoranda of association. The National Steel Corporation will be empowered (a) to hold the securities which vest in them; (b) to carry on any activities which the nationalized companies are or have been authorized to carry on by their memoranda of association; and (c) to form or acquire by agreement other companies whether engaged in iron and steel or other activities. The Corporation will also have power, subject to the Minister's approval, to purchase compulsorily land required for their own purposes or those of the nationalized companies.

28.   The nationalized steel industry will be able to diversify its activities when this appears commercially advantageous. Diversification is a common practice among private companies, including the steel companies, and has advantages. It enables an industrial organisation to adjust its activities to keep pace with changing technologies and market conditions. The government think that the efficiency of the national economy as a whole will be improved by giving the nationalized industries an opportunity to diversify.

29.   The nationalized iron and steel industry will acquire a firm basis of diversified experience on which to build through the acquisition of the wider interests of the Dorman Long and Lancashire Steel groups and certain other companies, particularly Stewarts and Lloyds. A major extension of its activities outside the iron and steel field will, however, not be solely a matter for the commercial judgment of the Corporation. It may raise issues of national policy. Both the Corporation and the nationalized companies will, therefore, be required to obtain the consent of the Minister of Power before acquiring interests in companies outside the iron and steel field; and the Corporation will be required to obtain similar consent before themselves undertaking activities outside that field.

Duties of the National Steel Corporation

30.   The specific duties of the Corporation will be to:

(a) promote the efficient and economic supply of iron and steel products in such quantities and at such prices as may seem to them best calculated to meet the reasonable demands of consumers and to further the public interest;

(b) avoid, and ensure that the nationalized companies avoid, undue preference or unfair discrimination between customers but without prejudice to such variations in the terms and conditions on which their iron and steel products are supplied as may arise from ordinary commercial considerations or from the public interest;

(c) promote the safety, health and welfare of their employees and the employees of the nationalized companies, and consult with appropriate organizations about the establishment of machinery for negotiation and joint consultation;

(d) promote the export of iron and steel products and any other products they or the nationalized companies produce;

(e) promote research and development in iron and steel activities and in any other activities which they or a nationalized company carry on.

Finance

31. The Corporation will be statutorily responsible for the finances of the nationalized industry as a whole, including the service of debt to the Exchequer. They will be required to ensure that the industry's revenues are not less than sufficient to meet outgoings properly chargeable to revenue account, taking one year with another, and to establish and maintain a general reserve. The Minister of Power will be empowered to give the Corporation specific directions about the disposal of surplus revenue and the establishment and management of the general reserve. It is the government's intention to apply to the nationalized steel industry the principles and procedures set out in the White Paper on the Financial and Economic Obligations of the Nationalized Industries[1] under which financial objectives are agreed with the boards concerned.

32. The nationalized iron and steel industry will be required to borrow on a long-term basis from the Minister alone. It will be empowered to borrow on a temporary basis from the Minister or, with the consent of the Minister, from other persons, and the Treasury will be able to guarantee such borrowings by the Corporation. Total outstanding borrowings, in addition to the industry's commencing capital debt,[2]

---

[1] Cmnd. 1337.

[2] The commencing capital debt will be made up of an amount for the compensation to private holders of securities in companies to be nationalized, the value as shown in their 1963–64 accounts of the securities held by the Iron and Steel Holding and Realization Agency in Richard Thomas & Baldwins Ltd, the amount of the Agency's outstanding loans to this company at vesting date, and the amount of the Minister of Power's loans under Section 5 of the Iron and Steel Act, 1953, to Richard Thomas & Baldwins Ltd and to Colvilles Ltd, all of which loans and securities will be transferred to the Corporation on vesting date.

will be limited to £300 million. This limit should be sufficient to meet the industry's need for borrowing to finance capital expenditure already planned and to re-finance certain loans to the companies concerned from outside bodies, and should also allow a margin for any further plans over a period of about five years. However, it will be provided that the industry cannot borrow more than £200 million without a resolution of the House of Commons.

33. The Minister will be empowered to give the Corporation specific directions about servicing the nationalized industry's commencing capital debt and any further sums advanced. The Minister will be required to send a yearly account of payments and receipts to the Comptroller and Auditor General, who will be required to lay it before Parliament together with his own report on it.

34. The Corporation will be required to keep proper accounts and each year to submit their audited accounts and those of the nationalized companies to the Minister, who will be required to lay them before Parliament.

The Role of the Minister

35. In addition to the powers to give the Corporation specific directions referred to in paragraphs 26, 31 and 33 above, the Minister of Power will be able to give the Corporation directions of a general character on matters which appear to him to affect the national interest and specific directions to discontinue or restrict activities or dispose of production facilities, other than iron and steel activities or production facilities in Great Britain. The Corporation will be required to obtain the Minister's approval for the general lines of their programmes of capital development and research and development, to provide any information the Minister requires and to submit an annual report to the Minister who must lay it before Parliament.

Protection of Consumers

36. The increased efficiency resulting from nationalization of the main part of the industry should benefit consumers of iron and steel through prices lower than might otherwise be necessary and through improvements in the quality of products and services. The nationalization measure will impose no restriction on imports of iron and steel. Consumers will be free to buy from the private sector any products it can provide. The nationalization measure will provide for the establishment of a Consumers' Council and consumers will be further protected by the specific duties to be imposed on the Corporation described in paragraph 50 above. Although the nationalization measure will not give the Minister any specific powers on prices, he can be expected to be

concerned with questions of price policy in the nationalized iron and steel industry in the same way that the responsible Ministers in successive governments have been concerned with questions of price policy in the other nationalized industries.

The Private Sector of the Iron and Steel Industry

37.   Although the main part of the industry will be nationalized, the private sector will still consist of about 210 companies[1] having an annual output valued at about £200 million and employing nearly 100,000 people. The government regard it as important that the private sector should have a healthy and efficient life of its own and so make a full contribution to the national economy. The private sector will have a particularly important role in those specialist finishing operations which lie on the borderline between the steel and engineering industries, but it will be represented in most sections of the industry. The government propose to abolish the controls now operated by the Iron and Steel Board. In the interests of proper planning of the investment programmes of the industry as a whole, the Minister will retain a reserve power to control substantial development projects by the private companies in the basic fields of iron- and steel-making alone. The Minister will also be responsible for collecting and publishing statistics relating to the industry as a whole.

38.   There will be a need for arrangements for appropriate consultation and co-operation between the nationalized and private sectors. The precise form of these arrangements will be a matter for consultation between the two sectors of the industry, the trade unions and the government; but the government envisage that there might be established on a non-statutory basis:

(a) an advisory committee including representatives of the two sectors of the industry, the trade unions and government Departments, to provide for the participation of the whole industry in national economic planning;

(b) a joint forum between the nationalized and private sectors to discuss matters of a more commercial character which are inappropriate to the advisory committee;

(c) an advisory council on research and development appointed by the Minister of Power and covering both the nationalized and private sectors.

39.   The nationalization measure will specifically permit joint action by the nationalized and private sectors in negotiations about terms and

[1] There will also be about 90 steelfounding and 1,200 ironfounding establishments outside the nationalized part of the iron and steel industry.

conditions of service and in the fields of safety, health and welfare. The arrangements for the supervision of training in the whole industry by the Iron and Steel Industry Training Board, appointed by the Minister of Labour under the Industrial Training Act, 1964, will not be disturbed.

2. PUBLIC TRANSPORT REORGANIZED[1]

6. All the studies carried out so far from the Buchanan Report onwards suggest that our major towns and cities can only be made to work effectively and to provide a decent environment for living by giving a new dynamic role to public transport as well as expanding facilities for private cars. Unless we recognize this we shall pull down the centres of our towns in an attempt to get rid of congestion; and at the end of the day we shall find congestion still with us, and the character of our towns destroyed. We have neither the physical space nor the economic resources to rebuild our cities in such a form that all journeys can be made by private car; and in any case we must provide for the large number of people – particularly many of the old, the young, the housewives, the poor – who will not have the use of cars.

7. To provide an attractive and efficient system of public transport is therefore vital to deal with the immediate and pressing problems in our cities. We must also see how far public transport can offer new opportunities in the renewal of our urban areas. The pattern of the growth of London in the past century was largely determined by the building of the suburban railways and tubes; the structure of many provincial cities reflects the pattern of the electric tram-ways. New rapid transit systems for our major cities might provide an attractive basis for new patterns of development.

II. THE PRINCIPLES OF ORGANIZATION

8. Five main consequences flow from this approach. First, the basic planning of local public transport must clearly be a function of local rather than central government. Local authorities are responsible for the planning of their areas and the development of their local road networks, and they cannot do these jobs effectively unless they also have a broad responsibility for public transport.

9. That is why the government has rejected the idea of establishing nationalized Area Passenger Transport Boards responsible to the Minister of Transport and organizing local transport services independently

[1] From White Paper, *Public Transport and Traffic*, December 1967, Cmnd. 3847, paras. 6–70. Reprinted with permission of the Controller of Her Majesty's Stationery Office.

of the local authorities in their area. A clear distinction must be drawn between the national transport network (designed to handle movement between cities) and the short-distance local movement of people which needs to be a local responsibility.

10.   Secondly, all the transport matters for which local authorities are to be responsible – the improvement of the local road network, investment in public transport, traffic management measures, the balance between public and private transport – must be focused in an integrated transport plan, which in its turn is related to the general planning for each area. Otherwise a series of unrelated schemes will come forward without a unifying policy. This will create difficulties for central government in seeing which investment projects should be given priority.

11.   Thirdly, investment in local public transport must be grant-aided by central government just as investment in the principal road network of our cities and towns receives capital grants of 75 per cent from the Exchequer. Otherwise the renewal and extension of public transport systems will be held up, while the money available is concentrated on road schemes because they are grant-aided. But responsibility for deciding what public transport developments are needed must rest in the first place on local communities.

12.   Fourthly, the main network of public transport is no longer an appropriate activity for private companies whose prime duty must be to their shareholders, even though they are subject to public regulation. Indeed it has long been recognized that these basic passenger transport services could only be effectively provided through public ownership – whether local or national. Most of the major cities have established their own public transport services. London's transport was integrated in a public Board in 1933. Since 1948 the British Transport Commission and later the nationally-owned Transport Holding Company (THC), as owners of the Tilling and Scottish Groups of bus companies, have been by far the dominant providers of bus services outside London and the big cities. Today the THC own over 14,000 buses and coaches and have a large share (averaging 40 per cent) in the companies of the British Electric Traction Group (BET), which own about 11,000 buses and coaches. In all, 80 per cent of stage bus passengers in Britain are carried by publicly owned undertakings, and there is a substantial public stake in a great part of the other services. Less than 10 per cent of these passengers are carried by wholly privately owned companies.

13.   To complete this process of bringing the basic network of local passenger transport services under public ownership and control would facilitate a radical rationalization of the pattern of public transport. It would enable the finances of public transport to be considered without

unfair treatment of individual shareholders. In particular it would be possible to consider the financing of local rail and bus operation together and not in entirely separate compartments.

14.   Finally, the planning and operation of public transport can only be done intelligently over areas which make sense in transport terms. This means the planning must cover not only a large city or town but also the area around it from which large numbers of people travel to the centre for work, shopping or pleasure. Such an area is far larger than that of any existing urban individual authority outside London. Indeed it is clear that one of the major factors making for the reorganization of local government is the need to create local authority units big enough to tackle the sort of problems, like transport, which they ought to tackle if local government is to survive as an effective force. Any such change in local government structure in England and Scotland must, of course await the reports of the Royal Commissions on Local Government. But the reform of local government is a complex matter and may well take several years. In the meantime the traffic situation of the major urban areas is so serious, and the prospects for public transport are deteriorating so rapidly, that the reorganization of the transport system cannot wait.

III. THE REORGANIZATION OF PUBLIC TRANSPORT

15.   Sections III to VI of this Paper set out the government's proposals for reorganizing public transport outside London on the basis of the principles described in paragraphs 8–14.

16.   First, powers are to be sought in the Transport Bill to set up, by Order, Passenger Transport Authorities (PTAs) in any area where it seems to the Minister concerned they are required for the effective organization and planning of public transport. The traffic problems of the major conurbations are already critical and their continuously built-up areas call for unified planning of transport under a single Transport Authority. Yet at present they are served by a multiplicity of operators, large and small; and the absence of any single transport authority inhibits the satisfactory planning of public transport in the area. In the Greater Manchester area, for example, there are eleven municipal bus operators with fleets ranging in size from over 1,200 vehicles down to 12. In these major conurbations suburban rail services play a substantial part in the movement of peak hour traffic; and full integration of the planning of rail and road services is a pressing need. Here too the role of new fixed-track transport systems (intended to serve areas wider than any single local authority) needs to be investigated thoroughly and quickly.

17.   To meet these needs new Transport Authorities must be set up to take responsibility for the whole area and for all kinds of passenger transport – rail, tube, bus and ferry – as well as new forms of rapid transit which may be developed. It is therefore proposed as soon as the Bill becomes law to proceed with the establishment of PTAs in Greater Manchester, Merseyside, the West Midlands and Tyneside. Consultations will be held with the local authorities concerned on the delineation of the area to be covered by the PTA in each case.

18.   In much of the rest of the country the problems are somewhat less acute and the question of establishing PTAs can perhaps wait until the future shape of local government is clearer. Immediate improvements can, however, be made by the effective co-ordination of bus services on the lines of the agreements at present operating in Bristol, Plymouth and elswhere. . . .

19.   In Scotland nearly all the buses outside the four main cities are already run by the Scottish Bus Group owned by the THC. Scottish local transport problems differ in nature from those in England and Wales. Separate proposals for Scotland including the establishment of a Scottish Transport Group (STG) are described in section VI.

IV. PASSENGER TRANSPORT AUTHORITIES

20.   The procedure for establishing Passenger Transport Authorities, and a description of their powers and functions, is set out in detail in the Annex. In England the Minister of Transport will be responsible for establishing PTAs; in Scotland and Wales the Secretary of State will exercise the responsibilities. The constitution of the PTAs is designed to secure two ends: first, the control of policy and finance by a body responsible to the local authorities in the area concerned; and secondly the delegation of day-to-day management to a professional Executive appointed by the controlling Authority and answerable to it. The relations between the Authority and the Executive will in many ways be similar to those between a Minister and a nationalized industry. The Authority itself will be composed almost wholly of people appointed by the local authorities. It will appoint its own Chairman, with the approval of the Minister concerned. Since the Authority and the government will be working closely together on many aspects of transport policy, with the help of substantial Exchequer grants, the Minister will appoint two or three members of the Authority, but not more than one-seventh of the total membership.

21.   The Authority will appoint the Executive on terms it will decide. The Authority will settle the broad lines of policy, including policy on services and fares. It will be for the Authority to choose, therefore,

whether public transport in its Area should be self-supporting or whether, because of wider transport considerations, it should be assisted through precepts on the local authorities in its Area. The Authority will be free to grant 'concessionary' fares throughout its Area.

22. The viability of public transport will clearly be affected by the extent to which it is related to the general planning of the Area which is the responsibility of the local authorities who are appointing the Members of the Authority. The Authority and the Executive must therefore plan public transport so as to fit in with a unified plan including land use, highways and traffic management.

Responsibilities of the Executive

23. A major task for the Executive will be to prepare a Plan, for approval by the Authority, setting out proposals for the development of a system of public transport capable of serving the needs of the Area. The Executive will also be responsible for the provision of services, partly by operating them itself and partly by entering into agreements with the National Bus Company (or its subsidiaries), with the Railways Board or with other operators. One of its most urgent tasks will be to reorganize the bus undertakings in the Area. As an essential first step it will take under its control all the municipal bus undertakings in the Area. Reorganization will also be made easier by the fact that all, or nearly all, the other major bus undertakings will be in public ownership under the control of the National Bus Company or the Scottish Transport Group, which will each be given a statutory duty to co-operate with Executives. This development now makes it unnecessary to give PTAS the compulsory powers of acquisition originally visualized.

24. The Executive will not however be just a body to organize or run bus services. Its primary job will be to plan the public transport system of the Area as a whole in the context of the development and traffic plans of the local authorities. The Executive must comprise men of vision and wide experience; and they must employ staff skilled in the latest techniques of transport planning and development, not only by road but by all means of transport. It will be the job of the Executive to work out with the local authorities a practicable balance between private and public transport, to integrate the bus and rail services in the Area and to evaluate the costs and benefits of major new investment in public transport, whether in fixed track systems, reserved routes for buses or by other means.

25. A first Plan for the development of public transport must be prepared by the Executive for approval by the Authority and for publication within two years. Such a plan, set in the context of the development plans of local authorities, will help the Minister or Secretary of State in

deciding on the capital grants to be made to the Executive for investment in major new projects.

Organization of the Executive's Own Bus Undertakings

26.   The Executive will need to regroup the municipal bus undertakings transferred to it (and any other bus services which it may acquire by agreement) in a way which will enable them to be operated with maximum efficiency. The total number of buses owned by each of the Executives in Greater Manchester, Merseyside and the West Midlands may well be of the order of 2,000 or even more. Although there is no evidence that there is any particular optimum size of bus undertaking (the optimum size almost certainly varies considerably in different conditions) there is a general consensus of view in the bus industry that the problems of effective management steadily increase as the number of buses in an undertaking rises above 1,000 . . . .

27.   Although the Authority and the Executive will be free to choose the method of organization they think right, there would clearly be advantages in grouping their assets in a number of subsidiary undertakings of a size which can be effectively managed; in the circumstances of the conurbations this would probably be of the order of 500–1,000 buses. These subsidiary undertakings could be organized as companies wholly owned by the Executive. The Executive would naturally control the general policy of the subsidiaries and would make sure that their activities were properly integrated. But within this general policy the management of each subsidiary would have plenty of scope to adopt policies fitted to its own local conditions.

28.   Such an arrangement would ensure close contact between each subsidiary undertaking and the local community which it served. It would be open to the Executive to appoint to the Board of Directors of these local undertakings some persons from the local authorities in the area, particularly those which had previously been running their own bus undertakings. In this way the existing interest and pride in the local bus services could be retained in the new system, and the undertakings themselves would be more responsive to local needs. The arrangement would also ensure that each subsidiary had a close link with those responsible for traffic policies, which can have so marked an effect on the efficiency and attractiveness of bus services.

29.   The arrangement would also ensure a sound system of financial responsibility in the individual parts of the Executive's undertaking. Each subsidiary would produce its own financial accounts and would have its own financial objectives set by the Executive and the Authority. Costs of running buses may vary widely over the Area, and these variations should not be masked in an overall average for the whole of a

monolithic undertaking. If costs in a particular part of the Area are relatively low, then it would seem right for the travelling public in that part to enjoy the benefits. Although therefore the Authority would establish a general fares policy for the Area as a whole, there is no reason why the individual and detailed fares scales of particular subsidiaries should be identical. There should be room for local variation in the light of local conditions and costs.

30.   In this way the Executive would be able to secure the substantial advantages of grouping the bus undertakings which it owns in units of an effective and manageable size with clear financial responsibilities, and yet retain those advantages of management, centralized purchasing and other common services which spring from single ownership and a control of broad policy.

Agreements with the National Bus Company

31.   The National Bus Company will own several individual companies operating in each of the first Passenger Transport Areas. The NBC will have a statutory duty to cooperate with the Executives in the reorganization of bus services. This could in some cases involve transfers of bus services between the Executive and the NBC. But in any case working agreements will be needed to avoid creating problems of severance or irritating restrictions (which often occur at present) on the way in which people inside and outside the Area can use the various bus services. The agreements between the NBC and each Executive must be of a kind which provides for full integration of services on a financial basis satisfactory to both parties.

32.   Although agreements with the NBC will not need the approval of the Minister concerned, details of them will be sent to the Minister as part of the reorganization plan for the Area referred to above (para. 25). Full control of bus services in the Area, which will be exercised by the Executive in place of the Traffic Commissioners, will not be given to the Executive unless the Minister is satisfied that a fair agreement has been made with the NBC.

Agreements with British Railways

33.   The suburban services operated by British Railways play a substantial part in the provision of public transport in the conurbations, particularly in the movement of commuters. These services must be integrated into the passenger transport system of the Area. In the conurbations the Executive will therefore be given a specific duty to prepare an agreement with British Railways which will set out the part which suburban railway services are to play in the comprehensive

transport plan for the area. This agreement will need the approval of the Authority.

34.   The precise nature of the agreements made by the Executive with British Railways may vary from Area to Area. But certain features would be common to all. The level of fares to be charged must be a matter for the Authority (taking account of railway fares on related services). Clearly an Executive will not be able to draw up an effective transport plan unless it is able to influence fares policy on all types of public transport in its Area. It might, for instance, wish to stimulate rail travel by fares concessions which would add to the losses made on the services. Moreover, it would not have the same incentive to reduce the loss on rail services by integrating them more effectively with other forms of transport if it did not have financial responsibility for that loss.

35.   The ultimate goal must therefore be for the PTA to take responsibility for paying grants for any continuing losses on the suburban rail services it decides are necessary as part of its comprehensive transport plan. But progress towards this goal will necessarily be slow and can only take place in the context of government policy designed to give local authorities greater financial help for public transport than they have at present. For this reason the government will be making special grants to Executives in connection with their agreements with British Railways, details of which are set out in Section VII.

Agreements with other Bus Operators

36.   Although nearly all sizeable bus companies will be publicly owned, a great many small privately-owned undertakings will remain. The Executive cannot be expected to plan transport services in its Area unless in the last resort it can control all Area bus services. It is therefore proposed that certain powers at present exercised by the Traffic Commissioners should be given to the Executive. . . .

Machinery for Negotiation and Consultation with Workers

39.   The Transport Bill will be laying on the Railways Board, the NBC and the STG a duty to consult the Unions with a view to setting up the necessary machinery for consultation and negotiation with their workers on terms and conditions of employment, measures affecting safety, health, welfare, and proposals for improving efficiency . . . .

40.   A similar duty will be placed on each Executive to make agreements with the Unions for suitable machinery to deal with these matters. . . .

Financial Position of Executives

42.   The financial position of the Executive will depend in the first

place on the efficiency with which it conducts its own business. The merging of the various municipal bus undertakings will present opportunities for reduction in the total cost of management, and for savings from the rationalization of services. Nor will the Executive, whose role will be mainly a planning one, require a large HQ staff. In the longer term, rationalization of garage and maintenance facilities, centralized purchasing and standardization of vehicles and supplies should also provide significant economies.

43.   Moreover for the first time public transport will be enjoying capital grants towards the cost of new transport projects, including the cost of new buses, together with a reduction in fuel duty, and these should reduce operating costs (see section VII).

44.   One of the most important factors affecting the running costs and attractiveness of bus services is the traffic conditions in which they operate. These will be under the control of the local authorities who appoint the members of the Passenger Transport Authorities and it will therefore be within their own power to create the conditions in which the services offered to passengers can be improved, and the strain on bus workers relieved. So great is the importance of effective traffic management to the viability of bus services that the government proposes to place full responsibility for traffic management on local authorities as described in section X.

45.   The finances of the Executive will be strengthened by the fact that they will have power to engage in a wide range of activities, including tours and excursions, hiring of buses and cars, and power to provide all the facilities needed to complement the basic public transport system and so improve its attractiveness and convenience for the travelling public. (Fuller details are given in the Annex.)

46.   The major factor in costs is the level of wages and other payments made to employees. At present there are significant differences in wage levels and conditions of employment in the various undertakings, both municipal and company owned. The principle of common conditions for those engaged on comparable work is obviously right. But it may well be thought that the conditions of work for bus staff are by no means identical throughout the whole of a Passenger Transport Area; and it may be that there will be a case for paying premium rates in certain parts of the Area where conditions of work are most trying and consequently it is particularly difficult to obtain enough staff. Clearly progress towards uniformity of conditions must depend, like all increases in pay, on the rate of increase in productivity in the bus industry.

47.   For these reasons the government believes that the establishment of PTAs and the transfer of municipal undertakings to Passenger Transport Executives will provide opportunities for a reduction in the

costs of providing public transport. Whether public transport in their Areas is able to cover its costs, or requires a rate precept, will depend partly on the quality of the people appointed to the Authority itself, partly on the management skills of the Executive which it appoints and partly on the readiness of the constituent local authorities to see that the traffic conditions in which buses operate are such that they can do their job efficiently.

V. NATIONAL BUS COMPANY

48.   Although this is not always recognized, a large part of the network of ordinary bus services throughout the country has for nearly 20 years been provided by undertakings which are nationally owned or in which there is a large public shareholding. Companies which are wholly owned by the Transport Holding Company own over 14,000 buses and coaches. The THC also owns an equal share with the British Electric Traction Company (each owning from one-half to one-third of the shares) in nearly all the companies in the BET Group, which owns about 11,000 vehicles. Although there are some 25,000 other privately owned public service vehicles in the country, less than one-third of the mileage run by these vehicles is on ordinary stage bus services; the remainder is on long-distance coach services, tours and excursions and contract hire work. And although there are hundreds of small companies engaged in this kind of work there are (outside the BET Group) only four privately controlled companies operating stage bus services which have more than 60 buses.

49.   The THC took the view that it would be desirable for them to purchase the shares they did not own in the BET Group, thus bringing under the control of a single body nearly all the main bus companies in Great Britain. They considered that apart from other intrinsic advantages this ought to enable that body to participate with each Passenger Transport Executive in the reorganization of bus services without damaging the economic and financial viability of the bus companies already owned or partly owned by the THC. It would also facilitate the useful reorganization of services in other areas. The THC therefore asked the government whether they considered it desirable for the THC to make an offer for the purchase of these shares. The government shared the general view of the THC on this matter. They also considered that the reorganization of public transport which they had in mind through the establishment of Passenger Transport Authorities, and of the National Bus Company and the Scottish Transport Group referred to below, would be carried through more smoothly and fairly if this were done.

50. It was agreed, however, in view of the scale of the transaction, combined with the fact that the government was considering the transfer of the THC bus assets in Scotland to an autonomous Scottish Transport Group, that if this was to be done the THC should ask for a formal direction to carry out the purchase as soon as the necessary legislation had been passed. With the authority of the government the THC has made arrangements for the purchase of the shares owned by the BET Company in bus companies in the BET Group. The price – some £35 million – represents the THC's estimate of the value of the underlying assets. The THC has agreed to offer to buy the other privately owned shares in these companies on a comparable basis. The THC has also acquired in recent months control of two sizeable independent bus companies in Yorkshire (the West Riding Automobile Co. and the Executors of S. Ledgard). The government will introduce legislation for the extension of the borrowing powers of the THC to enable the purchase to be completed.

51.   It is intended to establish a statutory National Bus Company, to which will be transferred all the THC interests in bus undertakings in England and Wales, including their interests in firms manufacturing buses. The THC has in any case to be reorganized since its road haulage interests are being transferred to the National Freight Corporation. It is therefore more convenient to establish a body specifically responsible for passenger transport. Like the THC the NBC will be run on commercial lines. It will continue to operate through locally based subsidiary companies. It will be expected to pay its way, providing out of revenue for the interest on its capital loaned by the Exchequer and for the renewal of its assets. The financial duty of the NBC will therefore be basically the same as that of Passenger Transport Executives. The THC interests in the operation of bus services in Scotland will be transferred to a separate Scottish Transport Group as described in Section VI. The National Bus Company and the Scottish Transport Group will maintain close relations to ensure that a common policy is adopted on broad issues affecting road passenger transport throughout Great Britain; and also that there is full co-operation in detailed matters affecting both bodies. Such close relations could be facilitated, inter alia, by the appointment of some people to be members of both the NBC and the STG.

52.   The THC and its successor body, the NBC will use the opportunity created by the control of the BET companies to rationalize the operations of their various subsidiaries in a way which has not proved practicable so long as the Tilling Group of bus companies was wholly owned by the THC while the BET Group was partly owned by the THC but effectively controlled by a separate company. Although there has been progress in

some areas, there is obviously scope for economies (apart from other improvements) by rationalization of services.

53. The NBC will have the power to acquire voluntarily bus undertakings which fit in with the rest of their services, but small private operators in many areas will continue to play a useful part in the provision of services particularly in country areas. The NBC will co-operate with other bus operators (and also with the Railways Board and the London Transport Board in respect of their services) to ensure the provision of the necessary public transport services for the community in as efficient a way as possible.

54. The NBC will have a specific duty to co-operate with each Passenger Transport Executive, in carrying through the necessary reorganization of public transport in the areas concerned. As described above (paras. 31–32) the subsidiary companies of the NBC in each Area will make agreements with the Passenger Transport Executive. These agreements will provide for integrated operation of services in and near the Area over which the Executive has a responsibility for planning public transport.

55. Such agreements should not of course just freeze the existing pattern for providing services. . . .

56. Where they are operating bus services wholly within a Passenger Transport Area the NBC companies will operate under the terms of their agreement with the Executive and not as at present under the jurisdiction of the Traffic Commissioners. . . .

59. More important, the Railways Board also have the responsibility for securing the provision of those bus services which have to be provided as a condition of the consent of the Minister of Transport to the withdrawal of rail passenger services. This responsibility has in many cases involved the Board in the negotiation of continuing contracts with bus operators; and under these contracts the Board paid subsidies to those bus operators of more than £500,000 in 1966. When the acquisition of BET undertakings by the THC is complete, over three-quarters of these subsidies will be payable to companies which will be owned by the NBC or STG and which they will be running as part of their general network of services.

60. The negotiation of contracts for bus services is not an activity which is proper to the functions of the Railways Board. It is therefore intended to transfer to the NBC or STG the obligation to arrange for the provision of those bus services which are required as a condition of the Minister's agreeing to the withdrawal of rail passenger services. The services so provided will naturally be subject to such amendments and variations, as Ministers may from time to time decide and the Traffic Commissioners approve.

61. The cost of providing these services has been taken into account in settling the financial duties of the NBC and STG. The NBC and STG will not, however, necessarily provide the services through one of their own subsidiary companies; they may find it more economic to contract with another operator to run a particular service. . . .

62. The NBC is being established to make easier the reorganization of bus services to meet the needs of each area. It will not be a centralized board but in effect a holding company owning a large number of local subsidiaries which will be responsive to local conditions and problems and will co-operate closely with the communities they serve. Although it will act commercially, its financial responsibilities will not be such as to inhibit it from taking a broad view of proposals for co-ordination whether in a Passenger Transport Area or with a municipal bus undertaking. In short the establishment of the NBC will provide a sound basis for developing on a rational basis the provision of bus services throughout England and Wales.

VI. PASSENGER TRANSPORT IN SCOTLAND

63. An efficient system of passenger transport in Scotland is essential both on social grounds and as a means of promoting economic growth. The pattern of services must be flexible enough to respond to movements in population, the development of industry and of tourism, increased car ownership and the different needs of the Central Belt and of the sparsely populated areas. In addition to rail and bus services, shipping and air services provide essential components of the Scottish transport system, especially in the Highlands and Islands.

64. Passenger transport in Scotland is to a large extent already in public ownership, although through a number of different agencies. Apart from the municipal services in Aberdeen, Dundee, Edinburgh and Glasgow the main bus services are provided by the Scottish Bus Group, which is a subsidiary of the Transport Holding Company. The THC also shares in the ownership of David MacBrayne Ltd., whose shipping and road services in the West Highlands are assisted by the Secretary of State for Scotland. Certain shipping services in Orkney and Shetland, as well as the new air service to the North Isles of Orkney, are assisted in the same way. Shipping services in the Clyde are provided by the Caledonian Steam Packet Company, a subsidiary of the Railways Board.

Proposed Organization

65. The Government considers that the overall planning objectives for Scotland will be achieved more effectively, especially in the field of

transport investment, if the whole of the road and sea passenger network in public ownership is developed by a single organization responsible to the Secretary of State. The Transport Bill will therefore provide for the establishment of a new undertaking to be known as the Scottish Transport Group (STG). Initially this organization will take over the Scottish Bus Group, the THC's shares in MacBrayne's, the Caledonian Steam Packet Company, and the ships at present chartered to the subsidized shipping companies by the Secretary of State. The Government hopes that the current discussions about a possible lease of the Glasgow Corporation's transport undertaking to the Scottish Bus Group will soon be successfully concluded. The STG will also have power to acquire by agreement any other undertakings needed to provide an effective passenger transport system, and to provide ancillary facilities such as hotels, car parks and piers.

66. The STG will operate mainly as a holding company, the various bus and shipping companies being operated as subsidiaries with the fullest possible measure of commercial freedom. It will have the same obligation to balance its accounts financially as the National Bus Company (see section V). Essential shipping services will where necessary continue to receive assistance under the Highlands and Islands Shipping Services Act, 1960, which it is proposed to extend to cover the Caledonian Steam Packet Company services in the Clyde. Cross-subsidization between bus and shipping services will be avoided as far as possible. Like other transport operators, the STG and its subsidiaries will be eligible to receive the various grants to be provided for in the Transport Bill. . . .

Passenger Transport Areas

70. The Government believes that these proposals will provide Scotland with a more cohesive system of public passenger transport which will be able to meet the rapidly changing needs of the community in both urban and rural areas. Studies which are now being made of the future transport requirements of various parts of Scotland will show whether it may be necessary to strengthen further the machinery for matching the transport system to the planning requirements of the area concerned. The Transport Bill will accordingly empower the Secretary of State to establish Passenger Transport Areas in Scotland, but a decision will be deferred for the time being on whether this power should be exercised and, if so, in what areas. The STG will have a statutory duty to co-operate with any Passenger Transport Executive which may be set up in Scotland, and it is envisaged that its subsidiaries would make an agreement with any Executive for the provision of bus services in the area concerned. The economies of scale achieved by the national

network could in this way be combined with the matching of services to local needs by the Executive.

3. THE NATIONAL FREIGHT CORPORATION[1]

1. The basic objective of government policy must be to improve the efficiency of the whole transport system. Nowhere is this more urgent than in the field of freight. Quick, convenient and economical means of moving goods are vital to industry. At the same time wider social and economic interests must not be overlooked. Only in this way will the nation's resources be put to their best use.

2. The White Paper on Transport Policy, 1966,[2] described the distribution and expected trends of freight traffic and outlined the government's new plan for freight. Since then, in the light of further statistical studies in the Ministry and of the wide-ranging consultations which have been held, the government has evolved its freight policy in greater detail. This Paper describes the proposals on which the forthcoming legislation will be based.

3. As the 1966 White Paper showed, rail freight traffic has declined over the years, mainly because of a large and continuous reduction in coal traffic, although this trend was offset between 1963 and 1965 by the railways' share of growth in the traffic generated by the steel industry during that period. By contrast, road transport has been growing fast with the rapid growth in the industries that are big users of road transport. In 1966 the fall in rail ton-mileage was resumed primarily because in addition to the continued decline in coal traffic, there was a sharp fall in steel traffic (see Appendix 1). Although the use of road transport increased less last year than in previous years, it is clear that there is going to be a further rapid rise in demand as soon as industrial production picks up again. The government recognizes that the flexibility which road transport offers means that this sector must continue to play a vital, and indeed a dominant, role in the service which the transport industry provides to the community. Because of the changes that are taking place in the type of service which industry needs, the dependence on road transport is increasing and will continue to increase. But the growing pressure on road space, together with technological changes in the railways themselves, emphasize the importance of making the fullest economic use of the railways where, in their modernized form,

---

[1] From White Paper, *The Transport of Freight*, November 1967, Cmnd. 3470, paras. 1–33. Reprinted with permission of the Controller of Her Majesty's Stationery Office.

[2] Cmnd. 3057, HMSO, 1966.

they can give an efficient service and can save road space and congestion costs.

4. The drive to cut costs and increase efficiency throughout industry has accelerated the trend towards handling and moving goods in larger units. With through transport becoming the key to efficiency and economy, the importance of container service for non-bulk goods is growing rapidly. With the steady expansion of freightliner services during the past year British Rail is adapting itself to play its full part in these developments. Similarly, the government has made proposals for increasing the maximum permitted length of articulated goods vehicles for general use on the roads to help them carry containers of the largest international standard size more safely. Containers enable the transport of goods to be treated as one integrated movement from origin to destination, not only by road and rail for domestic traffic, but also by road, rail, sea, and even air, internationally. The full impact of the introduction of container operations has not yet been felt; this will happen in the early 1970s. On the short sea routes to Europe there is also the alternative of roll-on/roll-off services. These too are expanding; and in the longer term the building of the Channel Tunnel would also affect the pattern of movement of the growing trade between the United Kingdom and Europe.

5. These technical developments highlight the need to ensure that wasteful competition and duplication within the publicly-owned transport system are eliminated. Road and rail services which perform the same function must be integrated to improve their efficiency, and those which should be complementary must operate in a framework which encourages co-ordination. The road haulage industry must be freed from the outdated restrictions of the licensing system under which it operates; but it must at the same time reorganize itself to meet the challenge of the higher standards which the nation now demands of it. Similarly, the commercial and social aspects of the railways' obligations must be clearly differentiated, and the White Paper on Railway Policy,[1] just published, shows how this is to be achieved.

6. The trend of traffic away from the railways at a time when they are adapting themselves to handle it more efficiently, the need for a new framework within which road and rail transport can work together and the simultaneous introduction of new concepts and techniques for the through handling of freight, in which there is a clear role for both road and rail, all point to the vital importance of integrated planning of the total transport system. Such planning must embrace all the processes in the transport chain: shipping, docks, inland transport and air services.

[2] Cmnd. 3439, HMSO, 1967.

The nationally-owned road/rail services are a vital link in this chain. They must be reorganized to take full advantage of the new techniques for handling freight and to meet the challenge of the container age.

The Objectives of Freight Policy

7.   Thus, within this broad field, the government has set itself six main objectives:

(i) to offer the customer a more efficient freight service in the public sector – including a comprehensive, efficient and more economic door-to-door road/rail service, facilitating and exploiting the use of containers;

(ii) to eliminate wasteful and inefficient competition between publicly-owned road and rail services for the same traffic;

(iii) to use existing road and rail assets and manpower more efficiently through the reorganization of structure and management and the adoption of new techniques and other improvements in productivity, as well as through the co-ordination of new investment;

(iv) to make the maximum economic use of our railways as well as our roads by promoting the transfer of all suitable traffic from congested roads on to the railways; and at the same time to make available to industry generally the full benefits of the new freightliner system;

(v) to improve the safety and efficiency of road haulage by means of a modern and effective system of carrier licensing and a revised and improved control of drivers' hours of work; and

(vi) to secure the willing co-operation of transport workers in these developments by associating them more closely with managements at all levels.

The Form of Integration

8.   One way of securing the integration of the publicly-owned transport services would be to set up a new national transport authority to which both the railways and the nationalized sector of the road haulage industry would be responsible. There are, however, grave objections to this. In the first place, as the Introduction to the 1966 White Paper pointed out, the problems of integration in the freight field are quite different from those for passenger transport, where the needs of the customer demand a more individual service and where, therefore, regional and local considerations necessarily play a greater part; in consequence the solutions the government is proposing are different, too.

9.   Second, it will be apparent from the report of the Joint Steering

Group annexed to the White Paper on Railway Policy that very substantial problems over a wide field of its activities will demand the full attention of the Railways Board in the next few years. These tasks will be urgent, exacting and over and above those arising from the integration needed in the freight field. If a national transport commission were to be established, with authority over the whole freight field, it would, whether it was given the direct responsibility for the operation of services or not, have to divide its energies between solving these railway problems and planning the organisational structure needed to provide the most efficient freight service in the various fields where road/rail integration was required.

10.   Moreover, such a new authority would take some time to find its feet and to work out a scheme for reorganization. In doing so it would inevitably go over much of the ground already covered by the government with the help of outside experts. At a time when the need is urgent for reorganization of our inland transport system to meet the coming challenge of container operations, valuable time would in fact be lost.

11.   The lesson of the British Transport Commission between 1947 and 1962 was not that the concept of integration was wrong but that a body of that size and range of responsibilities found it difficult in practice to get to grips with the basic problems of reorganization to achieve road/rail integration. The Government intends that the publicly-owned freight services shall operate on strictly commercial lines. But, if this is to be done, and be seen to be done, it is important that the various freight activities should be broken down for operating purposes into units which make functional sense and which can be held financially accountable for the work that they do. Only in this way will it be possible to cost their work precisely and openly, to eliminate undesirable cross-subsidization and to achieve real economies by integrating like with like.

12.   The nature and degree of the integration required between road and rail must vary according to the type of business. In some types of freight activity – removals, for example – there is little or no rail element. In others, such as the parcels service or the liner train services, there are obvious advantages to be gained by integrating road and rail. The first step, therefore, must be to differentiate the specialized freight activities so that reorganization can be carried out in a meaningful way. It is equally urgent to do this for road as for rail.

II. THE NATIONAL FREIGHT CORPORATION

The Field of Responsibility

13.   It is for these reasons that the government believes that a

separate and distinct body is needed to integrate the publicly-owned freight services. The forthcoming legislation will provide for a new National Freight Corporation (NFC), which is to be a free-standing corporation responsible to the Minister. Its first task will be the further rationalization of the functional groupings of the Transport Holding Company's (THC) freight activities as a precursor to integration with the corresponding rail activities where this would be sensible. To this end it will take over from the THC all its general and specialist road haulage services, together with its shipping services (excluding its interest in MacBraynes). It will take over from the British Railways Board (BRB) the assets – depots, vehicles, warehouses, containers and other equipment (but not the trains) – employed in the freight-liner and sundries services, and the BRB's other cartage vehicles. This will enable it to take commercial responsibility for all the movements which originate by road leaving the BRB responsible for both the marketing and operation of freight traffic – full train loads, company trains and wagon-load traffic – originating by rail.

14. In this way integration will be concentrated on the areas where it will be most productive: general merchandise and parcels and sundries. These are the fields where rationalization of road and rail services is most urgent if the railways' deficit is to be reduced. In 1966 the BRB lost £25 million on its sundries traffic and, in preparation for the legislative changes which it is hoped that Parliament will approve, BRB and THC are already engaged in discussions to bring the sundries service of the BRB and the parcels service of the THC together under unified direction so as to produce an expanding, efficient and more economical service. The Joint Parcels Organization which they have created, in consultation with the trade unions, will in due course be incorporated within the NFC.

15. The BRB is also incurring a heavy deficit in the handling of general merchandise – £36 million in 1966. Here the basic need is to reorganize old-fashioned methods. The carriage of unsuitable traffic by rail must be eliminated and better methods must be developed of collecting, bulking and distributing both consignments of wagon-load size and those traffics which present themselves in smaller quantities. These are the traffics which incur most of the losses. An important element in this reorganization will be the provision by the NFC of a modern and efficient through service from door to door, using road for collection and delivery, with traffic grouped at the terminals for trunk movement in bulk by rail, thus exploiting to the full the new rail freightliner services for the carriage of traffic in containers.

16. The Transport Holding Company has been conspicuously successful in tackling the problems of handling general merchandise and parcels traffic of this kind. At the same time the BRB has been

developing the imaginative freightliner concept as the most efficient method of road/rail haulage for a wide range of merchandise. The combination in one organization of the THC's experience of road haulage and the BRB's freightliner concept will pave the way for a vigorous new service to industry, commerce and the public. Using both the THC's vehicles and the BRB's cartage fleet to best advantage the flexibility and door-to-door facility of road haulage will be combined with the speed and economy of rail over long distances.

The Arrangements for the Freightliner Service

17.   The key to this road/rail development will be a Freightliner Company which, as a subsidiary of the NFC, will have the commercial responsibility for the marketing and management of the freightliner services. Transfer of this responsibility to the NFC is essential in order to enable the Corporation to make the most efficient and economic use of road or rail for the trunk haul. However, since the railways will still have a direct interest in the development of the freightliner service, as an important means of attracting a substantial volume of trunk haulage to rail, and in order to ensure that both organizations have a clear incentive to develop the service to the maximum economic extent, the legislation will provide for the BRB to have a substantial interest in the Freightliner Company, consisting of 49 per cent shareholding and an appropriate number of seats on the Board. The Board will be appointed by the Board of the NFC, the Railways Board nominating the BRB members. The BRB's interest in the Tartan Arrow Service will be safeguarded by transferring the Board's shareholding to the Freightliner Company with that of the THC.

18.   The Freightliner Company will have commercial freedom in determining its charging policy. It will normally employ a standard charging system available to all but will be free in the usual way to incorporate discounts for quantity, regularity, etc. As well as selling through services direct to the consignor it will offer a transport advisory and contract service to industry. It will also sell space on the freightliners to other hauliers. The freightliner terminals will continue to be open to the private haulier and to the own-account operator without discrimination either as to the charges levied or the services provided.

19.   The aim of the Company will be to exploit the full potentialities of the freightliner. Through its stake in the Company the BRB will be associated with the formulation of policy for the conduct and development of the service. Joint ownership will not only facilitate joint working between the BRB and the NFC and the free exchange of information between them, but will enable them to work more closely together on planning and investment. This will be important because the decisions

on the mode of transport in which investment is to take place will be expected to take account not only of the statutory financial duty which each undertaking will have, but also of the need to send freight by rail where it is economic to do so. This will be reflected in the statutory duty which the NFC will have to make the maximum economic use of rail. The two undertakings will be expected to invest in new freightliner services wherever the return on capital to them jointly would be better than if the investment were not made and the traffic continued to go throughout by road. The Railways Board will levy a charge for providing and hauling the trains, which will be negotiated on a commercial basis, since the Railways Board will have a financial duty to break even and must, therefore, in relation to the freightliner services as elsewhere, cover its long-term avoidable costs and secure an adequate contribution towards its indirect costs, including track costs. In addition, the profit made by the Freightliner Company will be divided between the BRB and the NFC in proportion to their shareholdings in the Company.

20. These arrangements will give the two undertakings a strong incentive to invest in the freightliner network to the maximum economic extent, and, once the investment has been made, to make the fullest use of the service. It will pay both undertakings to fill the train.

The Structure of the NFC

21. The role of the NFC Board will be to set the framework within which its various subsidiaries will operate, rather than to manage them. Freight transport is not a single, indivisible industry: its numerous parts vary enormously. Flexibility is therefore essential, and the new Board will be given the task of devising the structure most appropriate to its many sided activities. Its duty will be to expand vigorously as a commercial enterprise and it will seek every opportunity, as the THC has done, to acquire new businesses by voluntary agreement and to integrate them with its functional subsidiaries. The Board of the NFC will pay particular attention, over the whole field of its activities, to financial matters, the selection of management and its performance, conditions of service of all the staff and industrial relations generally, and public relations. There will be coordinating machinery within the NFC to ensure that common policies are followed on these matters and that the subsidiary units do not act against each other's interests, and so that of the NFC as a whole. There will also be arrangements at national level to permit co-ordination with other operators and the provision of central marketing services for the largest industrial users.

22. For these purposes a non-executive Board is required to plan the overall strategy of the undertaking and to co-ordinate the policies of the

subsidiaries. Its composition, and the subsidiary structure of the NFC will reflect the government's aim of securing closer association of the workers with the processes of governing and organizing undertakings of this kind. The most effective ways of doing this are matters for discussion between the NFC and the trade unions concerned.

23. In this way the NFC will be developed to provide a comprehensive, country-wide, road/rail service in conjunction with BRB, with links to Ireland and Europe, by both container and roll-on/roll-off service. On the deep sea routes, too, new container ships are coming into service with cargo concentrated for through transport with minimum handling. The NFC will develop road and rail inland transport links to serve these ships and the new and expanding network of inland clearance depots, in which the NFC will have a stake.

Financial Targets

24. The NFC will have a financial duty, similar to that given to other nationalized industries, of at least breaking even, taking one year with another, after making proper charges to revenue, including proper provision for depreciation or renewal of assets. Specific targets will be set for the NFC on the lines set out by the government in its recent White Paper *Nationalized Industries: A Review of Economic and Financial Objectives*. The road haulage and shipping activities taken over from the THC and the freightliner services taken over from the BRB will be operated on a commercial basis from the start and are expected to make a positive contribution to the Corporation's overall financial results.

25. But there is one area where it will be impossible for the NFC to break even in the early years. This is the sundries service which the Corporation will take over from the BRB. The Railways Board already have in hand a major reorganization of this traffic including the rationalization of depots, the trunk haul of some traffic by freightliner, and the transfer of some traffics to road throughout where this is more economic. This reorganization is expected substantially to reduce last year's £25 million deficit on sundries before the NFC takes the service over, and it will then be the responsibility of the NFC by further rationalization, higher productivity, and in due course by integrating the service with that of BRS Parcels Ltd, to eliminate the loss altogether. It will inevitably take some years for the NFC to achieve this end. In the meantime continued assistance will have to be given by the Exchequer, at least in the early years, to meet this loss.

26. It is therefore proposed that, subject to an overall limit to be imposed by the Transport Bill, the NFC should be given a grant in respect of the full loss on this sundries service, as estimated in advance, in each of the first three years after Vesting Day, two-thirds of the

estimated loss in the fourth year and one-third in the fifth year. On this basis the NFC would have to finance an increasing part of any loss on the sundries service in its fourth and fifth years, and any losses thereafter, from its profitable activities and from accumulated profits. The effect would be to concentrate Exchequer assistance in the period when it is most needed and subsequently to provide the maximum incentive to eliminate the remaining and probably most intractable element of the loss. . . .

III. THE FREIGHT INTEGRATION COUNCIL

31.   In order to assist the Minister of Transport to promote integration over the whole freight field, a Freight Integration Council (FIC) will be established by statute. This will be a small body consisting of the Chairman of the BRB, the Chairman of the NFC, two representatives of the trade unions representing road and rail workers and two independent members under an independent Chairman. The independent members will be people of standing who can bring relevant specialized knowledge to the Council's tasks. The Council will have a secretariat of its own provided and paid for by the Ministry of Transport.

32.   The Council's primary function will be to review and to report to the Minister periodically, or at her specific request, on the application in practice of the policy and arrangements for freight integration described in this White Paper. This will be particularly important during a period when the network of nationalized freight services will be undergoing extensive reorganization and development. The Council will also supplement the arrangements already described for co-ordination between the BRB and the NFC, particularly in the investment field. The FIC will seek to find generally acceptable solutions to issues on which the two undertakings have failed to reach agreement. Where it also fails it will be able to refer the matter to the Minister with its advice. In addition the Council will be able to propose measures that it considers would promote the integration of freight transport in the public sector. It would also examine any matters concerning freight integration referred to it by the Chairman of any of the other nationalized undertakings. The Minister will meet the Council to discuss its reports and recommendations, or any other matters of common concern, as appropriate.

The Minister's Powers

33.   The existence of the FIC will not affect the Minister's powers in relation to the BRB and the NFC, which will follow the normal pattern for nationalized industries in relation to such matters as investment and finance. However, in addition to these powers and the power to give the

Boards directions of a general character in relation to matters which appear to her to affect the national interest, the Minister proposes to take powers to give specific directions to the NFC and the BRB on matters which appear to her to require such directions and which arise from recommendations made to her by the FIC. Powers similar in form already exist in relation to matters reported to the Minister by the Transport Users' Consultative Committees.

4. POST OFFICE BECOMES A CORPORATION[1]

1.   The Post Office provides two major public utilities – posts and telecommunications – which play a vital part in the economic and social life of the nation. Its operations are correspondingly vast. During the last financial year it

- handled transactions to a total value of £7,900 million.
- invested £210 million – or more than any other public undertaking except Electricity Supply.
- dealt with 11,300 million letters and 6,900 million telephone calls.

At the end of the financial year the written-down value of its fixed assets was over £1,400 million. Its staff form nearly 2 per cent of the working population or about half the non-industrial Civil Service.

2.   Trading operations on this scale must be managed on commercial lines if they are to be efficient. Successive governments have sought to adapt the status and structure of the Post Office to meet this requirement. This began with the important changes in organization which followed the Bridgeman Report in 1932. Since 1955 the Post Office has been responsible for balancing its own income and expenditure, and has been explicitly encouraged to conduct its business as a commercial enterprise. In 1961 its finances were separated from the Exchequer. Since then it has been subject to financial disciplines similar to those applying to the statutory nationalized authorities. But constitutionally it is still a government Department, with a Minister at its head who must answer to Parliament for its day-to-day operations.

3.   The government have carried out a fundamental review of the Post Office, set against the challenging future of change and expansion which faces many of its services. Its present structure and methods are those of a Department of State. These have been evolved primarily for the formulation and execution of government policy, and are geared to

---

[1] From White Paper, *Reorganization of the Post Office*, March 1967, Cmnd. 3233, paras. 1–31. Reprinted with permission of the Controller of Her Majesty's Stationery Office.

the discharge of ministerial responsibility to Parliament. They are unsuited to the running of the postal, telecommunications and remittance services, and the new Giro service (Cmnd. 2751). The government concluded that the process begun in 1932 should be carried to its logical conclusion. A public corporation should be created to run these great businesses with a structure and methods designed directly to meet their needs, drawing on the best modern practice.

4.   The Postmaster General announced this decision in Parliament on August 3, 1966. In November 1966 he told Parliament that the Post Office Savings Department would remain as part of the Civil Service and would report to Treasury Ministers. It will be known in future as the National Savings Department.

5.   The government undertook that when the House of Commons' Select Committee on Nationalized Industries had completed its enquiry into the Post Office, and after consultation with representatives of the staff, the Postmaster General would present a White Paper to Parliament. This would set out proposals for the reorganization. The Select Committee presented its Report on 28 February 1967.

ESTABLISHMENT OF THE CORPORATION

6.   The Post Office is a major Department of State. Practically the whole of it is involved in the constitutional change. This is an undertaking without precedent. Moreover, Post Office services are an integral part of the nation's life. In addition to communications, the Post Office provides part of the machinery of the Social Security system, and many other kinds of business are transacted at Post Office counters. The government's objective is to create an authority which will

- be responsible for developing the most efficient services possible, at the lowest charges consistent with sound financial policies.
- carry on in a worthy manner the Post Office tradition of service to the public.
- develop relations with its staff in a forward looking and progressive way.

Ministerial Organization

7.   The Government have decided that a single Minister of the Crown will bear ministerial responsibility for the new Corporation and for the residue of the Postmaster General's functions (except Savings). An announcement as to which Minister will assume these functions will be made in due course.

Titles and Insignia

8.   The Corporation will be known as 'The Post Office'. Her Majesty The Queen has been pleased to approve that the title 'Royal Mail' should continue, and that the Corporation should use the Crown and the Royal Cypher as the Post Office does at present. The Sovereign's head will continue to be included in the design of stamps and postal orders. Postage stamp designs will be considered jointly by the Corporation and by the Minister and submitted to Her Majesty by the latter.

Legislation

9.   The government intend to introduce a Bill establishing the Corporation in the 1967–68 Session. The members of the Corporation will be appointed as soon as possible after the Bill becomes law. As soon as possible after that – on 'vesting day' – the Corporation will take over active responsibility for the services and will assume the appropriate assets and liabilities of the Post Office.

Position in Northern Ireland

10.   The Corporation, like the Post Office, will operate in Northern Ireland as in other parts of the United Kingdom.

THE OBLIGATIONS OF THE CORPORATION

11.   The essential purpose of the change will fail unless the Corporation has effective freedom of a kind appropriate to a nationalized authority. Yet the special role of the Corporation's services in the social fabric of Britain, and its monopoly of providing many of them, must carry special obligations. The government intend that these requirements should be reflected, both in the legislation and in the relationships of the Corporation with its users, with Parliament and with the Minister.

The Services

12.   The Corporation's most important responsibilities will be to provide letter and telephone services for the country as a whole, and to meet the needs of commerce and industry for inland and overseas communications.

13.   Post Office counter services play a vital part in the national Social Security system. The government consider it essential to provide statutory safeguards for the future functioning of this system. The Bill will confer on the Minister a reserve power to give directions to the

Corporation to make its own counter facilities available for central government and government of Northern Ireland services.

Financial Obligations

14.   The Corporation will have the same sort of financial obligations as other nationalized industries. It will be expected, as the Post Office is now, to pay its way with a sufficient margin between income and expenditure to make suitable allocations to reserves. It will observe the criteria set out in paragraphs 19–23 of the White Paper on the Financial and Economic Obligations of the Nationalized Industries (Cmnd. 1337). The Minister will settle targets with the Corporation to provide a stimulus to efficiency and to ensure that it generates an appropriate proportion of its own capital requirements. The Minister will discuss these with the Corporation as soon as possible.

15.   The Corporation will inherit a number of public services which cannot be made financially viable at any reasonable level of charge. The outstanding example is the inland telegraph service, which has run at a loss for many decades and cannot hope to pay for itself as its use continues to decline. Obligations of this kind are normally taken into account when financial targets are fixed.

16.   At present the Post Office provides agency services to the Government at 'cost' which includes the overheads of the services themselves but excludes a proper contribution to the Post Office's overall financial obligation. In future, the prices charged for agency services should make such a contribution to the achievement of the Corporation's financial obligations and the Corporation will negotiate with client Departments contracts designed with this object in view. The Minister will be given a reserve power to determine the charge to be made in the event of disagreement.

THE POSITION OF PARLIAMENT

17.   The constitution and responsibilities of the Corporation will be embodied in legislation. Its accountability to Parliament will be different from that at present. There will no longer be a Minister answerable to Parliament for its day-to-day activities. But both Houses will have the opportunity to consider the Report and Accounts of the Corporation when these are laid before Parliament every year. The work of the Corporation will be subject to scrutiny by Committees of the House of Commons. Increases in the total amount it may borrow will need to be approved by the House of Commons.

18.   The Minister responsible for the government's functions in relation to the Corporation will be answerable to Parliament for the

discharge of these functions and for the exercise of his powers (see paragraph 37 below).

SAFEGUARDS FOR THE USER

19. Parliament and public have a right to expect guarantees that the Corporation will be responsive to the social and business needs of users and sensitive to their opinion. For this reason, the government attach great importance to the arrangements to be made for user consultation.

20. The keystone of the consultative structure will be a national Users' Council to be established by legislation, with a secretariat independent of the Corporation. In appointing the Council the Minister will take account of the desirability of having members who are familiar with the special requirements and circumstances of the various parts of Britain. Arrangements will be made to ensure that there is effective consultative machinery below national level. The Council will represent the interests of all users. It will be able to make recommendations about the services. It will consider proposals put to it by the Corporation, and any complaints from individual users which may be remitted to it from below national level. The user consultative machinery as a whole will be flexible and readily adaptable to change.

21. The Bill will require the Corporation to consult the Council about all major proposals affecting its main services, in so far as these affect users. This will extend to proposals to vary, introduce or discontinue main services on a national scale. Its function in relation to charges and conditions of service is explained in paragraph 24 below. The Users' Council will have access to the Minister if it disagrees with the Corporation. The government will do all they can to foster a successful working relationship between the Corporation, the Council and the other consultative organs.

CHARGES AND CONDITIONS

22. The Corporation, like all other businesses and the nationalized industries, will be expected to have regard to the requirements of the national prices and incomes policy and its charges will be subject to prices and incomes legislation. It will also be expected to follow the informal arrangements for consultation about substantial changes in the level of prices between the Boards of nationalized industries and the Ministers concerned, currently formalized in the arrangements for early warning of increases in prices or charges described in the White Paper – *Prices and Incomes Policy: An 'Early Warning' System* (Cmnd. 2808).

23. Subject to these general considerations, the Corporation will itself have statutory power to fix charges for its services and facilities and

the conditions on which they are to be provided. It will be required to publish these charges and conditions.

24.   The government intend that the advice of the Users' Council, as the principal organ of consumer interest, should play an important role in the fixing of the Corporation's charges and conditions of service. But these will necessarily cover a very wide range indeed, including both the major elements of the main services – like the charge for a letter or telephone call charges – and those for minor and ancillary services and facilities, used only by relatively few people, but requiring to be set out in great detail. The government believe that it would hinder rather than help the work of the Council if the Corporation were obliged to follow a uniform consultation procedure for charges over the whole of this great range, regardless of their importance. They would naturally expect the Corporation to make suitable working arrangements to keep the Council informed about all developments in the field of charges and conditions. But the legislation will impose an obligation on the Corporation to consult the Users' Council only about proposals for major changes in the charges or conditions for the main services. It will provide for disagreements between Corporation and Council about interpretation of this provision to be referred to the Minister for decision.

THE POWERS OF THE CORPORATION

25.   The Corporation will be equipped with the statutory powers, including the financial powers, it needs to run the Post Office services which are to be transferred to it, including the Giro.

26.   The Corporation will brorow long term exclusively from the Minister, and will be empowered to borrow temporarily from the Minister or with his consent from other persons. The Treasury will be able to guarantee short term borrowing from the banks under this provision. Total outstanding borrowings in addition to the opening capital debt will be given a specific limit. As has been said earlier, any increases in the total amount which the Corporation may borrow will need to be approved by the House of Commons.

27.   The Bill will confer various ancillary and general powers on the Corporation, including power to manufacture anything used in connection with the exercise of its powers. The Corporation will also have power to form subsidiaries and to engage in joint undertakings with other organizations. It will be expected to consult the Minister if it proposes to undertake on a large scale any manufacturing work which the Post Office had not done previously.

28.   The Postmaster General's existing monopoly of the carriage of letters under the Post Office Act 1953 and his telecommunications

monopoly under the Telegraph Act 1869 extend to the United Kingdom, the Channel Islands and the Isle of Man. The Bill will confer on the Corporation a corresponding monopoly of the carriage of letters and, in a modernized form, of telecommunications within the United Kingdom. The question of the continued application of the postal and telecommunications monopolies to the Channel Islands and the Isle of Man will be discussed with the Insular Authorities in the Channel Islands and with the Government of the Isle of Man.

29. The Postmaster General's existing telecommunications monopoly is generally speaking confined to communications between one person and another who is not the former's servant or agent. The government do not intend that the Corporation should have a wider monopoly in this respect, so that the position of private networks operated at present outside the Postmaster General's monopoly will not be affected. The monopoly will not extend to broadcast transmissions from radio stations direct to the general public.

30. The Postmaster General's legal monopoly extends to inland telecommunications only, though in practice he is able to exert certain controls over the activities of overseas telecommunications operators in this country. The government have decided that, subject to the limitations expressed in the preceding paragraph, the Corporation's monopoly should extend, within the area of the United Kingdom (and – dependent upon the outcome of the negotiations referred to in paragraph 28 – the Channel Islands and the Isle of Man) to overseas telecommunications to, from and via that area. They have reached this conclusion because, with the rapid technological developments that are taking place in this field, overseas and inland telecommunications systems are becoming increasingly integrated from the operational point of view. Thus, for example, the International Subscriber Dialling and national Subscriber Trunk Dialling networks are interdependent to the point, where, to the user, they are virtually one system. The government believe that in these circumstances it is right for the Corporation's monopoly to extend to overseas telecommunications.

31. The Corporation will be empowered to grant licences under its monopolies, subject to the consent of the Minister, and to charge royalties on them. The reorganization will not affect any vested rights of the Corporation of Kingston-upon-Hull existing on vesting day to operate their own local telephone system, or other rights then existing under telegraph licences. Nor will it mean that overseas telecommunications operators will lose any rights in this country which they then have. But the Corporation's licence will be required for any renewal of such rights, and for the operation of any new telecommunication facilities within its monopoly.

5. OWNERSHIP OF BRITISH AIRLINES[1]

SHOULD THE PUBLIC SECTOR HAVE A SPECIAL ROLE?

493.   These paragraphs are really written for the avoidance of doubt. It is important to distinguish between what the public sector will be doing because of the tasks that happen to be assigned to it in the aviation field, and what it may be doing because it is publicly owned.

494.   On the first point, one thing is clear. BOAC and BEA are the leading British carriers and will therefore carry the burden of responsibility that falls to leadership. In IATA, for example, they are bound to be our principal representatives and will carry a large burden of IATA work. Similarly in technological development they, like large airlines everywhere, will carry the responsibility of innovation.

495.   On the second point, the fact of public ownership should not give the Corporations either advantage or disadvantage as against their private sector colleagues. They should be encouraged to act commercially in the same sense that large and efficient private sector undertakings would do – i.e. taking into account the long view which might mean accepting losses in certain areas in the short-term. If, because of the tasks assigned to them or for any other reason, they are precluded from behaving commercially in any field they should be relieved of the special non-commercial burden of this. Similarly, the fact that they are publicly owned should not cause them to receive any privilege or enjoy softer treatment than their private sector colleagues, or by contrast to labour under competitive inhibitions and administrative frustrations. The avoidance of any sense of unfairness should be an important point of policy if the industry is to work well in future. From time to time we shall have need to come back to this in other chapters.

SUMMARY

(1)   Our attitude to public and private ownership is pragmatic rather than philosophical. We believe that it is not ownership as such that is crucial to the quality of performance: it is the drive, enthusiasm, skill and dedication of the managements and their teams that really determine whether an airline is good or bad. These qualities will be encouraged or inhibited according to the environment and according to the behaviour of Parliament, Ministers and civil servants; we believe that competition and rivalry, where these can be secured without loss of scale economies, have an important part to play.

[1] From Report on *British Air Transport in the Seventies* (Edwards), May 1969' Cmnd. 4018, Chapter 9, pages 124–25, paras. 493–end. Reprinted with permission of the Controller of Her Majesty's Stationery Office.

(2)   We believe that there is no case for a policy of denationalization and recommend that airlines based on BEA and BOAC should continue to be publicly owned. We see little merit in artificially contriving a private minority holding. But we would certainly not oppose private stakes should there be good practical reasons.

(3)   There is a place in the industry for privately owned airlines and for airlines of mixed ownership.

(4) With the exception of the 'second force', in which the State should have a right to invest in convertible loan stock, no private airline should be forced to accept partial State ownership. The private sector when rationalized will need to be financially strong if it is to play its part. There may well be scope through BAS for airlines to which the public sector and the private sector can both contribute.

(5) It is an important point of policy that, if a mixed economy is to work well, everything should be done to avoid a sense of unfairness either in the public or the private sector.

CHAPTER III

ECONOMIC POLICIES AND ASSESSMENTS

The performance of any industrial body, reckoned in economic terms, must be central to its existence. Whether or not the reckoning should be exclusively economic is an issue that concerns this chapter and the two that follow. More important for this chapter, however, is the nature of the economic reckoning itself. What should be the economic aims or objectives of the industries? What criteria should be used to assess their economic performance?

At some stages of the debate about the purposes of nationalized industries, it has seemed as if the only issue lay between a 'purely economic' or 'commercial' viewpoint on the one hand, and a 'social' or 'wider objectives' view on the other. This is an oversimplification. The economic objectives themselves need formulation. The classical statement of the 'purely economic' position in the Herbert report on electricity supply in 1956 did not go into any sort of detail. It declared that (unless otherwise instructed) those running the boards should keep to a purely economic course, but apparently felt no need to say more.

It is perhaps relevant to stress that the question of objectives is not all that obvious for private enterprise concerns either. There is of course a certain respect for profit-making, but whether it will be *maximum* profit is unlikely to be very clear. In some cases firms will formulate, for their own guidance, some notion of a desirable return on capital for a few years ahead. Some firms proclaim an ideology of social purpose for themselves. For any private business, however, objectives will be internally generated; and here lies the main distinction in this matter between private and publicly owned concerns.

To begin with, it may be thought that aims once specified as purely economic, are self-evident. But if what is supposed to be evident is profit-maximization, this will not do for statutory bodies with monopoly rights. The events of the 1950s also showed the simple rule about covering costs, taking one year with another, to be inadequate. What provision for investment is to be made? What scale of operation is to be aimed at?

The first attempt to deal with the problems brought about by this situation is found in the government's White Paper of 1961. Extracts from this are to be found in Professor Hanson's earlier volume of readings (p. 273), but its basic importance requires its further inclusion here.

This White Paper dealt with a number of sore points of the 1950s. It specified the break-even period at five years; it clarified the methods of capital-raising, set up a system of financial targets and gave some indication of possible government acknowledgment of its responsibility for prices. It did not, however, set out any criteria for the guidance of the industries in determining their investment, nor did it deal with the issue of pricing policy. In 1967 another White Paper, *Nationalized Industries: a review of economic and financial objectives*, attempted to remedy these deficiencies. It added two policy guidelines: a principle of investment appraisal by discounted cash flow techniques at a prescribed test rate of discount; and a declaration that, in addition to recovering accounting costs, prices should be 'reasonably related' to marginal costs. A considerable extract from this White Paper is printed here. Together, these two papers constitute the core of general doctrine about economic policy for nationalization in Britain.

Central to these principles is the technique of investment appraisal, and current methods were explained by the Treasury in evidence to the Select Committee on Nationalized Industries in 1967. Incorporated in the 1967 White Paper was a suggestion that the appropriate test discount rate would be 8 per cent. An explanation of how this figure was arrived at is provided in the next extract, again from Treasury evidence to the Select Committee.

The extract that follows contains a discussion of policies about investment and prices – the new economic framework of 1967. This is taken from the Select Committee's report on *Ministerial Control* of 1968. There is a great deal of useful information about the practice of various methods of control in chapters 9 and 10 of the report, for which there is no space here. Similarly, there has been a long pre-occupation with the distinction between direct costs and benefits of an industry and its social consequences, and this is thoroughly discussed in chapter 14 of the Ministerial Control report.

The economic material in the report on Ministerial Control was partly a matter of exposition; but it was also a commentary. It was therefore itself subject to comment, and the economically relevant parts of a critique by Professor Robson and of the government's White Paper replying to the report constitute the next two extracts. One attempt to ease the financial problems of the industry was the creation of 'exchequer dividend capital' in BOAC in 1966 and 'public dividend capital' in the British Steel Corporation in 1969. This device is explained and discussed in the two extracts which follow.

The final contribution in this chapter is an article by Richard Pryke, of the University of Liverpool, defending the efficiency of the nationalized industries, by reference to their record in labour productivity and other criteria, published in 1970. The issues are discussed at length in Mr. Pryke's book *Public Enterprise in Practice* (Macgibbon and Kee, 1971).

Though there is no space to include them in this volume, mention should be made of two other contributions to the question of objectives. In a study of *Comparative Returns from Investment in Nationalized Industries* published by the Institute of Economic Affairs in 1968, George Polanyi discusses the possibility of a profit-maximization remit to the public corporations. Again, in chapter 2 of the Edwards report on *British Air Transport in the Seventies* plural objectives are set forth, and there is a discussion of wide interest, for – as the report says – the question of objectives 'is not as simple a matter as it might appear'.

6. THE 1961 WHITE PAPER[1]

4.   The industries, which were subject to the nationalization measures in the years 1946 to 1950 had very different histories and differed considerably (as they still do) in their prospects. Their economic strength also differed and they had to carry varying burdens of non-commercial, and generally unprofitable, obligations. Their economic and financial rights and obligations, as prescribed by the nationalizing statutes, followed a fairly standard pattern. This was based on the view that they were neither straightforward commercial concerns nor social services, but a combination of both: and perhaps on the hope that the ability to borrow at government rates would enable them to meet the limited financial obligations prescribed by statute and also to carry out their non-commercial obligations. For a variety of reasons (many of which have been outside the control of the undertakings themselves) their financial performance has generally fallen short of these hopes.

PAYING THEIR WAY

5.   The undertakings have, in common parlance, been expected to pay their way and most of the nationalizing statutes contain a require-

[1] From White Paper, *The Financial and Economic Obligations of the Nationalized Industries*, April 1961, Cmnd. 1337, paras. 4–9 and 17–33. Reprinted with permission of the Controller of Her Majesty's Stationery Office.

ment to this effect. Their statutory obligations prescribe that their revenues should, on an average of good and bad years (or similar phrase) be not less than sufficient to meet all items properly chargeable to revenue, including interest, depreciation, the redemption of capital and the provision of reserves. Thus the Acts prescribe a minimum performance and not a maximum. Moreover, this performance is defined in terms of a surplus or deficit, which differs from the ordinary definition of profit or loss inasmuch as provision is required to be made from revenue for all the items mentioned above before a surplus in the statutory sense arises. The undertakings were thus expected to make some profits in the ordinary sense of that term in order to accumulate reserves from them.

6. It was envisaged that in some years the nationalized undertakings might have a surplus and in other years a deficit. This provision was inevitable, for fluctuations in general business conditions were bound to affect their financial results, and there is no equity capital to act as a buffer. But if deficits are inevitable in some years surpluses must be accumulated in good years; and the period over which an average of surpluses and deficits is struck must not be unduly prolonged.

7. The wording of the Acts implies that the industries should provide out of revenue not only for payment of interest on capital but also both for depreciation and the redemption of capital. If these requirements were stringently interpreted they would impose upon the industries the responsibility not merely of providing from revenue for the maintenance of their capital assets but eventually of ridding themselves of capital liabilities. In practice, with the agreement of successive governments, the industries, like their predecessors, have not been required (nor have they sought) to make provision on this scale.

8. Their practice has varied according to their economic strength, their traditions and the precise nature of their individual statutory obligations. In general they calculate the provision for depreciation in their accounts on the historic costs of their assets. Most of the Boards recognize in their reports that, following the practice generally adopted by industrial concerns, it would be prudent to make some additional provision out of revenue to meet the difference, which emerges when prices rise, between depreciation at historic cost and at replacement cost and as a reserve against obsolescence.

9. The Acts also provide for the building up of general reserves and give Ministers power to issue directions as to the amounts. Although some of the undertakings show general reserves in their balance sheets these are in some cases entirely obliterated by accumulated deficits on revenue account. The total retained income of all these industries taken together (including supplementary depreciation provisions, capital

redemption funds and reserves) has not been sufficient to provide for the replacement of assets used up in the production processes, and this is also the case in most of the individual industries concerned. . . .

A NEW FINANCIAL FRAMEWORK

17.   In the government's view there would be no advantage in altering the basic financial and economic principles which the nationalized undertakings are by their statutes required to observe. If, however, these principles are to provide a satisfactory basis for their operation in the public interest they need to be intepreted more precisely in the form of financial objectives for the nationalized undertakings generally.

18.   The main heads under which clarification or re-statement of the obligations and relationships envisaged in the nationalizing Acts is needed are as follows:

> Revenue Account.
>
> Capital Account.
>
> Prices and Costs.

REVENUE ACCOUNT

19.   The government consider that the financial objectives of the nationalized undertakings under their Statutes should now in general be interpreted on the following lines:

(a) Surpluses on Revenue Account should be at least sufficient to cover deficits on Revenue Account *over a 5-year period*: in arriving at the surpluses and deficits for each year there should be charged against revenue the items normally so chargeable (including interest, and depreciation on the historic cost basis).

(b) Provision should also be made from revenue for:

> (i) such an amount as may be necessary to cover the excess of depreciation calculated on replacement cost basis over depreciation calculated on historic cost as in (a) above.[1]
>
> (ii) adequate allocations to general reserves which will be available *inter alia* as a contribution towards their capital development and as a safeguard against premature obsolescence and similar contingencies.

[1] The undertakings would not be required specifically to make good now any under-provision (i.e. on account of the difference between the historic cost basis and the replacement cost basis), which has already occurred in years prior to the operation of these new arrangements.

20. It is the government's view that in general anything more than a five-year period as the balancing period for the formula in paragraph 19 would be too long for effectiveness. They propose, in consultation with each board which has financial autonomy under the Acts, to agree a framework on the above lines for the next five years as an experimental period, but the operation will be subject to review each year in the light of events inside and outside the industry. This procedure will be applied in all the major nationalized industries,[1] including the Post Office.

21. The wide differences in the economic conditions of the various nationalized undertakings have been emphasized earlier in this paper. Their earning power, total depreciation provision and reserve requirements will vary according to their prospective commercial, technological and financial development. The criteria in paragraph 19 would be consistent with the general run of the existing statutory obligations, but they cannot be expressed as one standard formula to be applied to all nationalized undertakings alike.

22. Experience has shown, however, a general need for nationalized industries – even those which were at one time reckoned to be relatively free from commercial risk – to build up adequate reserves to deal with contingencies which may affect their capital as well as their revenue accounts. Moreover, there are powerful grounds in the national interest for requiring these undertakings to make a substantial contribution towards the cost of their capital development out of their own earnings, and so reduce their claims upon the nation's savings and the burden on the Exchequer: this is particularly so for those undertakings which are expanding fast and which have relatively large capital needs. In normal circumstances, the desirable level of reserves should be related to the amount of capital employed in the business.

23. It follows from all these considerations that the State, as owner or guarantor of the capital of the nationalized industries (which are investing over £800 millions a year, more than half of which comes from the Exchequer), would expect capital employed in this kind of business to earn a higher rate of return than the cost of the money to the Exchequer. The objective for each undertaking will be determined in the light of its own circumstances, needs and capabilities in relation to the criteria in paragraph 19. For some, the objectives may be expressed in terms of progress towards an appropriate level of self-financing of their capital expenditure, concurrently with the provision of suitable contributions to reserve. For others, the objective may be in terms of a specified rate of return on capital employed.

---

[1] Separate proposals have been made (Cmnd. 1248 of December 1960) for some of the nationalized transport undertakings, including the railways.

CAPITAL ACCOUNT

24. The existing procedures for discussion and authorization of matters concerning investment and borrowing will be continued and can be codified as follows:

(i) The government will each year discuss with the undertaking and approve the general lines of its plans for development and capital expenditure for the next five years ahead and be ready to agree to long-term commitments as appropriate.

(ii) In the light of (i) the government will each year fix an upper limit on the amounts to be spent on investment by the undertaking during the two years ahead.

(iii) The government will approve proposed borrowings on the basis of an annual reasoned estimate submitted by the undertaking.

(iv) The government will require to be kept informed of the extent to which the undertaking is proposing to invest new capital in projects which are expected to yield a relatively low return.

25. These requirements flow from the government's responsibility to keep public sector investment generally within the nation's resources, as well as from the government's role as provider of public capital. It would be the government's task to satisfy themselves that the procedure within each organization for scrutinizing and approving capital expenditure was effective.

26. The existing arrangements under which capital expenditure in excess of the approved ceiling, or borrowing in excess of the estimates, are subject to investigation and discussion between the undertakings and the Departments would continue. These procedures fit in with the recent arrangements under which Parliament has been given more detailed information about the estimates of investment and borrowing from the Exchequer and the government's undertaking to inform Parliament of the reasons for any marked variation between the estimate and the out-turn.

27. While the proposed arrangements are adapted to the present system, under which the industries resort to the Exchequer for their long-term capital requirements, the proposed clarification of financial obligations and the improvement in financial performance would be necessary and desirable in any event. The reasons which caused the government to discontinue in 1956 the procedure of borrowing from the market, with the support of a Government guarantee, and to withdraw the financing of the transport, gas and electricity industries from the market into the Exchequer are still valid. While the government recognize the force of the arguments in favour of requiring national-ized bodies to raise money from the market on their own credit, they see

no possibilities of an early move in this direction. They accept the view of the Committee under the chairmanship of Lord Radcliffe on the Working of the Monetary System (Cmnd. 827, paragraph 595) that such unguaranteed borrowing is not a realistic alternative, at least for the present. The amounts of money needed are much too large to be raised in the open market without government support and the industries are, of necessity, closely associated in the public mind with the government, so that it would be difficult for the market to regard them as independent financial concerns. Whatever may be the possibilities for the future, an improvement in the financial record as contemplated under the present proposals would be a prerequisite.

28. The procedures in paragraphs 20 to 26 would be applicable as long as the financial performance and prospects of the undertaking were satisfactory in terms of the new financial framework. In other cases the government would be bound to take a closer interest. Thus inability or prospective inability to meet the requirements in paragraph 19 (a) would be regarded as falling so far short of the objectives that the undertaking would be required to propose specific measures for righting the situation: it would naturally consult the Minister about these and the Minister would expect to be satisfied on various issues, including the financial justification for major investment proposals. Even if the undertaking were fulfilling the requirement in paragraph 19 (a), inability to achieve the objective set for it under paragraph 23, would be regarded as inadequate performance. In this case, the undertaking would be under an obligation to inform the Minister of the general plans for preventing the situation from deteriorating further and for making up the leeway.

PRICES AND COSTS

29. A clear definition of each Board's financial obligations inevitably raises the question of the extent to which the Boards should have freedom in their pricing policies. Although the government possess no formal power to fix prices in the nationalized industries, nationalized undertakings have, in fixing their prices, given great weight to considerations of the national interest brought to their attention.

30. Increased prices would not be the only way in which nationalized undertakings could carry out the prescribed financial obligations. For a variety of reasons, such as fructification of investment and reduction of unprofitable activities, combined with continuing improvements in commercial efficiency, some of the industries will be capable of increased productivity, part of which should be available to improve their financial results. The aim of the industries generally will naturally be to secure

the necessary additions to their net revenue as far as possible by reduction in costs. The government recognize, however, that the industries must have freedom to make upward price adjustments especially where their prices are artificially low.

31. While recognizing the case for greater freedom and flexibility in the pricing policies of nationalized industries the government must interest themselves in the prices of these goods and services which are basic to the life of the community and some of which contain a monopolistic element. In addition to the formal arrangements for the representation of consumers' views through Consultative Councils in the various industries and for the regulation of fares and charges in certain cases, the existing informal arrangements are that the Chairman of the Boards ascertain in advance the views of the appropriate Ministers when they prepare to make substantial changes in the level of their prices. In the government's view these arrangements should continue. If a Board decided to modify their own proposals by reason of views expressed by the Minister it would be open to them to require a written statement of those views, which could be published by the Minister or the Board, and to propose an appropriate adjustment of their financial objectives where, in their opinion, this modification would significantly impair their ability to meet them.

32. Financial performance is affected not only by the level of prices but by the level of costs. Costs may in turn be significantly affected by the amount of commercially unprofitable activities carried on by individual undertakings. These activities will, so far as practicable, have been taken into account in fixing the financial standard for each undertaking. To the extent that commercially unprofitable activities are subsequently imposed from outside, a Board would be entitled to ask for an adjustment of its financial objectives.

CONCLUSION

33. The nationalized industries are from their size and nature bound to play a major role in the economic life of the country. They cannot, however, be regarded only as very large commercial concerns which may be judged mainly on their commercial results: all have, although in varying degrees, wider obligations than commercial concerns in the private sector. The object of these proposals is to find for each industry or Board a reasonable balance between these two concepts. The government believe that the closer definition now proposed for the financial and economic obligations of the industries should help improve their performance and morale. It should also reduce the occasion and need for outside intervention in the affairs of the industries and enable them

to make the maximum contribution towards their own development and the well-being of the community as a whole.

7. THE 1967 WHITE PAPER[1]

2.   The statutory duties of nationalized industries are set out in the nationalization Acts. Broadly they are to meet the demand for their products and services in the most efficient way and to conduct their finances so that over time they at least break even, after making a contribution to reserves. The statutes however gave no guidance on what was meant by efficiency in economic terms, and prescribed only a minimum standard of financial performance. This was defined in terms of surplus (or deficit); it differs from the ordinary concept of profit (or loss) in that provision must be made for all items properly chargeable to revenue under the statutes.

3.   It was later found necessary to make this requirement more specific; and further guidance for the industries was set out in the White Paper on the Financial and Economic Obligations of the Nationalized Industries in 1961 (Cmnd. 1337). This interpreted the statutory provisions as meaning that industries should aim to balance their accounts 'taking one year with another' over a period of five years, after providing for interest, and depreciation at historic cost. Provision should also be made for the difference between depreciation at historic cost and replacement cost and allocations to reserve sufficient to make some contribution towards the industry's future capital development programme (which would otherwise fall on the Exchequer) and as a safeguard against premature obsolescence and similar contingencies. Financial objectives or 'targets' were to be determined for each undertaking in the light of its needs and capabilities in relation to these criteria. In practice targets have normally been expressed as a rate of return on the undertaking's assets though other methods of expressing them were not ruled out.[2]

4.   In the six years since 1961 much has happened. There have been important technological changes and discoveries of new natural resources which affect the long-term prospects of the fuel industries. There have been changes in the pattern of demand which affect the transport and aviation industries. Despite contractions in one or two industries,

[1] From White Paper, *Nationalized Industries: a review of economic and financial objectives,* November 1967, Cmnd. 3437, paras. 2–40. Reprinted with permission of the Controller of Her Majesty's Stationery Office.

[2] A list of the financial objectives currently in force is at Table 1 (not reprinted).

the overall capacity of the nationalized sector has been growing fast to meet increased demand. All this has led to investment on a scale far greater than was foreseen six years ago. In consequence, calls upon scarce resources of manpower and capital are now very heavy; and the need to measure these calls, to assess priorities, and to allocate resources upon an economically and socially rational basis has become even more important.

5. The government's objectives for industry are to increase the productivity of both labour and capital employed; to raise the rate of new capital formation; to ensure that new equipment is as technologically advanced as possible and is effectively deployed; to increase the profitability of new investment; and to obtain the maximum return in terms of the production of goods and services. The nationalized industries have a vital role to play in the attainment of these objectives as well as in the development of the government's wider social and economic policies. With the nationalization of steel, their net assets are now valued at nearly £12,000 million and they invest annually around £1,700 million, over half of which is at present financed by the Exchequer. Their annual investment is equivalent to the whole of that for private manufacturing industry; they contribute about 11 per cent of the gross domestic product and they employ around 8 per cent of the total labour force.[1] When the government's proposals for further nationalization in the docks are implemented, they will provide most of the economy's basic needs for energy, transport, communications, steel and export facilities; and the efficiency with which so large a sector operates will have a significant impact on the evolution and rate of growth of the whole economy. In their case the objectives outlined above cannot be achieved merely by maximizing the financial returns of each industry: significant costs and benefits can occur which are outside the financial concern of the industry and it is the special responsibility of the government to ensure that these 'social' factors are reflected in the industries' planning.

INVESTMENT

6. Investment is fundamental to economic growth and largely determines the way in which industries develop. The investment programmes of the nationalized industries are framed in the light of the

[1] Table 2 (not reprinted) gives for each industry for 1966/67 (the latest year for which figures have been published) figures of net assets, net income, fixed investment, Exchequer loans and total employees. Tables 3 and 4 (not reprinted) respectively show net and gross income as a percentage of average net assets for each industry and for each year over the period 1955/56–1966/67.

75

Government's policy for the sector (fuel, transport, etc.) concerned. Investment is often a necessary condition for the achievement of reductions in costs, and the choice between different ways of satisfying consumer demand requires careful and sophisticated calculations. The development plans for industrial sectors must greatly influence investment decisions made by individual public corporations, and, conversely, the pattern of investment decisions that is expected provides some of the basic information on which broad industrial policies are formulated by the appropriate government departments in consultation with the industries. There is no simple automatic rule for ensuring the consistency of decisions, and it will remain the job of sponsoring Departments to ensure that the strategy of economic development for their sector evolves appropriately in the light of changing circumstances and technological advances. Within the framework set by these strategies, investment decisions must be made against the appropriate criteria.

7. Investment projects must normally show a satisfactory return in commercial terms unless they are justifiable on wider criteria involving an assessment of the social costs and benefits involved, or are provided to meet a statutory obligation. Subject to these considerations, the government's policy is to treat the industries as commercial bodies and the underlying concept behind the control of nationalized industries' investment by rate of return is that the most efficient distribution of goods and services in the economy as a whole can be secured only if investments are made where the return to the economy is greatest. This holds true whatever the level of investment in the economy. The rate of return on new capital is not the same as the overall return on net assets; the two may diverge quite widely, for reasons discussed below.

8. The government expects the nationalized industries to use the best possible methods of appraisal. Discounted cash flow techniques, which are already widely used by the nationalized industries, are recommended for all important projects. By taking account of the effects of the timing of cash outlays and receipts, these techniques enable proper comparison to be made between alternative projects. They can be applied in different ways, and the industries are free to adopt whatever method suits them best, but the government will expect projects which are submitted to it for approval to be expressed in present values by the use of a test rate of discount.[1]

9. This test rate of discount must be sufficient to ensure that resources are efficiently used, and represents the minimum rate of return to be expected on a marginal low-risk project undertaken for commercial

---

[1] For a detailed discussion of discounted cash flow techniques see Appendix A of Treasury Memorandum to Select Committee on Nationalized Industries (Sub-Committee A), Session 1966/67 (H.C. 440/VIII, pages 291–8).

reasons. It is essential that the nationalized industries should use consistent methods of appraisal and should adopt the same test discount rate.

10. The government have decided that 8 per cent is a reasonable figure to use for this purpose in present circumstances. The figure is broadly consistent, having regard to differing circumstances in relation to tax, investment grants, etc., with the average rate of return in real terms looked for on low-risk projects in the private sector in recent years. Some nationalized industries have been using similar rates for investment appraisal in recent years. Following discussions with the industries about the application of these methods to their individual circumstances, the government is now asking the nationalized industries to use this rate until further notice. It is intended to apply to expenditure and receipts related to investment projects before allowing for tax; this is appropriate in the case of nationalized industries which although subject to tax in the same way as private industry, do not receive investment grants on their main activities.[1]

11. The test rate of discount is different from the rate of interest which the nationalized industries will pay on new borrowing from the Exchequer since they borrow at rates reflecting government credit. Access to this source of funds should not imply any relaxation of the economic criteria appropriate to investment for commercial purposes. The surplus over their interest liabilities provides part of the finance for the industries' investment programmes.

12. The test rate of discount, being a uniform rate for all industries, does not include allowance for the risks of individual investments. Exercising judgment as to what risks are worth taking is essentially a function of management. Whenever possible, estimates should be made of the likely range of outcomes, and investment undertaken only when management judges that prospects are, on balance, favourable. In these calculations the cost of capital should be taken as 8 per cent, so that prospective gains and losses can be compared in a consistent way. In some types of case, however, it may be impossible to make meaningful estimates of the degree of risk in quantitative form, and in these cases it will be desirable to use a more stringent criterion – that is, a higher test discount rate than the recommended one – in appraising exceptionally risky projects. Normally, the alternative receipts and outlays assumed in discounted cash flow calculations themselves represent the various possible expected outcomes. Risk is thus built into the cash-flow

---

[1] The rate to be used by the British Steel Corporation has yet to be settled. As part of manufacturing industry the Corporation will receive investment grants and these will have to be allowed for in determining the appropriate test rate of discount.

figures used and there is no need to allow for it separately in the discount rate chosen. Similarly the test rate of discount does not include an allowance for inflation; it is therefore necessary to base investment appraisals on the assumption that the prices of inputs and outputs are not affected by changes in the general price level. (Clearly, however, it is necessary to allow for expected changes in relative prices.)

13.   The use of this test rate of discount in investment calculations does not of course imply that nationalized industries should never invest new capital in the supply of goods and services which do not show a return of at least 8 per cent in real terms on the capital employed. There are circumstances in which it is desirable for social or wider economic reasons to provide such services; and it is desirable in a few cases to provide services at some direct financial loss. But all projects need to be assessed in a systematic way allowing for uncertainties in the forecasts of demand and of technological developments so that their direct return can be estimated before any other considerations are taken into account.

14.   The economic value of investments cannot always be measured by reference to the financial return to the industry concerned. Many investments also produce social costs and benefits which can in principle be valued in financial terms and which, when taken into account, will provide a good economic justification for them. Examples of these are extensions to the underground network in London which take account of congestion costs. Equally so there are cases like the railway branch lines where the government may take social and regional considerations into account in requiring an industry to undertake continuing operations which are themselves unprofitable; but these generally involve current rather than capital expenditure. Again, the demands of the nationalized industries for capital goods often exercise considerable influence on the pattern of their suppliers and of regional employment. These are factors which the government and the nationalized industries must take into account. Often the social costs and benefits arising from a particular investment are not significantly different from those associated with other investments offering similar financial returns, and to measure an investment by its financial return can for most practical purposes be regarded as giving a reasonable approximation to its value to the community. But where there are grounds for thinking that the social costs or benefits do diverge markedly from those associated with the alternatives the government will take this into account when assessing the investment. Indeed it must take a wider view than that of the industry itself, since the government's objective is to secure the maximum social return on the capital invested, while the industry's concern is properly with the financial return.

15.   Techniques of social cost/benefit evaluation are being developed

though there are often difficulties and uncertainties involved in making the calculations. Social cost/benefit studies may prove valuable in comparing investments within broad sectors of the economy (transport, fuel, etc.) where comparison cannot be made on financial terms because pricing arrangements in different parts of the sector are not comparable; they may also be necessary to assess the return to the economy of certain very large projects. Some of the costs and benefits, however, lie in fields where nationalized industries are not in a position to make estimates; and in order to be sure that assumptions are applied consistently, overall cost/benefit studies of major projects are best carried out by the government Departments concerned, in collaboration with the industries.

16. Equally, it does not follow that all investments passing the test rate are automatically undertaken. The test rate of discount is essentially a device to ensure that the calls of the public and private sectors upon resources do not get out of line with each other over the long term. After a nationalized industry has prepared an investment programme based on the demand it expects to meet at rational price levels, and appraised in the way just described, the government then has to consider it in the light of developments elsewhere in the economy, especially short-term ones, and of other calls on resources. The government are thus concerned with the phasing of investment which needs to be considered in the light of real resources available. The sums involved are now so large in relation to other public and private sector expenditure that there may also be special problems of financing. Alternative public sector borrowing arrangements will be kept under review, but nothing would be gained by going back to separate stock issues for the nationalized industries. These would involve serious problems of market management and would not create any additional savings. If therefore some easing of pressure in the short term is indicated, the government may arrange for the deferment of desirable but not immediately essential investment. But if in the long term the level of investment in the nationalized industries as a whole is considered excessive, then the proper course would be to adjust the test discount rate.

PRICES

17. The use of correct methods of investment appraisal will only be effective if the nationalized industries also adopt, within the context of national prices and incomes policy, pricing policies relevant to their economic circumstances. The circumstances of different industries vary greatly: much depends on the competitive environment, domestic or international, in which they operate. Nevertheless there are certain general considerations. The government's policy here starts from the

principle that nationalized industries' revenues should normally cover their accounting costs in full – including the service of capital and appropriate provision for its replacement. But important though this is, it is not in itself sufficient to produce a rational pricing policy. Prices, if they are to contribute towards a more efficient distribution of resources, must also attract resources to places where they can make the most effective contribution to meeting the demands of users.

18.   It is therefore important that, while covering overall accounting costs wherever possible, pricing policies should be devised with reference to the costs of the particular goods and services provided. Unless this is done, there is a risk of undesirable cross-subsidization and consequent misallocation of resources. The aim of pricing policy should be that the consumer should pay the true costs of providing the goods and services he consumes, in every case where these can be sensibly identified. There are of course exceptions to the general rule. In some cases there will be good commercial reasons for charging prices which differ from costs. In others it may be simply impracticable to cost separately relatively minor operations. In a few cases, cross-subsidization may be justified by statutory requirements or by wider economic or social considerations. But – these cases apart – to cross-subsidize loss-making services amounts to taxing remunerative services provided by the same undertaking and is as objectionable as subsidizing from general taxation services which have no social justification.

19.   Another reason for charging prices different from costs may arise when there is persistent spare capacity, either for relatively long periods or at certain times, places or seasons. This capacity is unlikely to be used economically unless charges adequately reflect the difference between the costs of meeting additional demand where spare capacity exists and the higher costs where additional capacity has to be provided to meet demand. Thus where there is additional demand which could be met without major investment in new plant, it is desirable that prices should be reduced if this would stimulate demand – if necessary to the level where the escapable costs of particular services are just covered. If this is not done a requirement for new investment may be created in industries supplying competing services without surplus capacity.

20.   In some industries – such as electricity and commuter services of the railways – the load at periods of high demand rather than the growth of total sales determines the need for new capital investment. In such cases plant may be under-utilized for much of the time and so far as is administratively possible the price system recognizes this characteristic of demand by providing adequate incentives to encourage users to shift from peak to off-peak. Provided off-peak charges do not fall below the levels needed to cover the variable costs incurred, differen-

tiation can be increased with advantage until the balance between peak and off-peak is economically most efficient. The effect on revenue is neutral so long as lower receipts from off-peak users are offset by higher receipts resulting from higher charges made to peak-time users; indeed a net revenue gain is likely. Two-part and differential pricing systems are also used to improve financial results without distorting the allocation of resources when there are important elements in costs which cannot easily be allocated to specific services or products (e.g. costs incurred jointly by several services or costs which do not vary proportionately with output). In apportioning these costs among consumers, there is a wide choice of methods ranging from complex multi-part tariffs designed to ensure that each customer pays for the costs he imposes, to simple, quantity discounts which may be appropriate in cases where large quantities are more economical to supply than smaller amounts. The actual calculation of the different elements of such a price system is itself a complicated task; but the broad objective is clear enough.

21. In addition to recovering accounting costs, prices need to be reasonably related to costs at the margin and to be designed to promote the efficient use of resources within industry. Where and when there is spare capacity, as there may be at some points in the business cycle, or excess demand, short-run marginal costs (i.e. the additional costs of increasing output in the short-run) are relevant; the object is to persuade customers to make use of spare capacity or to curtail excess demand. In the long run, the main consideration is the cost of supplying on a continuing basis those services and products whose separate costing is a practical proposition (i.e. long-run marginal costs), though the problems of transition to a new technology or to a new source of supply may imply the need, in the medium term, for prices to diverge from long-run costs. These long-run marginal costs naturally include provision for the replacement of fixed assets needed for the continued provision of services, together with a satisfactory rate of return on capital employed.

22. New technological developments can greatly reduce the long-run marginal costs of providing some services, and it is right to have regard to these in pricing policy. But a gradual adjustment of prices in the light of reasonable expectations is generally preferable to sudden large changes occurring discontinuously when major assets are replaced. Strict adherence to long-run marginal costing in such circumstances could lead to a period of revenue deficits requiring a temporary but heavy subsidy from general taxation, and this would be difficult to justify. The systems of large public undertakings are in any case of such a size that there are practical limits on the rate of modernization, and

unless plant is well tried, rapid innovation may lead to breakdowns and heavy costs. Too rapid a reduction in prices might stimulate demand so much that shortages would result or demand could be met only by costly measures to increase supply in the short run. It might also react on demand for the products of other nationalized industries; prices need to be set in the framework of government policy for the sector as a whole.

23.   Not all costs can be allocated to specific services or activities, and some industries, where the area of the unallocable costs is large, may find difficulty in going all the way towards a pricing structure which accurately reflects the costs of particular services while at the same time covering total costs. Two-part pricing is a device commonly employed to reconcile the two objectives, and in other cases a sufficient incentive to attract customers to areas where costs are lower might be provided by making prices proportional to costs at the margin but at a level sufficient to cover total costs.

24.   It will be clear from the preceding paragraphs that there is nothing rigid or doctrinaire about the pricing policy which the industries are expected to follow. Indeed the whole system of financial objectives within which the industries operate is a very flexible instrument. Targets are set for a period of years (usually five) at a time; and provided that industries, on balance, meet their targets over the period as a whole, they can, and should, carry out their pricing so as to fit in with the government's general policy for prices and incomes. In so far as the industries observe the principles set out in the White Paper, the government does not intend to interfere in the day-to-day responsibility of management to propose increases, and will endeavour to leave management the maximum discretion in adjusting their price structure to meet competition and to take advantage of commercial opportunities.

25.   Nevertheless, nationalized industries supply many of the basic needs of consumers and private industry; successive governments have, therefore, maintained a very close interest in the pricing decisions of the industries, and, in practice, Ministers have been consulted and given an opportunity to comment before final decisions have been taken to increase prices on any significant scale. Price stability in this sector is of especial importance to the economy. On the other hand, if nationalized industries' prices were allowed to get seriously out of line with costs this would lead to artificial stimulation of demand and a heavy burden of support on the general taxpayer.

26.   Arrangements for consultation with Ministers on prices have now been formalized as part of the voluntary early warning system described in the White Paper *Prices and Incomes Policy: An Early Warning System* (Cmnd. 2808). The powers of the Prices and Incomes

Act, 1966, apply to the nationalized industries in the same way as to private industry. But because of the importance of the industries to the economy, and the need to demonstrate that the public sector is co-operating to the full in carrying out the Prices and Incomes policy, the Government has decided in future to refer all major price increases in the nationalized industries to the National Board for Prices and Incomes (NBPI). In examining such cases – against the background of the industry's overall financial objective – the NBPI will consider the underlying justification for any increase, its timing and the extent to which costs could be reduced by increased efficiency.

COSTS

27.   To make the best use of resources, it is not enough merely to ensure that prices properly reflect costs, important though this is. Continuous and critical attention has to be paid to costs themselves in order that an industry must play a full part in bringing about a more efficient and faster-growing economy. It would obviously be wrong if any industry, public or private, were allowed to exploit a degree of monopoly power so as to attain satisfactory financial results by covering unnecessarily high costs by equally unnecessary price increases. The objective of price stability can only be reconciled with the important aim of earning a proper return on capital if costs are kept under firm control. Since it is likely that, for a variety of reasons, the prices of some of the resources, especially manpower, will rise from time to time, management's task is to seize every opportunity of reducing costs by employing improved methods or techniques. This calls for imagination, careful planning, and a willingness to experiment. New plant technology, automation and better use of manpower will all play their part.

28.   The principles of the productivity, prices and incomes policy apply equally to workers in the public and private sectors. It will therefore be for management and workers in the nationalized industries to continue to strive to increase efficiency and productivity and thus to meet the cost of pay increases while ensuring that the community as a whole benefits from higher productivity. Nationalized industries have a good record in this respect. Nevertheless, there is always scope for further improvements and it is clear from international comparisons (though these must always take account of different circumstances in different countries) that we still have some way to go in using manpower more efficiently. There is a national shortage of qualified engineers of which the nationalized industries are large employers and they therefore have a special obligation to employ engineers economically and to use their talents fully. There is also a shortage of certain kinds of skilled

worker and the industries are expected to make the most of their human resources, both by using less skilled labour so far as possible and by continuing enlightened training policies.

29. One of management's main tasks is to look continuously for possibilities of labour savings, and to encourage at all levels a positive attitude towards ideas of all kinds that might reduce the quantity of labour needed to provide the required level of service. This involves effective consultation and collaboration between management and men with a view to using labour more efficiently by improved organization of existing plant and methods, and introducing new plant and methods which require less labour. In appraising both investment proposals and suggestions for reorganization, the government will expect the industries to make allowance for the likelihood that the real cost of labour will rise continuously through time as general productivity increases. This means that industries will have to become gradually less labour-intensive in their methods over time. Similarly, if an appreciable rise in the relative prices of any of their other inputs is expected, management will rightly take this into account in its long-term operational and investment planning.

30. Normally the best use cannot be made of new plant and equipment unless changes in working methods are accepted by management and employees. When costly automated equipment is installed the optimal utilization rate should be higher than it was when less expensive plant was used, and in some cases tariff structures may need revision with the object of keeping the equipment fully used. All this requires considerable flexibility of approach by both sides of industry to manning questions, and there can be no room for inefficient, out-dated or restrictive practices, particularly in the operation of costly and technologically advanced equipment.

31. In view of the rapidity of technological changes, and the necessity of making the best possible use of scarce manpower resources, it is essential that the nationalized industries should continue to plan their future manpower requirements and keep these plans under review in the light of their own changing demand and the anticipated supply position for the categories of manpower which they require. Where manpower plans indicate a long-term reduction in total manpower requirements, appropriate measures should be taken (i.e. by control of recruitment and wastage) so that the planned reduction can be effected with the minimum of dislocation and redundancy.

32. The government has, of course, had frequent discussions in the past about productivity and labour utilization in the nationalized industries. In view of the great importance of productivity at the present time – and the fact that successful investment depends upon it – the

government has reviewed its policy in this area and has taken a number of important decisions. In the first place (as was announced on 7 September) the NBPI will be strengthened to enable it to make all necessary enquiries into the efficiency of the industries whose proposals for price increases are referred to it. These enquiries will cover the industries' machinery for keeping down costs including the appropriate forecasting and decision-making techniques. The Board plans to recruit a small number of specialist staff to concentrate on this work and to provide continuity. This staff will be reinforced as necessary by outside consultants. In addition the Government Departments directly concerned will continue to develop, in consultation with the industries, indicators of performance which will provide regular and systematic information about each industry's success in controlling its costs, increasing efficiency, and economizing in the use of manpower and capital resources. The government intends to pay particular attention to the trends shown by these indicators in the course of the annual Investment Review discussions with each industry. The main object will be to discuss with the industries what they have done in the past year and what they plan to do over the period of the review to improve efficiency in all its aspects and to add to the common pool of experience. Furthermore the nationalized industries should often be able to pass on to other parts of the economy the fruits of their experience in this field. The government hopes therefore that the nationalized industries generally will exchange views among themselves, and will make public as much information as they can about successful productivity techniques, and in particular, will give some account in their annual reports of what they have achieved in the past year and what they plan to do in the coming years.

FINANCIAL OBJECTIVES

33.   Clear financial objectives will continue to be necessary so that the industries know what is expected of them by the government. Thus they serve both as an incentive to management and as one of the standards by which success or failure over a period of years may be judged. The alternative would be an indefensible lack of control over the return achieved on a very substantial public investment. There are, inevitably, simplifications and compromises to be made in formulating an overall financial objective for a large industrial undertaking in the form of a simple figure. It is not always possible in practice to reconcile a prescribed rate of return on new investment, and a system of pricing which accurately reflects costs, with a predetermined overall return on total assets. Deviations may be inevitable if there are sudden developments in

technology affecting the lives or the use of large amounts of existing assets. Nevertheless, despite these difficulties the system of financial objectives has proved its value in practice: it cannot provide a perfect formula for the resolution of all pricing and investment decisions, but it does give a framework within which such decisions can be reached.

34. For these reasons the setting of objectives for those industries which have not got them or the replacement of those which expire cannot be solely an arithmetical exercise, and in its discussions with the industries the government will take into account the considerations – return on new investment, soundly based pricing policy, social obligations not covered by a subsidy, efficient operation, national prices and incomes policy – mentioned above. Unlike the common test rate of return on new investment, these objectives will in practice be different for each industry and for the various Area Boards because they will reflect different statutory and social obligations, conditions of demand, domestic costs and other factors peculiar to the individual undertaking. It will not be true therefore that a higher target necessarily indicates a more efficient industry.

35. The financial target system described above is essentially a flexible one. It has already been explained in paragraph 24 that industries are required to fulfil their obligations over a run of years taken together, and not necessarily to meet their targets every year. This in itself is a valuable means of reconciling financial discipline with reasonable price stability. But the target system can also be adopted to meet the varying circumstances of individual industries. Targets have so far been set mostly in terms of a percentage return on the net assets of the whole undertaking, which is readily comprehensible and provides an accepted standard by which to assess efficiency in the use of capital. It also takes some account of changes in the scale of an undertaking. But this is not the only criterion which can be devised. Objectives for different parts of an industry's operations, or expressed in other ways, might be appropriate in certain industries and at certain times. It might for instance be desirable to express an objective as a fixed money sum; though this would require more frequent revision with changes in the scale of operation or in the value of money, it could not be confused with the return to be expected on new investment or the rate of interest on borrowings. It will also be desirable to set some targets for a shorter period than five years. Finally, it follows from the fact that targets should reflect sound investment and pricing policy and not vice-versa that if there are significant changes in the circumstances of an industry the government would be ready to review its target within the period for which it has been set and revise it upwards or downwards.

36. In certain cases the circumstances of a particular industry

coupled with government approval to the application of wider economic and social factors, may involve overall losses. But even here a clear financial objective will be necessary as an aid to management and it will be desirable to set this in a way which will provide a realistic incentive to efficiency and morale within the industry. A two-part objective – providing for a certain determined level of losses, possibly subject to specific subsidies, on part of the operations and seeking an adequate return on the rest – is one possibility; tapering subsidies are another.

THE ROLE OF THE INDUSTRIES

37. The aim of strengthening the United Kingdom economy can only be achieved if resources are more economically used and more efficiently deployed than in the past and all undertakings fully observe the government's policy on prices and incomes. Nationalized industries, which command much greater resources than all but the very largest private undertakings, should expect to be numbered among the most progressive and efficient concerns in the country. Where there are significant social or wider economic costs and benefits which ought to be taken into account in their investment and pricing these will be reflected in the government's policy for the industry: and if this means that the industry has to act against its own commercial interests, the government will accept responsibility. (Where necessary the government will make a special payment to the industry or make an appropriate adjustment to its financial objective.) Except in such cases the industries should provide goods and services which consumers want and are willing to pay for at prices which reflect their own costs as accurately as possible, and keep these costs at the lowest levels consistent with providing satisfactory conditions of employment and earning a proper return on capital. In planning their future investment, the industries should have regard to the considerations set out in paragraphs 6 to 16 above, and should take into account economic forecasts prepared by the responsible government Departments. In their approach to problems of pricing, cost reduction and staffing, the industries should have regard to what is said in paragraphs 17 to 32 above.

THE ROLE OF THE GOVERNMENT

38. Though the responsible Ministers and their Departments are in frequent contact with the nationalized Boards about matters affecting government policy, it is not the government's intention to interfere in the day-to-day management of the industries. Nevertheless the government must accept a large measure of responsibility for the general lines

of economic development which are followed in this vital sector of the economy, and in its relations with the nationalized industries will have in mind the considerations outlined in this White Paper, and in particular that increases in costs should whevener possible be absorbed by greater efficiency rather than be passed on to the consumer, and that price increases should be capable of being publicly justified.

39. The annual Investment Review provides a regular occasion for reviewing the state of each industry. Then the government normally gives firm approval for the agreed level of capital expenditure for the forthcoming financial year and provisional approval (subject to some limitation on the extent to which funds are to be committed) for the following year; and also gives its views on the outline of investment proposed for subsequent years. The programmes for most industries extend five years ahead, and with industries in which investment takes a long time to mature, this longer-term look is of key importance. The implications of the investment programmes for the Exchequer – and hence for the short- and long-term balance of the economy – must always be considered, though it is not intended to express financial objectives in terms of self-financing ratios. It is also during the Investment Review discussions that the government is able to take account of the general balance of investment between individual nationalized industries, and between them collectively and the rest of the economy, in order to ensure co-ordinated development in the context of planned growth of the economy.

CONCLUSION

40. This White Paper is intended to show how investment, pricing and efficiency policies will be taken into account in setting financial objectives, rather than to make any change in the basic relationship between the government and the nationalized industries. It reviews the features and principles which are common to all nationalized industries and which underlie their relationship to the government. The circumstances of the industries are however very diverse and will be taken into account in formulating detailed policies for the sectors concerned.

8. TREASURY APPRAISAL OF INVESTMENT[1]

1. This Annex reviews the principles and methods which the Treasury, following discussions with the responsible Departments and

[1] From Select Committee on Nationalized Industries, session 1967–68, *Report on Ministerial Control of the Nationalized Industries*, vol. II, July 1968,

the industries, expects the nationalized industries to have in mind when assessing individual projects. It does not, of course, provide any automatic process of selection to replace the exercise of judgment. No attempt is therefore made to go beyond a general statement of principles because the precise nature of individual investments varies enormously from one industry to another and within industries. It is left to managements to develop their own methods having regard to the considerations set out below – and many have in fact been using these or similar techniques for some time.

2. Paragraph 12 of the covering Memorandum pointed out that cost/benefit studies may be necessary in appraising some large investments and in comparing investments in different parts of the economy where comparisons cannot be made in financial terms. These techniques are being developed but should only be used by nationalized industries in consultation with the government. Cost/benefit studies are not therefore discussed in this appendix.

ALTERNATIVES

3. The first step is to make sure that all the alternatives are really considered. If an asset wears out it is not sufficient to decide to replace it with a similar asset. Other ways of carrying out the activity – expansion as well as renewal, continued patching of existing equipment, and ceasing to carry out the activity at all – should be considered. Alternative courses of action include investing at different times. Even when an investment seems attractive if started today, it is possible that it would show an even higher return if postponed for a year or two.

THE UNDERTAKING AS A WHOLE

4. Costs and revenues relevant to any investment project are the difference between what the total costs and revenues of the undertaking would be with the project and what they would be without it. It is important to consider the difference which the project would make to the undertaking as a whole and not just that part of the system immediately concerned. This may call for consultation with related industries, and consideration of future plans for the industry in question in order to establish the contribution of an individual project to the future of the undertaking. Only rarely can new investments be considered in isolation. For example, the construction of a new power station will

H.C. 371–II, pages 14–18. Note by the Treasury on Appraisal of Nationalized Industries' Investment Projects. Reprinted with permission of the Controller of Her Majesty's Stationery Office.

affect the merit order of existing generating plant and a new transport service may affect revenues on other services.

DISCOUNTING

5.   If the distribution of receipts and outlays over time was the same for all alternatives it would be necessary only to average annual net receipts and relate them to initial capital costs. Clearly £9 per year on an investment of £100 would be better than £8 a year. But things are not usually so simple. Postponement of expenditure always carries an economic advantage, while postponement of receipts is always a disadvantage. If the average return over the life of two alternatives is the same; an investment where returns start high, and decline gradually as the asset grows older, is preferable to one where returns start at a low level and build up as the economy grows. This may seem obvious, but some methods of estimating returns do not allow for this important timing point.

6.   The simplest way to resolve these difficulties is by discounting all outlays and receipts to a common base year. The net present value of an investment in the base year is found by subtracting total discounted cash outlays, including both capital and operating outlays, from discounted receipts, including eventual scrap or disposal value. Capital outlays should be included in costs at the time when they are expected to occur. Provision for depreciation is unnecessary and interest, during the construction period and after, is allowed for in the discounting process.

7.   The discounted present value of any sum in any future year can be found from tables, just as the accumulated value of any capital outlay on which interest has been paid can be found from compound interest tables. The only difference is that the present value of a sum invested in the past is found by multiplying it by a factor greater than 1, while the present value of a sum due in the future is found by multiplying it by a factor less than 1. Thus, if interest is 5 per cent, the present value of £100 invested last year is £105, while the present value of £100 due next year is £95 4s. 9d. – the sum which, invested this year at 5 per cent interest, will be worth £100 next year. (Further notes on present value, with numerical examples and tables, can be found in Part III.)

8.   As was explained in paragraph 11 of the covering Memorandum, the Treasury recommends that a test rate of discount of 8 per cent should normally be used by nationalized industries in appraising their investments. The use of this rate will establish at once whether or not, in the absence of special considerations, the investment qualifies as a candidate. If the present value of receipts exceeds the present value of costs, the rate of return must exceed 8 per cent.

9. The actual rate of return on any investment is calculated by finding the discount rate that equates the present value of all receipts to the present value of all costs. Establishing the internal rate of return is useful in some circumstances. It is close to the businessman's normal approach to investment decisions in that it assesses the true earnings of the capital invested over its expected life making allowance for the timing of revenues and costs. As a general criterion, however, the rate of return on an investment is not a reliable guide when comparison has to be made between alternatives. Multiple solutions sometimes occur, depending on the time pattern of the stream of revenue less costs, and this may make it impossible to say what the rate of return is.

10. Nationalized industries should normally therefore use the net present value approach and should proceed with the alternative which shows the highest positive net present value. The net present value itself appears as a capital sum which may be thought of as the capitalized value of the stream of profits expected over the life of the investment with depreciation and interest at a rate equal to the discount rate.

DIFFERENT LIVES

11. But provided an investment offers a return higher than the test rate of discount, its net present value will be greater the longer its expected length of life. Every future year in which receipts exceed outlays adds to the present value. So where a long-term investment has to be compared with a shorter-lived alternative fulfilling the same function, a simple comparison of net present values would bias the calculation in favour of the longer-lived alternative. Provided that the short-lived investment can be renewed at the end of its useful life, the proper comparison should be between the net present value of the long-term investment and the net present value of a series of short-term investments supplying the same need over the same number of years.

12. Comparison can be made directly, but it may call for rather cumbersome and artificial calculations, particularly if the lowest common multiple of the respective lives is a large number. A simple short cut is to convert the capital sums in which present value is measured to equivalent annuities, calculated at an interest rate equal to the test discount rate, extending over the assumed useful lives of the respective investments. This is explained in paragraphs 35 and 36.

RISK

13. The techniques discussed above are useful as aids to judgement because they bring into focus complex changes in revenues and costs

spread over the expected life of a project. But the techniques are only as good as the figures and forecasts on which they are based. They do not produce the 'right answer' of themselves; their primary use is to arrange the relevant information in as effective and explicit a way as possible.

14. It is particularly important to be clear how the risks associated with different projects should be embodied in the calculations. The test rate of discount, being a uniform rate for all industries, does not include allowance for the risks of individual investments. The assessment of risk should therefore rest on a careful evaluation of the receipts and outlays expected from the project. Normally this would require the production of alternative figures based on optimistic and pessimistic assumptions. But sometimes it may be advantageous to take a single best estimate of present value and test its sensitivity to changes in assumptions about future costs, prices and sales.

15. In some circumstances it may be desirable to weight the test rate of discount as an alternative method of allowing for risk. This approach is less specific about the risk element in particular investments and involves treating a number of totally different risks as though they would all be satisfactorily discounted by a higher rate of return. Nationalized industries should therefore only use this method in exceptional cases – for instance when new activities are being undertaken and there is little experience to draw on in estimating risks associated with particular assumptions or where, as in some projects in the coal industry, unpredictable geological difficulties are likely to be encountered.

16. The existence of uncertainty imparts a new dimension to the problem of choice. The range of uncertainty may be so wide that a choice has to be made between a low-risk investment offering a modest return and a more ambitious scheme which, while potentially more profitable on optimistic assumptions, entails a greater risk of loss if things go badly. It is impossible to give general guidance on how to deal with these cases; selection must depend on the attitude to risk which management consider proper for the undertaking in each instance. Flexible projects do however have some advantages. The choice of fuel-using equipment, for example, would be affected not only by a best guess of the future relative price of different fuels, but also by the cost of conversion if the best guess turns out to be wrong.

TIMING

17. In considering their investment programmes, nationalized industries will need to compare the effects of undertaking particular

projects at different times. The economics of postponing or bringing forward projects can be established by comparing present values as of now if work is commenced on each of the years in which it is reasonable to contemplate beginning. Major new developments in working methods which cover a range of assets sometimes produce opportunities for cost-savings which could not be achieved by piecemeal replacement. In these cases the replacement of single assets may be justified sooner than if they were considered on their own – though it should always be borne in mind that technical progress may make postponement worthwhile until improved equipment is available.

18.   Where the phasing of expenditure is not governed by the need to fit into wider plans, the best time to choose will be that which maximizes the present value of the project. It may however be impossible to proceed in a given year with all projects which show a satisfactory rate of return. In this case projects whose value would be greatly reduced by postponement may be put in before higher yielding investments whose postponement would cause no serious difficulties or loss of present value.

REPLACEMENT INVESTMENT

19.   At some stage decisions will have to be taken about replacing existing assets. All assets deteriorate eventually with age and become less efficient and more costly to operate. And even before there is much deterioration, assets may become obsolete as they become more costly to operate in comparison with more modern equipment. Decisions about major investments for replacement purposes involve the same considerations as any other large investment – whether to invest and when to invest. Once an asset has been installed, the choice before an undertaking is between continuing to use it and incurring the cost of operating and maintaining it; or replacing it with some new type of asset; or scrapping it without replacement.

20.   The return on replacement investments will usually be in the form of cost savings rather than increased revenues. Comparison should be made between the costs of continuing to maintain and operate existing assets, and the costs (including capital costs but minus the disposal value of the old assets) of maintaining and operating the new equipment together with any increased revenue-earning power. If replacement would not show a positive net present value when the returns are discounted at the test rate, the possibility of discontinuing that particular activity should be seriously considered. In the great majority of cases, however, where services show a satisfactory rate of return, the main question will be when to replace.

21. Occasionally assets become physically worn out. Replacement is then obligatory if the activity is to be continued. Usually, however, replacement will be considered before existing assets become useless. In these instances it will involve an avoidable or postponable net capital outlay (allowing for the disposal value of the old assets). The return from replacing now rather than later should be calculated by reference to the period over which it is practicable to postpone replacement – the ultimate length of which is set by the prospective future life of the existing asset. It would not be sensible to extend the calculation beyond the point at which existing assets would have fallen to bits. In many cases a one year period of comparison would be adequate because the relative merits of the old equipment will almost always decline with time. Such a comparison would show whether it would pay to carry on with the old equipment for another year. It if does not pay replacement is indicated. If it does pay to carry on, the case can be examined again in subsequent years.

22. Replacement decisions are in many ways simpler than new projects particularly when the latter involve ventures into new markets. There is likely to be less uncertainty about the prospective level of demand, cost comparisons between old and new assets can be made with a fair degree of precision, and the cost of many new pieces of equipment is often known in advance (though this may not be true of large replacements involving new construction work). But technical progress and obsolescence involve a management in difficult questions of judgement. The more rapid the rate of technological change, the greater will be the apparent return from replacing soon rather than later. And if technical progress is expected to continue at a rapid rate the new assets must be expected to have a short life before it, in turn, becomes obsolescent. This means that it will not pay to replace until the expected discounted cost savings are so large that the outlay on the new assets will be recovered very quickly. It also has to be borne in mind that investing today means foregoing the chance of taking advantage of superior plant and equipment which may become available next year or the year after.

23. The book value of assets at any time has no direct relevance to decisions about replacement. Some assets remain in good order long after they have been fully amortized. Where they have not become obsolete the most profitable course would be to keep them in use so long as they remain serviceable. On the other hand, technical progress may render assets uneconomic long before they have been written down to their disposal value; this may indicate that the original investment was ill-considered and may point to the need for greater caution in judging future projects.

SMALL PROJECTS

24. Detailed analysis applicable to large projects may not be appropriate for smaller investments necessary to maintain the operational efficiency of services which show a good rate of return. Most nationalized industries will wish to devise simplified criteria to enable the merits of numerous minor items of capital expenditure to be assessed quickly at all levels. This will save time and reduce the number of projects which higher authority is required to examine. These simplified criteria must be consistent with procedures followed in major projects, and should be reviewed from time to time to check that they are not producing inferior decisions. Moreover it becomes all the more important that the return on major new projects should be thoroughly established if, once the programme is launched, the scope for applying full tests to small parts of it is necessarily limited.

9. THE TEST DISCOUNT RATE[1]

1. The White Paper issued in 1961 set out the procedures for discussion and authorization of matters concerning nationalized industries' investment and borrowing in the light of the government's responsibility to keep public sector investment within the nation's resources. The White Paper went on to say that it would be the government's task to satisfy themselves that the procedure within each organization for scrutinizing and approving capital expenditure was effective (Cmnd. 1337, paras. 24–25).

2. In considering these matters officials took the view that all investments made by nationalized industries should be appraised in a consistent way, and in order to do this it was clearly desirable to set a minimum rate of return which all investments justified solely on financial grounds should be expected to earn. This rate of return would also serve as a reference standard to assess the economic cost of any financially unprofitable investments that might be undertaken for social reasons.

3. In deciding how this rate should be determined, one factor was the recorded opinion of the Committee that the return should be more than the interest on the relevant loan capital. In support of this view it had been argued elsewhere that, since private firms could not borrow on gilt-edged terms, allowing nationalized industries to invest for a return which was no more than enough, after depreciation, to pay

[1] From Select Committee on Nationalized Industries, op. cit., vol. III, pages 27–28. Appendix on the Test Discount Rate. Reprinted with permission of the Controller of Her Majesty's Stationery Office.

interest on loan capital raised in the gilt-edged market would lead to too great a proportion of the limited resources available for investment being invested in publicly owned industries, leaving too small a proportion available for private investment. In a fully employed economy total investment is limited by resources. By measures designed to act on public and private consumption the government can and does ensure that a certain quantity of resources is available for investment but these resources will not be deployed as effectively as they might be if the criteria for investment in industries that are publicly owned are markedly less stringent than those in private industry.

4. It therefore seemed desirable, with a view to getting the best possible allocation of investible resources between publicly owned and privately owned industries, to aim at a test discount rate for the public sector similar to the minimum return which would be regarded as acceptable on new investment by a private firm. It was plain that no single figure could be expected to apply to private companies of all sizes and types, but it seemed reasonable to set a rate for public corporations which corresponded to the cut-off rate likely to be used by a large private firm of good standing and engaged in low risk business. A study of some of the available writings on the subject, and discussions held with a number of large private sector undertakings, revealed some differences of opinion (as was to be expected); however most of those who had thought about the subject carefully, and used discounted cash flow methods of appraisal to calculate returns on investment, were of the opinion that the minimum return acceptable would be something between 6 per cent and 8 per cent after tax, at constant prices. On the basis of the tax arrangements in force at the time (before the change to Corporation Tax) we calculated that the corresponding gross of tax return would be below the range 12–16 per cent, which would have been indicated by simply grossing up the range 6–8 per cent by a margin sufficient to allow for income tax and profits tax. This was because the combined effect of investment allowances, initial allowances, and the common practice of calculating annual depreciation allowances at a constant proportion of the reducing balance of cash invested meant that little if any tax would become payable in the first years in which profits were earned, the effective rate of tax on a given profit level increasing steadily as the amounts allowed for depreciation diminished. Since profits earned in early years are weighted more heavily than those earned in later years when discounted cash flow methods of appraisal are used, the effect is to reduce the difference between rates of return before and after tax below what it would be if there were no investment allowances or initial allowances and if annual allowances were given only on a straight line basis. Bearing these factors in mind, it seemed that a

rate of return before tax within the range 8 per cent to 10 per cent would be appropriate. In the light of the government's policy of encouraging investment that would lead to higher productivity and faster growth, it seemed appropriate to take the lower end of this range rather than the centre, and the figure chosen was therefore 8 per cent. This is the figure which was used in the Treasury's early discussions with the Departments and the nationalized industries.

5. After the change to Corporation Tax, the withdrawal of investment allowances, and the introduction of investment grants, the position became more complicated. Since nationalized industries normally raised all their capital requirements in the form of loan capital, the interest on which is deducted from profits before liability for Corporation Tax arises, the tax position of public and private undertakings was thereafter somewhat different. Again, since nationalized industries (before steel nationalization) did not receive investment grants on their main activities, another difference was introduced. The effect of these differences was to create a wide gap between the rate of return (before considering investments grant or tax) that would be acceptable to a private firm contemplating, for example, an investment in a manufacturing plant in a development area, and another firm considering investment in the service sector or in manufacturing outside the development areas. A number of calculations were made of the profitability, after Corporation Tax and investment grant (where applicable), of a number of 'typical' investments yielding 8 per cent before tax and grant. These investments were all supposed to yield a steady rate of return over 10 years, equivalent to 8 per cent in discounted cash flow terms. The result was a spread of returns ranging from 6 per cent after Corporation Tax where no investment grant was payable but a 30 per cent initial allowance applied to a maximum of 14 per cent where the whole cost of the investment qualified for an investment grant at the higher rate payable in development areas. (The apparent paradox that the return after tax is higher than the return before tax comes about because, on a marginal investment yielding relatively low profits, the present value of an investment grant payable about a year after the money is laid out can and frequently does exceed the present value of taxes that will only become payable in future years on the difference between profits and the annual amounts allowed for depreciation.) The centre of this range, 10 per cent, corresponded closely with views expressed by industrialists to the effect that the minimum return required by a large company in the new situation would be between 9 and 10 per cent after Corporation Tax.

6. There therefore seemed no case for disturbing the original 8 per cent test rate, the more especially as the introduction of Corporation Tax

and investment grants had certainly not been intended to discourage either publicly or privately owned industry from investing. It is however necessary to note that a somewhat higher rate than 8 per cent would have been indicated if the returns on private investment had been weighted by the approximate proportion of total investment qualifying for investment grants at the various rates. Only a very small proportion would attract grant at the maximum (Development Area) rate on its whole cost, and taking the centre of the range of outturns described in the last paragraph may be held to attach undue weight to this extreme result. On the other hand, if a rate much higher than 8 per cent had been prescribed for general use, nationalized industries might sometimes have been prevented from carrying out investments in development areas which would have been financially attractive to private firms.

7.   In the light of these various considerations it was decided not to make any immediate change in the 8 per cent rate.

10. SCNI REVIEW OF THE NEW ECONOMIC FRAMEWORK[1]

THE ECONOMIC CRITERIA

203.   The principal economic criteria mentioned in the 1967 White Paper relate to pricing, investment, financial objectives, costs and cost–benefit analysis.

204.   The Treasury evidence tended to put the first emphasis on pricing policy and their witnesses claimed that this marked the principal advance of Cmnd. 3437 (Q. 2091). 'It is therefore important that . . . pricing policies should be devised with reference to the costs of the particular goods and services provided. Unless this is done, there is a risk of undesirable cross-subsidization and consequent misallocation of resources. The aim of pricing policy should be that the consumer should pay the true costs of providing the goods and services he consumes' (Cmnd. 3437, paragraph 18). Prices, therefore needed to be 'reasonably related' to costs at the margin. (The Committee regret that the meaning of 'reasonably related' is not explained in the White Paper.) Sometimes, as where there is spare capacity, short-run marginal costs may be more relevant. But in general the main consideration is the cost of supplying additional output on a continuing basis, i.e., the long-run marginal costs (paragraph 21, and see Evidence pages 5–6).

---

[1] From Select Committee on Nationalized Industries, op. cit., vol. I, Report, pages 49-57. The New Economic Framework. Reprinted with permission of the Controller of Her Majesty's Stationery Office.

205.   There is much argument among economists about the proper measurement and use of marginal costs, and whether prices should normally 'be related to', 'reflect', 'be based on' or 'be equated with' short-run or long-run marginal costs (see Evidence, pages 589–90, 593–4, 597–8; Q. 1388, 1444–8, 2025–8, 2045, 2091, 2092–3). But the Committee have some sympathy with the point made by Mr Munby when he wrote 'Pricing policies are much too complicated to be codified in the form of a simple criterion, such as "long-run marginal costs", which is likely to become more of a slogan than a rational guide to economic policy' (Evidence, page 594).

206.   The Committee do not wish to become slogan-mongers and are well aware of the complications. They certainly are not qualified to discuss the more detailed economic aspects of marginal cost pricing, which in any event are largely irrelevant to the Committee's examination, in this Report, of Ministerial control. As they emphasize in Chapter VI, what type of policy should be applied in what circumstances is primarily a matter for Ministers. And on some issues more thought may yet be required. For example, the possibility of short-run variations in price to meet short-run demand variation clashing with long-run pricing and financial objectives is a serious one which was not dealt with in the 1961 White Paper; although the Treasury, in the 1967 White Paper, show themselves aware of this problem they do not yet appear to have found the solution. All the Committee are concerned to emphasize, at this stage, is that the Treasury, at least, have accepted the desirability of moving towards the eventual adoption of marginal cost pricing (Q. 2091, 2093, 2115).

207.   The other important new criteria advanced by Cmnd. 3437, and by the Treasury evidence, relate to investment. The industries have long attempted to measure in some way the return to be expected from new investment projects. For some time several of the industries, in common with a number of firms in the private sector, have been using some form of discounted cash flow (DCF) technique for investment appraisal. Details of this technique, its variations and some examples, are given in the evidence (Evidence, pages 14–22; Appendix 34, Annex C).

208.   DCF can be used wherever there is any choice of decision – between alternative investment projects, for example, or between renewing, patching-up, or even not replacing a piece of equipment. The investment choice may be whether to invest or not, whether to invest now or later, whether to invest more or less. The alternative to a particular project may lie within the industry, or it may lie in some other industry. DCF can be used on both new projects and replacement investment (Evidence, pages 14, 17). The main advantage of DCF is that

it enables true comparisons (in the sense of comparing like with like) to be made of investment alternatives with different time profiles, by expressing the receipts and outlays attributable to them in terms of present value, by means of a discount rate (Evidence, page 3).

209.   Following long discussion with the sponsoring Departments, the industries, and experts in academic and industrial circles, the Treasury have now decided to recommend to all the industries that they should use DCF techniques (Cmnd. 3437, paragraph 8; Evidence, page 3).

210.   The choice of discount rate employed in a DCF calculation is obviously of great significance. A high rate will favour low capital cost projects, or those with early earning prospects or deferred costs. A low rate would have the opposite effect. More important, the higher the discount rate, the more profitable a project has to be to show a positive present value; therefore the higher the discount rate, the fewer the projects that will be justified commercially. The Committee discuss in paragraphs 255–62 how the DCF rate was selected and the conditions for varying it.

211.   It is most important, however, that all the industries use the same rate of discount for their DCF appraisals. If this were not done, projects might pass a DCF test in one industry that would fail in another. This would lead to a misallocation of capital. If investment resources are to be properly allocated, the returns on marginal investment in each industry should be equal, for otherwise more value could be obtained by transferring investment from one industry to the other. It also seems desirable to the Committee that the test applied in the public sector should be broadly in line with that applied in the private sector, otherwise theoretically there could be a misallocation of capital between the two sectors (Evidence, page 595; Q. 51, 55–6, 2048–9). But some witnesses thought this less important (Evidence, page 591; Q. 2049–52).

212.   The Treasury have therefore recommended to all the nationalized industries that they should appraise all new investment using the same test rate of discount. This test rate 'represents the minimum rate of return to be expected on a marginal low-risk project undertaken for commercial reasons' (Cmnd. 3437, paragraphs 8–9; Evidence, pages 3–4). It has been calculated to be 'broadly consistent, having regard to differing circumstances in relation to tax, investment grants, etc., with the average rate of return in real terms looked for on low-risk projects in the private sector in recent years'. The government have decided that 8 per cent is a reasonable figure for the test rate of discount in present circumstances (Cmnd. 3437, paragraphs 10–11). The Committee consider the calculation of this figure in chapter VI (paragraphs 256–7).

213.   It is important to note three things that the test rate of discount is *not*. It is not the same as the financial objective. Financial objectives

expressed as returns on net assets relate to all investment, past and present; and they vary from industry to industry. The test rate of discount relates to new investment at the margin only, and is standard for all industries. Secondly, the test rate of discount is not the same as the actual price of capital to the industries, i.e. the current borrowing rates. The discount rate is a test rate, to decide what merits investment by comparison with the accepted opportunity cost of capital, i.e. the return that could be earned by investing elsewhere, whatever the current cost of borrowing, and irrespective of the method of financing involved (Evidence, page 3; Q. 2109).

214.   Thirdly, the test rate of discount is not a piece of computer magic that spirits away all difficult management or Ministerial decisions. Allowance will have to be made for risk and uncertainty (for in all cases both costs and benefits are at best estimates, and in some cases, especially for long-lived projects, are little more than informed guesses). This will usually be done in deciding the input and output data for the DCF calculation, but, exceptionally, by adopting a higher discount rate (Cmnd. 3437, paragraph 12; Appendix 8). Some projects may be justified for social or wider economic reasons that cannot earn 8 per cent DCF on the basis of purely commercial data but may be found to pass the test if further social costs and benefits are taken into account (Cmnd. 3437, paragraphs 13–15). And some investments that pass the test may still be refused or postponed for public interest reasons, such as the phasing of public investment (Cmnd. 3437, paragraph 16; Q. 2096–7).

215.   It should be emphasized that a DCF calculation, and hence the operation of the test rate of discount system as a control of investment, depends on the accuracy and correctness of the data fed into it. As far as accuracy is concerned, this is largely a question of accurate forecasting of demand and hence of receipts. The cost side of the equation is, in principle, reasonably easy to determine. But there is an essential assumption to make about correctness of data. The revenue-earning powers of the investment are dependent on the prices charged. If prices are not correctly related to costs, but are determined by some less relevant criterion, or even arbitrarily, then investment decisions based on the use of the test rate of discount will be equally unrelated to actual costs, and a misallocation of resources will result (Evidence, pages 4, 591).

216.   The last point about the test rate of discount is the important one. Unlike the system of financial objectives, this test relates not to the sum of performance past and present taken together but to current investment decisions. It is concerned with the marginal return on assets, not the total. It is thus both a guide to sound management and, in so far as it can be adjusted, an instrument of Ministerial control over the overall

level of investment in the public sector. As the Head of the Government Economic Service said, the adoption of marginal cost pricing and of the test rate of discount would mean a common approach to future pricing and investment, and this is more important than a common standard based on past decisions (Q. 2212–13).

217.   The remaining economic criteria are better known and can be mentioned more briefly. Financial objectives, the Treasury believe, will continue to be necessary so that the industries will know what is expected of them by the government (Cmnd. 3437, paragraphs 33–4). And they can be a useful tool for management in setting objectives for their industries (Q. 1658). But as will be seen (paragraphs 223–32) government thinking still appears somewhat confused about the role and significance of financial objectives.

218.   The fourth set of criteria, emphasized for the first time in the Treasury's evidence and by the White Paper of 1967, relates to costs (Evidence, page 6, and Cmnd. 3437, paragraphs 27–32). As the White Paper says, 'To make the best use of resources it is not enough merely to ensure that prices properly reflect costs, important though this is. Continuous and critical attention has to be paid to costs themselves . . . The objective of price stability can only be reconciled with the important aim of earning a proper return on capital if costs are kept under firm control' (paragraph 27). The Committee discuss cost-control in Chapter IX.

219.   And lastly regard will have to be paid to wider social costs and benefits than those calculated by the industry (Cmnd. 3437, paragraphs 14–15). These may often be relevant to investment decisions and sometimes to pricing policies. For example, the then Minister of Transport deliberately held down fares in London while the future of London Transport was being considered (Evidence, pages 224–6). Such factors may also determine who shall pay for services or investments. Even if the total price be properly related to marginal costs, it would be possible, on social grounds, for the price to the consumer to be reduced, and for the balance to be borne by the government or some other body. The Committee return to this subject in Chapter XIV.

THE INTERRELATIONSHIP OF THE ECONOMIC CRITERIA

220.   There are three principal interrelated criteria – pricing policies, investment criteria and financial objectives. Any of these could be treated as paramount, with the others being decided so as to conform with it. This was roughly the position under the 1961 White Paper, when pricing and investment policies had to be devised to enable the industries to achieve their stated objectives. For example, the Electricity

Council said that investment in their industry was mainly determined by financial objectives, and price levels geared to attain these objectives (Appendix 36, paragraph 2). Alternatively, two of the criteria could be independently laid down, and these two together would determine the third. For example, the use of a test discount rate for investment and a specified financial objective would jointly determine the prices to be charged to achieve these ends. Or, as is envisaged in the Treasury evidence, the adoption of a specified pricing policy and the use of a test rate of discount must spell a certain financial result (given certain assumptions about costs and demand), and this will become the financial objective. As the Treasury said, the financial objective 'should express in a simple way the sort of performance which an efficient undertaking should achieve over a period of years while pursuing sound investment and pricing policies' (Evidence, page 2). In so far as this is so, the objective would be calculated and not prescribed as a controlling factor. It would be a residuum (Q. 1658, 2091, 2093–4).

221.   What cannot be done is to attempt to lay down all three criteria independently. Or at least, if this is done, it will only be by a lucky accident if they prove compatible. Therefore, as several witnesses pointed out, the criteria are essentially interrelated (Q. 1790, 2000–2, 2091–4).

222.   Nearly all the witnesses who dealt with this topic were agreed that, of the three factors, pricing policies and investment criteria were the most important in economic terms and that financial objectives, in some measure, should simply be the residuum (Evidence, pages 581–2, 589, 678; Q. 1658, 1790, 1912, 2000, 2005–7, 2093–4, 2243, 2264).

223.   The theory is admirably clear; but it is not being clearly implemented. Running through both the White Paper of 1967 and the Treasury evidence is a conflict between the earlier and the new economic thinking. Indeed the Treasury appear loth to accept some of the consequences of their own thinking. For example, one Treasury witness said that they feared that, without financial objectives, the industries would lack guidance and would slip back into earlier bad habits of low earnings (Q. 2202). But the concept of marginal cost pricing was designed to give just this guidance and to avoid that kind of result. What does a financial objective add except a measure of past performance?

224.   The Head of the Government Economic Service, when questioned about the relationship of the three principal economic criteria, emphasized the limited scope of pricing and investment criteria when looked at as instruments of control; they could not give the precise answer to all pricing and investment questions. In particular, long-run marginal cost pricing does not determine the proper rate of adjustment of actual prices to changes in costs. In making such changes account might also have to be taken of the effect on the industry's surplus, and

hence the setting of a financial objective might properly influence the prices to be charged in the short run, 'although in the long-run you would want to be guided by the movement of long-run marginal costs'. Financial objectives could also make the industries 'a little bit keener . . . to get down to a level of costs which achieve the surplus set'. There was, therefore, he argued, 'an element of play in the three factors, and it would be a mistake to regard any two of them as sufficient for present purposes' (Q. 2093). He agreed that in practice all three factors would be fixed independently and then some of them would be treated elastically to ensure that all three fitted together (Q. 2094). (To the Committee this appears to amount to no more than saying that one should lay down criteria of pricing and investment and calculate the financial objective from them, but if this produces a result which one does not like one should go back and fiddle the arithmetic.) The Chief Secretary of the Treasury went further: abandoning the desiderata accepted by other witnesses he was prepared to argue that financial objectives were so important that at least in the short-run, pricing, and not the financial objective, became the residual factor (Q. 2396).

225. The divergent elements in the government's thinking were revealed most clearly when they were confronted with the possible dilemma of sticking to a marginal cost pricing policy which would result, at least in the short run, in an industry earning reduced surpluses or even incurring a deficit; or of abandoning marginal cost pricing for the sake of achieving enough revenue to cover total costs, such as might be required by a financial objective, at the expense of charging the new consumers of the product more than its cost and hence inhibiting the optimum allocation of resources. This could be the dilemma of an industry, such as the gas industry today, which has achieved a technical breakthrough, with the result that long-run marginal costs may for a while fall below the level of average costs (Evidence, pages 678–9).

226. Some of the academic witnesses discussed this problem and emphasized the need to put marginal cost pricing in the forefront of policy, but were not dogmatic about what should be done if this should result in deficits (Evidence, pages 588–9, 596). Mr Aubrey Jones was quite categorical: if there was a conflict, marginal cost prices should have priority (Evidence, pages 678–9; Q. 2317, 2240–1). As he said, 'this means reconciling oneself to the fact that past investment . . . has been overtaken by a new set of events' (Evidence, page 679).

227. The Head of the Government Economic Service was notably less than categorical in his view. But he came down eventually in favour of giving priority to pricing policies. Under some circumstances marginal cost pricing could produce large surpluses; under other circumstances it could result in large deficits. If a loss was unavoidable whatever prices were charged (as seemed to have been the case with the

railways in recent years), there was no escape from the dilemma; under these circumstances one simply had to ask 'what was the rational way to set about it?' If there was a great pressure of demand or shortage of capacity, the adjustment of prices to marginal costs should be made gradually. But, if, on the other hand, observance of marginal cost pricing – in a period when rapid technological development was making existing equipment obsolete – was liable to result in a substantial loss, then 'I think we would be prepared to face that'. It would be wrong to deprive consumers of the benefits they would receive if the service had been left in the hands of competitive industry, where competition would probably force prices down to the level dictated by the new costs of production without regard to the costs of earlier investment (Q. 2115).

228. The Ministries of Power and Transport also gave evidence about pricing policies. (The Board of Trade are less concerned, because of the unusual position of the Air Corporations in regard to tariffs (Appendix 21, Annex VII).) The Ministry of Power said that, 'while marginal cost pricing is a desirable aim of policy' there were practical obstacles to its implementation – in particular in some cases, the statutory duty to avoid making losses. Therefore, 'until now it is average costs rather than marginal costs which have determined the level of tariffs'. But marginal costs have been used to guide the allocation of costs between different types of consumer and different types of load; two-part tariffs, for example, reflected marginal costs (Evidence, page 355).

229. It seems, therefore, that the Ministry of Power would still probably put average cost financial objectives before marginal cost pricing policies, if they came in conflict; to do otherwise would be detrimental to the Treasury's interests they said (Q. 1790). They had not been able, therefore, to accept fully marginal cost pricing: 'Our enthusiasm for marginal cost pricing has to be matched against our enthusiasm for a reasonable degree of financial probity' (Q. 1388). There was, however, much scope for tidying up tariff structures and for a great deal of adjustment towards marginal cost pricing. This was being actively considered (Q. 1388). And they were trying to arrange for the fuel industries to have roughly the same methods of reflecting marginal costs in their prices (Q. 1390). It was a real problem at that time (July 1967), because the price of electricity for the potential new industrial user even then appeared to be above the long-run marginal cost of production (Q. 1790).

230. The Ministry of Transport said that because the nationalized transport industries experience some competition, 'a pragmatic rather than a theoretical approach to pricing policies is . . . often dictated by circumstances'. With this qualification, it was the policy of the Ministry to encourage the industries to formulate their pricing policies 'on a basis

which has close regard to the full long-run costs of the provision of the services which they offer' (Evidence, page 422).

231. The Ministry of Transport witnesses emphasized the need for economic criteria to give guidance in the place of the normal business criterion of profit maximization, which was not suitable for nationalized industries. It was necessary to relate prices to marginal costs so as to avoid cross-subsidization or artificially low prices (Q. 1912). Because of the deficit on the railways, however, they had been obliged to adopt 'a pragmatic pricing policy', charging what the market would bear, rather than one based on marginal costs (Q. 1444–7, 1913). Marginal cost pricing might result in pricing a service out of the market (Q. 1448). And regard had to be paid to competition (Q. 1911). With these qualifications, however, the concept of making prices proportional to marginal costs was meaningful and could help an industry to clarify its objectives (Q. 1912).

232. The main source of uncertainty, however, about what priority Ministers really intend to give to marginal cost pricing policies is the White Paper of 1967 itself. Some examples serve to indicate the un-readiness of the Treasury to accept or to reject a clear priority for marginal cost pricing where this conflicts with objectives expressed as a surplus or as a positive return on total assets. Paragraph 17 states a starting principle that 'nationalized industries' revenues should *normally* cover their accounting costs in full'. But paragraph 18 gives more emphasis to covering marginal costs – 'while covering overall accounting costs *wherever possible*, pricing policies should be devised with reference to the costs of the particular goods and services provided'. Then paragraph 21 states, '*In addition* to recovering accounting costs, prices need to be reasonably related to costs at the margin' (the Committee's italics in each quotation). Confusion deepens, when the White Paper of 1962 first says that 'the system of financial objectives . . . cannot provide a perfect formula for the resolution of all pricing and investment decisions, but it does give a framework within which such decisions can be reached' (paragraph 33), but then goes on to say 'targets should reflect sound investment and pricing policy and not vice-versa' (paragraph 35). Are, then, objectives to be a determining framework which conditions pricing and investment decisions, or simply a residuum, reflecting them ? The White Paper simply is not clear. Its authors try to eat their cake and have it.

CONCLUSIONS

233. The Committee were concerned at the extent to which the economic thinking of the Ministries of Power and Transport, particularly regarding the priority to be given to marginal cost pricing, might

be at variance with the policies advanced by the Treasury (see Evidence, pages 5–6). In so far as the policies have been at variance, the Committe believe that the Treasury should be held responsible. They are the Department responsible for taking the lead in developing and formulating for the government new economic and financial policies. But the Committee fear that the Treasury themselves were handicapped by indecisiveness at certain vital points (see paragraphs 223, 232).

234.   The Committee recognize that, as Cmnd. 3437 says, there should be 'nothing rigid or doctrinaire about the pricing policy which the industries are expected to follow' (paragraph 24). Of course policies must be flexible and adjusted to the particular circumstances of each industry. In some cases or for some periods the covering of total costs may have to be paramount; in other cases the competitive position may make marginal cost pricing difficult to pursue; elsewhere some measure of cross-subsidy may be unavoidable or socially justified. But totally flexible guidance is no guidance at all.

235.   The power to determine the economic obligations of the nationalized industries is one of the most important instruments of control that Ministers possess. It enables them to condition the size, prices and profits of the industries. This Ministers must be able to do. But the obligations selected must not be ambiguous. The industries must know what is expected of them. And Parliament and the public must know what guide lines Ministers have laid down.

236.   The Committee therefore welcome the emphasis now placed by Ministers on efficient pricing and investment criteria rather than on the achievement of a predetermined financial objective. They note the clarity and firmness of the criteria that the industries are being required to employ for investment appraisal. They consider, however, that although the government have accepted the desirability of moving towards the adoption of marginal cost pricing by the nationalized industries (Q. 2091, 2093, 2115), there is still ambiguity about what pricing policies they will apply in practice. The Committee would welcome a further statement by the Treasury on the Government's pricing policies for the nationalized industries and particularly on the priority that Ministers intend to give to marginal cost pricing when such a policy conflicts with covering total costs.

237.   The Committee also recognize, however, that there are practical problems to be faced in constructing the desired economic framework, and that there are wider economic consequences of the new thinking which has been discussed in the White Paper and in this chapter. The practical implementation of these economic policies is considered in Chapter IX. The Committee turn to consider the wider economic consequences in the next chapter.

11. PROFESSOR ROBSON'S CRITIQUE[1]

W. A. ROBSON

THE SETTING OF FINANCIAL TARGETS

The present system of financial control stems from the White Paper of 1961 on 'the Financial and Economic Obligations of the Nationalized Industries' (Cmnd. 1337). This introduced a series of specific annual financial targets laid down quinquennially for each of the public corporations, after consulting the Board and taking into consideration all the relevant circumstances likely to affect its performance. It is quite true that the ability of a public corporation to achieve its target, or even the target figure itself, cannot be regarded as a reliable index of efficiency. A deficit may equally well be due to adverse circumstances rather than bad management. Nevertheless, the introduction of targets was generally welcomed as a great improvement on the vague statutory enactments which required the nationalized industries not to make a loss on current account taking one year with another – and left it at that.

Economists have criticized the setting of financial targets as lacking significance. They contend that if correct methods of appraising investments are used, and correct pricing policies applied, the financial result of the year's trading is irrelevant. The weakness of this analysis is that it ignores the demoralizing effect on the personnel and directors of a large industrial undertaking of substantial deficits on the annual trading account. It also ignores the extreme importance attached to an annual surplus or deficit by business men, the Press, politicians and the general public. To the man in the street and to most politicians success or failure in public enterprise is judged to no small extent by whether a public corporation shows a profit or a loss.

INVESTMENT AND PRICE POLICY

In 1967 a second Treasury White Paper appeared dealing with the 'Economic and Financial Objectives' of nationalized industries (Cmnd. 3437). This introduced the notion of scrutinizing investment programmes by means of the discounted cash flow method with a test rate of return of 8 per cent. Any proposed capital investment which survived this test would be approved; any which did not would be rejected,

[1] From W. A. Robson, 'Ministerial Control of the Nationalized Industries', *Political Quarterly*, vol. 40, No. 1, January 1969, pages 105–8. Reprinted with permission of the author and the editor of *Political Quarterly*.

unless it could be justified on non-commercial grounds. The object was a simple one: to prevent the misallocation of national resources by allowing public enterprise to embark on investments which would yield less advantageous returns than other forms of capital expenditure in either the public or private sectors. The DCF method is to be associated with the highly speculative cost-benefit analysis which attempts to assign a money value to everything in the world, including the imponderables. Professor William G. Shepherd, an American economist who has made a special study of public enterprise in Britain, remarks that the calculations rest on predictions of cost and revenue which are little more than guesses. 'Screening the resulting predicted rate of return is often therefore an empty exercise.'[1] Also, why should a uniform test rate of return be applied to projects which differ greatly in risk?

The 1967 White Paper dealt at length with pricing policy. It urged that while prices should cover overall accounting costs wherever possible, they should reflect the costs of particular goods or services. There could be justifiable exceptions to this based either on grounds of principle or of practical expediency; but cross-subsidization is in general undesirable because it means taxing remunerative services in order to cover the losses on other services. The Treasury gave several instances where charges could justifiably differ from costs. Then followed the statement: '*In addition to recovering accounting costs*, prices need to be reasonably related to costs as the margin and to be designed to promote the efficient use of resources within industry. Where and when there is spare capacity, as there may be at some points in the business cycle, or excess demand, short-run marginal costs (*i.e.*, the additional costs of increasing output in the short run) are relevant; the object is to persuade customers to make use of spare capacity or to curtail demand.'[2] This was followed by a warning that strict adherence to long-run marginal costing in, let us say, gas or electricity when new technological developments can greatly reduce long run marginal costs, would lead to substantial revenue deficits requiring heavy subsidies from general taxation which would be hard to justify. Moreover, the huge public industries cannot be modernized quickly and a rapid reduction of prices might stimulate demand and cause a breakdown on the supply side.[3]

MARGINAL PRICING THE ROAD TO UTOPIA

The Select Committee has transformed this farsighted and balanced

[1] 'Alternatives for Public Expenditure', in *Britain's Economic Prospects*, by Richard E. Caves and Associates, pages 388–9.

[2] *A Review of Economic and Financial Objectives*, Cmnd. 3437/1967, para. 21. [My italics.]

[3] Ibid., para. 22.

statement into a series of dogmatic statements which they assert with all the fervour of converts to a new-found faith.

A Treasury witness had said that without financial targets the nationalized industries would lack guidance and revert to the bad habit of low earnings of earlier years.[1] But, asked the Committee, 'what does a financial objective add except a measure of past performance?' – as though this was a useless and unnecessary indicator. Sir Alec Cairncross, then Head of the Government Economic Service, stressed the limited scope of pricing and investment criteria as instruments of control, and insisted on the importance of financial targets in instilling keenness and cutting costs. He urged that the interactions of all three factors should be considered together. This remark by a distinguished economist with much practical experience the Committee dismissed contemptuously as meaning no more than that 'one should lay down criteria of pricing and investment and calculate the financial objective from them, but that if this produces a result one does not like one should go back and fiddle the arithmetic'.[2] It is this kind of remark which reveals the lack of common sense or political sensibility in the Report.

The responsible Ministries saw quite clearly the political and other difficulties of fully accepting the doctrine of marginal pricing as the only road to salvation. To abandon the covering of average costs would in some instances contravene the statutory duty to avoid making losses. The Ministry of Power said their enthusiasm for marginal cost pricing had to be matched against their enthusiasm for a reasonable degree of financial probity. The Ministry of Transport had been forced to adopt a pragmatic pricing policy charging what the traffic would bear – as the railways had so often done under private ownership. They had to pay attention to competition, and marginal cost pricing might result in pricing a service out of the market.[3]

Any uncertainty or faltering in subscribing to their new-found faith seemed to the Select Committee a heresy based either on confusion of thought (a frequent term of censure in the Report) or on a failure to accept the pure and undiluted doctrine of marginal cost pricing. The probable or possible results of its application were nowhere considered. They ignored the political consequences both inside and outside Parliament of heavy deficits in industries which may be capable of making a surplus by other methods; and they did not consider the effect on the popular image of nationalized industries caused by their failing to show up reasonably well on their annual trading account.

Even more striking is the absence in the Report of any of the reservations, qualifications or opposition to marginal cost pricing which have been expressed by economists.

[1] Report, para. 223. [2] Para. 224. [3] Para. 231.

A recent article in *Economica* puts one powerful argument against it as follows: 'The standard case for marginal cost pricing by a public enterprise requires, among other things, that prices equal marginal costs in the rest of the economy, and it implicitly assumes that any resulting profit or loss is acceptable. In fact, the requirement is not met, and the assumption is invalid. There is often a close relationship between a public enterprise and private industries which do not sell at marginal cost, and public enterprises are normally set financial targets'.[1] The Select Committee nowhere inquire into the question whether private industry applies marginal cost pricing, and if so to what extent. And if it does not, whether this affects the position of public enterprise. The report assumes that if the theory is applied in the public sector alone the optimum allocation of resources will result. The Report makes no reference to the theory of the second best which has been the subject of much discussion among academic economists. A well-known article by Professor Lipsey and K. J. Lancaster, published more than ten years ago, demonstrated mathematically that in the real world with its imperfect markets the determination of output on the basis of marginal cost pricing is as likely to lead away from the optimum allocation of resources as towards it.[2] In other words, 'to apply to only a small part of the economy welfare rules which would lead to Paretian optimum if they were applied everywhere, may move the economy away from, not toward, a second best optimum position. A nationalized industry conducting its price-output policy according to the Lerner-Lange "Rule" in an imperfectly competitive economy may well diminish both the general productive efficiency of the economy and the welfare of its members'.[3] Nancy Ruggles, in her article on marginal cost pricing which Ralph Turvey has reprinted in his recent collection of readings on public enterprise, concludes that the search for a panacea in the shape of a single simple rule by which to guide all conduct in these matters, is a vain search and even a foolish one. 'A set of tools', she remarks, 'is available with which to accomplish a complicated job. A better job can be done if each tool is used where it is appropriate, instead of throwing away all but one and expecting it to serve all purposes.'[4]

Yet this is just what the Select Committee have done. After reviewing

---

[1] 'Second-Best Rules for Public Enterprise Pricing', by R. Rees, *Economica*, August 1968, page 260.

[2] 'The General Theory of Second Best', by R. G. Lipsey and K. J. Lancaster. *Review of Economic Studies*, vol. XXIV – 1956–57. See also 'The Influence of Marginal Cost Theory on Pricing and Investment in British Nationalized Fuel Industries', by Sheila Bhalla, *Applied Economic Papers*, Osmania University (March 1964), vol. 4, No. 1.   [3] Lipsey and Lancaster, page 17.

[4] *Public Enterprise*, ed. by R. Turvey (Penguin Modern Economics), page 43.

a number of exceptional circumstances which might justify a departure from the norm, they conclude that 'in the long run, the economically justified pricing policy for most of the nationalized industries would be marginal cost pricing. They are satisfied that, if this pricing policy was applied wherever possible, the efficiency of the industries would be improved and the optimum allocation of resources secured'.[1] The Committee therefore recommend that 'the use of marginal cost pricing policies and the use of DCF appraisal . . . for investment control should be the *standard* policies for the economic control of the nationalized industries'.[2] [Their italics.]

It is difficult to avoid a suspicion that the members of the Select Committee were taken for an intellectual ride and being on unfamiliar ground they lost their way and were overready to accept simple solutions to complex problems.

12. THE GOVERNMENT'S RESPONSE[3]

PRICING POLICIES

20. The government welcome the Committee's general endorsement of the policy for pricing set out in Cmnd. 3437. The Committee has suggested that this policy has not been laid down with sufficient clarity to be an unambiguous guide to the industries in making individual pricing decisions. The government point out that the White Paper was intended only as a statement of general principles, in which it was necessary to set out a series of possible qualifications of the marginal costing principles.

21. As explained in paragraph 34 of the White Paper, the government intend to elaborate these principles and qualifications as necessary in working out, with the industries, individual pricing policies for each industry. The detailed application of these policies is for the industries themselves. It was explained in evidence that the Treasury and departments concerned will be pursuing these questions with the industries.

22. These discussions will in many cases be linked to the renegotiation of financial objectives as these fall due for renewal. These objectives, and the pricing and investment criteria which they will reflect, will of course be reported to Parliament by the responsible Ministers as new agreements are concluded. This will, the government believe, meet the intention of the Committee's recommendation (paragraphs 396 and 418)

---

[1] Para. 276. [2] Para. 280.

[3] From White Paper, *Ministerial Control of the Nationalized Industries*, May 1969, Cmnd. 4027, paras. 20–37. Reprinted with permission of the Controller of Her Majesty's Stationery Office.

that standard pricing policies should be laid down for each industry and published.

23. The Committee recommended in this connection (paragraph 417) that Ministerial control over pricing policies should be given legislative sanction.

24. The government do not accept this proposal, which would in their view be likely to lead not only to undesirable interference in day-to-day management but also to serious practical difficulties in its application to those industries which provide a wide variety of goods and services. The pricing policies of the industries will, however, be considered by Ministers in the course of the settlement of financial objectives and it will, of course, be open to the government to influence these policies indirectly by the use of statutory directions on the level of reserves.

25. The Committee proposed (paragraph 803) that the Air Transport Licensing Board should be abolished. The government will bear this recommendation in mind during its consideration of the report of the Committee of Enquiry into Civil Air Transport.

26. The Committee proposed (paragraph 409) that within the pricing policies to be laid down by Ministers (whether statutorily or, for the present in most cases, extra-statutorily) industries should have a measure of freedom to make changes in price without the need to seek Ministerial approval. The Government accept this proposal in principle; industries need, and currently have, a measure of flexibility in setting individual prices (subject to the general prices and incomes policy). It would however be difficult to define the limits of these powers in any precise way, and as the Committee recognizes any such limits would need adjustment in the light of experience.

INVESTMENT POLICIES

27. The Committee agreed (Chapter V) with the policy laid down in Cmnd. 3437, under which investment decisions are based upon discounted cash flow calculations and the use of a test discount rate derived from the estimated returns to investment in the private sector. The government welcome this endorsement of their general policy towards investment. They accept the Committee's recommendation (paragraph 257) that periodic reviews should be made of the evidence available from the private sector. Such a review is at present in process.

28. At the same time it must be appreciated that the investment criteria just referred to are not automatic but depend on the skill and capacity of management. Within the general lines laid down for the exercise of strategic control there remains a need for the government to

scrutinize the overall level and pattern of investment, and in some cases, if their strategic control is to be effective, and well-informed, the government may also need to scrutinize large individual investment projects. Where an industry has a well-established and approved plan of development there will in general be the less need for scrutiny of individual smaller projects. But an informed judgement on investment programmes as a whole is seldom attainable without some examination of major projects from time to time. In some cases Ministerial approval of individual investment decisions is required by specific statutory provisions, and it is also necessary in other cases where important social or economic considerations are involved.

29. The Committee recognized the importance for investment decisions of correct demand forecasting; the government accept the recommendation in paragraph 455 that further discussions of this subject should be initiated to supplement the extensive work already undertaken in some industries.

30. The government also accept responsibility for issuing general guidance to the industries about economic planning assumptions upon which demand forecasting can be based (paragraph 581); the government will keep the industries fully informed of their economic assumptions.

31. But at the end of each annual investment review decisions have to be made about the level of investment to be approved for each industry, towards the setting of which the investment criteria of Cmnd. 3437 offer only partial guidance. Some individual investment decisions may on occasions have to be reserved for Ministers. For this reason, a capital rationing scheme of the kind proposed in paragraph 274 may not be the only way in which changes in investment programmes should be made. Nor would the development of such a scheme be free from practical and technical difficulties. But the government agree that an effort should be made to devise a capital rationing system, for use when reductions in investment are needed to maintain the balance of the economy, which would distribute total cuts between the industries in the least harmful way, while leaving the industries the maximum practicable freedom to choose the items to be cancelled or postponed. They propose to discuss this problem further with the industries.

32. The Committee proposed (paragraph 592) that cost–benefit studies should be made of all major projects proposed by the industries which could not be justified on commercial criteria alone, or which, while commercially profitable, imposed significant social costs upon the community. The government announced their intention, in paragraph 14 of Cmnd. 3437, of taking externalities into account in appraising investment projects. Cost–benefit studies are, and will continue to be,

made wherever this seems desirable in order to reach an informed decision.

33. The Committee proposed (paragraph 597) a further supplement to the existing investment controls; comparing the actual outturn of projects with the returns which were forecast when the investment was decided. It recommended that the Treasury should initiate discussions with departments and industries about this proposal. In fact, inter-departmental discussions of this topic had recently begun, based on information available about the techniques already in use in the industries. These discussions have now been extended to include the industries themselves.

SOCIAL OBLIGATIONS

34. In paragraph 282, and in greater detail in Chapter XIV of the Report, the Committee recommended that 'where extra social or wider public interest obligations are imposed on or undertaken by the industries, they should be publicly identified, quantified and appropriately financed by the Ministers concerned'. It will not always be practicable to identify or quantify such obligations precisely. Nor, having done so, would it always be necessary or desirable to make special payments accordingly. Nevertheless, as indicated in paragraph 37 of Cmnd. 3437, where an industry is required to act against its own commercial interests the government will take responsibility and, where appropriate, make a special payment to the industry or make an adjustment to its financial objectives.

FINANCIAL OBJECTIVES

35. The Committee accepted (paragraph 483) the policy set out in the White Paper, under which financial objectives should become the financial expression of the pricing and investment criteria already laid down. The governments are already working out the consequences of this policy for settling new financial objectives for the gas and electricity industries, and financial objectives for the other industries will fall to be fixed, or revised, from time to time. In this process the views expressed by the Committee in paragraphs 485–498 about the quantification and expression of objectives will be borne in mind. To a considerable extent these views reflect the government's existing thinking on these subjects as expressed in evidence to the Committee.

36. The Committee recommended (paragraph 496) that objectives should be set for each of the fuel industries as a whole and not for

individual Area Boards. So long as the Area Boards enjoy financial autonomy under the statutes, the Minister concerned must formally settle financial objectives with each of them. Where, as in the gas industry and in the electricity industry in England and Wales, there is a Council for the industry, the Minister will seek the advice of the Council before settling the individual objectives.

CAPITAL STRUCTURE AND BORROWING

37.   The Government note the views expressed by the Committee in chapter XI, which in general accord with their own policy. They accept the recommendation in paragraph 628 that the Treasury should initiate studies of the terms and conditions of the industries' borrowing powers. They agree that the existence of public dividend capital should not be allowed to obscure judgement of economic performance, but consider this experiment in the form of capital structure to be worth making.

13. EXPERIMENTS WITH EQUITY CAPITAL[1]

(a) The SCNI on Exchequer Dividend Capital, 1968

611.   The present system of financing the capital requirements of the industries by fixed interest loans means that, if they fail to earn a large enough surplus to cover their interest charges, they have to raise more capital from the Exchequer in order to pay the interest due to the Exchequer (unless they accept a capital reconstruction). Thus the consequences of low earnings in the past are carried forward to add to the burdens of the future. One way of avoiding this is to cease to carry forward automatically all debts on capital. This has been tried.

612.   As an experiment, a new form of capital financing was introduced for BOAC in 1966. £35 million, about half of their capital, takes the form of non-redeemable Exchequer dividend capital on which BOAC are required to pay an annual 'dividend' instead of fixed interest. Details are given in the evidence (Evidence, pages 11, 191–2; Appendix 21, Annex IV, paragraphs 8–11).

613.   The dividend on what BOAC call their equity capital is to be 'such amount as may be proposed by the Corporation and approved by the Minister with the consent of the Treasury, or such other amount as the Minister may, with the approval of the Treasury after consultation

[1] From Select Committee on Nationalized Industries, op. cit., vol. I, Report, pages 133–4, Exchequer Dividend Capital. Reprinted with permission of the Controller of Her Majesty's Stationery Office.

with the Corporation, determine' (Evidence, page 192). For 1965–66 BOAC paid a dividend of 10 per cent (Evidence, page 191); for 1966–67, they paid 15 per cent (BOAC Report and Accounts, 1966–67, page 3). This was more than they would have paid on fixed interest loans (Q. 654). BOAC were very anxious that the dividend should always be agreed and not imposed (Evidence, page 192). The Committee do not doubt that the Board of Trade and the Treasury will normally keep their compulsory powers in reserve.

614. Other industries, notably BEA (Evidence, page 277; Appendix 31; Q. 989–90) and British Railways (Evidence, page 165), have expressed a wish to have some sort of 'equity' capital. The Committee have therefore considered the relevance of this method of capital financing to problems of Ministerial control. They note the Treasury's view that more experience of the system is needed before they could consider its extension to other industries (Q. 2214–15).

615. As the Committee of 1967 indicated, when they considered the idea of extending Exchequer dividend capital to BEA (Report of 1967 on BEA, paragraphs III 29–41), the main significance of Exchequer dividend capital is psychological rather than economic or administrative. Its purpose – and presumably principal effect – is to enable the financial results of industries which are fully viable, but which are especially subject to fluctuating returns, to be evened out over the good and bad years. Hence it would appear unsuitable for industries which are in regular deficit: they could never pay a dividend, and Exchequer dividend capital would be for them little more than an interest free, non-repayable advance (Evidence, page 11; Q. 654–5). The main effect of this system is therefore on the final results on the profit and loss account i.e. the results after paying interest and dividends and not on the operating surplus or on the net return on capital.

616. This means that Exchequer dividend capital should have no relevance to operations designed to achieve a financial objective expressed either as a net surplus before interest charges etc. or as a net return on capital. Nor should it be relevant to pricing policies related to marginal costs, because the Exchequer dividend, being itself uncertain until a balance is struck between revenue and expenditure, cannot at the same time be treated as a cost. The marginal costs for these purposes should be derived from the opportunity cost of capital, namely the test discount rate. Nor should it be relevant to investment decisions, because these should be based on the use of the test discount rate and not the market price of capital (see chapter V). This analysis was confirmed by the Chairman of BOAC, who said that the existence of this form of capital did not make any difference to the way they run their business (Q. 655–6).

617.   The Committee conclude, therefore, that this form of financing has little significance for either the management of the industries or for Ministerial control of their activities. Exchequer dividend capital creates the appearance of a financial partnership; the Exchequer helps the industry in bad years, and the industry gives the Exchequer a bonus in good years. (But even this arrangement would be artificial in so far as an industry were dependent on Exchequer loans for financing its investment; for the higher the dividend paid to the Exchequer the lower would be the retained surplus and the more the Exchequer would have to advance to pay for investment, and vice-versa; for an industry which can borrow elsewhere, as BOAC can, for example, overseas, it may have more significance.) It also reduces the chance of occasional deficits, and hence may have some of the psychological advantages referred to in paragraphs 609–10. On the other hand, by imposing a distorted reflection of an industry's actual financial results and by distracting attention from the financial objective as the proper measure of performance, this new system of capital financing could retard the proper judgement of the economic achievements of the nationalized industries. Of this the Committee would disapprove.

(b) Equity capital structure for the British Steel Corporation, 1969[1]

Under the Iron and Steel Bill, now before Parliament, the capital structure of the British Steel Corporation is to be radically altered.

The present long-term capital of the Corporation as established by the Iron and Steel Act 1967 consists mainly of debt, known as 'commencing capital debt', of some £834 million due to the Minister. Under this Act this debt, the greater part of which reflects the compensation paid by the government to the shareholders of the fourteen scheduled companies on nationalization, was assumed by the Corporation on vesting date (28 July, 1967) and carries interest from that date at a fixed rate determined by the Minister, regardless of the industry's earnings. The Act also provides for the repayment of the principal of the debt.

This form of capital structure is common to virtually all the nationalized industries established since 1946, but in 1966 the Government introduced, by way of a five-year experiment, a new form of capital into BOAC, namely Public Dividend Capital (PDC).

What is PDC? To use the government's own words:

---

[1] From 'Equity Capital Structure for BSC', *British Steel*, May 1969, pages 2–3. Reprinted with permission of the editor of *British Steel*. This article does not necessarily reflect later policies of the Corporation.

This is a form of capital corresponding to equity. . . . The remuneration of such capital is by way of variable dividends at a level approved by the Government in the light of the industry's earnings for a particular year and of its resources, rather than by way of interest at a fixed rate.

In other words, PDC is, for a nationalized industry, the equivalent of equity capital in a private sector company.

The government's stated policy on PDC is that it is

. . . only suitable for those nationalized industries which are fully viable but which are subject to fluctuating returns as a result of their trading conditions, the nature of their assets, etc. It would not be suitable for nationalized industries which have difficulty in breaking even taking one year with another because it would become little more than an interest-free, non-repayable advance.

It is on the basis of this declared policy that the government have agreed to make a further five-year experiment with PDC by introducing it into the Corporation.

The principal arguments put forward by the Corporation for PDC were:

The fluctuating nature of the Corporation's business and, in particular, the varying profitability which inevitably arises in an industry which is subject to intense international competition and technological change and the resulting need to have a form of capital that can accommodate such fluctuations. These are vividly demonstrated in the aggregate results of the fourteen companies nationalized by the 1967 Act.

The Corporation is a sound financial and commercial proposition with the ability to generate resources for profitable trading, taking one year with another, sufficient to reward adequately the government's investments in it and to maintain and develop its business.

The need for comparability with its competitors at home and abroad, most of whom have a substantial proportion of equity in their capital. In the absence of such comparability, i.e., if the Corporation were financed entirely by loan capital, its results could not be compared with those of its competitors, could give a misleading and damaging picture to the world of its performance and thus impair morale in the industry and its relationships with customers in this country and abroad.

Moreover, as is pointed out in the booklet *Finance for Steel* published by the Corporation:

If the Corporation's capital is not reconstituted with PDC it could only pay interest on the commencing capital debt out of post-vesting earnings. There was no surplus out of which to pay such interest from vesting date to September 1968 and there is little prospect of earning an adequate surplus in the current financial year, which will end in September 1969. If interest were to be charged and paid by the Corporation on the commencing capital debt from vesting date to the end of the current financial year, the Corporation would be in deficit at September 1969 to the extent of over £100 million. . . .

In putting forward these arguments, the Corporation was satisfied that it met the government's requirements for PDC in that it was both fully viable and subject to fluctuating returns. There was, therefore, no question of the introduction of this form of capital's being designed to relieve the Corporation of the liability to reward adequately the government's investment in the industry. On the contrary, the shared expectation both of the Corporation and the government is that the financial returns to the latter under the new capital structure will be at least equal to, and probably more than, the returns they would have received by way of fixed interest on a wholly loan capital.

The government accepted the Corporation's case and the current Iron and Steel Bill gives effect to this further experiment with PDC.

What does the Bill provide and how will PDC operate?

The starting point is the provision in the Bill which establishes, as from the vesting date, the commencing capital debt of the Corporation at £134 million instead of £834 million and the balance of £700 million as PDC. Interest on the £134 million loan capital continues to be payable at a fixed rate determined by the Minister.

In considering the clauses in the Bill which provide for the payment of dividends on PDC the sequence of the steps leading up to the determination of the amount of the dividend to be paid in respect of a financial year is significant. As a first step, the Bill requires the Corporation to propose a dividend to the Minister at the end of each of its financial years.

If the Corporation's proposed dividend is acceptable to the Minister and the Treasury then that is the dividend payable for the year in question. Alternatively, if the Minister is satisfied that no dividend should be paid, then the Corporation is under no obligation to pay a dividend in that year. However, if the Corporation's proposal is not satisfactory to the Minister and the Treasury, nor can the Corporation satisfy the Minister that no dividend should be paid, the Minister is given power, with the approval of the Treasury and after consultation with the Corporation, to determine a dividend in respect of the year in question. The Corporation is then under a duty to pay such dividend.

The procedure envisaged by the Bill highlights two important points – namely, that the initiative for proposing a dividend in any year is with the Corporation and, secondly, that if the Corporation's proposals are not acceptable to the Minister, the Corporation must be consulted before an alternative solution is imposed by his direction.

The Bill, in addition to converting £700 million of the Corporation's commencing capital debt into PDC and providing for the payment of dividends, empowers the Minister:

> within the limits laid down in the Bill, to pay the Corporation further sums by way of PDC, and
>
> after consultation with the Corporation to direct that some or all of the reserves of the Corporation and the publicly-owned companies shall be capitalized and treated as notional payments of PDC on which dividends will be payable.

The Bill also substitutes for the existing general financial duty in Section 16 (1) of the 1967 Act (' . . . to secure that the combined revenues of the Corporation and the publicly-owned companies are not less than sufficient to meet their combined charges, properly chargeable to revenue account, taking one year with another'), a more precise duty aimed at achieving a specified rate of return on net assets to be determined by the Minister after consultation with the Corporation.

To the government, the introduction of PDC into the Corporation is a further experiment with this type of capital in a nationalized industry. To the Corporation it is not only a most welcome innovation but a pre-requisite for an industry which has to establish itself, in the face of intense international competition, in the forefront of the major steel industries of the world.

14. THE GROWTH OF EFFICIENCY[1]

RICHARD PRYKE

During the first decade of nationalization, the industries had a disappointing productivity performance. Between 1948 and 1958 their output per man-hour increased by only 16 per cent. This was slightly less than the rise of 20 per cent achieved by manufacturing industry, though even this was a very modest gain. During the second post-war decade the rate of productivity growth has accelerated in both the public

---

[1] From Richard Pryke, 'Productivity performance and public ownership', *British Steel*, November 1970, pages 4–8. Reprinted with permission of the author and the editor of *British Steel*.

and the private enterprise sectors, but the increase has been far more spectacular in the nationalized part of the economy. Over the period 1958–68 output per man-hour rose by 68 per cent in the public enterprise sector compared with a rise of 44 per cent in manufacturing and a still smaller increase in the private sector as a whole.

If attention is confined to the last five years of the period (1963–68) it is found that productivity has been rising about 50 per cent faster in the public enterprise sector than in manufacturing. Moreover there is only one manufacturing industry – chemicals – where, over the last decade, productivity has increased more than it has in the public enterprise sector and only one nationalized industry – buses – whose productivity has increased less than that of manufacturing.

These facts naturally provoke the question of why the nationalized industries' output per man-hour has been increasing so fast and of whether there is some special explanation for the exceptionally rapid progress which they have been making. As I showed in an article which appeared in the Spring 1970 issue of the *Moorgate & Wall Street Review*, the sector's favourable performance does not appear to have been due to any of the more obvious factors which might explain it away. It has been shown time and again that large gains in production and productivity go together, but it is clear that the public enterprise sector's productivity lead over manufacturing has not, for the most part, been due to the advantage of rapidly rising production. Nor does it appear that the nationalized sector owes its lead to exceptionally heavy investment and the substitution of capital for labour on an exceptional scale. Productivity calculations which take the use of capital into account serve to confirm, rather than throw doubt on, the picture which emerges from comparisons of the growth in output per man-hour.

Even when allowance has been made for the various factors which, managerial efficiency apart, usually explain differences in the growth of labour productivity, the doubt persists that a comparison between different industries is no more instructive than a comparison between chalk and cheese. The scope for productivity gains may vary from one industry to another because the rate of technical progress is not uniform and because scientific advances can be applied more easily in some industries than in others; though it is interesting to observe that heavy research expenditure and large productivity gains tend to go together, which suggests that to some extent industries may themselves determine their rate of technical progress. Fortunately international productivity comparisons throw some light on the question of whether the nationalized industries have been blessed by fortune to an exceptional degree and afforded more scope than other industries for making productivity gains. International comparisons are difficult to make and are not easy to evaluate but they do have the advantage that they approximate to a comparison of like-with-like.

International productivity comparisons can be made for four of the nationalized industries – electricity, coal, railways and airways. The results of these comparisons relate to the period 1958–68 . . . In manufacturing industry, however, there were 12 foreign countries where manufacturing productivity grew at a faster rate than in this country, and that for the most part their lead over Britain was more than marginal. In four of the countries (Japan, Italy, Sweden and Holland) the rate of productivity growth appears to have been over 50 per cent higher than in Britain and there were five other countries (Germany, Austria, Belgium, Norway and France) whose rate exceeded our own by between 30 and 50 per cent. On the other hand, there were only two foreign countries (USA and Australia) where manufacturing productivity grew more slowly than in Britain. The poor showing of British private industry is not explained by the malfunctioning of a few particularly backward industries but by a general tendency for productivity to rise at a slower rate than abroad. Indeed there appear to be only one or two 'manufacturing industries which are at, or near, the top of their productivity leagues and it is interesting to observe that chemicals – the one British industry to have made larger productivity gains than public enterprise – was not among them. The nationalized industries' relative performance turns out to be strikingly different from that of the rest of British industry . . . the nationalized industries' productivity gains compare extremely favourably with those which have been made in the same industries abroad. The British electricity industry's sales per man-hour have risen as fast or faster than those of all but one of the six major foreign suppliers for which figures have been obtained. During the past decade only Belgium, with a productivity growth of 10.4 per cent per annum, advanced more rapidly than the British electricity industry whose productivity increased at a rate of 7.7 per cent. The German electricity industry turns out, at 7.6 per cent a year, to have done about as well as Britain, but Electricité de France and the American investor-owned utilities, at 7.3 per cent and 7.1 per cent respectively, appear to have had a slightly inferior performance. That of the two other foreign countries, Norway and Italy, was decidedly worse.

The NCB, like the British electricity industry, was beaten by only one of the foreign countries for which a comparison has been made. Over the period 1958–68 the tonnage produced per man-hour increased at a rate of 7.1 per cent in Germany and by 5.9 per cent in Britain and Belgium. However, Belgium has only advanced as rapidly as it has because of the extensive pit closures in its southern coalfields where productivity is exceptionally low. If attention is confined to the Campine, which is the northern coalfield, it appears that Belgian productivity has risen by only 5.3 per cent per annum. The other major European producers had still slower rates of advance. In Poland, the figure was 5.0 per cent, in Holland 4.7 per cent, in France 3.1 per cent and in Czechoslovakia only about 3 per cent (over the period 1956–58).

The figures for railways are less firm than those for electricity and coal, but it appears that once again productivity in Britain increased as fast, or faster, than it did in all save one of the continental countries. Sweden was at the top of the international rail league with a rise in traffic per man-hour of about 6 per cent per annum over the period 1958–68. However, this figure probably gives an exaggerated impression of the rate at which productivity was growing because of the change which occurred in the composition of Swedish freight traffic, for which my production index does not allow. Sweden was followed by the German Federal Railway and British Rail, both of which made productivity gains of about 4.5 per cent a year. The railways whose productivity seems to have increased less fast than that of British Rail were the Swiss and Belgian, whose output per man-hour appears to have increased by a little over 4 per cent per annum, the French, whose productivity rose by about 3.5 per cent (between 1958 and 1967), and the Italian and Austrian railways, whose productivity increased by about 3 per cent and 2 per cent respectively.

The air corporations' performance also turns out to have been a good one. Three major international airlines increased their productivity at a faster rate than BEA and BOAC, whose results have been combined, but six made less progress than the corporations. The aviation league was headed by Lufthansa, Alitalia and KLM whose productivity, in terms of passenger miles per worker, increased by about 10.5 per cent per annum between 1958 and 1968. Then came the British air corporations with an increase of 9.8 per cent per annum when allowance is made for the effects of the BOAC pilots' strike in the final year of the period. The airlines whose productivity increased less were Quantas and Pan American Airways, whose productivity increased by about 9 per cent each year; SAS, Air France and Japanese Air Lines, where the increase was between 7 per cent and 8 per cent; Swissair with an increase of about 6.5 per cent; and finally Sabena, with an even lower rate of progress.

The fact that these nationalized industries, which account for 84 per cent of the net output of the public enterprise sector, have performed so well in comparison with the same industries abroad, lends no support to the idea that the sector's fast rate of productivity growth has been due to the ease with which productivity gains can be secured in this part of the economy. If, despite public enterprise's favourable showing compared with British manufacturing industry, the nationalized industries had made smaller gains in productivity than the same industries abroad, this would be *prima facie* evidence that they happen to be operating under especially favourable conditions. No such case can be made out but, on the contrary, the way in which manufacturing turns out to be almost at the bottom of its productivity league indicates that it has had ample scope to make faster progress.

It is of course possible that there have been special factors at work which on the one hand have made it easy for the nationalized industries to do better than most of the foreign industries in their fields, but on the other have made it difficult for our manufacturing industries to match the performance of their competitors. For instance, it is often argued that Britain's low rate of productivity growth by international standards is due to 'stop–go' and the relatively slow rate at which output has increased in this country. If the nationalized industries have had the advantage that their production has increased faster than that of the same industries abroad, their performance will seem less remarkable.

It is clear, however, that the nationalized industries' favourable showing cannot be explained in this way. British Rail has laboured under the disadvantage of declining traffic while none of the continental railways have experienced a fall, and most have had the benefit of a significant increase. Similarly the sales of all but one of the foreign electricity suppliers with which the British electricity industry was compared have increased at a more rapid rate. Again, the air corporations have secured a somewhat larger increase in productivity than was to have been expected from the growth in their traffic. There were six foreign airlines which had a larger increase in traffic than BEA/BOAC but only three which obtained a larger rise in output per man.

Another possible explanation for the nationalized industries' rapid progress by British and foreign standards is that these industries were exceptionally backward and have simply been catching up. However, there is no evidence to suggest that those who have fallen behind will be able to accelerate without difficulty. If this were the case the underdeveloped countries would not present such an intractable problem. Moreover, since the level of manufacturing productivity is now considerably lower here than it is in the other advanced nations of Western Europe, British productivity should, if it was an advantage to be behind, now be growing at a rapid rate. It would also be wrong to assume that the nationalized industries are relatively inefficient . . . their level of productivity relative to that of the same industries abroad now appears to be higher than that of the rest of British industry. Despite this, the nationalized industries continue to make rapid progress.

Finally, it might be argued that the nationalized industries should not find it difficult to secure larger productivity gains than have been made abroad because their foreign counterparts are for the most part in public ownership and therefore likely to be inefficient. However, the available evidence suggests that foreign public enterprises tend to be model undertakings. For instance, Professor Kindleberger of the Massachusetts Institute of Technology concludes that in France 'the public corporations, especially in railroads, aviation and electricity, have been among the leaders in increasing efficiency and improving technology'.[1] Again, the efficiency of the Italian state holding companies has become a by-word as the British steel industry, faced with the example of Finsider, will need no reminding. . . .

[1] *National Economic Planning*, edited M. F. Millikan, page 285.

CHAPTER IV

POLICIES IN THE
MAJOR NATIONALIZED INDUSTRIES

The previous chapter was concerned with matters of general principle or performance of the nationalized industries. This chapter is concerned with particular industries, or with major sectors such as power or inland transport. It serves to illustrate the working of the broad generalities in industrial practice, and to emphasize that there are considerable differences in the nature of the various industries and in the problems they have experienced. It is not possible in this space to provide a full treatment; the chapter is mainly a review of the official literature, and only a few extracts are printed.

THE NATIONALIZED POWER INDUSTRIES

Most of Britain's fuel and power industries, both primary and secondary, are nationalized. The exception is the petroleum industry. Policy making for these industries is therefore very largely a public sector operation.

The decade was one of controversy about national fuel policies, and the controversies focused on the attempts of the Labour government to formulate agreed principles. The decisions were likely to be crucial for the coal industry, and since the Labour party had in the past drawn much of its support from coal-mining constituencies, policy-making in this subject was a delicate political matter.

The first attempt was set out in a White Paper (Cmnd. 2798) of October 1965, not reprinted here. This reviewed the recent history of the fuel industries and considered their future prospects. In the 1950s the expected rise in demand for coal had not materialized, and difficulties had arisen because stocks of small coal had built up. There was increasing use of fuel oil for many purposes. In 1961 a duty of 2d. a gallon was placed on fuel oil for revenue purposes, and its continuance provided some protection for coal. Estimates of the future need for energy were based on the National Plan of 1965. For coal, it foresaw a continuing rundown, steadied by a measure of protection, through the fuel oil tax and the ban on coal imports. Consumption of oil was expected to increase, but in view of the risks to security attempts should be made to secure diverse sources of supply. The nuclear power programme was to proceed, based on the advanced gas-cooled reactor, which it was hoped would produce electricity more cheaply than other types. The two secondary fuel industries, electricity and gas, were to continue their expansion in general competition.

One of the concomitants of this policy review was the acceptance of the need for special measures to deal with the situation in the coal industry. Of general interest for the role of nationalized industries was the acknowledgement that, having pursued a policy of expansion with active government support, the corporation should be relieved of debt arising from investment which had turned out to be unnecessary. The grounds for this capital reconstruction were explained in a White Paper, *The Finances of the Coal Industry* (Cmnd. 2805) of November 1965.

The first extract in this chapter is from a second White Paper on *Fuel Policy* (Cmnd. 3438) which was published in 1967. It announced that 'though the predominance of coal and oil as primary fuel sources will continue for many years to come, they will in future be competing for the market with nuclear power and natural gas. We are moving from a two-fuel to a four-fuel economy'. The White Paper discussed mainly the primary fuels, and the main new factor to be considered was the introduction into the market of cheap natural gas from the North Sea. The significance of the policy lay in its attempt to ensure that full economic advantage was taken of this development, and of the predicted developments in nuclear power. The extract printed indicates the prospects as the government saw them. This analysis did not satisfy the National Coal Board, especially as it related to the period after 1970, and an extract from an annual report of the NCB shows the grounds of the disagreement.

The conditions of several of the power industries were reviewed in the decade by the Select Committee on Nationalized Industries. The electricity industry was investigated in 1963, and the National Coal Board in 1969. The Select Committee considered the gas industry in session 1960–61 (H.C. 280, not reprinted) and in 1967–68 it turned to the exploitation of North Sea gas, a crucial factor in the new fuel policy. The extract printed is from this later report, and it explains the decision to make this large capital investment.

There is no space for material about nuclear power developments, but these were a second major factor in the new fuel policy. The capital costs of nuclear power stations are very high but their running costs are low. Considerable controversy surrounds the calculations of the costs of generating electricity in the 1970s by nuclear stations, compared with using coal- or oil-burning apparatus. In addition the United Kingdom Atomic Energy Authority is an unusual nationalized concern since it is largely financed by government grant and works closely with the relevant central government department. The position of the industry was reviewed twice in the period by the Select Committee on Science and Technology (H.C. 381 of session 1966–67, and H.C. 401 of session 1968–69) with particular attention to problems of cost, exports, and industrial structure. This was part of a long preoccupation with the structure of the industry, as noted in chapter 2, and in the event not finally resolved by 1970.

INLAND TRANSPORT

The 1960s were years of great change in the public transport systems in Britain. They were years of particular crisis for the railways, but there was at the end of the decade a fundamental reorganization of public road transport as well, embodied in the Transport Act of 1968.

In December 1960, in the time of Mr Ernest Marples' tenure as Minister of Transport, there was published the White Paper of *Reorganization of the Nationalized Transport Undertakings* (Cmnd. 1248), and a critique of this paper by Mr Ernest Davies is reprinted in Professor Hanson's volume (p. 106). This volume takes up the study with work of Dr Richard Beeching as chairman of British Railways, and an extract summarizing his report on the *Reshaping of British Railways* (1963) is here reprinted. This concludes by hoping that much of the railway's financial deficit would be eliminated by 1970. However, by the mid-sixties it became clear that even the vigorous prosecution of Dr Beeching's policies would not bring this about, and further measures were necessary. The development of ideas on road transport was furthered by other government reports, notably the Buchanan report on *Traffic in Towns* (1963) and the Geddes report on *Carriers' Licensing* (1965).

By this time the Labour government was engaged in a wide-ranging restructuring of transport services, described in a White Paper on *Transport Policy* (Cmnd. 3057) of July 1966 (not reprinted). This described a set of intentions for each aspect of transport, to adapt it to the age of the motor vehicle. In November 1967 the implications for *Railway Policy* were further elaborated in a White Paper (Cmnd. 3439). This expounded a new policy of identifying particular services to be supported by the government on social grounds, and of ending the grant to meet recurrent deficits with the aid of a further drastic capital reconstruction.

The economic implications of other aspects of the new transport policies are seen in an extract from another White Paper, *Public Transport and Traffic* (Cmnd. 3481) of December 1967. An extract printed earlier in this volume was concerned with extensive proposals for restructuring and the creation of new public corporations. The extract here deals with financial assistance – capital grants, bus grants, fuel grants and so on – with which the central government proposed to promote the re-equipment and efficiency of local transport.

Another nationalized industry which needed new policies in the decade was British Waterways. It was decided to maintain unified management, but in addition to commercial operation of part of the system, a new emphasis was put on their possible amenity uses. This was explained in a White Paper of 1967 (Cmnd. 3401).

AIR TRANSPORT

The two nationalized airlines have special economic problems – they are subject to competition from foreign airlines, and yet the routes they fly and the prices they charge are fixed by administrative process. The beginning of the decade saw one of them, the British Overseas Airways Corporation, slipping into financial crisis. The situation showed very well the difficulties of relationships between Ministers and board chairmen (one chairman, Sir Matthew Slattery, was asked to resign in 1963), and the problem of distinguishing the Corporation's interest from the national interest. There was a government-sponsored enquiry by an accountant, Mr Corbett, in 1963 and the financial situation was reported to the House of Commons in a White Paper (H.C. 5 of session 1963–64). An investigation by the Select Committee followed, and the conclusions this came to are found in its report of 1964 (H.C. 240 of session 1963–64). British European Airways was the subject of a Select Committee enquiry in 1967, not reprinted here. The general background of the airline industry is reviewed in the report of the Edwards committee, *British Air Transport in the Seventies*.

Finally, there is the communications industry – the Post Office. Before it became a public corporation in 1969, it was investigated by the Select Committee on Nationalized Industries (H.C. 340 of February 1967).

15. FUEL POLICY IN 1967[1]

74. Table A below illustrates in round figures the likely pattern of fuel use in the mid-1970's on the assumptions indicated in the footnote.

[1] From White Paper, *Fuel Policy*, November 1967, Cmnd. 3438, paras. 74–75, 86–110. Reprinted with permission of the Controller of Her Majesty's Stationery Office.

TABLE A

Trends of Primary Fuel Use

	Million tons coal equivalent (m.t.c.e.)		
	1957 (*Actual*)	1966 (*Actual*)	1975
Coal	212.9	174.7	120*
Oil	36.7	111.7	145
Nuclear and Hydro-electricity	1.7	10.2	35
Natural Gas	—	1.1	50
Total Inland Demand for Energy	251.3	297.7	350

* Exports of coal estimated at about 2 million tons.

FOOTNOTE – The main assumptions underlying the pattern of primary fuel use in 1975 shown in Table A are that North Sea gas reserves would support a level of production at an average rate of 4,000 m.c.f.d. and that the price of the gas would be such that it could be sold; that there would be no conversion of coal-fired power stations to oil; that the second nuclear power programme would be fulfilled; that oil tax would be at a rate of 2d. a gallon; and that no coal would be imported. Gross domestic product is assumed to grow at an average rate of 3 per cent per annum.

75. Projections for so long a period ahead are inevitably subject to considerable uncertainty and the figures should be regarded as illustrating trends, not as setting targets. It is important to note the assumptions on which they are based, as summarized in the footnote to the table. The considerations involved are further discussed elsewhere in the White Paper. But, subject to this proviso, the indications are that:

(a) By 1975 nuclear power and natural gas may be supplying as much as a quarter of all our energy requirements. How much natural gas will eventually be produced will not be known until much more exploration is completed; but studies of nuclear energy point to nuclear power making a rapidly increasing contribution in the later 1970s, possibly amounting to almost a quarter of our total energy requirements by the end of the decade.

(b) The inescapable result of the growing use of these new fuels will be to limit the market for coal; but even without them coal would have continued to decline unless it were still more heavily protected.

(c) In order to alter relative prices in favour of coal sufficiently to slow down its decline significantly, it would be necessary to protect it at a level which would lead to misuse of resources and would put British industry at a disadvantage with its competitors.

(d) The decline in the demand for coal, which is already faster than was anticipated in the 1965 White Paper,[1] could therefore only be reversed by deliberately holding back the expansion of nuclear power and the introduction of natural gas, and by heavy additional protection or a massive subsidy.

(e) Oil is unlikely to maintain its fast growth of recent years; but with growing consumption for transport and similar exclusive uses, it will hold or slightly increase its present share of the total energy market. . . .

CHAPTER 7. LONG-TERM POLICY

86. The first decision for the government is whether a pattern of energy supplies in the mid-1970s of the general shape indicated by Table A[2] is desirable. As explained in paragraph 75, the figures in that table are in no sense production targets for the various primary fuels, but rather an illustration of the balance between them which underlying trends are likely to have brought about by the mid-1970s. They also point the direction in which the fuel sector is likely to develop in the still longer term: a continuing contraction of the coal industry, a slower rate of expansion for oil, rising use of nuclear power and perhaps further growth in natural gas.

87. The developing pattern of primary fuel supplies offers substantial benefits. The introduction of the newer fuels will mean cheaper energy. In the coming years they will not only take up the natural increase in Britain's energy requirements, but will also capture some existing markets from oil and coal. The recent growth of oil, both in new markets and in displacement of coal, has been very rapid: over the past nine years oil rose from 15 to 37 per cent of our total energy use and, if the introduction of nuclear power and natural gas were impeded, oil would inevitably gain an increasing share of the energy market. In a two-fuel economy, the time might have come when, despite oil's advantages as a fuel and its value in so many other roles, dependence on foreign sources for so much of our energy became a matter of serious concern.

88. The experience of the Middle East war emphasizes the importance of developing the new fuels on grounds both of security and cheapness. North Sea gas and nuclear power will slow down the advance of oil

---

[1] Cmnd. 2798.   [2] See para. 74.

and they will take up some of the markets which coal would otherwise be likely to lose to oil. To the extent that they do so, there will be benefits to the balance of payments and an improvement in the security of fuel supplies. With a four-fuel economy the proportion of its energy requirements for which the country has to rely on imported fuel in the mid-1970s would be little higher than it is today, and there should be no greater need to consider limiting the growth of oil on security grounds. It should be noted that oil prices already reflect the cost of existing diversification and oil stockpiling by the companies.

89.   Further decline in the markets for coal could not be prevented even by holding back the expansion of nuclear power and the development of natural gas unless the present level of coal protection were raised to an extent which would lead to a big increase in the general level of energy prices, or unless coal prices were heavily subsidized. But excessive protection for coal would lead to a misallocation of manpower and capital to the detriment of the economy as a whole.

90.   We cannot afford to penalize our competitive standing as a nation by adding unnecessarily to our energy costs. Developments in recent years have reduced our competitive advantage in fuel costs *vis-à-vis* Europe: and American fuel costs are markedly lower than ours. It follows that we need to take the fullest advantage of the new primary sources of energy – natural gas and nuclear power – in order to assist industry in its competitive struggle; and that it is essential for the coal industry to continue its drive for greater efficiency and lower costs, so that it too can play its part in the provision of cheaper energy.

91.   Nevertheless, while the balance of payments position is difficult, as at present, some discrimination against oil is justifiable to conserve foreign exchange. But as indicated in paragraph 80 the present rate of tax on oil already represents a high level of protection for coal.

92.   The other major potential constraint on accepting a shift to the cheaper fuels is the rate at which it is practicable for the coal industry to contract and for the government and the industry to deal satisfactorily with the resulting employment and social problems. The government consider that a contraction to the level of demand for 1975 suggested by Table A should be manageable, but they have accepted the advice of the National Coal Board that the rate of contraction implied by the corresponding figures for 1970[1] would cause unmanageable difficulties for the industry during the next few years. It might also cause serious difficulties for the economy in this period.

93.   The government have decided that it is in the national interest to accept the long-term trends implied by Table A as a basis for planning. However, the figures in Table A make no allowance for the possible

[1] See Appendix I, Table D (not reprinted).

conversion of coal-fired power stations to oil or for any relaxation in the present virtual ban on foreign coal imports. It will be necessary to consider at a later date whether to relax these measures and what effect on coal demand in the 1970s this would have. For the present, the problems raised by the already fast rate of contraction of the coal industry up to 1970 preclude such relaxation; and during this period it will be necessary to take additional measures to help the industry and to secure an orderly transition. These measures are described in the next chapter. The longer-term decisions implicit in the government's general conclusions are as follows.

Natural Gas

94. Natural gas is to be introduced rapidly into the economy. Strategy on gas absorption will continue to be evolved as more knowledge is gained about reserves, prices and markets. At this stage a rapid build-up in supplies is envisaged, on a basis allowing for the absorption of all that the fields so far discovered are expected to produce in the mid-1970s, with a modest allowance for additional discoveries. Most of the natural gas available will go to the premium markets where it will largely be displacing oil, but there will be some supplies to bulk industrial users, to assist the early build-up in supplies and to balance load thereafter. In these markets there will be some displacement of coal as well as oil.

95. This policy will mean a shorter life for the gas fields than a policy of slow depletion and will involve using some of the gas in markets where the resource savings are relatively low. The government believe that these disadvantages are outweighed by the value of giving an incentive to the further exploration needed to improve our knowledge of the ultimate reserves available, and by the benefits to the economy and the balance of payments which a fast build-up of supplies will bring.

96. Rapid absorption of natural gas will not bring dislocation or chaos to the energy market. The 4,000 m.c.f.d. assumed to be available in 1975 will represent only about 15 per cent of the total demand for energy; an important slice of the market but not revolutionary in its impact. But, for the gas industry, it does represent a revolution involving the wholesale displacement of existing gas-making plant and methods, a nation-wide conversion programme, and an expansion of sales by nearly fourfold between now and the mid-1970s.

Nuclear Power and Power Station Fuel Use

97. In the last few years, in recognition of the strong interest it has in the well-being of the coal industry because of the many coal-fired power stations which will remain in use for many years ahead, the electricity

industry has been giving preference to coal in operating its stations. The government have decided on a new scheme extending to 1970–71, the details of which are given in paragraphs 116–17 below.

98.   The 1965 White Paper[1] established for planning purposes a second nuclear power programme of 8,000 MW and the government envisage the completion of that programme by the mid-1970s. That White Paper also stated that proposals for oil-fired power stations would be the subject of special scrutiny. In order to keep down costs and prices it is important that the electricity industry should be able to make use of cheap sources of primary energy. Power stations not yet started cannot at the very earliest come into commission before 1973. For future power stations, the government have now decided that the generating Boards should base their choice of fuel on an economic assessment of the method of generation which will enable them to supply electricity at the lowest system cost consistent with security of supply and load balancing. In deciding whether to give consent to new stations, the Minister of Power and the Secretary of State for Scotland will also take into account such wider economic considerations as may be relevant.

99.   It would be consistent with this policy for the generating Boards to seek consent in the longer term for the conversion of stations from one primary fuel to another where this would reduce system costs. The electricity industry will, however, require very large quantities of coal in the 1970s and has a strong, continuing interest in the health of the coal industry. For this reason, linked as it is with the short-term structural problems of the coal industry, the government do not in general envisage the conversion of coal-fired stations to other fuels in the next few years, though there may be scope for some use of natural gas on a seasonal basis and there may be cases where the requirements of clean air dictate conversion from coal to other fuels.

Oil

100.   Although the government have decided, particularly in the light of the current balance of payments position, that it is right to continue to favour indigenous fuels against oil, it remains their broad policy to avoid discrimination between oil companies trading in the home market. Good progress has been made towards the goal of home refining capacity to match the country's requirements and this remains a major objective of policy, though with recognition of the fact that some trade in oil products between countries will still be necessary for the oil companies to balance their international refining operations. The home refining policy depends also on the maintenance of a reasonable and balanced level of demand for the various oil products.

[1] Cmnd. 2798.

101. The repercussions of the Middle East war could have significant implications for certain aspects of oil policy. As stated in paragraph 50, the government are conducting a thorough re-examination of ways of strengthening the security of our supplies. They nevertheless consider it right to base fuel policy on the expectation that regular supplies of oil at competitive prices will continue to be available and they believe that it would be wrong to deny to British industry the advantages that oil can bring. The greater part of the expected growth in demand is due to the growing needs of those markets, notably transport, where oil has no substitute; in the competitive part of its markets oil's rate of growth is expected to slacken. Although oil use as a whole in 1975 is expected to represent a higher percentage of total energy requirements than now, the increase will be small by contrast with the past. Subject to the outcome of the re-examination now in progress, no greater discrimination against oil should prove necessary on grounds of security.

Coal

102. The government have concluded from their analysis of coal's position and prospects in relation to competing fuels that, on any tenable view of the longer-term pattern of energy supplies and costs, the demand for coal will continue to decline. This is not the result of government policy; it reflects a continuing trend in consumer preference.

103. The government do not underrate the difficulty of the task confronting management and men in trying to maintain and increase the efficiency of an industry which is gradually contracting. But because coal will continue for a long time to provide such a large and indispensable part of the country's fuel supplies, it is of the greatest importance for the efficiency of the industry to be still further increased and costs reduced. The government have concluded that the modernization of the coal industry and its concentration on the most economic coalfields and collieries must go forward. Only in this way can the coal industry remain viable.

104. The precise level of coal demand in the 1970s will depend on the extent to which productivity can be raised and costs brought down: without a substantial rise in productivity and the consequent saving in manpower, the cost of coal will be so high that coal demand will fall more quickly than implied by Table A. Either way, a further decline in colliery manpower is inevitable.

105. To the extent that manpower, and hence production, are not reduced in step with rising productivity and falling demand, undistributed stocks will rise above the level necessary to ensure proper distribution and security of supply; this has recently begun to happen on a

large scale. With the present outlook for demand, there is serious risk of these additional stocks remaining unsold indefinitely. In any case they are a large additional burden on the Exchequer, which has to finance them, and a continuing discouragement to the men and management of the industry. The government therefore consider it important that production should be continually adjusted to the level of demand and that excessive stocking should be avoided. However, time will be needed both for the industry's management to make the necessary adjustments inside the industry and for the men becoming redundant to be redeployed into other employment. Similarly, time must elapse before the measures now being taken by the National Coal Board can result in cost reductions. The greater the Board's success in reducing costs, the higher coal demand is likely to be in the mid-1970s.

106.   Most of the colliery closures will be in the older coalfields in development areas. The measures it is proposed to take to improve the benefits to men leaving the industry or transferred to other collieries, and to facilitate the redeployment of ex-miners to other suitable work in the transitional period, are set out in the next section; for the longer term, the government's regional policies take full account of the trends of mining employment.

107.   The government have decided that protection for coal cannot be reduced at the moment, but they have reviewed the existing forms of protection. At present, apart from the assistance from the electricity industry, there is the protection afforded by the 2·2d. a gallon tax on oil and the virtual ban on imports of coal. Imports of coal competing with home production would add to the difficulties of the United Kingdom coal industry and the lifting of the import ban cannot be contemplated at the moment, but the Government will keep this question under review.

108.   An alternative to action against other fuels to protect coal would be a general subsidy for coal. The cost of a subsidy sufficient to have the same effect as the present tax on oil would be very heavy, representing a significant increase in taxation; and if it were to replace the oil tax the revenue so lost would additionally have to be made up from new taxation. A subsidy would reduce energy prices but would not alter the real costs of energy supplies to the country. It would also have the effect of protecting coal against natural gas and nucelar power. The government have concluded that a general subsidy for coal is undesirable for these reasons, but they have accepted certain commitments for the transitional period as explained in the next chapter.

109.   Taking a broad view of the industry's prospects in the long term, the Government are satisfied that it should be able to provide on an economic basis a substantial though declining part of the country's

fuel requirements. Over the next few years, however, the industry will need continuing assistance.

110. In neither of the last two financial years were the Board able to generate from their earnings all the funds needed for colliery investment: the higher revenue secured from the coal price increase in the spring of 1966 was entirely absorbed by rising costs. Any further substantial addition to prices would tend to depress the demand for coal still further and so increase the difficulties of dealing with manpower. In these circumstances the Board cannot be expected to find from their own resources all the finance for the expensive modernization programme or to bear a large proportion of the cost of the measures necessary to ensure that the reduction in manpower is conducted without undue hardship. Parliament will therefore be asked to provide further investment funds to continue the financing of the industry's modernization, in so far as these cannot be provided from current revenue without undue increases in the price of coal. The proposed financial arrangements for the measures needed to deal with manpower in the transitional period are set out in the following chapter.

16. THE COAL BOARD DISSENTS[1]

18. The White Paper on Fuel Policy (Cmnd. 3438), published in November, 1967, marked the transition from a two-fuel to a four-fuel economy. Within the White Paper there are really two policies – a longer-term policy for the period to 1975 based on an estimated demand for coal in that year of 120 million tons, and a transient policy to moderate the rundown of the coal industry to 1970–71. The Board are bound to report, with regret, their disagreement with the longer-term policy. While the Board were fully consulted for the period to 1970–71, there has not been adequate discussion on the period beyond. The policy for that period would involve the displacement of such a large number of men as would be inconsistent with maintaining good industrial relations.

19. The Board acknowledge that the formulation of a long-term fuel policy is essential if the fuel industries are to plan the deployment of their resources of capital, technology and manpower in the way most beneficial to the national interest. Nevertheless, they would stress the importance of not taking irrevocable decisions today, in relation to

[1] From National Coal Board, *Annual Report and Accounts 1967–68*, paras. 18–26. Reprinted with permission of the Controller of Her Majesty's Stationery Office.

natural gas and nuclear power, which will prevent the use of cheap coal in the competitive market in the 1970s. The demand estimates in the White Paper appear to be based on rates of development which drastically reduce the scope for flexibility, however much coal improves its competitive position.

20. The coal industry, in which a large state investment has already been made, could produce a greater quantity of coal at competitive costs in the 1970s than the White Paper indicates and an unduly rapid rundown in the industry's productive capacity will have extremely serious economic and social consequences. Where decisions which substantially affect the balance between competing fuels have to be taken, they should be based on a complete evaluation of the total costs to the nation, direct and indirect, economic and social, of the various alternatives. This, in the Board's view, the White Paper has failed to do.

21. The development of nuclear power in the 1970s has particularly serious implications. Any error here, leading to a decision precluding the construction of further coal-fired generating capacity, will involve the nation in abortive capital investment totalling hundreds of millions of pounds. The Board have explained both to the Select Committee on Science and Technology and to the Ministry of Power the reasons for their reservations about the size of the AGR programme and the relative cost estimates on which it is based. The present nuclear programme, of which half is already committed, will require an investment of between £240 million and £320 million more than a similar programme of conventional stations; this avoidable investment should be expected to earn a larger than normal return. To recover the additional capital expenditure through lower running costs will take ten, or more probably twenty years; a relatively small divergence from expected performance could make its recovery impossible. Because there are identifiable areas of technical uncertainty in the AGR system and because nuclear cost estimates are not sufficiently comprehensive, such a divergence is, in the Board's opinion, a real risk.

22. In all the circumstances, the Board consider that there is strong justification for a full, independent enquiry into the technical and financial basis of nuclear power. A policy of total dependence on nuclear stations for new generating capacity would result in a preponderance of capital-intensive capacity. This capacity would have to operate at the highest possible load factor, to the exclusion of conventional capacity, in order to justify the investment; even then, because of the limited summer load, not all the capacity would be able to operate at the high load factor which is technically and economically desirable. A more balanced generating system would include provision for new conventional capacity. Moreover, the hypothetical cost advantages of nuclear

power, after taking into account the probability of lower costs in conventional generation arising from improvements in the methods of operation and from advances in mining and in coal transport, are, at best, narrow. If coal is excluded from the electricity market to the extent envisaged, any such advantages will be outweighed by the effects on the coal industry's finances and the cost to the nation of the social consequences of the resultant colliery closures. The Board wish to make it clear that they are entirely in support, from the nation's point of view, of further technical progress being made in the field of nuclear development. They consider, however, that, so far as the AGR programme is concerned, this progress can adequately be achieved through the stations already committed; and, because of the massive economic and social problems involved, any further commitment should not be undertaken until the enquiry suggested above has been completed.

23.   On natural gas, the White Paper states that uncertainties about price and reserves have so far prevented the formulation of a firm long-term strategy for its absorption, although the construction of a nation-wide transmission system has already been authorized. The estimates in the White Paper of primary fuel use in 1975, however, put the consumption of natural gas at 50 million tons of coal equivalent. Absorption at this level presupposes the existence of substantial bulk outlets for gas, particularly in the summer when demand from other consumers is low. The possibility of converting conventional power stations to burn natural gas in the summer and other fuels in the winter is at present under consideration. The Board would encounter serious problems to the extent that natural gas displaced coal in this way; not only would the overall market for coal be reduced but the disparity between summer and winter demand would also be increased, with heavy additional coal stocking costs. Rail freight services would be adversely affected and investment made by British Rail in large capacity wagons would be jeopardized. There is therefore a strong case for a total sum approach, covering all the consequential costs, before final decisions are reached on the rate at which natural gas should be absorbed in the 1970s, with particular regard to the bulk markets.

24.   The impact of the Fuel Policy on the coal industry will be severe and the White Paper recognizes that the rate of contraction for the period to 1970–71 should, as far as possible, avoid disruption within the industry and hardship in the mining communities. The government have accepted that the rundown for the period has to be held within tolerable limits and have agreed that, on the Board's estimates of productivity, this will imply an output in 1970–71 of 155 million tons. To ensure that this output is absorbed rather than stocked, it has been agreed that, during the period to the end of 1970–71, the gas and

electricity industries should use more coal, in preference to other fuels, than they had planned. The Coal Industry Act, 1967, which followed the White Paper, provides that the additional costs of these measures to the industries concerned, up to a maximum of £45 million, may be borne by the government. To provide especially for the extra stocking of coal during the period, the Act raises the limit on the Board's borrowing powers from £750 million to £950 million.

25.   The Act also provides for special assistance to men made redundant after reaching 55 years of age, for an increased contribution to the Board's redeployment costs and for reimbursement of the losses incurred by the Board in deferring individual colliery closures at the government's request (*see* Chapter VII). While these measures will reduce hardship arising from the contraction of the industry, its impact, particularly on development areas, will be serious and the replacement of lost employment opportunities for boys and men will be particularly difficult.

PROSPECTS

26.   The Board are quite clear that their whole policy must be directed towards maximizing the size of the industry by reducing costs and being thoroughly competitive in the 1970s. As this and previous Reports have shown, the efficiency of the industry has been substantially improved year by year, but the full effects of this improved efficiency cannot be realized until the high-cost collieries are closed. They cannot be closed any more quickly than the present programme and indeed at this level the Board are bound to report that it is placing a great strain on management and men.

17. PLANNING FOR NORTH SEA GAS[1]

THE REASONS ADVANCED FOR EXPLOITING NORTH SEA GAS

I. 1.   The clearest and most obvious advantage in exploiting North Sea gas lies in the direct saving to the gas industry from using natural gas instead of manufacturing gas as is done at present to make what is known as town gas. The Gas Council submitted a Memorandum (Appendix 7) setting out some of the considerations involved in their appraisal of their investment in North Sea gas.

---

[1] From Select Committee on Nationalized Industries, session 1967–68, *The Exploitation of North Sea Gas*, July 1968, H.C. 372, pages ix–xi and xiii–xv. Planning for North Sea Gas. Reprinted with permission of the Controller of Her Majesty's Stationery Office.

I. 2.   The Memorandum explained that, subject to the validity of the basic assumptions of their calculations, the Council expect the return on the investment included in the industry's current capital programmes to show a satisfactory margin above the test rate of discount of 8 per cent laid down by the Government in the White Paper *Nationalized Industries: A Review of Economic and Financial Objectives* (Cmnd. 3437). Over the full life of the North Sea reserves a 'Discounted Cash Flow' rate of return of not less than 10 per cent on capital employed is indicated on the basis of the necessarily more tentative assumptions implicit in such a long-term assessment (Appendix 7, paragraph 7).

I. 3.   But while this clearly appears to constitute a satisfactory investment from the point of view of the gas industry, it is obviously necessary to study the effects of exploiting natural gas on other fuels as well. The Ministry of Power were therefore invited to give their assessment of the effects of exploiting natural gas on fuel policy as a whole.

I. 4.   The Ministry of Power said that they had endeavoured throughout all their work on fuel policy to measure the benefits of various lines of policy in terms of the resources used (Q. 34); and they submitted a memorandum (Appendix 2) which explains more fully what they mean by this concept of resource costs.

I. 5.   The Memorandum says that the true cost of supplying the nation with the energy it needs is measured by the value of the resources employed – manpower, capital material and foreign exchange. And while in general the prices of fuel will reflect the cost of the resources used in supplying the fuel, in certain circumstances prices may diverge from the true cost in terms of resources.

I. 6. As the Ministry of Power explained, the divergence between money costs and resource costs in meeting the nation's energy might arise because some fuel prices reflect elements which are not true resource costs but rather transfer payments; the oil tax for example is an element in the cost of oil which is not directly related to the cost in resources in supplying it. Money costs might also diverge from resource costs when part of the costs of supplying a fuel cannot be saved by reducing the supply of any one fuel; the capital invested in existing assets is an example of a cost which it may be impossible to save. Money costs might also diverge from resource costs, depending on how manpower can be re-deployed; for example if miners cannot be profitably employed other than in mining for some time, then in the short term the resource cost of the coal they mine is less than the accounting costs of its production; but conversely if the miners can in the longer term be more profitably employed elsewhere, there will be a saving in resources (Appendix 2, paragraph 2).

I. 7.   To follow the advantages claimed for natural gas and the divergence of resource costs from money costs, it is necessary to examine the three sectors of the fuel market to which North Sea gas may be supplied. The first of these sectors is the traditional market of the gas industry, commonly referred to as the 'premium market' because in this market gas, since it is clean and easy to control and needs no storage, can command a premium over an equivalent amount of heat from coal or oil.

I. 8.   In this 'premium' sector of the gas market, savings will arise from using natural gas instead of manufacturing town gas, as at present. These savings in money terms will be reflected in the profitability of the Gas Council's investment (see paragraphs I. 1 and I. 2). And they imply no off-setting cost in terms of resources, for the use of coal to make gas is being rapidly phased out already (see paragraphs IV. 10 and 12) quite irrespective of the exploitation of North Sea gas (Appendix 2, paragraph 5).

I. 9.   In addition to the traditional market of the gas industry, new outlets commonly called the 'semi-premium market' are expected, where consumers will be prepared to pay some premium for gas over crude fuel prices, though these consumers would not have been prepared to pay a sufficient premium for gas sold at the price which would have had to be charged if North Sea gas had not been available.

I. 10.   In this market the fuel likely to be displaced is mainly the lighter oil products, so the money savings do not imply any substantial offsetting cost in terms of resources on account of any displacement of coal. The savings here in fact would amount to the difference between the cost of supplying this market with North Sea gas and the cost of supplying the alternative fuel, and the premium value attached to the gas (but deducting the premium value, if any, attached to the alternative fuel) (Appendix 2, paragraph 6).

I. 11.   In both the premium and the semi-premium markets for gas the displacement of coal is small, and there will be a very substantial saving in foreign exchange, in addition to the money savings and the domestic resource savings already referred to. For the gas industry of the future without the use of North Sea gas would have had to supply the premium market with gas made from oil, and the semi-premium market would have used mainly the lighter oil products in preference to gas. Savings in these markets will include substantial savings where conversions would have been made to oil, but, with the advent of natural gas, will be to that fuel instead.

I. 12.   The Ministry of Power estimate that the direct foreign exchange savings from natural gas will be of the order of £50 million a year by about 1970–71 (Q. 676). But the savings cannot be assessed with precision at present, partly because the price to be paid for most of the gas already discovered has not yet been settled, partly because the rate of absorption of the gas depends upon whether or not further discoveries are made (see paragraph II. 10), and partly because in the event of further discoveries the question of the national ownership of the successful company would be very material (Q. 49).

I. 13.   The third market for natural gas is the bulk industrial market, where gas may have little or no special advantage over any other source of heat except that of price. Here the savings from natural gas will often not be much more than the difference between the cost of natural gas and the cost of the alternative fuel (Appendix 2, paragraph 7).

I. 14.   Neither the White Paper on Fuel Policy (Cmnd. 3438) nor the Ministry of Power's Memorandum is able to quantify the whole of the saving in resources arising from the exploitation of natural gas; but, as the Memorandum says, while it is often difficult to put precise figures on the resource costs of a particular pattern of development, it is usually possible to estimate the order of difference between alternative courses (Appendix 2, paragraph 3).

I. 15.   The Ministry of Power in fact were fully satisfied that there would be savings in terms of resources in all three sectors of the future market for gas. In the premium market the resource savings arising from the use of North Sea gas would be very large, for they would arise from the displacement of oils for gas-making, and these oils are among the high-priced oil products. In the semi-premium market there would be a range of saving in resources, with a substantial saving at the upper end and, even at the lower end, savings which would be 'strong, positive and desirable' (Q. 676). In the bulk industrial market the resource savings would remain positive, although they would be lower and in some cases very slight. The resource savings envisaged were considered both as compared with the use of oil for the immediate future and for the possible displacement of coal, which would not arise on any significant scale until the 1970s; and in both cases in the bulk energy market there would be positive savings in resources, although they would be smaller than the savings in the other sectors of the market (Q. 676).

I. 16.   Accordingly, while the process of calculation of resource costs and resource savings was an extraordinarily difficult one in some respects (Q. 34), the Ministry, 'looking to 1975 saw a fairly clear picture of reasonable certitude that the type of pattern they had sketched out should be the best and most viable' (Q. 665). An expanding amount of energy would be supplied at lower cost of resources, both in the premium market and the semi-premium market; of that there was no doubt whatsoever. There was less precision in the forecasts for the bulk market, but there again in many cases the use of gas would certainly represent a more economical use of resources (Q. 700). And as the

Ministry of Power pointed out, while some of the savings in the near future might be small, the smaller savings obtainable in the next few years from the bulk use of some of the gas might clearly be worth more than the discounted 'present value' of the greater savings obtainable from reserving that gas beyond a certain point in time for possible use in premium markets (Appendix 1, paragraph 28). . . .

THE CAPITAL COST OF NORTH SEA GAS

I. 25.   The whole of the gas industry's capital investment in fixed assets from 1962–63 to 1967–68 has amounted to £856 million, and their estimate of further investment in fixed assets up to 1972–73 is £1,221 million, but it has not been possible to apportion all this investment between town gas and natural gas (Evidence, page 27, Table V and paragraph 48). As the Minister of Power announced in the House on 22 May 1968, when moving the Second Reading of the Gas and Electricity Bill, this figure of £1,221 million represents about three-quarters of the industry's total estimated capital requirements for the period, which amount in all to £1,600 million. The Minister said that about £500 million of this latter sum will be met from the industry's internal resources (H.C. Deb. (1967–68) 765, c. 544).

I. 26.   Estimates of capital requirements beyond 1972–73 are not possible; but, as the Chairman of the Gas Council said, any forecast of a decline in capital requirements to be expected beyond 1973 depends upon whether the absorption rate of natural gas continues at the figure at present planned (see Chapter II), or whether it is further expanded. This in turn depends on whether or not more gas is found (Q. 139). Under the system of annual investment reviews, the rate at which the capital is actually invested is extremely flexible (Q. 794).

I. 27.   The rate of amortization of the total capital costs of the introduction of North Sea gas varies according to the object of the expenditure. At present it is planned to spread each year's cost of conversion of consumers' equipment forward over a 15-year period (Q. 123, 286). For other new assets the rates of depreciation are at present being reviewed (Q. 174), but on current plans capital equipment for the pipes of the national transmission system are depreciated on the basis of a 30-year life (Q. 197).

I. 28.   Your Committee have already referred to the return expected on this capital expenditure (see paragraph I. 2); and they note that for the future the industry's plans envisage the making of operating surpluses, small perhaps in the first five years but thereafter increasing rapidly (Appendix 6, paragraph 10). With government approval for their loans, together with the finance provided from their own resources, the Gas Council have no inhibitions and feel they can go ahead with their plans (Q. 117).

CONCLUSIONS

I. 29. Investment in North Sea gas undoubtedly represents a very large capital commitment, but the Gas Council foresee large operating surpluses after the first five years (Appendix 6, paragraph 10). In considering the investment cost, moreover, it has to be remembered that in the absence of North Sea gas very considerable investment would be needed in conventional gas-making equipment, which would require more capital per therm of gas made than North Sea gas requires.

I. 30. Your Committee are satisfied that, as long as the present test rate of discount for capital investment by the nationalized industries is set at 8 per cent, the exploitation of natural gas as at present planned must be accepted as a fully justifiable capital investment in financial terms as far as the gas industry is concerned. For the gas industry expects the return on its current capital programmes to show a satisfactory margin above that test rate, subject to the validity of the basic assumptions they have made; and over the full life of the North Sea reserves a 'Discounted Cash Flow' rate of return of not less than 10 per cent is indicated on the necessarily more tentative assumptions implicit in such a long-term assessment (Appendix 7, paragraph 7). In other words, gas can be supplied substantially more cheaply by exploiting North Sea gas.

I. 31. Your Committee also welcome the Ministry of Power's approach of assessing the merits of exploiting North Sea gas on the basis of the resource costs and savings involved. By this approach it is possible to take into account all the factors involved, and to give proper weight on an 'avoidable costs' basis to charges for coal production and transport, as well as on a 'transfer payments' basis to charges for any measures to assist in promoting alternative employment in areas affected by the closing of coal mines, and to give weight to the whole question of re-deployment of manpower resources.

I. 32. Your Committee are not themselves qualified to assess whether the Ministry's calculations are open to further questioning, but they wish to draw attention to the Ministry's claim that while all such calculations are in a sense speculative, the Ministry have tested their calculations in every possible way, and that there is no real doubt about them (Q. 849). For the merits or otherwise of exploiting North Sea gas ultimately depend upon the validity of the calculations; and if the calculations are right, the cheaper gas resulting from the exploitation of

North Sea gas will not be outweighed by greater total expense in the whole energy market.

I. 33. The foreign exchange saving arising from the displacement of oil by natural gas will of course be partially off-set where coal is displaced by natural gas. Your Committee, however, wish to draw attention to one particular consideration in connection with savings of foreign exchange, which, however theoretical it may seem today, may have importance at a later date. They believe that even if the likely saving of foreign exchange can be assessed accurately, the value of that saving is itself a variable quantity; for any special value that may be attached to savings of foreign exchange will vary according to the size of the surplus or deficit on the balance of payments at any particular time.

I. 34. As Your Committee have said, however, they welcome the Ministry's approach to the assessment of the merits of North Sea gas. They consider that if, as the Ministry claim, the calculations have been tested in every possible way, the Chairman of the National Coal Board is not justified in his view that a total sum has not been attempted, for a full assessment of resource savings represents just such a total sum.

I. 35. This Report deals in Chapters IV to IX with the effects of the exploitation of North Sea gas on individual industries. But it is convenient to deal here with the further general argument of the Chairman of the National Coal Board (Q. 451) that the exploitation of North Sea gas was an example of the unecessary competition between the fuel industries which overall had led to hundreds of millions of pounds of state capital having been invested abortively (see paragraph I. 21).

I. 36. The truth is that it is not more economical to persist with a more expensive process, however much capital has been invested in it, if it can be shown that some other process produces the same product substantially more cheaply. The concept of cost-savings by means of replacement is clear enough when looked at within a single enterprise, and it is equally valid for the whole of the energy market.

I. 37. The decision to embark on a new process in any particular case must naturally depend on confidence in the calculations of the relative costs of the processes concerned. But if the Ministry of Power are satisfied that from an economic point of view the replacement of one source of energy by another produces a margin of saving which represents an acceptable net return on investment, they cannot be criticized on general economic grounds for approving that replacement. As the Ministry witnesses said, in general it is the duty of any undertaking to make suitable provision against the impact of technical change. It is characteristic of the whole history of industry in this country and elsewhere that an industry has to take account of the prospects of technical change and to provide for them either in its policy or depreciation or alternatively in its policy for putting profits to reserve (Q. 841). Any error in investment lies not in investing in the new process which shows an economic return, but in having in the past over-invested in processes which now prove uneconomic.

18. BEECHING REPORT ON BRITISH RAIL[1]

SUMMARY OF THE REPORT

The Report describes the investigations carried out, the conclusions which were drawn, and the proposals which are made for the purpose of reshaping British Railways to suit modern conditions.

The thought underlying the whole Report is that the railways should be used to meet that part of the total transport requirement of the country for which they offer the best available means, and that they should cease to do things for which they are ill suited. To this end, studies were made to determine the extent to which the present pattern of the railways' services is consistent with the characteristics which distinguish railways as a mode of transport, namely: the high cost of their specialized and exclusive route system, and their low cost per unit moved if traffic is carried in dense flows of well-loaded through trains. As a result, it is concluded that, in many respects, they are being used in ways which emphasize their disadvantages and fail to exploit their advantages.

The proposals for reshaping the railways are all directed towards giving them a route system, a pattern of traffics, and a mode of operation, such as to make the field which they cover one in which their merits predominate and in which they can be competitive,

To this end, it is proposed to build up traffic on the well-loaded routes, to foster those traffics which lend themselves to movement in well-loaded through trains, and to develop the new services necessary for that purpose. At the same time, it is proposed to close down routes which are so lightly loaded as to have no chance of paying their way, and to discontinue services which cannot be provided economically by rail. These proposals are, however, not so sweeping as to attempt to bring the railways to a final pattern in one stage, with the associated risks of abandoning too much or, alternatively, of spending wastefully.

Although railways can only be economic if routes carry dense traffic, density is so low over much of the system that revenue derived from the

[1] From British Railways Board, *The Reshaping of British Railways* (Beeching report), 1963, HMSO, Part I, pages 57–60. Reprinted with permission of the British Railways Board.

movement of passengers and freight over more than half the route miles of British Railways is insufficient to cover the cost of the route alone. In other words, revenue does not pay for the maintenance of the track and the maintenance and operation of the signalling system, quite apart from the cost of running trains, depots, yards and stations. Also, it is found that the cost of more than half of the stations is greater than the receipts from traffic which they originate.

Amongst traffics, stopping passenger services are exceptionally poor. As a group, they are very lightly loaded and do not cover their own movement costs. They account for most of the train miles on much of the lightly loaded route mileage, but also account for a considerable train mileage on more heavily loaded routes, and are one of the main causes for the continued existence of many of the small and uneconomic stations.

Fast and semi-fast, inter-city passenger trains are potentially profitable and need to be developed selectively, along with other forms of traffic on trunk routes. High peak traffics at holiday periods are, however, very unremunerative. They are dying away and provision for them will be reduced.

Suburban services feeding London come close to covering their full expenses, but give no margin to provide for costly increases in capacity, even though they are overloaded and demand goes on increasing.

Suburban services feeding other centres of population are serious loss makers, and it will not be possible to continue them satisfactorily without treating them as a part of a concerted system of transport for the cities which they serve.

Freight traffic, like passenger traffic, includes good flows, but also includes much which is unsuitable, or which is unsuitably handled by the railways at present. The greater part of all freight traffic is handled by the staging forward of individual wagons from yard to yard, instead of by through-train movement. This is costly, and causes transit times to be slow and variable. It also leads to low utilization of wagons and necessitates the provision of a very large and costly wagon fleet.

Coal traffic as a whole just pays its way, but, in spite of its suitability for through train movement, about two-thirds of the total coal handled on rail still moves by the wagon-load. This is very largely due to the absence of facilities for train loading at the pits, and to the multiplicity of small receiving terminals to which coal is consigned. Block train movement is increasing, but substantial savings will result from acceleration of the change. This depends, in turn, upon provision of bunkers for train loading at the pits, bunkers for ship loading at the ports, and of coal concentration depots to which coal can be moved by rail for final road distribution to small industrial and domestic consumers.

Wagon-load freight traffic, other than coal, is a bad loss maker when taken as a group, but over half of it is siding-to-siding traffic, much of which moves in trainload quantities, and this makes a good contribution to system cost. One third of the remainder moves between sidings and docks, and this falls just short of covering its direct costs. The remaining 30 per cent of the whole passes through stations, at one or both ends of its transit, and causes a loss relative to direct expenses which is so large that it submerges the credit margin on all the rest.

Freight sundries traffic is also a bad loss maker. It is handled at present between over 900 stations and depots, which causes very poor wagon loading and a high level of costly transhipment of the freight while in transit. Railways handle only about 45 per cent of this traffic in the country, and do not select the flows which are most suitable for rail movement. If they are to stay in the business, British Railways must concentrate more upon the inter-city flows and reduce the number of depots handling this form of traffic to not more than a hundred.

Study of traffic not on rail shows that there is a considerable tonnage which is potentially good rail traffic. This includes about 8 m. tons which could be carried in train-load quantities, and a further 30 m. tons which is favourable to rail by virtue of the consignment sizes, lengths of haul, and terminal conditions. In addition, there is a further 16 m. tons which is potentially good traffic for a new kind of service – a Liner Train service – for the combined road and rail movement of containerized merchandise.

Preliminary studies of a system of liner train services, which might carry at least the 16 m. tons of new traffic referred to above and a similar quantity drawn from traffic which is now carried unremuneratively on rail, show such services to be very promising and likely to contribute substantially to support of the main railway network, if developed.

The steps proposed, to achieve the improvements referred to above, are:

(1) Discontinuance of many stopping passenger services.
(2) Transfer of the modern multiple unit stock displaced to continuing services which are still steam locomotive hauled.
(3) Closure of a high proportion of the total number of small stations to passenger traffic.
(4) Selective improvement of inter-city passenger services and rationalization of routes.
(5) Damping down of seasonal peaks of passenger traffic and withdrawal of corridor coaching stock held for the purpose of covering them at present.
(6) Co-ordination of suburban train and bus services and charges,

in collaboration with municipal authorities, with the alternative of fare increases and possible closure of services.

(7) Co-ordination of passenger parcels services with the Post Office.

(8) Increases of block train movement of coal, by:

   (a) inducing the National Coal Board to provide train loading facilities at collieries;

   (b) inducing the establishment of coal concentration depots, in collaboration with the National Coal Board and the distributors.

(9) Reduction of the uneconomic freight traffic passing through small stations by closing them progressively, but with regard to the preservation of potentially good railway traffics, and by adjustment to charges.

(10) Attraction of more siding-to-siding traffics suitable for through-train movement by operating such trains at the expense of the wagon forwarding system and by provision of time-tabled trains, of special stock, to meet customer requirements.

(11) Study and development of a network of 'Liner Train' services to carry flows of traffic which, though dense, are composed of consignments too small in themselves to justify through-train operation.

(12) Concentration of freight sundries traffic upon about 100 main depots, many of them associated with Liner Train depots, and carriage of main flows of sundries of Liner Trains, probably coupled with passenger parcels, and possibly Post Office parcels and letters.

(13) Rapid, progressive withdrawal of freight wagons over the next three years.

(14) Continued replacement of steam by diesel locomotives for main line traction, up to a probable requirement of at least 3,750/4,250 (1,698 already in service and 950 on order at present).

(15) Rationalization of the composition and use of the Railways' road cartage fleet.

These various lines of action are strongly interdependent. If the whole plan is implemented with vigour, however, much (though not necessarily all) of the Railways' deficit should be eliminated by 1970.

19. PUBLIC TRANSPORT FINANCE[1]

71.   Public transport both in our cities and in the countryside cannot

[1] From White Paper, *Public Transport and Traffic*, December 1967, Cmnd.

be expected to play its necessary role without new measures of financial support. The Government stated in the 1966 White Paper on Transport Policy (Cmnd. 3057) that it intended to take powers to provide financial help for public transport. Proposals have now been worked out in detail.

GRANTS TOWARDS CAPITAL EXPENDITURE IN PUBLIC TRANSPORT

72.   The government will take powers in the Transport Bill to make grant towards the cost of capital investment in public passenger transport – just as grants are at present given towards the cost of major highway construction and improvement. This major new development in government policy is intended to correct the present imbalance in government financial support for transport in urban areas, where improvements to the principal road system attract Exchequer grants but expenditure on public transport does not.

73.   The grants will be made towards the cost of approved projects 'for the provision, improvement or development' of public passenger transport in cities and towns. Eligible projects will include:

(a) major improvement or extension of railway-lines – track, stations, signalling systems, re-equipment with stock special to the project and associated investment for local railway services;
(b) provision of new fixed track rail and bus systems (e.g. tube railways, monorails, busways):
(c) construction or major improvement of:
(i) bus stations and depots,
(ii) terminals and vessels for local passenger ferry services,
(iii) interchanges, including car parks, for people transferring to and from public transport systems.

The costs of preliminary work and the preparation of proposed projects will be eligible for grant.

74.   In England the Minister responsible for making grants will be the Minister of Transport, and in Scotland and Wales the Secretary of State. The rate of grant will be 75 per cent of the approved cost of major projects, such as those described in (a) and (b) above (i.e. the same rate as for grants for major road investment).

75.   In deciding whether a project shall be approved for grant the Minister concerned will expect it to be set in the context of local plans for handling the transport problems of the area. Grant will not be approved for isolated projects which cannot be clearly related to general

3847, paras. 71–101. Reprinted with permission of the Controller of Her Majesty's Stationery Office.

transport planning. Investment in public transport projects – particularly in fixed track systems – is long term in its nature, and the investment once made is irreversible for several decades. These projects must therefore fit in with plans for the structure of the area, the land use pattern, the road and rail network, the balance between public and private transport – in short with the basic planning of the locality. The land use/transportation studies in the conurbations will provide a basis for assessing major projects.

76. The financial return on the investment will clearly be one of the considerations in deciding whether a project should attract grant. But in evaluating a project the Minister will also take into account the total benefits which would accrue to the community, including any reduction in congestion costs, the value of savings in journey time (not only for those using the new or improved services but for all travellers in the area) and all other factors in social cost/benefit analysis. Investment in local public transport may well be highly advantageous in these terms even if the extra revenue attributable to the improved services would not cover the full cost (including the high capital charges often involved.)

77. The new grants will be of particular value in helping to finance the cost of new railways and tubes in London and the main conurbations, where complete reliance on buses for public transport is not practical. In most other towns, buses using the ordinary highway will continue for the foreseeable future to provide the great bulk of public transport, with only a limited contribution from local railways. Here the grant system will help with the provision of interchanges and the improvement of terminals so as to make public transport more attractive and more efficient. In these cases too the projects must be shown to fit in with the transport planning of the area.

78. Application for grant will normally be made by the body responsible for the project. This may be a national body – the Railways Board, the London Transport Board, the National Bus Company, the Scottish Transport Group; or it may be a local body – a Passenger Transport Executive or individual local authorities. In a Passenger Transport Area the Minister will expect a project to be submitted by or through the Executive so that it can be related to its overall plan for public transport in the Area. Whether in a Passenger Transport Area or not, the project will have to be the subject of full consultation with the local planning authorities. There will also be provision to empower local authorities to contribute to the capital cost of projects of benefit to their areas.

79. The contribution by the government to public transport under this scheme will be substantial and is likely to grow steadily through the next decade. The first projects for consideration will be in London,

where the government has already approved the building of the Brixton extension of the Victoria line and will be considering the project for grant under the scheme. But soon projects are likely to be coming forward from the main conurbations. The Manchester Rapid Transit Study, commissioned by the Minister of Transport and the Manchester Corporation last year, has been published, and this describes the kind of public transport developments which may be needed in a large conurbation. The next stage will be to proceed with the detailed planning of an underground railway providing direct rail access to the heart of Manchester. This and other rail developments will be assessed in the Southeast Lancashire and Northeast Cheshire transportation study which is being undertaken by a joint Ministry and local authority team. Similarly on Merseyside preparatory work is going ahead on the proposed Mersey railway extension under central Liverpool, and this proposal too will be assessed in the land use/transportation study for that area.

NEW BUS GRANTS

80.   The capital grants for fixed investment in public transport will not be of major importance to bus operation. Yet in all areas outside central London the bus is likely to continue to provide the bulk of short distance public transport services and in many areas it will be the only available form of public transport. Any moves to help and improve public transport must therefore include a radical effort to increase the attractiveness of bus services by comparison with the private car, and to increase as far as possible economy and efficiency of the operation of bus services.

81.   It is clear that these aims can be achieved only by a considerable increase in expenditure on the re-equipment of existing bus fleets with new vehicles. The cost of this re-equipment programme can be so large that individual operators need financial incentives to encourage them to embark on it. The rapid extension of 'one-man operation' of buses is essential to hold down costs of operation in the face of rising labour costs and the fall in passengers. If 'one-man operation' is to be introduced as quickly as it should be, this will require the replacement – earlier than customary – of existing buses not suitable for such operation, and the additional capital charges can swallow up a large part of the savings in the early years. In the cities the installation of fully automatic equipment for fare collection would greatly facilitate one-man bus operation. This too would involve substantial additional capital expenditure.

82.   Apart from this, developments in bus services may well require

an increase in the use of specialized types of buses for specific purposes – limited-stop commuter services, feeder services to stations, standee buses, small buses for town centre use. This again may well justify replacement of existing buses before the normal date.

83.   Moreover, if buses are to compete more effectively with the private car, passengers must be offered higher standards of comfort – quality of ride, warmth, air-conditioning, convenience of boarding and so forth. And bus drivers in the future will need additional measures, such as fully automatic transmission, for helping their work, particularly when they are operating without a conductor. All this will raise the cost of the individual bus.

84.   The government proposes therefore to take powers to introduce a grant scheme for buying new buses. The rate of grant will be normally 25 per cent of the cost. These new bus grants will be made only for buses of types approved by the Minister of Transport, suitable for ordinary stage services. They will not apply to luxury coaches and long-distance express buses.

85.   The aim of the new scheme is to encourage the purchase of standardized buses of high quality. It is a major weakness in the manufacture of buses for the British market that each operator tends to produce his own detailed specification, varying not basically but in many details from the buses ordered by other operators. This makes large production runs impossible and so increases costs. Basic specifications for a limited range of models will be laid down in consultation with manufacturers and operators, and only vehicles conforming to these specifications will normally be eligible for grant. The grant will, however, also be payable for experimental vehicles in approved cases, so as to stimulate new development.

86.   The Minister may lay down certain conditions (apart from compliance with safety conditions of the Construction and Use Regulations and international standard recommendations) for buses to be eligible for grant. Discussions will be opened immediately with bus manufacturers and operators on the conditions of eligibility. The scheme will apply to buses delivered to operators from the autumn of 1968 onwards. As soon as the conditions of eligibility have been settled, the Minister will be prepared to consider grant applications for buses for which orders have already been or will be placed. All bus operators (Passenger Transport Executives, municipal bus undertakings, NBC, STG and London Transport, and private operators) will be eligible for the grants. Operators will normally have to make a refund of grant if they sell the bus, or cease to use it on stage services, within five years of its delivery new. The scheme will be introduced for a period of seven years. It may be extended beyond this period if the need still exists to encourage faster replacement.

87. Expenditure on new buses primarily for use as stage services is at present running at something like £20 million a year. This is based on an average life of about 15 years. If replacement is speeded up the total expenditure will increase. The economies of standardization should offset some increase in the costs due to higher standards. The government's help to the bus industry through these grants is likely to be at least £5 million and probably more a year – a substantial contribution towards the capital costs.

BUS FUEL GRANTS

88. Representations have been made repeatedly by bus operators that fuel duty represents a heavy burden on bus services and that it ought to be removed. Stage bus services have of course been insulated from recent increases in fuel duty by the payment of an offsetting grant by the Minister of Transport now totalling 10d. a gallon. The government has carefully considered the representations of bus operators, but it has concluded that it would be wrong to exempt stage bus services entirely from taxation on the fuel they use. Bus operators have access to a track which has been provided at the public expense and for which they make no direct payment. In economic terms it is right that bus operators should meet a charge at least as high as the cost of providing the track which they use.

89. However, the government does not consider it desirable in the light of its policy of helping public transport to seek to raise fuel taxation on stage bus services in excess of a proper contribution to expenditure on the track provided for their use. Moreover the weight of fuel duty has had an unfortunate side-effect on the design of buses. Operators have sought to keep fuel consumption as low as possible and this has led to the use of power/weight ratios for most buses considerably lower than that for many buses used in other countries. In present traffic conditions buses need better powers of acceleration, automatic transmission, power steering and other characteristics which tend to increase fuel consumption.

90. The government has therefore decided to increase the grant paid to operators of stage bus services by a further 9d. a gallon, bringing the total to 1s. 7d. a gallon. The additional payment will be made in respect of fuel on and after 1 January 1969. The government would not however consider it reasonable for the industry to press for a further reduction below this level. The extra grant will be worth some £7 million a year to the industry.

SUBSIDIES TOWARDS OPERATING COSTS

91. The capital grants for fixed assets and for buses, and the further grant to offset fuel duty, represent a large government contribution to help public transport. They will be available to public transport operators throughout the country within the terms already described. It is undesirable as a general principle for the central government to provide grants or subsidies out of national taxation to meet losses incurred in the operation of local urban transport services, except in the special circumstances set out below.

92. The reason for this is that whether a local public transport system operates at a loss or a profit will depend basically on local factors. Some – such as the efficiency of the management of the under-taking – will be within the control of the operator. Others – such as the traffic conditions under which buses have to operate – are within the control of the local authorities. Much will depend on the extent to which the local community demands – and is prepared to face the cost of maintaining – off-peak and Sunday services, which are very lightly loaded. It follows that any subsidies which are to be given to meet operating losses of public transport operators ought to be provided by local communities. This is why Passenger Transport Authorities are being given power to precept on the rates of local authorities.

SUBURBAN RAIL SERVICES IN PASSENGER TRANSPORT AREAS

93. However, as explained in section IV, Passenger Transport Authorities and Executives in Areas where railways are particularly important for local passenger movement (notably the main conurbations) will be required to assume responsibility for deciding what services should be provided by the railways in the context of their transport planning for their Areas. The present suburban rail services in the main conurbations outside London are losing in total several million pounds a year. These losses are at present met by the taxpayer through the rail-ways' deficit grant. It would obviously be impossible – and quite wrong – to expect the Passenger Transport Authorities, and through them the local communities, suddenly to take over responsibility for finding sums of this magnitude. Moreover, the Authorities will, at the very beginning, have little choice but to continue the existing pattern of services.

94. But in the course of time the Authorities and Executives will be taking many decisions which will fundamentally affect the cost of providing these services. As part of the integration of bus and rail

services they may decide to expand some rail services, create new ones and perhaps curtail others. The level of suburban rail fares will be settled by the Authorities as part of their general policy on fares. Some rail services which are at present not paying their way may become profitable if bus services are organized so as to make it more convenient to use rail. In the long run therefore the size of any losses on suburban rail services in the conurbations will be determined by local decision. It follows that the cost should ultimately be borne on the general accounts of the Executives.

95.   But help will be needed at first. Therefore the government proposes to make grants to Executives in respect of the costs of rail services covered by their agreements with the Railways Board. In the first year the grant will be 90 per cent of the estimated cost. The level of grant will be tapered over a period of years in the light of progress with the Executive's transport plan and of the rising level of other forms of government help to public transport.

RURAL BUS SERVICES

96.   Government help will also be given towards the cost of operating rural bus services through a scheme for rural bus grants. This scheme is intended to do something effective to implement the Report of the Jack Committee of 1961. The government proposes to give powers to local authorities to make grants to operators of bus services in rural areas where the essential services could not be provided on a commercial basis. Provided that the terms laid down by the Minister or the Secretary of State concerned are complied with, they will pay the local authorities 50 per cent of the grant paid to the bus operator. This scheme is designed to deal with the situation in remote country areas which can no longer sustain a bus service on a commercial basis simply because the number of people who need or want to use it is so small. In the government's view it would be wrong for areas like these to be deprived almost entirely of public transport, even though the number of people seriously affected may be relatively few. For general social reasons it is right that the central government should contribute towards the cost of maintaining some bus services in these outlying areas.

97.   The National Bus Company and the Scottish Transport Group will continue to maintain many services in country areas which do not cover their full cost of operation. But there are others where the receipts may be so low that neither the NBC, the STG nor private operators can be expected to maintain them without some form of grant or subsidy. In these cases the local community must decide whether the

service is so important that it is worth providing a continuing subsidy to keep it going. Applications from operators will therefore have to be made to the local authorities concerned, who will have to reach a decision. If the cost of subsidizing the service is small (less than £500 a year) the Minister concerned will give the local authority 50 per cent of the cost of subsidy without prior approval. In other cases a specific application by the local authority for grant will be considered on its merits. The general criteria to be followed will be worked out in consultation with the local authorities.

98.   Local authorities will be given powers to make grants not only towards operating costs but also for other suitable purposes, such as buying vehicles. The procedure for applying for grants will be simple and the powers flexible. Grants will not be given for services for which the demand is so limited that the benefits derived from the expenditure are too small; and so it will be necessary to review services after a period to see whether they are worthwhile. In many cases services to outlying villages can best be provided by private operators, who may well run a bus service in conjunction with other activities; and the service may be best provided with a relatively small vehicle. The government itself is experimenting on some postal services with the use of minibuses which will at the same time carry a few passengers. The procedure for obtaining a licence to run bus services with small vehicles will be simplified so that such operators will find it easier to undertake the job.

99.   The cost of the Rural Bus Grants scheme will no doubt build up slowly; much will depend on the views taken by individual local authorities as to the scale on which these country services should be maintained. The eventual cost is not expected to rise beyond about £4 million a year, in which event the Exchequer would be contributing £2 million of this. The Exchequer contribution will be a specific grant for the purposes of rate support grant.

FERRY SERVICES

100.   Arrangements similar to those in respect of bus services will be made to assist ferry services which benefit people living in rural areas. The principle of grant-aiding such services has already been accepted in legislation affecting the Scottish Highlands and Islands (whose special position is dealt with in section VI). Local authorities will be empowered to give grants towards capital or operating costs and may receive a contribution from the Exchequer. As the circumstances of the ferry services concerned vary more widely than those of bus services, no fixed percentage of the government's contribution will be laid down. In

other respects the administrative arrangements will be the same as for the Rural Bus Grants scheme.

CONCLUSIONS

101. The schemes described above represent a new and large scale programme of government assistance to local passenger transport services. Over and above anything which is now being contributed by the government, they may well amount to at least £20 million in the first full year, rising thereafter as the preparation of approved major capital projects goes forward. They should provide a powerful incentive to develop and re-equip public transport and to increase its operating efficiency.

CHAPTER V

ACCOUNTABILITY AND CONTROL

If economic performance can be said to be fundamental to any enterprise, then accountability and control can be said to be a fundamental part of *public* enterprise. In Britain these topics have been given their special flavour by the dominance of the public corporation form. Their development up to 1961 has been described in Professor Hanson's volume and in chapter I of this one. After much hesitation, the House of Commons set up in 1955 a Select Committee on Nationalized Industries, and this in itself served as a means of improving the parliamentary accountability of the industries. In practice, moreover, one of the constant concerns of the Committee has been the other aspect of the problem – control by Ministers. This preoccupation continued into the 1960s, and resulted in 1968 in a long report of the SCNI on *Ministerial Control*. This report, the evidence to it, and the reactions to its proposals, will provide a large part of the material for this chapter.

It is worth stressing the dependence of much of what is printed here about 'control' on the economic material in previous chapters. In particular, the received theory of government control in the 1960s depended on rules of conduct for the industries set out in economic terms – in the White Papers of 1961 and 1967, and discussed in the SCNI report of 1968. An understanding of the extracts from these papers printed in chapter III is therefore crucial to what follows.

The state of accountability to Parliament is first reviewed. Information about parliamentary activity in practice is provided in a memorandum prepared by R. D. Barlas for the Select Committee on Nationalized Industries in 1967. A further extract from the oral evidence of Mr Barlas shows the vulnerability of the government department and the government-owned company to the parliamentary question.

The scope of the Select Committee itself is the question at issue in the following two extracts. The enquiry by the SCNI in 1968 into its own order of reference threw a great deal of light on forms of public enterprise not hitherto reckoned in the mainstream of nationalization. One of the principal matters of contention was the accountability of the Bank of

England. The material on this from the 1968 report has been omitted because it was eventually examined by the Select Committee in session 1969-70, and an extract from that report is reprinted here. It contains a valuable statement of the basic principles of public accountability. There was not much independent discussion of these principles in the decade, but an article by Ernest Pritchard (in *Parliamentary Affairs*, Autumn 1964) contained a basic and general argument about the efficacy of parliamentary concern. The difficulty, he suggested, has lain not in the nature of the relationship between Ministers and boards, but in the lack of a generally-accepted frame of reference in which discussion could take place.

The chapter then concentrates on the system of ministerial control, one of the main preoccupations of the decade. A general survey, not included here, may be found in Sir Ronald Edward's Stamp Memorial Lecture of 1967. Another survey was provided by Mr Aubrey Jones, at the time chairman of the National Board for Prices and Incomes, from a lecture delivered in Turkey in 1968, and published as evidence to the SCNI report on *Ministerial Control* (H.C. 371–II of 1968, page 682).

For information about how the British system operated in practice the reader is recommended to read chapters 2 and 3 of the SCNI report on *Ministerial Control*, too long to include here. In evidence to the Select Committee, the then Chief Secretary to the Treasury (Mr J. Diamond) said (Q. 2407) that it is the responsibility of the industry to make sure that it is efficiently run; it is the responsibility of the sponsoring department to make sure that the industry has 'taken pains' before concluding that it is efficient; and it is the responsibility of the Treasury not to provide large sums of money until it is satisfied it will not be wasted. This neat description needs considerable amplification, but it does indicate the distinctive standpoints of the institutions concerned.

Printed below are two extracts concerned with particular proposals put before the Select Committee. One of these is Mr W. Thornhill's plea for more open relationships between Ministers and the corporations, to be achieved by regular use of the power of General Direction. The other proposal is that for an Efficiency Audit Commission, set out here in an excerpt from the evidence of Professor W. A. Robson, though in fact similar proposals were made by Mr Thornhill and Professor Hanson. A number of statements opposing the idea were made by the corporations, in Volume III of the Report (Appendices 32, 33, 35, 37, 38, 40), not reprinted here. Further comments appear in extracts 25, 26, and 27.

The views of the SCNI on the role of the National Board for Prices and Incomes, and on efficiency studies and efficiency audits, are contained in chapter 15 of their report on *Ministerial Control*. It is important to remember that in this period the NBPI did develop functions of some significance for the nationalized industries, as well as for private industry and the trade unions.

The next group of extracts is concerned with the institutional proposals of the Select Committee's report. In the main these form a Part of the report called 'The Heart of the Matter', but a short extract from a previous chapter describes a proposal for periodic White Papers on each industry. The main proposals are in two chapters, one analysing 'What has gone wrong?' and the other setting out the scheme for a Ministry of Nationalized Industries in some detail. This was to be concerned with the efficiency of the industries; the Committee's proposals for policy-making machinery were not so clear, and were weakened even further when the Department of Economic Affairs was wound up shortly afterwards. Critical assessments of the plan are provided by Professor Robson and Professor Hanson, and the negative response of the government is recorded in an extract from the White Paper on the subject. It should perhaps be emphasized that subsequent reconstruction of the structure of government departments, in the last months of the Labour government and the first of the Conservative government, moved in the opposite direction. The Ministry of Power was broken up and disappeared into an enlarged Ministry of Technology, which later became an even larger Department of Trade and Industry. The Ministry of Transport became part of the Department of the Environment. This reconstruction was carried through on the basis of functional principles, as explained in the White Paper on *The Reorganization of Central Government* (Cmnd. 4506, 1970), and a department based on the ownership of its client industries would have run counter to this.

The proposals are followed by three pieces of comment. Some of Professor Robson's sharp criticisms have already been printed in chapter III; his criticism of the institutional proposals is given here. Professor A. H. Hanson was more receptive to the general tenor of the report, but nevertheless very critical of the idea of a separate department. The institutional part of the government's White Paper (Cmnd. 4027) concludes this chapter.

20. PARLIAMENTARY ACTIVITIES[1]

Memorandum submitted by the Clerk of the House (prepared by the Second Clerk Assistant)

1. The Sub-Committee have asked for a Memorandum on the

[1] From Select Committee on Nationalized Industries, session 1967–68,

extent to which Ministers are accountable to the House of Commons for the affairs of the Nationalized Industries and also for observations on the opportunities and procedures under which accountability is exercised.

2. The opportunities for parliamentary control in the House may be divided into the following heads:

(i) Parliamentary Questions
(ii) Motions for the [half hour] adjournment
(iii) Legislation
(iv) Debates on Reports and Accounts of the Industries and on Reports from the Select Committee, etc.

The greater part of this memorandum is devoted to Parliamentary Questions, since more attention has been paid in the House to this aspect of control.

QUESTIONS

3. Subject always to the rule that Questions are not in order which repeat in substance Questions to which an answer has been refused, any Question may be asked on a matter for which a Minister is responsible. Ministers' statutory powers are classified as follows in May's Parliamentary Practice (17th ed. at page 355):

'(i) Power to give a general direction in the national interest to the governing body of the industry or service concerned;
Provided that the direction is of general application a Question may therefore be asked regarding the exercise of this power.
(ii) Responsibilities in specific matters set out in certain statutes relating to particular industries – e.g. gas research, safety in mines and training schemes.
Questions are admissible on such matters.
(iii) Power to require information from the Boards or other governing bodies concerned.'

4. Though *prima facie* in order, Questions seeking to obtain information from the Boards on matters of detail were initially refused answers by Ministers. The effect of this refusal, and of refusals by successive governments, was to bring such Questions under the rule

Report on Ministerial Control of the Nationalized Industries, vol. II, July 1968, H.C. 371–II, pages 472–8 and 487–9. Evidence on accountability to the House of Commons by the Second Clerk Assistant, Mr. R. D. Barlas. Reprinted with permission of the Controller of Her Majesty's Stationery Office.

against repeating in substance Questions already answered or to which an answer is refused; in Session 1947–48, Mr Speaker Clifton-Brown stated, in relation to nationalized industry questions, that 'this rule prevents the admission to the Order Paper of all future Questions dealing with the class of matters dealt with by the Questions to which an answer was refused' (H.C. Deb. [1947–48] 449, cols. 1630–4).

5.   The operation of the rule was reviewed by the Select Committee on Nationalized Industries which reported to the House in October 1952 (H.C. [1951–52], 332). While expressing some misgivings at the system, the Committee observed that under their existing constitutions the Nationalized Industries were not subject to any direct control by Ministers in individual matters of detail. 'Your Committee, therefore, feels that without altering the terms of the Statutes under which the public corporations are constituted, which they are not empowered to recommend, Questions on matters of detail are inappropriate' (ibid. at Page ix).

6.   The rule was again reviewed by the Select Committee on Procedure which reported in the current Session (Fifth Report H.C. [1966–67] 410, pages vii to viii). For ease of reference their recommendation, contained in paragraph 9 of their report, is repeated here:

> Your Committee accept the opinion expressed in the Report of the Select Committee on Nationalized Industries in 1952 that allowing questions to appear on the Paper to which no answer could be expected would increase the sense of frustration of the individual Member and waste the precious time of the House at Question Time, particularly if it gave rise to complaints expressed as points of order. The Committee in 1952 remarked that if the change of practice were effective 'in the sense that it provided information to Members which under present arrangements cannot be obtained, this could only mean that the pressure on the Minister would have been passed on to the Public Corporation, and to meet it they would have to take all the steps which would be necessary if the Minister were answerable for such Questions. The worst possible situation would be created if the publicity resulting from the appearance of such Questions on the Order Paper had the effect of putting a check on initiative without adding any information.' Your Committee do not recommend any change in the existing practice in this regard.

7.   Although the rules governing Questions on Nationalized Industries remain basically the same as they were when the Select Committee considered them in Session 1951–52, the manner in which they operate has changed considerably. The developments of the last fifteen years have had the effect of allowing a wider variety of Questions

upon the Paper than formerly. These developments are explained below under the classifications given in May's Parliamentary Practice.

General Directions

8. Evidence was given before the 1951–52 Committee, that Questions calling for general directions were only in order if the point applied to a matter of 'large calibre' and that if there were a discrepancy of view between the Member and the Table the Speaker was asked for his view whether the point was of sufficient importance to merit calling for a general direction (H.C. [1951–52], 331 evidence, Q. 126).

9. The present practice, under guidance from the Chair, is no longer to attempt to make any subjective judgement whether a matter is of sufficient calibre or importance to justify calling for a general direction in the national interest. It is sufficient that a Question raises a matter of general and not particular application and is of national and not purely local significance. It is for the Member to determine whether the issues which he wishes to raise are of sufficient moment to justify a request for a general direction appearing on the Paper as a Question; it is for the Minister to decide whether to answer on the point of substance or to reply that the matter is one for the Board concerned. Neither the Chair nor the Clerks at the Table act as arbiter. Examples of Questions addressed to the Minister of Transport calling for a general direction which have been asked during the current Session are attached at Annex A. Questions asking for general directions addressed to other Ministers controlling nationalized industries have followed a similar pattern.

10. In this connection, the Sub-Committee may wish to have their attention drawn to a Ministerial statement made by the then Leader of the House (Mr R. A. Butler) on 25 February 1960 (H.C. Deb. [1959–60] 618, col. 577). After stating that, in addition to their specific statutory duties, Ministers might also be concerned with other Questions of broad policy affecting the industries, he continued: 'There is no hard and fast formula by which these matters could be identified and opened to Questions in the House but, provided that Questions on the Paper relate to Minister's responsibilities for matters of general policy, they will consider sympathetically the extent to which they can properly reply.'

11. This statement provided no indication as to the type of policy question which might receive a substantial reply; indeed it expressly disclaimed any such intention. Nor was 'policy' defined. Questions were put down to individual Ministers, following the statement, inviting them to define the areas of policy on which they were prepared to answer; but they replied that no precise definition could be given (see e.g. H.C. Deb. [1959–60] 621, cols. 3 and 4 written answers). It was, however, apprecia-

ted by the Clerks at the Table that unless a Question appeared on the Paper, the Minister concerned would be given no opportunity to decide whether a sympathetic approach could properly be made.

Responsibilities in Specific Matters

12.   Apart from the power to give general directions, numerous specific statutory powers and duties are imposed on Ministers by nationalization and other acts. A complete list is not given here, since it is understood that the Sub-Committee is already in possession of this information; a list showing the position at the time was published as an Appendix to the Special Report from the Committee in Session 1955–56 (H.C. [1955–56] 120); and references to powers have been made in subsequent reports on individual industries.

13.   Any Question on the way in which specific powers have been exercised, or pressing for the future exercise of the powers, is in order. Special mention should be made of Ministers' control over capital expenditure. Questions invoking these powers provide a ready means of keeping under regular review the expansion programmes of particular industries. In some cases, indeed, this control enables Questions to be asked about individual projects; thus, Questions have been asked about the purchase of aircraft by the air corporations and the electrification of particular railway lines.

Power to Require Information

14.   Although, in general, successive administrations have refused to answer Questions which would involve (if a strict legal view were taken) the use of the statutory powers to require information, the application of the rule that such Questions form a class to which an answer has been refused has been subject to so many exceptions that it can no longer be stated in simple terms. An indication of the present practice in allowing Questions is given below.

15.   On 31 July 1963 (H.C. Deb. [1962–63] 682, col. 450), the Leader of the House (Mr Iain Macleod) announced that Ministers would in future sympathetically consider giving answers to Questions seeking statistical information on a national basis about a nationalized industry. Since that date, Questions asking for such information have been placed upon the Paper, and the great majority have been answered by Ministers in successive administrations. On occasions, replies have been given that the information requested was a matter for the Board concerned; this may have been because the information was not regarded by the Minister as coming properly within the category of a national statistic – a term which in itself is no more capable of precise definition than 'policy'; and in any event, no undertaking was given that all Questions

on national statistics would be answered, but only that an answer would be sympathetically considered. The fact that a minority of Questions have been refused an answer has not, however, affected the practice in allowing any Question which can reasonably be assumed to be a national statistic to go on the Paper. Each Question is considered *ad hoc* upon its merits.

16.   National statistics are an example of where, despite the general refusal to answer, Ministers have agreed to answer on defined occasions. But there are other occasions where a Minister is assumed to be willing to make an implicit exception to the general practice. If, in reply to a supplementary on a detailed point arising out of a wider policy question, or indeed in any other way, a Minister gives any indication in the House of a willingness to answer, a Question will be allowed. The clearest way in which this can be done is by an express invitation to put the Question down; but it will be sufficient if the Minister says no more than that he will look into the matter. On this principle, Questions were allowed about individual tips following the Aberfan disaster. It should be noted here that although a door may be opened, it may also at a later stage be shut again. Ministers might have answered freely for a time, but later it might have become apparent that the situation had changed; and Questions which involved information on matters of detail within the responsibility of a Board have been disallowed on the assumption that they had returned to the category of a class of Questions to which an answer had been refused.

17.   Although a Question would not be in order which invited a Minister to intervene by advice in a nationalized industry matter where he had no statutory powers, if a Minister has in fact intervened a Question will be allowed. This is in accordance with a general principle adopted in other cases that, even where a matter may lie outside a Minister's strict powers and responsibilities, responsibility will be assumed where an intervention has taken place. An example of this practice can be found in the field of prices charged by certain nationalized industries. As the Sub-Committee will know, arrangements exist whereby Ministers are consulted in many instances. The extent of their intervention in relation to electricity tariffs is described in the 1963 report of the Nationalized Industries Committee (H.C. [1962–63] 236, paragraphs 42–44); the influence exercised by Ministers on gas prices is described in the 1961 report (H.C. [1960–61] 280, paragraphs 71–74); the position regarding London Transport fares is dealt with in the 1965 report (H.C. [1964–65] 313, paragraphs 66–73). Consistently with the principles mentioned above, Questions have been allowed on prices and fares.

18.   Questions are also allowed asking the Minister to elucidate or

amplify any statement made in a White Paper concerning a nationalized industry, notwithstanding the fact that the Question may concern the detailed administration of the industry. The theory underlying the allowance of such Questions is that the Minister is primarily being asked to explain his own White Paper and only secondarily being asked about the industry concerned. A considerable number of Questions under this head have appeared on the Paper; examples may be found following the publication of the White Paper on Transport Policy (Cmnd. 3057) in the summer of 1966.

Ministers' General Duties

19.   Finally, a Minister's general responsibilities in relation to the product or service provided by the industry concerned are taken into account. In the case of the Minister of Power, these are laid down by statute; he is charged with 'the general duty of securing the effective and co-ordinated development of coal, petroleum and other minerals and sources of fuel and power in Great Britain . . . ' (Ministry of Fuel and Power Act, 1945, Section 1). It was on this ground that Questions on competitive advertising in the gas and electricity industries and joint reading of gas and electricity meters were allowed. Again, the Minister of Transport has overall responsibility for transport, and, although a Question complaining of train services on a particular line would not be in order, it would be in order to make an allegation of defective transport facilities generally in the area concerned.

Application of Rules

20.   In the preceding paragraphs, the operation of the rules relating to nationalized industries has been analysed, and for the sake of clarity the rules have been set out under separate heads. In considering the admissibility of a Question, however, it is not usual to consider the rules in isolation from each other. They are for the most part interrelated and their application in combination will usually determine the form in which the Question may be asked.

Possible Variations in Practice

21.   The Committee will be aware that some industries are organized on a regional or federal basis with a central authority and semi-independent area boards (e.g. gas and electricity); in such cases, general directions can be given by the Minister both to the central authority and the area board concerned. The power of giving a general direction to an area board enables Questions to be put down about the regional aspects of the industries; and in some cases (where the subject of the Question is

concentrated in a small area), it will enable constituency issues to be raised as well. Other industries, notably British Railways and the National Coal Board, have only a central authority to whom the Minister may give general directions; and in these cases it is difficult to raise a regional issue.

22. If Ministers were given statutory powers to issue general directions to, or in respect of, the formations immediately below a central authority, despite the fact that those formations had no statutory independence, the balance would of course be redressed. Such a proposal would, however, involve factors outside the scope of this memorandum. Short of this, a measure of equality could be achieved if Ministers were willing to indicate their readiness to answer Questions asking for statistical information on a regional basis either in respect of those industries which have no regional autonomy or in respect of all industries. If Questions were answered in this manner for the National Coal Board and British Railways, Members would be provided with information which they could use in availing themselves of other parliamentary opportunities, even if they were still prevented from pressing for regional action in a Question by means of a general direction.

23. Apart from any consideration of redressing the balance of opportunities at Question Time as between the centrally organized industries and the remainder, it may well be that the provision of statistical information on a regional basis would provide a valuable service to Members without at the same time imposing an undue burden on departments or industries. Certainly, so far as the House itself is concerned, previous relaxation of the rules does not appear to have been followed by any abuse.

ADJOURNMENT MOTIONS

24. The affairs of Nationalized Industries may be raised on the motion for the half hour adjournment at the end of the morning or evening, or indeed on any other adjournment motion. The rules of order for Questions do not apply to matters raised on the adjournment, and issues of the minutest detail may be, and are put forward. Details of adjournment motions on Nationalized Industry matters raised during the current session are shown at Annex B.

25. Raising a matter on the adjournment is, of course, subject to competition. Five adjournment opportunities are available weekly, four subjects being chosen by ballot and the fifth being selected by the Speaker. At present, thirty Members on average compete every week.

LEGISLATION

Public Legislation

26. Public bills and statutory instruments are introduced from time to time to reorganize individual industries, or to alter their powers, or the powers of Ministers in relation to them. The scope of debate will depend in each case upon the content of the bill, or the instrument, and the opportunities for discussion of the industry will vary accordingly.

27. Borrowing Powers bills and orders are a regular feature of national industries legislation, and these give a periodic opportunity for a wide debate on the industry concerned. Since the power to advance additional capital is at issue, it is relevant to discuss any purpose for which the money may be required and to enquire whether money borrowed under previous powers has been properly spent. Any aspect of the capital structure of the industry may be brought under review.

28. Borrowing Powers bills, in fact, offer a double opportunity for debate on the industry concerned during their passage through the House. Such bills are often 'one clause bills' (i.e. they contain one effective clause plus the citation clause). The common form is for the effective clause to increase the former statutory limit of borrowing to $£X$ and to provide that the Minister may, by Statutory Instrument, increase the powers still further to $£X+Y$. The debate on second reading covers the ground mentioned in the previous paragraph. On the Committee Stage (which is usually taken in Committee of the Whole House), it is open to Members to move amendments reducing the new maximum figures and advantage is usually taken of this procedure. The same arguments are, however, relevant on considering reduction of the maxima in committee as were relevant on second reading. The result is that the Committee Stage of such bills is usually a repetition or amplification of the second reading stage, thus giving a double opportunity for debate.

29. Borrowing Powers orders are statutory instruments, subject to the affirmative procedure. The scope of debate on these orders is similar to that on bills of the same nature. Being subject to the affirmative procedure, no time limit is set to the length of the debate.

30. A list of recent Nationalized Industry legislation is not included in this memorandum, since it is understood that the Sub-Committee are obtaining details direct from Departments. But it may be of interest, as an example, to note the debates on the current borrowing legislation in force for the Gas Industry. The Gas (Borrowing Powers) Bill, 1964, which amended borrowing powers contained in Acts of 1948 and 1963, was debated for four and a half hours on Second Reading (H.C. Deb. [1964–65] 715, cols. 1996–2076) and for two and three quarter hours in

Committee (ibid. 716, cols. 1475–1530); there was no debate on Third Reading. An order raising the upper limit of borrowing was debated for two hours and ten minutes at the morning sitting of 7 June 1967, without bringing the debate to a conclusion (H.C. Deb. [1966–67] 747, cols. 977–1020). The order was finally agreed to on 19 June 1967, after further debate lasting four hours and ten minutes (H.C. Deb. [1966–67] 745, cols. 1297–1372).

Private Bills

31.   Private Bills are promoted by the Nationalized Industries for the same purposes as in the case of any other statutory company or private corporation, viz.: to confer particular powers, or benefits, upon themselves in excess of, or in conflict with, the general law (see May's Parliamentary Practice, 17th ed., at page 867). A list of bills introduced by the industries is attached at Annex C; bills which were debated in the House are marked separately.

32.   As in the case of public bills, the scope of debate on private bills depends in general upon the contents of the bill concerned. Special rulings have, however, been given in respect of the scope of debate on the Second Readings of bills promoted by Nationalized Industries. If a bill is of wide content, it is classified as a 'general purpose bill', and in that event debate will be in order upon the whole administration of the management responsible for the matters contained in the Bill (H.C. Deb. [1948–49] 641, cols. 1965–66; ibid. [1950] 473, col. 655, etc.). A general purposes bill, therefore, provides an opportunity for scrutiny of the detailed management of the industry or section of the industry concerned, despite the fact that the issues which a Member may wish to raise are not covered directly by the terms of the Bill. The only limit placed upon debate in such cases is that of time; as the Sub-Committee will be aware, the hours set apart for opposed private business are from 7 p.m. to 10 p.m.

33.   Although initially advantage was taken of this procedure in debates upon bills promoted by the British Transport Commission in the late forties and in the fifties, general debates are now somewhat rare. Of the last five general purposes bills promoted by Nationalized Industries, in only one case has there been a wide-ranging debate. . . .

Examination of Witness (12 July 1967)

Mr R. D. Barlas, OBE, Second Clerk Assistant, House of Commons, called in and examined

Chairman [Mr Ian Mikardo]

. . . Could I begin by asking some questions about Questions in the

House and the more or less unwritten rules regarding Questions to Ministers on Nationalized Industries which are applied ? Could I ask you whether many Questions which are put in by Members on the Nationalized Industries are ruled out of order by you and your colleagues, and in what proportion of cases, when they are ruled out of order, the member exercises his right of appeal to Mr Speaker ?——There are very few Questions which are ruled out of order in the sense that nothing ever appears on the Order Paper. A Member, particularly at the beginning of a new Parliament, who is ignorant of the rules, will come in perhaps with an individual case which we can always suggest to him can be re-phrased to bring out the matter of principle underlying the individual case, and in general we satisfy Members on that score. As to Questions going to the Speaker, I can only remember one Question going to Mr Speaker in the last three sessions, so that is not a very high proportion.

1692.   Does that mean that by and large Members are satisfied with the rules and do not feel frustrated, do not feel, as far as you can judge, unduly restricted by the rules ?——I would like to be rather cautious in replying to that. I can only speak as to the extent to which the dissatisfaction is voiced in the Table Office. It is not very much nowadays, certainly nothing like the dissatisfaction that was voiced 10, 15, 20 years ago. 15 to 20 years ago there was about one Question going to the Speaker a week on Nationalized Industries as compared with the situation today when, as far as I can recall, we have only had one Question going to Mr Speaker in the last three sessions.

1693.   That might mean, might it not, not that Members are happier, but that they are reconciled more than they were 10 or 15 years ago ?—— That might well be the position, that they have come to accept it.

Colonel Lancaster

1694.   Members are inclined to say – possible they do not say it to you – 'It is not worth putting down a Question about that', therefore they do not put Questions down because they feel either they are not going to get any satisfaction or they may feel, perhaps incorrectly, that the Question will not pass the Chair ?——They may well feel that, Sir, if they wish to raise an individual occurrence or an individual point in relation to a Nationalized Industry. They know that is not possible so they do not pursue it.

Chairman

1695.   Members do sometimes, however, do it in a Supplementary, what is in general, the result of that ? Do they get away with it ? Do they tend to get the information which they have asked for ?——If one may refer to that as a kind of acknowledged cheat that one puts in a Question

173

then asks one's real point in the Supplementary, that does not really occur very much in Nationalized Industry Questions. I have given an appendix of, I think, 64 Questions on general directions to the British Transport Commission, and in only two of those Questions was an individual instance underlying a question of principle raised in a Supplementary. I think on the whole Members do pursue only points of principle. You can get a good comparison between Questions on Nationalized Industries and other instances when you look at the Post Office Questions. The Questions to the Postmaster General are scattered throughout with Questions about individual post offices, individual call boxes, and so on. There are no questions about individual trains, individual stations, on the Order Paper, to the Minister of Transport, unless, of course, the station comes under the heading of a capital development. I think that was the case in the matter of St. Pancras and Snow Hill, Birmingham, for both of which capital approval was required.

Mr *Crouch*

1696. There have been Questions about individual lines. This is considered sufficiently general?——No, the Ministry has specific powers under the 1962 Act, it is section 56(7), I think, in regard to the closure of passenger lines.

1697. I did not mean regarding closure, I meant regarding performance, or the unevenness of the track, or something like that. Have there been Questions on that?——I do not think there have been Questions on the unevenness of individual bits of track. I can confirm that. There have been Questions about electrifications, but that, of course, comes under capital approval.

1698. I was seeking to find out how you determine in the Table Office this dividing line between the particular and the general?——It is a matter of exercising common sense. By and large we find that Members acknowledge the common sense approach as well.

1699. Does that mean you are able to steer an original Question that is too particular into being rephrased in a more general way so a general direction Question is asked?——Yes, Sir, exactly.

Mr *Ridley*

1700. What would you say was the main difference between Questions which are allowable about a Nationalized Industry and a private industry? You can ask a lot of questions about the boot and shoe industry or other industries which are not in public ownership. How would you describe the difference between the rules governing Questions about public concerns and private concerns?——To start with a

Minister is not empowered to give general directions to any private industry. Questions would be in order to the President of the Board of Trade asking about the welfare of any industry in general, but not in general about the activities of the particular firms within that industry.

1701.   You could ask him to do something or other in relation to a private industry or firm ?——Not in regard to a private firm, in regard to the industry as a whole.

1702.   To take the intermediate case, there are certain firms which are, in effect, owned by the Government but which are not a Nationalized Industry, for instance Fairfields and British Petroleum and Short Brothers. Now what do you do in those instances ? Do you give a bigger latitude than for purely private concerns, or not ?——Questions would be completely open. If there is a government majority shareholding interest we would regard any question about the activities of the firm as being in order. Indeed you will find from week to week a large number of Questions about the commercial enterprises of Short Brothers and Harland appearing on the Paper.

1703.   You would give a bigger latitude in the case of Short Brothers and Harland than you would in respect of the Electricity Council because that is, technically speaking, a Nationalized Industry ?——Yes, we would.

1704.   Is that position entirely fair in your opinion ? I know it is right, but is it fair ?——It seems to me, with respect, reasonable. In the case of a firm in which the Government have a 51 per cent share or more, the Government, as shareholders, have complete control over that firm.

1705.   But they have also in the Electricity industry, which is 100 per cent. Government owned ?——Their powers are circumscribed to a certain extent by statute.

Chairman

1706.   That is the difference, is it not, that the statutes on the Nationalized Industries have been drawn so as to give the industries concerned a certain immunity from the detailed accountability that is involved in specialized Parliamentary Questions ?——Yes, subject to the operation of the rule, which affects the statutory provisions, under which the Minister can require information from the industry on any matter whatsoever. That would, at its face value, allow a Minister to require information about any detailed or particular activity such as, for example, the running of a train, and it is in that regard that the initial refusal to answer continued by successive Governments, does operate.

1707.   Does it still apply with regard to, for example, Short and Harland, as it does to other matters, that a Minister can in the end say, 'I will not answer this Question' ?——Certainly.

1708. That always lies within the discretion of the Minister in any event ?——Certainly, there is no rule obliging Ministers to answer. It is not usual that they do not answer. Presidents of the Board of Trade will usually not answer if it is a matter which concerns commercial activities, purchasing and so on, of government departments or government industries, but that is merely because of giving information to competitors.

Colonel *Lancaster*

1709. When Members come to you and you think a Question is not likely to either be answered or indeed pass yourselves, do you ever advise the Member that he might well be advised to write to the Chairman of the Board itself to find out that particular information ?——Yes, we do. We do usually also advise him of the implications of privilege. You may perhaps know that communications with the Chairman of a Nationalized Board, or indeed with a Minister in regard to the activities of that Board, are not covered by parliamentary privilege.

21. OTHER NATIONALLY OWNED ENTERPRISES[1]

24. Your Committee have said . . . that they believe that it should be possible for the House to use its Select Committees to seek information about all areas of activity for which Ministers are ultimately responsible, both where the government is acting directly and where it is acting through agents which it actually controls or could control if it chose to do so. Your Committee also bore in mind that the main area not covered by the present Select Committees was the area of government-controlled bodies with income not 'provided by Parliament' which for one reason or another have been held not to be 'nationalized industries' within their Order of reference. It appeared to Your Committee that succeeding Nationalized Industries Committees had gained considerable experience in studying nationally-owned bodies with substantial commercial incomes and that accordingly many of these bodies at present exluded from examination might best fall to a Nationalized Industries Committee to examine.

[1] From Select Committee on Nationalized Industries, session 1967–68, special report, *The Committee's Order of Reference*, June 1968, H.C. 298, paras. 24–35, 63–129. Reprinted with permission of the Controller of Her Majesty's Stationery Office.

ORGANIZATIONS NOT RECOMMENDED FOR INCLUSION IN THE
COMMITTEE'S ORDER OF REFERENCE

25.   Accordingly the Treasury were invited to submit a Memorandum listing bodies engaged wholly or partly in activities of a commercial or trading nature, financed otherwise than through the Estimates, in which the government has a controlling interest. The Treasury duly submitted a Memorandum, which is set out as Appendix I. The Memorandum contains a list of 36 bodies, but when the Treasury came to give evidence they suggested that one of them ought to be removed from the list for consideration, as the government could not properly be said to control the body (Q. 95), and Your Committee accept this view.

26.   The Treasury also included in the list the Upper Clyde Shipbuilding Group in which Fairfields (Glasgow) is now merged, simply to explain what had happened to Fairfields (Q. 88). Under the merger the government held only $17\frac{1}{2}$ per cent of the equity, and the Treasury agreed that the government had in no sense a controlling interest.

27.   There remained then 34 possible bodies (or groups of bodies) which appeared to the Treasury to come within the terms of the original definition referred to in paragraph 25. However, it appeared to Your Committee, and the Treasury were able to confirm, that 13 of them were in fact so far financed out of provision from the Estimates as to make it appear *prima facie* reasonable that the Estimates Committee should investigate them if they thought fit. Equally, as provision is made in the Estimates, expenditure is brought to account in the Appropriation Accounts; and accordingly the relevant provision would fall to be considered by the Committee of Public Accounts. These 13 bodies are as follows:

National Building Agency (Q. 63);
Industrial Advisers to the Blind Ltd. (Q. 70);
Remploy Ltd. (Q. 70);
British Broadcasting Corporation (Q. 72);
Agrément Board (Q. 81);
Industry Boards (Q. 83);
National Computing Centre (Q. 84);
National Research Development Corporation (Q. 84);
Atomic Energy Authority (Q. 87);
National Film Finance Corporation (Q. 90);
Industrial Estates Management Corporations (Q. 90);
Forestry Commission (Q. 91);
Herring Industry Board (Q. 94).

28.   In present circumstances Your Committee see no reason to

recommend that their Order of reference should be widened, so as expressly to include the possibility of holding an inquiry into any of these particular bodies.

29. Of the original 34 bodies, a further eight appeared to Your Committee to be in the position either that their accounts were statutorily subject to audit by the Comptroller and Auditor General, or that accounts of receipts into the payments out of the Exchequer in respect of these bodies were so subject to his statutory audit. The Treasury were able to confirm the Committee's view, and it accordingly appears to Your Committee that these eight bodies may be regarded as within the traditional field of the Committee of Public Accounts.

These eight bodies are as follows:

Covent Garden Market Authority (Q. 36);
Sugar Board (Q. 40, Appendix 1);
Industrial Reorganization Corporation (Q. 46);
New Towns Development Corporations and Commission (Q. 62);
Housing Corporation (Q. 67);
Shipbuilding Industry Board (Appendix 1);
Scottish Special Housing Association (Q. 93);
Scottish New Towns Development Corporation (Q. 97).

30. Here again Your Committee see no reason at present to recommend that their Order of reference should be widened so as expressly to include the possibility of holding an inquiry into any of these particular bodies.

31. However, it may be that at some future time, some of these bodies – in particular the Covent Garden Market Authority, and the Industrial Reorganization Corporation – may effectively become self-financing; they would then no longer be regularly in receipt of Exchequer payments, or finance from the Estimates. If that position were to arise, the bodies concerned would no doubt cease to be clearly within the Order of reference of the Estimates Committee or the traditional field of the Committee of Public Accounts; and in that case, Your Committee believe that it would be desirable to consider whether they should be brought within the Order of reference of the Nationalized Industries Committee instead.

32. In evidence the Treasury explained that the British Sugar Corporation Limited, one of the bodies referred to in the memorandum, had publicly quoted stock, of which the government owned only $36\frac{1}{4}$ per cent (Appendix 1, Q. 41). While the Minister of Agriculture, Fisheries and Food, with the Secretary of State for Scotland where appropriate, can give directions in defined circumstances under the Sugar Act 1956, Board decisions are otherwise taken commercially and are not necessarily government policy (Appendix 1). Your Commit-

tee appreciate that in ordinary circumstances a 36¼ per cent holding of a company's equity may effectively give the holder control of that company; nevertheless they believe that it would not be appropriate to extend their Order of reference expressly to cover bodies over which the government has not *de jure* control, and accordingly they do not recommend that their Order of reference should be widened to include the possibility of an inquiry into the British Sugar Corporation Limited.

33.   The Treasury also listed the Horserace Betting Levy Board in their Memorandum. Your Committee appreciate that the Board has some trading income, but it is mainly financed from a levy on bookmakers and a contribution from the Horserace Totalizator Board (Q. 51). Its income is devoted to raising the general standard of horseracing.

34.   Your Committee regard the position as analogous perhaps to that of the Boards financed out of compulsory levies such as the Industrial Training Levy. While it may well be desirable that such bodies should be subject to the scrutiny of a Select Committee at some time, Your Committee do not believe that the experience of Nationalized Industries Committees is such as to make it appropriate that their Order of reference should be widened expressly to include the possibility of an inquiry into the Horserace Betting Levy Board.

35.   Of the original 34 bodies listed in the Treasury Memorandum, then, 11 remained for consideration, namely (in the order in which they appeared in the Memorandum):

Bank of England;
British Petroleum Company Ltd;
National Seed Development Organization Ltd;
General Practice Finance Corporation;
Horserace Totalizator Board;
Letchworth Garden City Corporation;
Independent Television Authority;
Cable and Wireless;
Beagle Aircraft Ltd;
SB (Realizations) Ltd;
Short Brothers and Harland.

This Report now discusses in detail the considerations which apply to these 11 bodies.

ORGANIZATIONS CONSIDERED FOR INCLUSION IN THE
COMMITTEE'S ORDER OF REFERENCE

(a) *The Bank of England* . . .

63.   It thus appears that the Bank of England is a publicly owned Corporation which is intimately concerned with the machinery of the

economic management of the country, and for which Ministers are ultimately responsible. Your Committee recommend that their Order of reference should be widened to include the Bank of England.

(b) British Petroleum Company Ltd

64.   As the Treasury Memorandum (Appendix 1) notes, the government now own 48.9 per cent of the ordinary shares of BP as well as a small number of preferred shares. Your Committee have explained (see para. 32) that whatever the realities may be of control of a company, where the government's holding is less than 50 per cent they would not normally regard a company as in government control. But in BP's case the government have control in a special sense; because they nominate two directors to the Board, and these directors have a right of veto (Appendix 1).

65.   The right of veto is to be exercised with due regard to the financial and commercial interests of the Company and only in respect of matters of general policy, such as the supervision of the activities of the Company as they may affect questions of foreign and military policy, any proposed sale of the undertaking or change of status of the Company, and new exploitation and other matters directly bearing on the fulfilment of current contracts for the Admiralty (Appendix 1).

66.   The Minister of Power explained that a controlling interest was originally obtained before the first world war with the object of securing fuel oil products for the Navy at a time when petroleum production under British control was very limited (Q. 102). As the Minister pointed out, the original controlling interest, in the sense of a holding of over 50 per cent, no longer obtains, for the Government's holding of shares has recently been allowed to fall below that; but the Government's power of veto, which is written into the company's Articles of Association, is still retained. However, it has never been used (Q. 102). The Minister suggested that the government had had no reason to dispose of its shareholding which had in fact been a lucrative investment (Q. 125).

67.   The Minister said that in his view the position of the Company was not analogous to that of a nationalized industry. His Department did not review its investment programme in the way that the programmes of nationalized industries are reviewed; nor did his Department suggest anything in the nature of a financial objective to the Company (Q. 107). The relationship was on all fours with the government's relationship with other oil companies except that BP informs the Treasury when the dividend is about to be declared, and holds consultations with the Treasury if new capital or new financial structures for the Company are under consideration (Q. 129). This description of the Company's relationship with the government was confirmed by the

Treasury. As their written evidence shows, there were only two official contacts in 1967 between the Treasury and BP in its capacity as a Company partly owned by the government, the occasion being the notification of the prospective dividend (see Appendix 6).

68.   The Minister was asked whether he objected to the proposal that the Committee's Order of reference should be widened to cover BP. His objection was based on the view that many of the concessionary authorities in countries where BP have or might have interests were prejudiced against firms which were government-owned or government-controlled (Q. 108–9). And he was anxious lest, if it were made possible for the Nationalized Industries Committee to investigate BP, the normal commercial transactions of what is an international company should be assumed to be those of a State-controlled undertaking (Q. 109). The Treasury also advanced similar views and suggested that it had been an advantage to BP that the government shareholding had been reduced below 50 per cent (Q. 31).

69.   Your Committee do not see great force in this objection. The Minister agreed that oil interests throughout the world were too astute to be unaware of BP's position, and that equally they were aware that there is no precedent for the Government's interfering at all with the commercial responsibilities or administration of the company (Q. 111). And Your Committee cannot accept that a decision by Parliament to allow one of its Committees to examine BP could in any way imply any extension of State control over the undertaking. The original decision of Parliament to set up the Select Committee did not lead to any increase in government control of the nationalized industries.

70.   Your Committee would see advantage (though the Minister did not (Q. 110)) in their having the power to discover by the ordinary process of taking evidence, both from the government and from the Company, the extent to which the limited powers of the government over the Company have been or could be used, and to inform the House accordingly. Thereafter further investigation would not appear desirable, unless at some time in the future the power of veto were extensively used.

71.   The inclusion of BP in the Order of reference seems therefore a logical consequence of the government's retention of the power of veto; and Your Committee, therefore, recommend that their Order of reference should be widened to include the British Petroleum Company Ltd. But in making this recommendation they have it in mind that, if the power of veto continues never to be exercised by the government, this fact will obviously give BP a very low priority in Your Committee's selection of matters to be considered by them. Moreover, they wish it to be clearly understood that they are not implying by their recommenda-

tion that there has been, should be, or is likely to be any change of any sort whatever in the traditional relationship between the government and the Company. Nor do they intend to imply a wish to inquire into any of the ordinary commercial transactions and relationships of the Company inside or outside the United Kingdom.

(c) *Cable and Wireless Ltd*

72.   Cable and Wireless Ltd and its seven wholly owned subsidiary companies form a group which operates telecommunications entirely overseas in 53 countries. The group owns and operates national telephone systems, coaxial submarine telephone cables, satellite earth stations, tropospheric scatter and microwave radio systems, high frequency radio stations and telegraph cables (Appendix 4, para. 11) as well as a fleet consisting of one cable-laying ship and five cable-repair ships (ibid., para. 12).

73.   The government acquired 2.6 million of the Group's shares under the Imperial Telegraphs Act 1938, and the remaining 27.4 million shares under the Cable and Wireless Act 1946 (Appendix 4, para. 8). The directors of the Group are appointed by the government (Appendix 1) but the Group is responsible for the day-to-day running of its services (ibid.) and Ministers have not intervened in the running of the Group (Q. 197); they have no special statutory right so to intervene but as the government are the only shareholders they are in fact in a position to intervene if they think it necessary (Q. 198–200).

74.   The Group raises all its capital from its own resources (Appendix 4, para. 15); nevertheless, every project of capital investment costing more than £100,000 must come before the Treasury for approval if it is not expected to earn an 8 per cent return (Q. 212), and a five-year advance forecast of capital expenditure is submitted annually to the Treasury (Q. 217). The Group is also required to follow the principles laid down by the government as regards the financial returns of nationalized industries (Appendix 4, para. 15).

75.   The Group's declared dividend has varied between 3¾ per cent and 6 per cent in recent years (Q. 219). The average share capital employed for the year 1966–67 can be derived from the Group's Accounts as £56.5 million.

76.   Cable and Wireless Ltd. was acquired under the 1946 Act following the conclusion of a Commonwealth Conference in 1945 that some fundamental changes should be made with a view to bringing more into the sphere of public ownership bodies dealing with external telecommunications in some Commonwealth countries including the United Kingdom (Q. 195).

77.   Your Committee note that the Group has many of the character-

istics of a 'nationalized' industry; it was acquired by the government as an act of policy, and the treatment of its capital expenditure and financial returns follows the principles of nationalized industries; and its controlling Board is appointed by Ministers of the Crown. The only doubts whether it is covered by Your Committee's present Order of reference arise from the question whether it can properly be said to be an industry (cf. para. 3), and whether it can properly be said to be 'established' by statute since it was, strictly speaking, acquired rather than established.

78. Your Committee, therefore, asked the Postmaster General whether he would have any objection to the Groups coming under the scrutiny of the Nationalized Industries Committee. In reply he pointed out that . . . no such examination had in fact taken place (Q. 223).

79. But his main objection was that the Group had built up an image of independence, and that foreign companies still thought the Group was an independent body (Q. 224). He agreed that foreign governments would be aware of the actual ownership, but maintained that the public of the countries in which the Group operated and many of the Companies there would not be so aware; and suggested that the Group's business might be affected (Q. 225–6).

80. Your Committee do not consider that these arguments justify the exclusion of Cable and Wireless Ltd from their Order of reference. The Group is sufficiently large to merit inquiry, and although Ministers do not intervene in the day-to-day running, the effect of requiring Ministerial approval for capital investment and of requiring adherence to Ministerial principles as regards financial returns is a matter which Your Committee regard as one of proper interest to Parliament.

81. In reaching this conclusion they, of course, wish to be understood, as they wish it to be understood in the case of the British Petroleum Company (see para. 71), that no change is implied in the principles on which the Group operates in regard to its customers, or in regard to the confidential nature of its agreements and, still more, of its communications. But, as in British Petroleum's case, they would see advantage in making public what the principles of operation are.

(d) The Independent Television Authority

82. The Independent Television Authority is a public Corporation incorporated by Act of Parliament (Appendix 4, para. 1). It provides and operates a television network and regulates the programmes which are provided by private companies in return for the right to sell advertising time (Appendix 1).

83. The Authority is financed by rental payments made by the

contracting companies. The Postmaster General appoints the Authority's Chairman and Members: he exercises control over the development of the transmitter network, and the number of hours of broadcasting and has a reserve power to prohibit any broadcast, but in practice he does not intervene in day-to-day affairs (Appendix 1).

84. The Authority submits its capital expenditure programme to the Postmaster General annually with a view to satisfying government policy on investment in the public sector (Appendix 4, para. 6), in much the same way as the investment programmes of the nationalized industries are submitted to Ministers (Q. 170–2). On the other hand the intention is that the Authority should cover its costs (Appendix 1) but no financial objective is set in the way that objectives are set for the nationalized industries (Q. 160–1). It is open, however, to the government to direct the Authority as to the disposal of any surplus that is made, and in fact the Government has directed the Authority to transfer to the Exchequer a total of £6.6 million over the last seven years (Q. 163); and the proportion of any surplus that is to be transferred in this way is within the discretion of the government (Q. 165–9).

85. The doubt whether the Authority might be held to be within Your Committee's present Order of reference again depends upon the interpretation of the word 'industry'; that apart, the Authority would appear to be covered.

86. In the case of the ITA, however, the interpretation of the word 'industry' assumed some importance; for the Postmaster General, in commenting on the proposal that the Authority should be included in the Nationalized Industries Committee's Order of reference, attached weight to his view that the Authority was not effectively a commercial body (Q. 162, 181, 184). Your Committee, however, consider it to be commercial in part, in that it may earn surpluses of varying amounts, and in that it rents facilities in the manner of a landlord to commercial companies (Q. 189).

87. The Postmaster General also questioned whether it was appropriate for the Nationalized Industries Committee to examine the Authority when the Committee of Public Accounts had already done so, and when the Estimates Committee had the power to examine how the Postmaster General discharges his own responsibilities for broadcasting (Appendix 4, para. 17 and Q. 184). He further pointed out that the ITA's statutory powers run for limited periods, and that before its Act is renewed it is the practice to subject it to a searching inquiry by an independent Committee of inquiry (Appendix 4, para. 19 and Q. 191).

88. Your Committee consider that it is a matter of doubt whether the Authority should be regarded as most suitably accountable through the Committee of Public Accounts. Their Accounts are not, in fact,

subject to audit by the Comptroller and Auditor General (see para. 11); but as Your Committee have noted (see para. 18), that Committee's Report of 1958–59 is one of the two which relate to Accounts not audited by the Comptroller and Auditor General, since a Nationalized Industries Committee was set up in 1956. Your Committee also bear in mind, however, that the Account of payments made by the contracting companies under the statutory levy are subject to the Comptroller and Auditor General's audit, and they do not wish to suggest that the field of commercial broadcasting is altogether outside the traditional field of the Committee of Public Accounts.

89. The question appears to be one which the House might wish Your Committee and the Committee of Public Accounts to decide between themselves, no doubt through the machinery of the Chairmen's Liaison Committee. Your Committee merely suggest that in view of the affinities of the LTA to a nationalized industry in the matter of Government approval of its investment programmes, and of Ministers' discretion in the disposal of surpluses, and of much of the Authority's partly commercial relationship to the contracting companies, it would be appropriate that they should be in a position to study as a whole the circumstances in which the Authority operates; they could then undertake an inquiry at some time in the future if it appears that the Committee of Public Accounts has no immediate intention of reporting on accounts in the field of television.

(e) SB (Realizations) Ltd, Short Brothers and Harland Ltd and Beagle Aircraft Ltd

90. The government own 69.5 per cent of the share capital of Short Brothers and Harland Ltd through their wholly owned company SB (Realizations) Ltd. The function of the Company is to manufacture aircraft and aircraft components (Appendix 1).

91. The Government have announced their intention to acquire the assets of Beagle Aircraft Ltd, and the provision enabling them to do so is contained in the Industrial Expansion Bill which was before Parliament at the time that Your Committee heard evidence (Q. 133), and which has now received the Royal Assent. Arrangements are in hand to set up a successor company in which the government will hold all the share capital (Appendix 1).

92. The two companies thus differ in that Beagle Aircraft is to be wholly owned while Short Brothers and Harland are not, but the Minister of Technology agreed that the principles of control, for the purposes of any inquiry by a Select Committee, were probably the same (Q. 133). The directive given to the Chairman and Directors of SB (Realizations) Ltd, in 1955 is similar to that to be given to the Chairman

of Beagle Aircraft's successor company. The Directors of SB (Realizations) Ltd, who are in turn Directors of Short Brothers and Harland Ltd, are required in carrying out their duties as Directors of Short Brothers and Harland to act in conformity with the best commercial principles with the object of making the company as efficient and financially sound an organization as possible. They are further required to seek the prior consent of the Ministry for substantial capital expenditure, for the authorizing of share issues, for any investment in subsidiary companies, and for the appointment of a Chairman and determining his terms of service and remuneration. There is also a requirement expressly laid on the Chairman to seek the approval of the Ministry before entering upon a course of action which, however appropriate to a purely commercial undertaking, might, in the case of one substantially owned by the State, raise controversial public issues. In the case of Beagle Aircraft, the company will be asked to act on commercial principles, but substantial capital investment in fresh activity outside the light aircraft sphere, the disposal of substantial assets or association with foreign companies abroad or at home or any matters which raise controversial public issues will need to be approved by the Ministry (Q. 136).

93. The Minister of Technology explained that Short Brothers and Harland were acquired by the government during the second world war because the Company was not being operated efficiently and the government could not allow it to collapse. Beagle Aircraft is to be acquired on grounds of public policy in order to ensure that a light aircraft industry is maintained in this country (Q. 157).

94. Your Committee note that periodical assistance has been given to Short Brothers and Harland by provision in the Estimates, and that the Committee of Public Accounts have examined items in the Appropriation Accounts relating to their affairs (Q. 135); further support will need to be provided in the immediate future (Q. 154). However, the Minister of Technology explained that it was not his intention that either company should be regularly subsidized (Q. 154). Your Committee, therefore, wish to consider the position as it will be if and when no further assistance is provided from the Estimates.

95. The Minister of Technology was asked if he would see any objection to the companies being brought within the Order of reference of the Nationalized Industries Committee. He drew a distinction between an inquiry into the relationship between the government and the companies, and an inquiry into the actual conduct of the companies' business (Q. 156). He suggested three possible objections to the Order of reference being widened to embrace this latter aspect.

96. First, he suggested that the companies should, subject to

certain conditions, operate commercially on their own and that the government was in fact deliberately limiting the degree of its intervention in order to allow a devolution of authority to the companies (Q. 140, 156); that at the same time there were very much closer links between the government and industry than there had ever been before with the result that relations with the government-owned companies and with private companies were becoming more similar (Q. 141, 156); and that if in these circumstances the management decisions of government-owned companies were subject to detailed scrutiny, this might destroy their independence of management (Q. 157).

97. Secondly, the Minister distinguished between individual companies with no monopoly position fighting for their survival, and the traditional nationalized industries (whether or not the latter were subject to competition). He thought that where these individual companies were obliged to take substantial commercial risks, the possibility of an inquiry by the Nationalized Industries Committee might lead Minister and Civil Servants to insist on weighing the risks themselves more than they otherwise would do (Q. 158).

98. Thirdly, the Minister suggested that if the Nationalized Industries Committee were given the right to investigate any Company in which the Government had a majority equity shareholding, it might encourage government participation in industry not to take the form of equity but of other means of participation which would not render the companies concerned liable to such examination (Q. 159).

99. All these objections appear to Your Committee to be generalized rather than particular to the cases of Short Brothers and Harland and Beagle Aircraft. Nevertheless, it may be convenient to comment on them here. Specifically, Your Committee are not convinced of the distinction between Companies fighting for their survival and the traditional nationalized industries. The government have acquired these Companies to enable them to survive, and they must accordingly be regarded as by implication to some extent underwritten in the same way as the nationalized industries.

100. Your Committee note the Minister's contention that he wishes to limit his intervention. That is a matter for him. But the extent to which he intervenes in the management of the Company has no bearing whatever on the question of whether the Company should fall within the Committee's Order of reference; the operative factor is that, as has been shown above (paragraph 92), he has undoubted control of some of the Company's major decisions. Thus, the first of the three points advanced by the Minister as purporting to be an argument against the Committee being empowered to examine the Company was in fact an argument against Ministerial intervention in the management of the company.

There is no connection between these two different concepts. The Committee believe that government control, whether or not it leads to frequent intervention, is likely to have effects on an undertaking which Parliament should be in a position to study.

101. In regard to the Minister's second objection, Your Committee would deprecate the possibility that an inquiry by them should in any way affect the amount of attention which civil servants devote to weighing the commercial risks taken by the Company; they trust that Nationalized Industries Committees in the past have distinguished between the sphere of management of the industry and the sphere of the sponsoring department, and have not held the latter responsible for errors of judgement in matters which they have left to the industry.

102. Your Committee are not convinced by the suggestion, contained in the Minister's third objection, that Minister's choice of means of participation in industry might be distorted. They can see no third course apart from (a) making some form of grant, which would imply liability to examination by the Estimates Committee and the Committee of Public Accounts, and (b) acquiring all or part of the equity of the Company, or otherwise providing the Company with an independent income of the kind discussed in this Report. Indeed Your Committee consider that if the question of examination by Select Committee is likely to distort the method of participation at all, distortions will surely be much more likely if Companies assisted in the way that Short Brothers and Harland and Beagle Aircraft have been assisted are excluded from examination by Select Committee.

103. Your Committee, therefore, consider that SB (Realizations) Ltd, Short Brothers and Harland Ltd, and Beagle Aircraft Ltd (or its successor company) should not be exempted from the principle which they are putting forward, namely that government-owned bodies which dispose of a commercial or trading income should be accountable to Parliament through the Nationalized Industries Committee.

(f) The National Seed Development Organization Ltd

104. The function of the National Seed Development Organization Ltd is to promote the development of plant varieties bred in the United Kingdom with the aid of public funds, to acquire plant breeders' rights in plant varieties and to exploit them commercially. The governing body is appointed by the Minister of Agriculture, Fisheries and Food, the Secretary of State for Scotland and the Home Secretary. The initial finance of the Organization is an interest-bearing Exchequer loan of £200,000 and the Company may use income from sales and royalties to defray expenses. Ministers have wide formal powers of control, but the Organization is autonomous in the day-to-day management of

commercial operations (Appendix 1). The turnover of the Company is at present about £130,000 a year (Q. 37).

105.   It appears to Your Committee that the Organization has thus many of the characteristics of a nationalized industry. Your Committee would certainly maintain that *prima facie* the Organization ought to be within their Order of reference. They have refrained from taking further evidence on the point solely on the ground that the Organization is not at present large enough to warrant an inquiry by the Nationalized Industries Committee, so that the question of its inclusion is to that extent academic.

(g) *The Letchworth Garden City Corporation*

106.   The function of the Corporation is stated in Appendix 1 to be to manage and carry on the undertakings of the Corporation, and the Minister appoints the Chairman and three of the six members of the Corporation. The Corporation is financed by borrowing in the open market, and Your Committee have no evidence that the government has any other means of controlling policy, or that it finances the Corporation.

107.   In the absence of any control over policy and in the absence of government finance, Your Committee would not regard the Corporation as suitable for deliberate inclusion within the Committee's Order of reference. If, however, any proposed wording for an Order of reference for the Nationalized Industries Committee should, technically, include the Corporation, Your Committee would not be unduly dismayed. They would merely regard it as highly improbable that a Nationalized Industries Committee would ever embark on an inquiry into the Corporation, whatever their Order of reference.

(h) *The General Practice Finance Corporation*

108.   The function of the General Practice Finance Corporation is to make loans to general practitioners for the provision, acquisition or improvement of practice premises. The Minister of Health and the Secretary of State for Scotland jointly appoint and dismiss the Chairman, Deputy Chairman and Members of the Corporation, after consultation with the medical profession, and approve the Corporation's schemes; they also have the power to give directions as to the performance of the Corporation's functions (Appendix 1).

109.   The Corporation's borrowing powers are limited to £10 million, extendable by statutory instrument to £25 million (Appendix 1); but at present it has actually lent £1 million at commercial rates of interest (Q. 50). Its expenses are met by grants from the Estimates; that for 1968–69 is £3,000.

110. Your Committee suggest that on balance the commercial rate of interest on £1 million might be thought to outweigh the grant of £3,000, and that accordingly the Corporation might appropriately be brought within their own Order of reference, rather than be left exclusively to the Estimates Committee.

111. They would not, however, wish to press the point; no doubt the Estimates Committee could mount a satisfactory inquiry if they thought it proper to do so; and Your Committee doubt whether a Nationalized Industries Committee would wish to undertake an inquiry unless the Corporation's borrowing increases considerably.

(i) The Horserace Totalizator Board

112. The function of the Horserace Totalizator Board is to operate totalizators in connection with horse-racing. The Chairman of the Board and three of its Members are appointed by the Home Secretary, and its activities are financed from the proceeds of the totalizator fund (Appendix 1).

113. The Treasury indicated in evidence that Ministers had no strong view on whether or not the Board should be included in their Order of reference (Q. 60), and the Home Office confirmed in a letter (Appendix 5) that there was no objection to the Board's inclusion. They pointed out that no public investment was now involved, as the original borrowing (by overdraft) had long since been paid off.

114. Your Committee welcome the co-operative attitude of the Home Office. The Board's Accounts are in fact published and laid before the House, but as they are not audited by the Comptroller and Auditor General, they may be regarded as outside the traditional field of the Committee of Public Accounts. Nevertheless, the Board appears to have a statutory monopoly and a substantial income arising from it, as well as a large number of customers among the general public who are entitled to be satisfied – so far as a Parliamentary Committee can satisfy them – that the Board's affairs are managed in accordance with the general interest.

115. Your Committee believe that such an inquiry could most appropriately be carried out by the Nationalized Industries Committee, and they therefore recommend that their Order of reference should be widened to include the Horserace Totalizator Board.

A NEW ORDER OF REFERENCE

(a) Defining the bodies to be studied

116. In the course of this inquiry the Treasury were consulted on the drafting of a new Order of reference, and they expressed the view

that it might be most suitable to list in any Order of reference the bodies to be examined by the Nationalized Industries Committee (Q. 99).

117.   Your Committee hope that, after further consultation, it may be possible to avoid any such idea. They believe that in this Report they have formulated a principle which the House can accept, namely that it should be able to examine through one of its Committees all bodies which are or could be subject to control by the government; and that where any such body, by reason of the fact that it disposes of an income arising from its operation, falls outside the Order of reference of the Estimates Committee or the traditional field of the Committee of Public Accounts, it should be brought within the Order of reference of the Nationalized Industries Committee. (If the principle is accepted, it might be desirable to change the Committee's name.)

118.   If the principle is accepted, Your Committee think that to list the enterprises concerned in their Order of reference would be unfortunate. They have referred in particular to the Covent Garden Market Authority and the Industrial Reorganization Corporation (paragraph 31), which may become self-financing in the future, and might then appropriately be brought within the Committee's Order of reference; and other new bodies may arise which might be in a similar position. Your Committee would think it unfortunate if they and the House were obliged to study any list of bodies contained in their Order of reference at frequent intervals to see that it was kept up to date.

119.   If there is to be any question of listing, therefore, Your Committee believe that the list should be of exceptions from the principle they have sought to establish, rather than listing the bodies to be investigated.

120.   On the question of a possible overlap with the work of the Estimates Committee and the Committee of Public Accounts, Your Committee have already noted that theoretically every one of the industries at present within their Order of reference are liable to examination by the Committee of Public Accounts, and several of them to some extent by the Estimates Committee as well.

121.   Your Committee are not aware that any major difficulties have arisen in the past from this overlap; and in the special case of the Post Office (see paragraph 4) where some doubts arose in this connection before the Nationalized Industries Committee began its inquiry in 1966, the result appeared to be perfectly satisfactory; the Post Office appeared before the Committee of Public Accounts to give evidence on certain matters within that Committee's traditional field, while its whole method of operation and plans for the future were studied by the Nationalized Industries Committee.

122.   Your Committee believe, therefore, that any question of over-

lapping can best be settled by the Committees themselves, and that there is no need for the House to try to define precisely the separate functions of the three Select Committees.

123. Your Committee have not attempted at this stage to put forward a form of words which might become their Order of reference; that will be a matter for detailed discussion when agreement has been reached upon the bodies to be included.

(b) 'Examining' Reports and Accounts

124. Your Committee have suggested that their Order of reference should be widened to include the various bodies referred to in paragraphs 36 to 115. But it is clear that the nature of the inquiries carried out into these bodies might differ widely. On the one hand they have suggested that any inquiry into BP would be likely to be confined to the question of the exercise or non-exercise of the Government's power of veto (see paragraph 70), and on the other hand an inquiry into the Independent Television Authority, for example, might be concerned not only with capital investment approval but also with the whole circumstances in which the Authority operates (see paragraph 89).

125. Your Committee have therefore considered whether it might be desirable to define their functions more precisely than is done by their present Order of reference, which merely enjoins them to examine Reports and Accounts.

126. Your Committee have no hesitation in recommending that no attempt should be made to define the nature of the Committee's enquiries. The history of the setting up of the Committee is set out in Erskine May (see paragraph 1); and as that history shows the original attempt to define the nature of inquiries led the Committee to make a Special Report to the effect that the form of their Order of reference precluded them from undertaking any useful inquiry at all.

127. In fact, Your Committee would go further; if their Order of reference is widened to cover the bodies referred to in this Report, the Order of reference should reflect the fact that some of their Reports and Accounts are not laid before Parliament and (in the case of the Bank of England) are not published at all.

128. Your Committee also believe that their present Order to examine Reports and Accounts is unsatisfactory in that it might be held to imply a duty to examine all relevant Reports and Accounts – whether formally or otherwise – every year; the Committee of Public Accounts have always interpreted Standing Order No. 79 which gives them their Order of reference in that sense. Your Committee therefore suggests that a less explicit Order, such as the House has given to the 'specialist' Select Committees, would be more appropriate.

129.   The Treasury have undertaken to help to find suitable wording for an Order of reference (Q. 99). Your Committee hope that it will be possible to agree upon a suitable wording in time for a Committee to be appointed in the opening days of the next Session of Parliament.

22. PUBLIC ACCOUNTABILITY AND THE BANK OF ENGLAND[1]

269.   The philosophy underlying Your Committee's insistence on the publication of accounts is based on more than a desire to satisfy public curiosity about, for instance, the cost of new branch buildings. Your Committee regard it as wholly inappropriate that a public body should be accountable to nobody. The Bank's argument that the Court is responsible for the proper running of the Bank appears to miss the point. It is not enough that a 'highly responsible body' such as the Court 'each and every member of which is appointed on the recommendation of the Prime Minister' should control what the Bank does (Q. 2014). The Boards of other nationalized bodies may be at least as responsible as the Court, but they, through their accounts and in other ways, have to give an account of their stewardship. The Bank up to now has had to give none. The Governor said that the Court of the Bank was responsible to the country for the proper conduct of the Bank (Q. 1082), but up to now the country has been quite unable to judge whether the Bank has been properly conducted.

270.   Your Committee's approach to the Bank and to other nationalized industries has been that Ministers and the industries should be publicly accountable. The Nationalized Industries Committee of 1967–68 defined public accountability, and what they said is worth quoting at length. 'Public accountability means that information must be published about the performance of the industries, and that the public, and particularly the representatives of the public in Parliament, should be able to test the success of the industries and to measure their management. It means that responsibilities for actions, successes and failures, should be publicly identifiable, and that Ministers should be accountable to Parliament both on their own behalf and to some extent indirectly on behalf of the industries. In addition, Parliamentary interest may result, as it has done, in the Boards being required to answer more directly to Parliament for the conduct of their under-

[1] From Select Committee on Nationalized Industries, session 1969–70, *Bank of England*, May 1970, H.C. 258, pages lxxxii–lxxxvii. The principle of public accountability. Reprinted with permission of the Controller of Her Majesty's Stationery Office.

takings' (H.C. 371–I (1967–68), para. 154). It remains to be discussed how the principle of public accountability should be applied to the Bank.

271. In its operations in the markets, in its implementation of monetary policy, and particularly in its giving of advice to the government the Bank acts very much as an arm of government (see Q. 298 and 2192). It is not, however, constituted like a government department. It would seem to Your Committee that if the Bank is to be publicly accountable for its work in these directions it should be so primarily through the Treasury or to the same extent as the Treasury. And it would seem to them entirely proper that accountability for the Bank's actions as agent for the government in all spheres of monetary and economic affairs should have increased since 1946 and be increasing all the time (see Q. 138).

272. In a discussion of what was lacking in the provision of economic and monetary information by the Treasury Mr Anthony Harris said, 'I cannot see that it is fair to expect the Bank of England, which operates as an arm of the Treasury, to be franker than the Treasury itself' (Q. 1795). Your Committee agree entirely. This opens up the question of whether sufficient light is shed on the whole process of economic management by monetary and fiscal means. All the journalists who gave evidence drew attention to the secrecy which surrounds this process in this country, and Mr M. H. Fisher in particular felt it would be wrong to think of secrecy and the withholding of information in terms of the Bank alone (Q. 1793). It was argued that perhaps the best way in which to combat this excessive secrecy was to consider the possibility of having a Select Committee on Economic Affiairs (see Q. 1803). Mr Peter Jay drew attention to the situation in the USA where 'the Federal Reserve is accountable publicly to the Congress and feels very acutely a sense of accountability to the public and . . . that if it moves more than a certain distance out of line with popular feeling its position will become untenable and it therefore needs to justify and explain what it is doing' (Q. 1779). It has not been within Your Committee's brief to consider policy matters, but rather the way in which the Bank carries out its functions including the implementation of policy decisions. Nevertheless it does seem to Your Committee that a strong case can be made for some closer form of parliamentary scrutiny, if not of policy, at least of the implications of policy. Your Committee were impressed by the attitude in the Federal Reserve System that, in addition to their own publications, the regular congressional appearances by the Board also greatly enhanced the level of public discussion of economic and monetary matters (see Appendix A). Your Committee also noted the view of one witness that the Bank's publications ought to be restricted

to fact and ought to eschew comment, since comment cannot be publicly answered by Treasury officials (Q. 1598). Your Committee take a less restrictive view, and consider that it would probably be much better that both sides should be able to be open in their comment on policy issues. Since civil servants traditionally are not in a position to make public comments, the best forum for discussion might well be a parliamentary Select Committee.

273.   The way in which the Bank advises the government may be one of its most important functions, but Your Committee are not qualified to comment on that advice. If a Select Committee were ever ordered to consider general questions of economic policy (involving the Bank) it would clearly be a very different committee from the Nationalized Industries Committee. The interest of that Committee in the public accountability of the Bank is limited to a narrower area, to the efficiency of the Bank of England in performing those functions which the Act of 1946 calls the 'affairs of the Bank' and which do not involve day-to-day liaison with Government – that is, those functions which it performs in a way most clearly analogous to the working of any other nationalized industry.

274.   The problem created by the Bank's specially privileged position is that apart from the Court there really is no judge of the efficiency of the Bank. The public, lacking any detailed information about the Bank's work, are not in a position to assess the success with which the Court is exercising the responsibilities with which it has been entrusted. 'At present an area of the Bank's activities – the Banking Department and what is sometimes called the affairs of the Bank – is left free of public supervision to an extent that is not usual in public industries' (Q. 2292). If, as Your Committee feel, this situation is no longer in harmony with present-day conditions the question 'to whom should the Bank be accountable for its "own affairs"?' remains to be decided.

Accountable to the Treasury?

275.   The Treasury are not in a position, nor do they want (Q. 2268 and 2277), to be responsible in great detail for the way in which the Bank manages its own affairs. The Treasury are, as the Permanent Secretary explained, a small department (Q. 298), and it may be that they do not have either the time or the manpower to carry the sort of watching brief that other 'sponsoring' departments carry in relation to the nationalized industries answerable to them. The Treasury take an interest, however, in the operations of other nationalized industries and undertake responsibilities for investment control. It is hard to believe that someone in the Treasury could not find time to evaluate, for instance, the Bank's investment programme: after all, public funds and national

resources are involved. Your Committee believe that it is possible that, had such investment as the rebuilding of the Bank's branches been submitted to the Treasury, the investment might have been reconsidered in some respects. They take the view that some attempt should be made to ensure that the Bank applies the same techniques of investment appraisal as are employed in relation to other nationalized industries. In the particular case of the branches it may well be that had such techniques been applied the continuation of the branches' note issue function would in fact have been justified because of the possibly high cost of any adequately secure alternative, although in the absence of the figures this is simply conjecture. If this investment had been shown to be justified in this way, similar attempts should, Your Committee believe, have been made to assess the value of the additional investment necessary to provide other facilities besides the note issue, including the industrial intelligence work.

276.   One way suggested to Your Committee to make the Bank more accountable to the Treasury would be for 'the head of the Treasury' to have a seat *ex officio* on the Court of the Bank (Q. 1558 and Appendix 32). This suggestion of Lord Balogh's raises a number of issues. In the first place it is clear that Lord Balogh's reasons for proposing it were primarily directed towards the supervision of the Bank in regard to its policy function. He personally seems little concerned about the domestic management of the Bank. Your Committee have already explained how limited the policy function of the Court is; as the Governor said, it is 'the Governor and his permanent lieutenants in the Bank' who form the body which gives advice to the government on general economic policy (Q. 1932). It is clear, however, that even without having a representative on the Court, the Treasury are in the closest touch with the Bank in a number of ways, through daily contact on the state of the markets and through various indepartmental committees. Additionally it is not the practice in this country that representatives of government departments should sit on the boards of public bodies. (The situation in this country is quite different from that in Germany, where members of the Federal Government may attend meetings of the Central Bank Council of the Deutsche Bundesbank (see Appendix B).) Accordingly, Your Committee would not recommend that there should be a Treasury representative on the Court of the Bank of England.

277.   The difficulty remains that the Bank should be accountable in its domestic affairs. In respect of those affairs Your Committee do not believe that accountability to the Treasury would be sufficient and they were pleased to note that the Chancellor of the Exchequer said that he would not be in favour of the Bank showing its accounts to himself or to the Treasury and not also showing them to the public (Q. 2268). Your

Committee have suggested that the Bank should publish accounts which would form a basis for discussion of the Bank's efficiency and its problems. In the case of other nationalized industries the publication of full accounts not only provides a discipline in itself for the industries concerned, but also forms a basis for informed public and parliamentary discussion of their problems.

Accountable to Parliament?

278.   The extension in the last session of Your Committee's order of reference to cover certain activities of the Bank of England means that (provided the order of reference remains the same) the Nationalized Industries Committee will in the future be able to examine the Bank of England from time to time. This, together with publication of accounts, would represent a valuable step towards the fuller accountability of the Bank for its own affairs.

279.   It is in the public interest that the facts should be known about public bodies. Your Committee believe that the proper interests of the Bank would in no way suffer if much of the traditional secrecy which has for so long surrounded its activities were to be dispelled. They have therefore recommended that the Bank should publish accounts (see previous chapter). Beyond this they believe that the Bank ought to be answerable to Parliament in much the same way as other nationalized industries. The *raison d'être* of an inquiry by the Select Committee on Nationalized Industries is to benefit Members of Parliament by informing them about what the industry does, how it does it, and how it sees its function in a wider context, and equally to benefit those under inquiry by testing their assumptions. In this connection Your Committee were pleased to note that the Governor said that he had found their inquiry a useful exercise, and liked to think that both sides had benefited from it, and would not have anything to say against repeating the exercise (Q. 2028 and see Q. 2306).

280.   Your Committee would hope that it would be possible for future Nationalized Industries Committees to review, with the benefit of full accounts, the work of the Bank from time to time in the same way as they would review the work of other nationalized industries. They do not believe either that this present inquiry has endangered, or that future inquiries would endanger in any way, the Bank's much-prized independence or its highly-valued relationships with the City. Nor do they believe that it need be any more difficult to preserve the balance between the rights of Parliament to seek to learn how the Bank is being managed and the rights of management to get on with managing, without outside interference, than it is in the case of other public corporations.

GENERAL CONCLUSIONS

281. Your Committee believe that in all principal respects the nationalized Bank of England, although unique in its status and responsibilities, should be treated with regard to its own affairs in the same way as other public corporations. The Bank should publish accounts. Its capital expenditure programme should be submitted to the annual investment reviews and the Bank should make use of the same objective criteria with regard to capital expenditure as do other public corporations. The Bank should make charges designed to recover costs for services, including those performed for the government. The profits of the Bank, after appropriate provision for working capital and reserves, should be surrendered to the government. In respect of its own affairs the Bank should be examined from time to time by future Nationalized Industries Committees. It is a matter for consideration whether in those areas where the Bank operates as an arm of government its activities, along with those of the Treasury, should be subject to examination by a Select Committee on Economic Affairs. Finally, while Your Committee incline to the view that part-time members should form a smaller proportion of the total membership of the Court of Directors of the Bank than they do at present, they have had so little detailed evidence about how much of their time the non-executive directors have to give that they are not in a position to make any positive recommendation in this connection.

23. USE OF THE GENERAL DIRECTION[1]

9. The general influence which a Minister can exercise is a combination of the various formal powers allowed him by the relevant statutes and the influence arising from the informal contacts between the Minister and his Department and the corporation and its staff. The latter includes of 'lunch-table directions' referred to by the Select Committee in its Report on the Post Office (H.C.P. No. 340, 19666/7). Some of these are routine powers of supervision which normally give rise to no controversy but which, equally, might be said to detract from the commercial freedom of the boards. It is possible, however, for a Minister to use his formal powers and informal influence to secure a considerable direction of the affairs of a corporation, sometimes to the detriment of the

---

[1] From Select Committee on Nationalized Industries, session 1967–68, op. cit., pages 539–40, paras. 9–11. Mr W. Thornhill on the use of the General Direction. Reprinted with permission of the Controller of Her Majesty's Stationery Office.

corporation's success in meeting the statutory requirements placed upon it. The most notable area of Ministerial influence is that over prices, which has been a frequent source of comment in the Reports of the Select Committee. Influences of this kind have the effect of subjecting the corporations to a degree of uncertainty about their objectives which makes the idea of commercial freedom seem remote. Such indeed was the complaint of a former board chairman in a public speech a few months ago, and more recently, that of the chairman of the British Railways Board when examined by the Select Committee in April. There is obviously a need to reduce the scope for frequent Ministerial influence of an 'unconvenanted' kind. One way to achieve this would be to limit Ministerial intervention to requirements expressed by formal direction – but this would require a new approach to the Ministerial power of direction.

10.   The general power of direction in the national interest has been used by Ministers on two major occasions only, and then in circumstances which provoked some political controversy. Partly because of this, partly because of the fact that the issue of a direction of a general nature would attract both publicity (with speculation about the possibility of underlying dissension between a Minister and the board) and accountability in Parliament, but mainly because Ministers have been able to exert pressure in other ways, the general power of direction has fallen into disuse. There is perhaps a popular tendency to regard it as a means whereby a Minister can have the final word in any dispute between himself and the board, and because of this the existence of a difference of opinion is regarded as the reason for the issue of the direction. This, however, is a negative approach; a more positive approach to the use of the general power of direction has not been adequately explored. There is no reason why the direction should not be used, not to settle differences between a Minister and a board, but to share and define their respective responsibilities for policies based on social and economic grounds on the one side and on commercial considerations on the other.

11.   If the general direction were to be seen in this light, its use should not be the occasion for heated political controversy, but it could be used, perhaps on an annual basis, as a means by which a Minister indicated to a public corporation the social and economic objectives within which he expected the industry to operate. The Minister's direction would then be debatable in Parliament on its merits, and the board would be left free to pursue its undertaking in a commercial manner within the limits laid down. The freedom of the board could be further protected by providing a statutory prohibition on any further intervention within the year by the Minister except on the ground of

urgent national importance. The use of the general power of direction in this manner would give to the framework of decision-taking the certainty which the boards have rarely enjoyed, and would bring Ministerial actions into the open so that they could when necessary be reviewed in Parliament.

24. AN EFFICIENCY AUDIT COMMISSION?[1]

14.   A question of great importance which has so far escaped serious attention is the audit of the accounts of the public corporations. The legislation assumes that firms of professional accountants will be appointed to audit the accounts and this has invariably been the practice. The late Sir Frank Tribe, where Comptroller and Auditor-General, made it quite clear to the Select Committee on Nationalized Industries that although his department could, if required, undertake the audit, he would not be able to report on their efficiency. He was certainly reluctant to accept the task. He stated that the professional auditors might be able, if required to do so, to provide Parliament with the kind of information which he gives to the Public Accounts Committee. The Institute of Chartered Accountants was opposed to this idea and no action was taken on the suggestion. The certificates given by professional auditors to the accounts of the nationalized industries resemble the unilluminating formula which applies to joint stock companies in the private sector.

15.   I do not believe that the professional audit used for the nationalized industries serves any important purpose beyond ensuring that financial regularity and honesty are observed in their administration. The time has come to reconsider the entire process of auditing and to see if it could be made to achieve more than it does at present. The relationship between a professional auditor and the company which is his client and pays his fees, is entirely inappropriate for a public corporation.

16.   I have advocated for many years the establishment of an Efficiency Audit Commission to assess the work of the nationalized industries, to draw attention to weaknesses and to make suggestions for improvement. The proposal was first put forward in my *Public Enterprise* (1937), pages 379–81. I developed the idea at greater length in *Problems of Nationalized Industry* (1952), pages 321–5. In the latter book I explained that my proposal

assumed that an audit commission would concern itself only with the

---

[1] From Select Committee on Nationalized Industries, session 1967–68, op. cit., pages 534–6, paras. 14–25. Professor W. A. Robson on the Efficiency Audit Commission. Reprinted with permission of the Controller of Her Majesty's Stationery Office.

efficiency of a nationalized industry operating within the framework of policy already laid down in the statutes, regulations and directions. It would not normally raise questions involving a change of fundamental policy, such as a different form of organization for the coal industry or the introduction of a subsidy for transport. There need not, therefore, be overlapping or duplication between an audit commission inquiring into the operating efficiency of a nationalized industry and an occasional investigation of a more fundamental character by an *ad hoc* committee. The audit commission would inquire into such matters as the character, quantity, and quality of goods or services provided; price policy; efficiency of administration; personnel questions, including pay, recruitment, and methods of promotion; relations between the board and the consumers; capital expenditure, and the methods of financing it, and so forth.[1] The *ad hoc* committees would be concerned with major policy and organization.

An important feature of the audit commission would be its ability to accumulate a store of knowledge about all the public corporations working in a variety of industries. It would build up a skilled staff possessing an unrivalled insight into the problems of nationalized industry and an unequalled ability to compare the methods adopted by the several boards for coping with them. There would be great advantages in having somewhere in our governmental system a clearing-house of knowledge and experience about the nationalized industries.

17. In *Nationalized Industry and Public Ownership* (1960) I again referred to the subject in Chapter VIII, and emphasized that the work of the Select Committee on Nationalized Industries would be 'immeasurably strengthened if they were supplied with the reports of an Efficiency Audit Commission or the advice of a highly qualified staff'.[2] I concluded that the accountability of the British nationalized industries is fully adequate, but nevertheless doubted whether it is possible to appraise their efficiency without the guidance of an expert body such as an audit commission.[3]

18. Mr Normanton in his recent work *The Accountability and Audit of Governments*,[4] points out that the British public corporations are unique in escaping any kind of constitutional control through audit. He regards this as a serious limitation on their accountability. 'The submission of annual reports and professionally audited accounts' he declares 'does not amount to accountability . . . It is of the very essence of accountability that the persons or bodies held accountable should not

[1] *Public Enterprise*, page 380.
[2] Page 202.   [3] Page 210.   [4] Page 311.

be able to dictate which aspects of their business will be examined; the initiative must be held by those to whom they are accountable.'

19. In France a special body known as the Commission de Vérification des Comptes des Entreprises Publiques was created in 1948 to audit the affairs of the nationalized industries. The members are drawn chiefly from the Cour des Comptes, which audits the accounts of government departments. The Commission has 26 members and is divided into four sections, dealing respectively with Power; Transport and Communications; Credit, Insurance and Information; and mechanical, chemical and other industries in the public sector. The staff of the Commission consists of a substantial body (the number rose from 70 in 1948 to 130 in 1960) of highly qualified rapporteurs, who carry out investigations on behalf of the Commission. They are drawn from the *grands corps* of the French Civil Service, the higher administration of the Departments, Engineers of the Ponts-et-Chausseés and the Mines, economists, controllers of insurance, etc. The rapporteurs are seconded to the Commission for a limited period, an arrangement which has certain drawbacks.

20. The rapporteurs carry out their investigations on the spot, as do the officers of our own Exchequer and Audit Department. Their reports are discussed freely with the managements of the public corporations at hearings in the various sections. The Commission has no powers of decision; it is only a reporting body. Its reports are submitted to the relevant Ministers, to the Cour des Comptes and to the parliamentary finance commissions.

21. I do not suggest that the Commission de Vérification has been set up in the best possible way, or that its composition or procedures are perfect, but it has unquestionably brought to light many defects and undesirable practices in French nationalized industries which would not be revealed in this country either by the Select Committee on Nationalized Industries, or parliamentary questioning, or the professional audit. I would refer the Select Committee to Mr. Normanton's account given in pages 343 to 354 of his book. French experience shows, he remarks, that 'an efficiency audit of State Enterprises is both feasible and useful'.

22. In the United States the General Accounting Office (the equivalent of our Audit and Exchequer Department) carries out the audit of Government Corporations. Each of the Corporations is required to prepare an annual budget, together with a plan of operations, for submission to the President and Congress through the Bureau of the Budget. These budgets may be considered by Congress but are not subject to a system of annual appropriations. The Corporations are audited on the principles applicable to commercial undertakings.

23. The Comptroller General's audit has brought to light many

matters bearing closely on the operating efficiency of bodies like the Panama Canal Company and the TVA.

24. India has one of the largest public sectors in any country with a mixed economy. Most of the public undertakings are in the form of joint stock companies. They are audited by professional auditors appointed in consultation with the Comptroller and Auditor General, under whose general direction they are required to work. He can issue instructions to them and also conducts a supplementary test audit.

25. Mr Normanton concludes that no one can seriously doubt any longer that 'a competent efficiency audit can make a really important contribution to parliamentary, public, ministerial and even managerial understanding of nationalized industries'. As the author of the idea, I commend these remarks by an independent expert who has studied foreign experience in a variety of countries, to the serious attention of the Select Committee, emphasizing once again that an efficiency audit would not duplicate their own work.

25. A MINISTRY OF NATIONALIZED INDUSTRIES ?[1]

White Papers on each Industry

867. The most valuable improvement, however, that the Committee believe could be made in the methods of Parliamentary accountability would consist in the periodic publication by the Minister of a White Paper in respect of each industry. In part this should be like the annual Post Office Prospects White Paper. It should set out the anticipated financial and productive performances of the industry for the forth-coming year, together with some information about pricing proposals, technical and other developments, the quality of service aimed at, etc., all of which would add up to a picture of how they intend to achieve their financial and other objectives in the coming years. Such a White Paper, together with the Board's own Report on its past achievements, should present a balanced picture of the industry.

868. In addition the Minister should use this White Paper as the medium for setting out the sector policies as they affect the industry and the policies for the industry itself, as recommended in chapter VIII (paragraph 366), and also the pricing and investment policies which he is requiring the industry to adopt, together with specified social obliga-

[1] From Select Committee on Nationalized Industries, session 1967–68, op. cit., page 188, paras. 867–869. White Papers on each industry; and pages 189–204, The Heart of the Matter. Reprinted with permission of the Controller of Her Majesty's Stationery Office.

tions, etc., in the terms recommended in chapter VI (paragraphs 280–3).

869.   Such White Papers, when presented to Parliament, would provide the clarification of the purposes and responsibilities of Ministers and Boards which is necessary for effective Parliamentary accountability.

Part III

THE HEART OF THE MATTER

Chapter XVIII

WHAT HAS GONE WRONG?

870.   The Committee do not pretend that this chapter sums up their conclusions on Ministerial control of the nationalized industries. If it were attempting to do so, its title might be different, as there are many successful aspects and welcome developments in the system of Ministerial control which the Committee have referred to in the course of their review. There are also specific failures and faults. But below the individual successes and failures, the Committee have sensed an underlying weakness – in particular a lack of clarity and certainty and purpose – to which the surface cracks owe their origin. It is the purpose of this short chapter to analyse this basic weakness. It is the aim of the next chapter to suggest the remedy.

871.   The central pillars of the system of government control of the industries are the sponsoring Departments. Whatever the importance of the Treasury – and their influence is enormous and their capacity for innovation has been welcomed – the brunt of the day-to-day supervision of the industries falls to the Departments. They inevitably stand at the centre of the system. And the Committee are of opinion that the underlying weaknesses in the system are mainly to be found in the sponsoring Departments.

872.   To be specific. The Committee regret that they heard little from the Ministers or their officials that indicated a readiness to look critically at the system of control in the large, to consider the very purpose of their existence or of their jobs or to look critically at the wider economic aspects of Ministerial control. There were exceptions; some had clearly faced the more awkward questions; but on the whole, all three Departments that gave evidence were more concerned to defend the details of their actions than to question or explain what was the purpose of these actions.

873.   Secondly, and this is the fundamental weakness, the Committee

have become aware of an underlying confusion touching all the elements in the system, but centring on the sponsoring Departments. Sometimes this has revealed itself as a confusion about purposes – what for example, is the real purpose of Ministerial control of investment? (chapter X, paragraphs 516–23). Sometimes it has been seen as a confusion about policies – for example is marginal cost pricing normally to have priority over covering total costs, or vice versa? (chapter V, paragraphs 220–36). Sometimes it has been a confusion about methods – what for example should be the methods of the Ministries in applying pricing policies? (chapter IX, paragraphs 384–93). But mainly it has been a confusion of responsibilities – what are the respective responsibilities of the Treasury and the sponsoring Departments regarding the totals of investment? (chapter X, paragraphs 529–41); what are the respective responsibilities of the Departments and the industries regarding the details of investment programmes? (chapter X, paragraphs 542–7); what are the responsibilities of Ministers in relation to staff and wage questions? (chapter XII); what are the respective responsibilities of Ministers and Boards regarding social obligations? (chapter XIV). And finally what should be the role of the NBPI (chapter XV). On all these matters, to a lesser or greater degree, confusion, uncertainty or lack of clarity has been shown by one or other or all of the parties involved. And this has sometimes led to considerable duplication of effort (e.g. scrutiny of the details of investment).

874.   Not surprisingly, this lack of clarity about purposes and responsibilities has revealed itself in a lack of understanding and in some cases, a breakdown of mutual confidence between Boards and Ministries. Some Board Chairmen, in particular, while ready to voice their complaints to this Committee had not discussed them with their Minister or his officials (paragraph 137). And this lack on the part of the boards of confidence in the sponsoring Departments has led some of them to press for more access to the Treasury (so threatening to confuse responsibilities still further), and others to criticize the staffing of the Departments (chapter XVI).

875.   Lying still deeper than this lack of clarity, this confusion of responsibilities and this breakdown of confidence remains a failure to understand and to work towards the fulfilment of the basic purposes of Ministerial control in respect of the industries. As set out in paragraph 74, these are first to secure the wider public interest – and secondly, to oversee, and if possible ensure, the efficiency of the industries.

876.   The implications of this demarcation, in the opinion of the Committee, were that it was the intention of Parliament that Ministers should be primarily concerned with laying down policies – in particular for the whole of their sectors of the economy – which would guide the

operations of the individual industries, and should not intervene in the management of the industries in implementing these policies.

877. The practice has revealed an almost reversed situation. Until fairly recently, Ministers appear, on the whole, to have given the industries very little guidance in regard to either sector policies or economic obligations such as pricing policies or investment criteria; clear policies on some of these matters, including pricing, are still lacking (chapters V, VIII). On the other hand they have become closely involved in many aspects of management, particularly in control of investment in some sectors (chapter X) and also in some aspects of pricing control (chapter IX) and control over staff matters (chapter XII).

878. The Committee do not wish to exaggerate. They have picked on the weaknesses to show where the fabric needs strengthening. They are well aware that because of the experience, loyalty, energies and, sometimes, wisdom of many of those involved in the work of the Departments and the industries, the work has gone on, the industries have expanded and developed, and the nation has frequently (although not always) had the benefit of a good service. But they are left with the firm conviction, as it was put by one Chairman of a Board, that 'we have not got yet the proper relationship between the nationalized industries, their sponsoring departments and the government' (Q. 583).

879. The Committee have made numerous specific recommendations designed to improve this relationship within the present structure of government. But they now turn to examine the structure of government itself, as it relates to the problem of Ministerial control.

Chapter XIX

THE STRUCTURE OF GOVERNMENT FOR CONTROLING THE NATIONALIZED INDUSTRIES

THE CASE FOR CHANGE

The Need for New Thinking about Institutions

880. The Head of the Government Economic Service said in evidence that he suspected more attention had been paid to economic issues than to organization issues (Q. 2192). The Committee believe this to be true. In recent years there has been much new thinking regarding the economic obligations of the industries, and a new relationship between Ministers and Boards has begun to emerge. The main characteristic of this relationship, as analysed and further advocated by the Committee in this Report, is the development of rationally determined strategic guidance, together with more autonomy for the Boards to interpret and comply with this guidance as efficiently as they can and by whatever

means they choose. This relationship has been advocated especially in respect of pricing and investment, which are the main economic regulators of the industries. And the acceptance of this new relationship implies some modification of the respective responsibilities and powers of all the bodies concerned – the Treasury, the DEA, the sponsoring Ministers, the industries and, now, the NBPI.

881. It is impossible, however, to alter the relationship between institutions in such a way as to alter their responsibilities and powers without calling in question whether those institutions are still the right ones for the task.

882. Approaching the issue by another route, the Committee come to the same question. If a basic confusion of purposes and of responsibilities exists, as has been demonstrated, between the industries, the Departments and the Treasury/DEA, could it be because different institutions are needed to do the jobs which have become confused?

883. The Committee have welcomed the new economic thinking and have sought to take it a step or two further in some respects. But they believe that the necessary institutional thinking, consequent on the new relationships, has lagged behind – at least among those from the Ministries and industries who gave evidence. The Committee therefore hope to help institutional thinking onwards by a few steps as well. Who should do what? And through what machinery?

The Responsibility of Ministers

884. It has already been argued that Ministers have a twin set of responsibilities *vis-à-vis* the industries. They are, first, to secure the public interest, and secondly, to oversee and to seek to ensure the industries' efficiency (paragraph 74). The Committee also recognize that sponsoring Ministers have two allied obligations; on the one hand they are the spokesmen for the interests and wishes of the industries in the Cabinet and in Parliament and on the other they represent the interests and wishes of the Cabinet and Parliament (and through them the general public) to the industries (Evidence, page 14). On the whole, although not completely, a Minister's responsibility for securing the public interest is allied with his role as spokesman for the government – he tells the industries what they are expected to do; his concern for an industry's efficiency finds expression in his role as spokesman for that industry (and see Evidence, page 334).

885. The new economic thinking implies some change in the balance of these responsibilities. Securing the public interest is essentially a Ministerial task which cannot be shared with the industries, and for which Ministers must be seen to take full responsibility, including often financial responsibility. Ministers may have to exercise direct, *ad hoc*

and specific controls to secure these interests, in regard to either investment, pricing or services to be provided.

886. The duty to oversee and to seek to ensure the industries' efficiency should be principally exercised by the use of certain economic policies and criteria, which as far as possible should be determined and applied equally to all industries (chapters V and VI). Therefore, in so far as the industries are operated as commercial bodies, they should be left as free as possible of detailed Ministerial control regarding prices (chapter IX) and investment (Chapter X). The government should not intervene in management (Cmnd. 3437, paragraph 38).

887. Therefore it will be seen that not only does each of the sponsoring Ministers bear a double responsibility, but that the nature of their exercising them differs. To combine the two sets of responsibilities in one man is bound to cause confusion in the minds of both Ministries and industries. There will either be a confusion of purposes (this appears to have happened in respect of the BEA aircraft replacement programme, when the Minister's concern for the public interest became confused with the quite separate desire for maximum efficiency) or, there will be a confusion of responsibilities between Ministry and Boards (such as the Committee believe has happened in the case of railway investment, where the Ministry's separate concerns for public interests and for the Railways Board's efficiency appear to have become hopelessly confused).

888. The first purpose, therefore, of the reconstruction of the Departments that the Committee will propose is to separate out these two sets of responsibilities. Until this is done, the Committee are convinced that confusion will continue. They consider that much of the complaint made by witnesses from the industries about the system of Ministerial control stems from a failure on the part of Ministers (and also, sometimes, Boards) to distinguish these responsibilities. In particular, a Minister who has to impose fairly heavy social obligations, perhaps on several industries and even on industries other than those for whom he has sponsorship responsibilities, must find it very hard to limit his concern for more commercial investment to the level that would be appropriate if his only responsibility was the oversight of their efficiency.

The Need for Concentration and Specialization

889. The second purpose to be secured by reconstruction is quite separate. As has been shown there is a fairly rapid turn-round of staff in the nationalized industry divisions of sponsoring Departments; there is little specialization; and there is little cross-fertilization of experience and ideas (chapter XVI). One object of Departmental re-organization should be to make better use of the staff of sponsoring Departments.

890. A parallel purpose should be to work for the adoption of common appraisal and control criteria, in the same way that the use of DCF at the test rate of discount was advocated and came to be adopted. There is a need for a concentration of this kind of work into some central body, and also for centralized study of social cost-benefit analyses, of the techniques of demand forecasting, of the methods of scrutiny of costs, and of the quantification of marginal costs.

THE COMMITTEE'S PROPOSALS

891. In this section the Committee make proposals for a re-arrangement of Departmental responsibilities designed to make a fundamental change and improvement in the system of Ministerial control of the nationalized industries. They have not, however, taken detailed evidence about the allocation of Departmental responsibilities, and in this regard, although the Committee are convinced of the merits of their main proposal, the suggested consequential changes must be more tentative.

A Ministry of Nationalized Industries

892. In the opinion of the Committee the purposes described in the last section could best be achieved by bringing together in the person of one Minister, to be called the Minister of Nationalized Industries, those responsibilities now exercised by the President of the Board of Trade, the Minister of Power, the Secretary of State for Scotland, the Minister of Transport and (after the creation of the Post Office Corporation) the Postmaster General that are chiefly directed at overseeing and seeking to ensure the efficiency of any of the nationalized industries. But only those responsibilities would be so transferred; the other functions of the Ministers would stay with the original Minister or be further re-allocated (see paragraphs 902–8).

893. The principal responsibilities of the Minister and Ministry of Nationalized Industries would be as follows:

(i) *The appointment (and dismissal) of the members of all the Boards.* While this instrument of control is basic to both 'public interest' and 'efficiency' purposes, the standing of Board Members is the primary expression of the autonomy of the industries; and the power to appoint or dismiss them is essentially associated with concern for the industries' efficiency.

(ii) *Laying down the adopted pricing and investment policies for the industry* (see paragraphs 280–3). This could be a two-part exercise. In so far as it was a matter of determining a pricing policy, say, appropriate for an industry, the Minister of Nationalized Industries would deal with the industry direct. But the stated policies could also contain adjustments required by other Ministers for social obligations and other public interest reasons.

(iii) *Agreeing the financial objective that follows from (ii) above.*

(iv) *Reviewing investment programmes and approving investment projects.* Again adjustments might have to be made in programmes, at the request of other Ministers, for social obligations. But it is hoped that, as far as possible, these obligations or services will be 'bought' by the beneficiary Department, and appear on the programme only for information and to enable the aggregate of investment to be reviewed (see paragraphs 743–7).

(v) *Approving capital structures and borrowing.*

(vi) *Furthering co-ordination and co-operation between industries in the interests of their commercial efficiency.* Co-ordination for other purposes, e.g. fuel policy, would be a matter for other Ministers.

(vii) *General oversight of the structure and organization of the industries with regard to their efficiency,* including the spread of new management techniques, e.g. critical path analyses, computerization, and the use of efficiency study units.

(viii) *Undertaking or making arrangements for efficiency studies* (see paragraphs 911–20).

(ix) *Approving research programmes, training and education programmes, etc.,* in so far as this is thought to be necessary for ensuring efficiency (see paragraphs 677–81).

(x) *Approving the forms of the Accounts.*

(xi) *Laying annual Reports and Accounts before Parliament.*

(xii) *Accounting to Parliament* for all their own activities and answering on the adjournment debates, etc., on the activities of the industries as commercial bodies. It might be desirable to have separate Ministers of State for the fuel and power, transport and civil aviation sectors. The new Minister would not be expected to attract nearly as many Parliamentary questions as the present sponsoring Ministers in total, first because the present Ministers have other responsibilities, e.g. roads, and secondly because he would not assume their responsibilities for fuel and transport policy, etc.

In addition the Minister of Nationalized Industries would need formal powers to give directions to give effect to government policies determined by other Ministers in the circumstances described in paragraph 901 below. But he would not normally exercise powers of direction on his own behalf.

The Advantages of a Single Ministry

894. One of the strongest arguments in favour of a centralized

Ministry of Nationalized Industries is that it would be able to make optimum use of the total staff available for this work. No doubt within the Department they would divide up by sectors, but the allocation of the staff between sectors should be much more flexible than is the case at present between the separate Ministries, and so they could be deployed to the best advantage and the greatest effort could be concentrated on whatever industries at any one time appeared to need such help or attention.

895.   The staff of the new Ministry would become experts in the affairs and problems of nationalized industries, as such, and so further the kind of specialization desired by the Fulton Committee on the Civil Service. Instead of spending three or four years in the railways division, say of the Ministry of Transport, and then moving, say to roads or road safety, officials would always be concerned with problems related to nationalized industries so long as they stayed in the Ministry at all. And since much of the work would have merits 'across the garden fence' (e.g. lessons learned about techniques for appraisal of investment in relation to aircraft would not be entirely useless when applied to locomotives), the consequent continuity of experience and sense of common purpose would be valuable. As the Permanent Secretary at the Ministry of Power said, 'comparative knowledge of all nationalized industries' is 'almost as important as knowledge of the one they are dealing with at the time' (Q. 1846). What better way could there be of achieving this than to have one Ministry?

896.   The Committee believe that a single Minister of Nationalized Industries would also develop a more consistent relationship towards all the industries than can the separate Ministers today. This would be reflected in the formulation of common policies and practices for such matters as the salaries and terms of appointment of Board members, and the methods of finding and selecting them. The single Minister would also be better placed than the present separate Ministers to plan the appointment of Board members between industries, for example to appoint someone as a part-time member of more than one Board, and so further the co-ordination of the industries' planning.

897.   One of the most important gains would be in the development and promotion of management and control techniques common to the industries. It might be desirable to set up a central development division in the Department with people drawn from work concerned with different industries, which would give particular attention to promoting the use by the industries of sound forecasting techniques and investment appraisal methods, the calculation and application of marginal costs, the further development of pricing policies and the longer-term calculation of financial objectives. The desirability of this kind of common con-

tinuing study of techniques was recommended by several witnesses (Evidence, page 593; Appendix 43, paragraph 29; Q. 1390, 2029–31, 2038). And the Treasury and Mr Aubrey Jones emphasized the need for centralized study and development of cost–benefit analyses, and particularly the use of common values in such analyses (Q. 225, 2397). All this could be done by the Ministry of Nationalized Industries. The new Ministry would be well placed moreover to act as a clearing house of information relevant to cost-benefit analyses in the public sector.

898.   The new Ministry would undoubtedly be more effective than the present separate Departments in securing the fullest possible co-ordination between the commercial policies of the industries, e.g. in considering the effects on the various industries of the development of the Channel Tunnel, of the electrification of railway main lines and of changes in the use of coal by the CEGB. They would be better placed to see that the correct assumptions regarding the prices charged by one industry were taken into account by other industries when preparing their demand forecasts and investment programmes (see chapter VIII). And the new Ministry would be well placed to seek economies of scale through fuctional co-operation between the industries, for example in the purchase of common stores and in arrangements for administrative training, in particular the organization of Staff Colleges. Need each industry make separate arrangements ? A single Ministry would make it their business to find out.

899.   Finally, the new Minister would act as the spokesman for all the industries to the Treasury and in the Cabinet. Unlike the present Ministers he would have to consider the interest of all the industries and not just of those within a particular sector. This should help the balanced planning of the industries' programmes. He would be able to judge the effect on the industries of policies imposed for social or other public interest reasons, to discuss with them how they should be implemented and to put the case for the industries to the Ministers concerned. He would thus look after the interests of all the industries equally, with an equal concern for their efficiency and fortunes.

The Role of Other Departments

900.   Other Government Departments would remain responsible for initiating policies towards or for the nationalized industries so far as these are required to secure wider public interests – i.e. wider than the purely commercial interests of the industries, or their consumers, as judged by those industries. As far as possible the Departments concerned should be those whose interests would benefit from such policies (at present such activities are not mainly undertaken for the 'benefit' of the sponsoring department). For example the Ministry of Defence,

the DEA, the Board of Trade, the Ministry of Employment and Productivity, the Ministry of Social Security, or the Ministry of Transport should be able for varying reasons to make a case for keeping open an unprofitable railway service. The Ministry of Employment and Productivity or the DEA could promote the use of coal by the CEGB in so far as a measure of coal preference was considered necessary for social reasons such as preventing unemployment, or to prevent too rapid a run-down of the coal industry for wider economic reasons. And the Scottish Office could take steps to ensure the continuation of unremunerative rail and air services in Scotland (for other examples, see paragraph 743).

901.   In all cases where another Department wished to initiate such a policy they would be responsible for any payments or compensation to be made to the industry concerned for the provision of the service. The cost would be borne on the vote of that other Department. As far as possible the price to be charged should be negotiable in the terms discussed in paragraphs 743–7. The Ministry of Nationalized Industries should be informed about all such proposals and arrangements. Only if mutually satisfactory terms could not be agreed should the Ministry of Nationalized Industries exercise power to require the provision of the service on behalf of other Ministers and on terms to be decided by the government. Parliament should be informed of all such arrangements. But whether these social obligations are agreed voluntarily or are imposed under formal powers, the Ministry of Nationalized Industries would be well placed to ensure proper co-ordination between all the Departments concerned.

The Consequences for the Present Sponsoring Departments

902.   The most important task remaining after the transfer of functions to the Ministry of Nationalized Industries would be the preparation, negotiation and formulation of sector policies. Thus the formulation of fuel, transport and civil aviation policies in so far as it was a question of determining their parameters – e.g. deciding the tax on imported fuels, giving some preference to the use of coal, selecting the margin of capacity of the electricity industry, transferring the carriage of freight to or from railways by varying the taxation of road haulage, and the operation of civil air transport licensing policies – would remain the responsibility of other Departments.

903.   Transport policy should probably remain the responsibility of the Minister of Transport, in view of the many duties of that Minister in respect of transport matters apart from the nationalized industries. This Minister would become responsible for taking a view of all means of transport, including possibly air transport. Responsibility for fuel policy, on the other hand, might not provide such a volume of continuing

work as to justify the retention of a separate Ministry with only policy and little executive functions. Fuel policy has considerable implications for both economic growth and regional development, and so might well become the responsibility of an economic planning Department such as the DEA.

904.   The Ministry of Power would then cease to exist as a separate entity. Their functions for overseeing the efficiency of the nationalized fuel and power and steel industries would go to the Ministry of Nationalized Industries, together with much of the work of their statistics, economics and Accountant General's divisions (that which was related to fuel policy would go to the Department responsible for that policy). Their 'safety' work (e.g. safety in mines) might properly go to the Ministry of Employment and Productivity to fit in with the present factories inspectorate (and in any event should a Department with an interest in production be responsible for safety ?), and work on standards might appropriately be transferred to the Board of Trade. Their duties in respect of the oil industry and North Sea gas would appear to fit in with their fuel policy responsibilities, and to be proper for the DEA or whatever Department was given these responsibilities.

905.   For the sake of completeness and to remove anomalies, the responsibilities of the Secretary of State for Scotland for the two Scottish Electricity Boards might also be transferred to the Minister of Nationalized Industries. Any residual electricity policy functions would then be transferred to the DEA or other selected Department. But the Secretary of State's duty to look after the interests of Scotland would, of course, be unaffected. On such matters the Secretary of State could deal direct with the Scottish Electricity Boards.

906.   The greater part of the Board of Trade's responsibilities for the Air Corporations and the British Airports Authority would be transferred to the Ministry of Nationalized Industries. Residual responsibilities for air transport policy – including, especially, licensing – could be assumed by the Ministry of Transport.

907.   The work of the Postmaster General as the Minister responsible for the Post Office (assuming the creation of the proposed Post Office Corporation) would be transferred to the Minister of Nationalized Industries. His broadcasting responsibilities might also be allocated to that Minister if the oversight of the BBC and ITA were assumed by the new Ministry. Otherwise they could be transferred to another Minister. A separate sponsoring Department for the Post Office and broadcasting would not be required.

908.   The work of the Ministry of Transport in overseeing the efficiency of the nationalized transport undertakings would be transferred to the new Ministry. The rest of their work might be little

affected. They would remain responsible for all forms of transport policy.

The Treasury, and other Central Departments

909. The work of the present central Departments should not be greatly changed by these proposals, initially at least, except in so far (as perhaps with the DEA), as they take over responsibilities from one or more of the present sponsoring Departments. In the long run the Ministry of Nationalized Industries would probably develop the experience and expertise to take over much of the Treasury's pioneering work in the development of control criteria and techniques. The Treasury should continue to have, however, the responsibility for giving economic guidance to the Ministry and to the industries before each year's investment review, for deciding the test discount rate, and for reviewing nationalized industry investment as recommended in chapter X. They would, in effect, remain as a policy department in respect of the industries, deciding and applying economic policy in much the same way as others would apply fuel or transport policies.

910. There would be one clear gain, however, for all these central Departments. They would have to deal with only one Department in relation to the nationalized industries. This should help the achievement of proper co-ordination in such matters as prices and incomes and regional development policies, and should reduce delays in the approval of individual investment programmes (see Appendix to Report, paragraphs 9–16).

Efficiency studies and the role of the NBPI

911. Within the context of a single Ministry of Nationalized Industries it is now possible to suggest an answer to the questions posed in chapter XV about who should be responsible for efficiency studies and to what extent an external, independent examination is required.

912. The Committee believe that the prime responsibility for looking critically at cost, for checking on efficiency, and for seeking to improve it lies with the industries themselves. Where the industries have anxieties about some systems, for example cost control or forecasting, they could employ as they do already, management and other consultants to give advice.

913. The Ministry of Nationalized Industries would look critically at the industries' costs, efficiency, and prices, starting from the information that would come to them in the course of investment reviews, particularly about the techniques used by the industries for investment control, but also about productivity and other performance statistics. If the Ministry were anxious about any aspect of a Board's work or

performance, their first approach should be to discuss the problem informally with the Board or their officers; next they might suggest that the Board seek the assistance of some outside expert or should encourage them to seek advice overseas where this appears to be desirable; and lastly they might themselves carry out, through a unit of their own, special studies in conjunction with the Board's officers of the problem concerned. The Committee have in mind such studies as those undertaken by officials of the Ministry of Power of the fuel and power industries' investment appraisal systems (Appendices 13, 14, 15, 16; and see paragraphs 424–8). The Ministry, in carrying out such studies, should also be encouraged to examine comparable institutions and systems overseas.

914. Sometimes a more formal study might be desirable. Here they consider that the formal reviews carried out by the Ministry of Transport together with the Railways Board and the London Transport Board, respectively, which also enlisted the help of experienced outsiders, set a good precedent.

915. In particular the Ministry might consider that the prices charged by Boards should be periodically examined. Here the chief interest would be to assure themselves that the prices charged by the Boards accorded with the pricing policies laid down by the Minister. The occasion for a formal study of this kind by the Department might well be when a Board wished to increase its prices (particularly if the increases went beyond the delegated powers given to the Board by the Minister (see paragraph 409)), but this should not be undertaken automatically for every price increase. As argued in chapter XV, the actual level of prices is often more important than price increases.

916. In cases where the Ministry have undertaken a formal study of an industry's prices, costs or efficiency, the results, together with as many of the facts as possible, should be presented to Parliament so that they can be examined by the Select Committee on Nationalized Industries – who could take such further evidence as they thought necessary – and debated if so desired. This would ensure that degree of publicity that is necessary if the public accountability of the industries is to be secured.

917. There might still be occasions and circumstances, however, when the Ministry would decide that an independent external study was required, whether of a particular price proposal, of an existing price structure, of the level of an industry's costs or of some other specific aspect affecting efficiency. This would be the appropriate occasion for a reference to the NBPI. In this way the nationalized industries would only be subject to examination by the NBPI (at least in respect of prices and incomes questions) on an equal footing with private industry. The

results of relevant efficiency studies made by the Ministry should, of course, be made available to the NBPI.

918. Looking at these proposals as a whole, it will be seen that the Ministry of Nationalized Industries would be much better placed to carry out the efficiency studies envisaged than would any of the present sponsoring Departments. As the Chairman of the NBPI pointed out, one benefit of having efficiency studies done by the Board rather than by the present Departments is that efficiency problems common to more than one industry can be studied as one problem; for instance, the use of coal-wagons by British Railways for supplying coal from the National Coal Board to the CEGB (Q. 2260). But a Ministry of Nationalized Industries could bring to bear all the same advantages, and even greater and more specialized experience, of the problems of all the industries.

919. The new Ministry would also be able to ensure that efficiency studies were concentrated on those areas of the public sector of industry where it appeared most necessary, which should make for a more balanced approach than is likely to come from Departments working separately. They could apply more easily to one industry lessons learned from their studies of other industries. And they could ensure that common standards were applied to all the industries.

920. To sum up. The Ministry of Nationalized Industries would first look to the industries to ensure and check on their own efficiency. However the Ministry's central responsibility is intended to be the over-sight of efficiency, and where they have anxieties they must therefore take what steps they consider necessary for ensuring this efficiency. These might include the reference of problems to outside advisers or to the NBPI. The NBPI would thus be an instrument for use by the Minister as it is at present, in other fields, for other Ministers. But this should never be regarded as detracting from the responsibilities of the Ministry for all the nationalized industries. A dissipation of responsibility could lead to duplication of effort and interference with management. It is to the Ministry that Parliament, as representing the owners – the nation – would look to ensure that the industries were performing all their obligations, both commercial and social, as efficiently and economically as possible. . . .

Mr Aubrey Jones's Proposals

931. Mr Aubrey Jones proposed to the Committee a new pattern of Ministerial responsibilities that was similar to that advocated by the Committee, with one important addition (Evidence, page 682; Q. 2320–45). He recommended that there should be a Minister of Nationalized Industries, but that between him and the Boards there should be a large state holding company rather like those that operate in Italy (Q. 2320–1).

He advocated this for two reasons. First to place the industries at one stage further removed from political influence. And secondly to build up a body with the sort of commercial experience and expertise that would reflect more closely the commercial background of the members of the various Boards: the normal background of civil servants was unsuited, he thought, for control of industrial spending and investment (Q. 2320). The functions of the present Boards would not be affected, he said (Q. 2333). The Ministries of Power and Transport could be abolished, and most of their work transferred to the Minister of Nationalized Industries (Q. 2334–41). The new Ministry would still exercise overall control over investment (Q. 2324–5). But there would be no case for both the Ministry and the holding company exercising detailed oversight over the industries, and he therefore thought that the Ministry's staff should be fewer than that of the holding company (Q. 2330).

932. The Committee do not believe that Mr Aubrey Jones's proposals are fundamentally opposed to their own. But they do not agree with the proposal for placing a holding company between the Minister and the Boards for several reasons.

933. First, they wonder whether the existence of such a holding company would lessen the ability of Ministers to impose social or public interest obligations on the Boards or in other ways to bring the public interest to bear. As the Committee have emphasized throughout this Report, whatever other desiderata there may be, this ultimate ability must be unfettered.

934. Secondly, it is possible that, if the Boards were made more remote and less subject to direct Ministerial control through the inter-position of a holding company, Ministers would be less accountable to Parliament for the acts and achievements of the Boards.

935. But thirdly, and in any event, the Committee are convinced that there is no room for a new tier between a Minister of Nationalized Industries and the Boards. What would the holding company do? If it attempted to oversee the efficiency of the industries – to review investment or to scrutinize price proposals, for example – it would be doing the task which Ministers must do if they are to be accountable to Parliament for public money and financial aspects of publicly owned bodies. If it did anything else – e.g. if it attempted to control in detail the execution of Ministerial policy – it would be doing the work of the Boards themselves. The Boards must know to whom they are responsible – it could be to a holding company or to a Minister: it cannot be to both.

LEGISLATION

936. Legislation would be needed to implement several of the proposals of the Committee, especially those relating to financial

obligations (if pricing policies and investment criteria are to be the determining factor, the present statutory financial duties become less relevant), Ministerial powers regarding prices, the power to give directions, and the proposals set out in this chapter.

937.   The Committee therefore recommend that legislation be introduced at an early opportunity to tidy-up and harmonize the present nationalization legislation and to give statutory authority to the financial and administrative framework of Ministerial control as recommended in this Report.

CONCLUSIONS

938.   The Committee have surveyed the present system of Ministerial control and found certain underlying weaknesses that appear to stem from the combination in sponsoring Ministers of two disparate – and even possibly conflicting – responsibilities and obligations. They are convinced that the best way to solve this problem is to go to the source of the difficulty and separate the two fundamental responsibilities at Ministerial level.

939.   The Ministry of Nationalized Industries which they have proposed would have clear responsibilities for which they would be accountable to Parliament; so would the remaining sector policy Departments. Furthermore the new Ministry, by bringing together experience and skills relevant to Ministerial control throughout the public sector, would be much better equipped to deploy these valuable assets in the most efficient way than are the four separate sponsoring Departments at present. Enriched by shared experience and guided by common standards, Ministerial control should be more consistent and more effective than that examined and criticized by the Committee in this Report.

940.   It is not claimed that these proposals solve all the problems about arrangements for Ministerial control of the nationalized industries. Some of the consequential implications for rearrangement of the work of the present sponsoring Departments clearly require fuller study. Changes in the attitudes of Ministers and civil servants towards the industries would also be required, and the right relationship would only emerge and develop with time and experience. But the clearer separation of Ministerial responsibilities for oversight of efficiency and for securing the public interest – without in any way prejudicing the achievement of these purposes – would be fully in harmony with the principles and criteria adopted in this Report. It would, it is suggested, lay the foundation for a much healthier and more efficient relationship between Ministers and nationalized industries than exists at present.

26. PROFESSOR ROBSON'S COMMENTS[1]

W. A. ROBSON

It is widely recognized that the relations between the government and the legislature on the one hand and publicly owned industries on the other is of central importance. I have closely observed public enterprise in many countries, and everywhere one finds the same problems arising in slightly different forms. One problem is how to give public undertakings of an industrial or commercial character a large measure of independence in their day-to-day activities, while reserving for the government the final decision in matters of major policy. Another problem is how to encourage or permit the management to follow commercial principles while ensuring that social, political and economic goals are pursued when the national interest so requires.

The tendency in Britain, as in other countries, has been for Ministers to intervene in many different ways, regardless of whether they possessed the legal power to do so. The government is usually in so powerful a position and has so many opportunities for persuasion or inducement at its disposal that it can almost always influence a public enterprise to do what it wants whatever the legal text may say.

This is the background against which the recent report from the Select Committee on Nationalized Industries on Ministerial Control should be seen.

Hitherto all the reports from the Select Committee have dealt with a single industry or undertaking. Now for the first time the Select Committee have carried out an inquiry across the board into Ministerial control of all the nationalized industries. This fact, combined with the importance of the subject, makes the report one which demands very serious attention.

The report is a curious document. It is highly abstract, doctrinaire, and non-political in the sense that it seems to leave out of account some essential political aspects of Ministerial responsibility for the nationalized industries.

The report deals mainly with two topics of the subject. One relates to the governmental structure through which Ministerial control should be exercised. The other relates to the kinds of control which Ministers should exercise and the methods, purposes and objectives which they should use. The Committee's aim has been to consider whether

[1] From W. A. Robson, 'Ministerial Control of the Nationalized Industries', *Political Quarterly*, Vol. 40, No. 1, January 1969, pp. 103–105 and 108–112. Reprinted with permission of the author and the editor of *Political Quarterly*.

existing institutions and procedures are well designed 'to fulfil the underlying purposes of the creation of public corporations responsible to Ministers'.[1] These purposes they deem to be that Ministers should to some extent exercise control, but that the public corporations should have some degree of managerial autonomy which would limit the scope of government intervention.[2] This is the nearest the Committee get to enunciating a theory of the public corporation or analysing the role of public enterprise – and it is not very far.

THE PRESENT SYSTEM CONDEMNED

The nationalized industries have a dual obligation: on the one hand to be mindful of the public interest and on the other to operate as efficient commercial bodies. The Committee declare that Ministers have duties to ensure that both these obligations are achieved as far as possible, though the two goals will sometimes conflict. The public interest is of course a vague expression which can include many different policies.

The Select Committee are highly critical not only of the manner in which Ministers have exercised control but of the whole system. They state that Ministers are not aware of the reasons for the powers they possess; that there is confusion about the purposes and methods of Ministerial controls; that there is an absence of coherent principles among sponsoring departments; that Ministers give little or no guidance on questions of policy but show an increasing tendency to encroach on the details of management; and that it is quite wrong to expect a sponsoring department to combine the twin functions of overseeing efficiency and of ensuring that public corporations observe the public interest. Indeed, the whole system of sponsoring Ministers is attacked and rejected. In reading this report one can see how wide of the mark Mr David Coombes was in his book[3] on the Select Committee in saying that it is an informative rather than an investigatory body, that it has sought to describe rather than to solve the main problems facing the industries. For in this report the Committee put forward what they regard as the proper lines on which Ministerial control should be conducted.

CAN MINISTERS 'ENSURE EFFICIENCY'?

It is in my view very doubtful whether Ministers either are or can be

[1] Para. 28.
[2] Paras. 33 and 60.
[3] *The Member of Parliament and the Administration.*

responsible for overseeing and ensuring the efficiency of the nationalized industries. There is certainly nothing in the legislation which places this duty on them. Ministerial powers are explicitly related to particular matters such as the appointment of chairman and board members, the approval of capital investment programmes, research programmes, training and education programmes, laying down the form of the annual report and accounts, appointing the professional auditors, and so forth. Ministers will, of course, normally exercise these powers with the intention of promoting the effectiveness of the undertaking, for this is in everyone's interest, including that of the government. But how far is it realistic to expect a government department to be able to ensure or promote the efficiency of British Railways or BEA or the BBC? They have neither the staff nor the know-how to be able to do so in any meaningful sense. The Post Office has been entirely controlled by the Postmaster-General, yet this complete and comprehensive Ministerial control did not ensure a satisfactory level of efficiency and so the government has decided to transform it into a public corporation. Why should the government now be able to ensure its efficiency when it was unable to do so previously? Why should the government be able to ensure the efficiency of the British Airports Authority when the Ministry of Civil Aviation and its successors made such a mess of the design, construction and administration of London Airport and have aroused almost universal criticism by its handling of the Stansted proposal?

The Select Committee do not ask, much less attempt to answer, awkward questions of this kind. They merely lay down a series of propositions which indicate what they regard as the criteria of efficiency. These consist almost entirely in the application of specified techniques for investment decisions and price policies. There are some general observations to the effect that Ministers must be concerned with the efficiency with which the industries carry out the public policies and financial, economic, and social obligations imposed on them, but there is no indication how this is to be done except in regard to investment and pricing policy (other than that Ministers should be authorized to carry out 'occasional special efficiency studies'). It seems to have escaped the Committee's notice that all the efficiency studies which have been carried out in the past have been made by outside bodies, such as the Herbert Committee on Electricity Supply, the Fleck Committee, the Stedeford Committee, the Pilkington Committee, management consultants, academic economists or political scientists. . . .

. . . The Select Committee are anxious to reduce or eliminate much of the intervention now commonly exercised by Ministers. They would like Ministerial control to be limited in the financial and economic sphere to laying down and ensuring the application of simple formulae such as those relating to investment criteria and pricing policy.[1] The whole process would then become largely self-operating and there would be no need for Ministerial scrutiny except as a check on whether the formulae were being strictly applied.

A MINISTRY OF NATIONALIZED INDUSTRIES

With this in view the Committee make sweeping proposals for changes in the machinery of government. Sponsoring departments would disappear, and the Ministry of Power would be abolished. In their place a Ministry of Nationalized Industries is recommended to deal with all the public corporations. It would be responsible for supervising and ensuring the efficiency of the entire range of nationalized industries. Its principal functions would consist of appointing and dismissing the members and chairmen of all the Boards; defining the pricing and investment policies to be adopted by each industry and agreeing their financial targets; reviewing investment programmes and approving capital projects; approving capital structures and borrowing; promoting co-ordination and co-operation between the nationalized industries to improve their commercial efficiency; conducting a general over-sight of the structure and organization of the industries, including the adoption of new management techniques such as critical path analyses, the use of computers, and so forth; making efficiency studies or arranging for them to be carried out by outside bodies such as PIB; approving programmes of research, training and education; approving the form of the accounts and being responsible to Parliament for the nationalized industries.

Any other Minister could try to secure that the public interest as he sees it is pursued by a nationalized industry. Thus, if a railway line were required to be kept open for military reasons, the Ministry of Defence would negotiate with British Railways and pay the cost. If BOAC or BEA are to be persuaded to purchase a foreign aircraft instead of a British plane the Treasury or the Ministry of Technology would compensate the airline for forgoing their preference. The Select Committee do not regard these payments as subsidies but merely as 'commercial transactions between the Ministers concerned and the Boards. The Ministers desire a service, namely the provision of certain social or public interest benefits; the Boards are able to provide it. The Minister concerned should therefore negotiate with the Board and agree a contract for the provision of the service . . . at a contracted price . . .'[2]

[1] Para. 407.
[2] Para. 744.

THE MODEL OF PRIVATE ENTERPRISE

Throughout their Report the Select Committee project public enterprise in the image of private enterprise. To them, nothing matters compared with commercial efficiency expressed in terms of marginal cost pricing and investment criteria based on a rate of discount designed to treat public enterprise on a par with private enterprise. Even the national interests which Ministers are expected to safeguard would be subjected to the higgling of the market and negotiated. The feeble system of professional audit is to be maintained, and the salaries of board members are to be increased substantially so as to bring them into line with those paid in private industry – regardless of what is paid to Ministers, civil servants, the higher judiciary, or the law officers.

Efficiency in any sense beyond the narrow economic criteria mentioned in the Report seems to be outside the Select Committee's comprehension. It would be quite possible for all their economic or financial criteria to be satisfied by the Post Office and yet for the telephone service to be as inefficient technically as it is today. The Committee believes that productivity is an inseparable part of general efficiency, but this is a matter which they consider should be left entirely to the management of the public industries. Yet the productivity of London Transport, for example, has been deeply affected by its failure to innovate in regard to the manning of buses or the introduction of new technology during the post-war years. Is a public corporation to be left in undisturbed somnolence in such circumstances as these?

A basic defect of the Report is therefore that while it claims that one of the two main objects of Ministerial control is to oversee and ensure efficiency of the nationalized industries, its concept of what constitutes efficiency is abysmally narrow and rigid.

To concentrate responsibility for, and power over, all the public corporations in a single Minister will mean that his department will know far less about the sphere in which each undertaking operates than the sponsoring departments do at present. On the other hand, a greater consistency of treatment might be achieved by a single department.

THE ITALIAN EXPERIENCE

It is odd that the Committee make no mention of the position in Italy, where a Ministry of State Holdings (Ministro della Participazioni) was created in 1956. The aim was the same as that which the Select Committee have in mind – to promote the operating efficiency of the public corporations and to achieve unified control. The Ministry was intended to be a supervisory body. What has happened in Italy is that a standing

Ministerial Committee, presided over by the Prime Minister, decide most of the important questions, such as the goals to be pursued by the State holding companies and indirectly by their subsidiaries. Amalgamations, disposals, the establishment or purchase of undertakings, the approval of new projects, etc., are generally decided by the Committee of Ministers, and not by the Minister of State Holdings. The Committee are not supposed to determine questions motivated only by technical or economic considerations, since the latter are for the management of the enterprise.

Only the Committee of Ministers are entitled to issue directives defining the aims of public enterprise; and it is they who see that funds are allocated for new projects. They also review the financial results of the great Italian public corporations (ENI and IRI). The Minister of State Holdings acts as a channel of communication between the Committee and the public enterprises, but he occupies a subordinate position. The chief centre of authority and policy-making lies in the interministerial Committee. I have described the situation in Italy more fully in an article in *The Times Business News* of 26 August 1968.

The Select Committee's proposal for a Ministry of Nationalized Industry was strongly opposed by the Treasury on several grounds described in the Report. It seems probable that the sponsoring departments will oppose the severance of responsibility for securing public interest from responsibility for efficiency, which the Treasury do not consider it possible to separate. The reaction of other departments is not, however, mentioned in the Report. The alternative of giving the Treasury wider functions is not considered, though much of the recent economic thinking about nationalized industry has been done in that department.

AN AMERICAN ECONOMIST'S COMMENTS

The limited outlook and superficial thinking of the Select Committee's report can be seen by comparison with the much more profound reflections of Professor William Shepherd, whose studies of British public enterprise seem to have escaped the notice of the Committee. In his book, *Economic Performance under Public Ownership. British Fuel and Power*,[1] he cast doubts on the much-vaunted principle of subsidies payable by government to public corporations for unremunerative activites by analysing some of its drawbacks, such as the possibility that such open and rational subsidies might become as entrenched, irrational, and deadening to efficiency as most subsidies to private industries already are (the position regarding housing subsidies is relevant here).

[1] Yale University Press, 1965, pages 48, 144.

He mentions several other drawbacks to the policy of payments from taxes for particular services and deliberately proposed cross-subsidization within the firm as an alternative. In his concluding chapter, Professor Shepherd declared that 'a preoccupation with internal efficiency for public corporations, especially from the viewpoints of commercial criteria, lends itself to superficiality, sterile controversy, and misemphasis among policies.'[1]

In his contribution to the Brookings Institute Study entitled *Britain's Economic Prospects*,[2] Professor Shepherd looks at some of the investment and pricing policies of the nationalized industries from a much wider angle than the Select Committee's report. He considers that the exceptionally and unnecessarily capital-intensive substitution of nuclear power for coal involves a use of limited resources which will yield only modest gains in fuel economy and a relatively small release of miners for other industries. He regards the investment programme for electricity, and especially for nuclear generation, as excessive and urges its reduction.[3] This is irrespective of the Treasury screening method and test discount ratio. A rapid expansion of gas investment during 1968–73, both for conversion and direct use, with a slowing down of colliery closures, could replace a substantial portion of the nuclear investment programme. The unit cost savings in the AGR nuclear cost estimates over conventional stations are only slight, but the capital costs are much higher.[4] 'Yet the electricity system's tendency to invest more, and to do so more capital-intensively, than energy policy requires would not be automatically corrected by raising the Treasury's test rate of return.'[5]

Professor Shepherd also makes some interesting comments on price policies. He considers British pricing policies in telephones, electricity and gas to be as efficient as any in the world. Further study might show that the deliberate overpricing of business postal services and subsidizing of some telecommunication services would promote long-run efficiency.[6]

Surely this is the breadth and quality of thinking we need to inform Ministerial control of the nationalized industries, rather than the narrow concepts and abstract formulae adopted by the Select Committee.

IMPLICATIONS OF THE REPORT

In conclusion, we may note one important reaction to the Report. *The Times* greeted it in a leading article which described it as 'a very good report'. Shortly afterwards *The Times* published a long first leader in support of Mr Enoch Powell's proposal to denationalize the industries by

---

[1] Ibid., page 145.
[2] George Allen & Unwin (1968).
[3] Op. cit., page 393.
[4] Ibid., pages 394–396.
[5] Ibid., pages 397–398.
[6] Ibid., pages 389, 403.

distributing shares to private citizens. The leading article contended that the Select Committee's report abolishes the original case for nationalization, which rested on the idea that the Government should be able to control or influence certain basic industries or services if they were state owned. The Report, wrote *The Times*,

'recommends separating these industries from political influences by detaching them from their present controlling Ministries. The effect of this is to create independent corporations which can pursue normal commercial policies. The principle is to commercialize industries which have been damaged by political interference. This in itself makes a strong case for denationalization. If what we want to do is to make the state undertakings resemble private corporations as closely as possible, then the obvious way to do it is to turn them into private corporations by disposing of the equity.'[1]

It is ironical that a Report issued by a Select Committee presided over by Mr Mikardo, usually regarded as a left-wing Socialist, should provide the opponents of public enterprise with so much ammunition. It is indeed true that the Report does at almost every point seek to make the public corporations resemble ordinary joint stock companies. This is seen in its recommendations on investment appraisal, price policy, the salaries of board members, the exaggerated emphasis placed on managerial autonomy, the rejection of an efficiency audit in place of the professional audit, the concentration on economic and financial factors as criteria of efficiency. Above all, the view that Ministers should negotiate, purchase, and enter into contracts with a public corporation in order to induce it to carry out social, political or economic activities in the public interest which it would not otherwise pursue, follows precisely the procedure which the Government observes in dealing with a commercial company. It would be interesting to know on what grounds the case for nationalized industry now rests in the view of Mr Mikardo and his Labour colleagues on the Select Committee.

It is greatly to be hoped that the Government will think not twice but several times before adopting the recommendations contained in this report.

27. PROFESSOR HANSON'S COMMENTS[2]

A. H. HANSON

. . . In the context of its major recommendations, however, these ambiguities are not very important; for the Committee is in no doubt what

[1] *The Times*, September 14, 1968.
[2] From A. H. Hanson, 'Ministers and Boards', *Public Administration*, vol. 47,

the sponsoring minister should in fact do and how he should do it, nor does it mince words on the subject of 'What has gone wrong' (chapter XVIII, pages 189–91). The burden of its song is that ministers have not adequately discharged their responsibilities for securing 'the wider public interest' and overseeing 'the efficiency of the industries'. Instead, they have tended to interfere, sporadically and sometimes harmfully, in matters which, in the interests of operational efficiency, ought to have been left to the boards. Although some ministries are more guilty in this respect than others, all have shown a disposition to use powers of control for 'tactical' rather than for 'strategic' purposes. This is not only contrary to the intention of the nationalization Acts but inherently undesirable.

> 'Until fairly recently, Ministers appear, on the whole, to have given the industries very little guidance in regard to either sector policies or economic obligations such as pricing policies or investment criteria; clear policies on some of these matters, including pricing, are still lacking (chapters V, VIII). On the other hand they have become closely involved in many aspects of management, particularly in control of investment in some sectors (chapter X) and also in some aspects of pricing control (chapter IX) and control over staff matters (Chapter XII)' (*Report*, page 190, paragraph 877).

In demanding that this situation should be radically changed, the Committee may not be entirely acquitted of baying the moon. The industries are part of the country's political system and therefore, from time to time, will inevitably be the victims of interventions that can be justified neither by considerations of economic rationality nor by those of long-term public interests; for the electorate as a whole does not understand economic rationality, and sometimes does not wish to understand it, and tends to be more impressed by ephemeral short-term advantages than by solid long-term ones. Nevertheless, the Committee is clearly right in its desire to minimize the 'politicization' of the industries, by laying down rules which, if consistently followed, will facilitate performance of a kind that may be regarded, in Rousseauan terms, as reflecting our 'real will'. These relate to the *point* at which the division of responsibility between minister and board should be *normally* fixed, by convention if not by law, and to the *methods and techniques* through which ministerial powers may be most creatively and consistently exercised.

The first type of rule is obviously the most difficult to formulate, for reasons already explained. All one can say – and all that the Committee

Spring 1969, pages 67–74. Reprinted with permission of the editor of *Public Administration*.

can say – is that once certain purposes have been agreed upon (or, in the last resort, imposed by the minister), the industries should be allowed to go ahead on their own, with full freedom 'to carry out the policies required of them as efficiently as possible'. There is an area, in fact, where the boards should feel at liberty 'to achieve their own successes and even to make their own mistakes' (*Report*, page 35, paragraph 143). If this were not so, there would be no point in having a public corporation as distinct from a government department. By implication, the minister should be prepared to *defend* the board's freedom in this area.

But if this is to work, the rules about methods and techniques become crucial; and it is significant that the Committee devotes the greater part of its report to them. Here its task is greatly facilitated by the fact that much of the basic new thinking on this subject has already been done by the Treasury. Briefly, the methods and techniques which the Committee sees as playing a key role are Discounted Cash Flow calculations (DCF), cost–benefit analysis, and marginal cost pricing (MCP). All three figured prominently in the Treasury's White Paper of November 1967 (Cmnd. 3437) which, as the Committee recognizes, developed a series of criteria much more sophisticated than the 'net return on total investment' yard-stick offered by the previous White Paper of 1961 (Cmnd. 1337). The use of these tools, the Committee considers, permits the making of rational economic choices with due regard to the fact that the industries have obligations wider than those of 'normal' commercial concerns. With their help, ministerial intervention can become purposeful, consistent and fully informed and the industries be accorded the degree of managerial freedom that they have always possessed in theory but rarely enjoyed in practice.

The importance of DCF calculations in respect of new investments is now, of course, fully accepted; indeed, the Committee was able to base its recommendations on an admirable Treasury memorandum (*Minutes*, pages 14–22) explaining the technique in language fully comprehensible to the reasonably numerate layman. Marginal cost pricing, moreover, is now no longer the highly controversial subject that it was when the 'Ridley' Committee reported. There is still room for differences of opinion about the circumstances when long-term MCP should be preferred to the short-term variety, and vice versa, and no one but a very hidebound economic theorist would claim that there are no 'wider public interests' that could possibly justify any departure from the principle. One of these is obviously the requirements of a government's prices and incomes policy (*Report*, page 60, paragraph 248). There are also, as always, political considerations to take into account, such as the unpopularity of the deficits that would be produced by the application of MCP in conditions of decreasing marginal costs. As a general principle, however, MCP stands pretty firm. The economists have clearly won the battle, if not the whole campaign. As for cost-benefit analysis, 'the technique that has been developed for the quantification of social obligations' (page 157, paragraph 722), the Committee admits that this is 'still in its infancy', but hopes that 'it will be rapidly developed as an invaluable aid to Ministers in taking decisions affected by wider social and economic factors' (page 158, paragraph 726).

What the Committee clearly expects is that, with the improvement of these methods and techniques, the questions that come up for purely political decision will be less frequent and numerous, and that the main *recurrent* function of the minister will be to satisfy himself that the managements under his supervision have done their homework properly. Control can then become really strategic in character, the area of managerial freedom considerably extended, and both Parliament and public more fully informed of the criteria by which the performance of a nationalized industry is being judged. Summarizing its proposals on this most central of the many subjects it discusses, the Committee writes:

> Pricing and investment policies must be unambiguous. The Committee accordingly recommend that the use of marginal cost pricing policies and the use of DCF appraisal at the test discount rate for investment control should be the *standard* policies for the economic control of the nationalized industries. Ministers should make this plain to the industries. And, unless otherwise requested, the industries would be expected to apply these policies as fully as possible.
>
> Where the use of marginal cost pricing does not appear appropriate, the proper pricing policy to be employed should be discussed by the Minister with the Board concerned, and their conclusions should be made public.
>
> Where extra social or wider public interest obligations are imposed on or undertaken by the industries, they should be publicly identified, quantified and appropriately financed by the Ministers concerned.
>
> And where, for any reason, Ministers require the industries to adopt pricing or investment policies different from the standard ones, they should make this fact public, should justify their departure from the standard policies, should explain the financial effects, and, where an industry suffers actual loss, should normally negotiate financial compensation with the Board concerned (*Report*, page 67, paragraphs 280–3).

All this, as the Committee says, sounds 'formal', and one does not need to be a professional politician to recognize it as a counsel of perfection. But, in my view at least, it offers guide-lines superior to any that have hitherto been laid out. Yet there is no conspicuous novelty about them. Although some of the techniques are newish, the 'philosophy' behind them is familiar enough. We are back with the old Webbsian specifics of 'measurement and publicity' – and I, for one, am certainly not going to criticize the Committee for that kind of old-fashionedness.

The only possible criticism is that the Committee displays over-confidence that the deployment of new techniques can provide quasi-automatic solutions for what are essentially political problems. Certainly, some of its formulations suggest a belief in econometric magic. On the other hand, one has to reckon with the very real possibility that the development and refinement of these techniques may eventually put to rest the old controversies about the nature and extent of ministerial responsibility. The report's 'technocratic' approach to the problem of the nationalized industries may have even wider implications. How far is it applicable to other fields of public administration ? And if it should have widespread applicability, what are the organizational consequences ? The Fulton Committee's suggestions about 'the desirability of "hiving off" activities to non-departmental organizations' (Cmnd. 3638, vol. I, page 106) would seem to draw sustenance from the present Committee's general line of thinking. But if this is to be the pattern of the future, how is the citizen to be effectively protected against those forms of malad-ministration of which the technocrat is likely to be even more guilty than the bureaucrat ? And what about 'participation' ? Ombudsmen, administrative courts and advisory councils are the stock answers. Ministerial responsibility, as conventionally understood, is quite obviously insufficient. To discuss these matters here, however, would take us much too far beyond the substance of the report.

What is certain is that if 'measurement' is to be the watchword, some form of efficiency check must be introduced into the system. One of the report's great merits is that it recognizes this necessity, even though – for reasons that I personally find unconvincing – it shies away from the concept of an efficiency audit.

Perhaps it is unfortunate that the Government, without waiting for the publication of the report, has already given responsibilities in this field to the Prices and Incomes Board. Having listened to evidence from Mr Aubrey Jones, the Committee takes an unexpectedly favourable attitude to the studies on which this body has embarked, which it might have regarded as competitive with its own. With only slight misgivings, it accepts the Board's assurance that it 'intends to avoid the restriction of making efficiency studies only in relation to specific price references' (*Report*, page 168, paragraph 773), expresses its satisfaction that the NBPI 'has brought to these problems new skills and a new approach – or at least skills and methods that appear to have been neglected before' (page 173, paragraph 797), and concedes that there may be 'appropriate occasions' when the services of the Board should continue to be enlisted (pages 199–201, paragraphs 917, 920).

The Committee is by no means satisfied, however, that the NBPI has the best tools for the job it would like to see done, and its own suggestions for the improvement of efficiency control are not only far-reaching but the most controversial thing in the whole report. What it envisages is the establishment of a Ministry of Nationalized Industries with responsibility for overseeing and ensuring the efficiency of all the public corporations. This new Ministry would also take over from the existing 'sponsoring' ministries (one of which, the Ministry of Power, would cease to exist as a separate entity) the following functions: the appointment and dismissal of board members; the determination of pricing and investment policies; the approval of financial objectives; the review of investment programmes and approval of investment projects; the approval of capital structures and borrowings; the furthering of co-ordination and co-operation between industries, in the interests of commercial efficiency; the approval of research, training and education programmes; and the approval of the form of accounts. When all these things have been hived off, the sponsoring departments – or those of them that remain – would keep as their 'most important task' the 'preparation, negotiation and formulation of sector policies'. Thus, while investment, pricing and 'efficiency' control (together with the crucial responsibility for top-level appointments) would go to the Ministry of Nationalized Industries, such matters as 'the formulation of fuel, transport and civil aviation policies, in so far as it was a question of determining their parameters, e.g. deciding the tax on imported fuels, giving some preference to the use of coal, selecting the margin of capacity of the electricity industry, transferring the carriage of freight to or from railways by varying the taxation of road haulage, and the operation of civil air transport licensing policies – would remain the responsibility of other Departments' (*Report*, pages 193–4, paragraph 893, pages 196–7, paragraph 902).

This recipe presupposes that the various nationalized industries have common problems of a kind that neither the Treasury nor the DEA are fitted to deal with, and that the co-ordination of their commercial policies can be clearly distinguished from the fitting of these policies into a plan for the whole national economy – for neither of which presuppositions is there any clear evidence. More seriously, it separates the power to appoint from the power to give directions, and the power to deal with matters of commercial efficiency from the power to determine general policies. How complicated and potentially damaging this division of responsibility could be is illustrated by the Committee itself in the comment that it appends to its recommendation that one of the duties of the new minister should be 'laying down the adopted pricing and investment policies for the industries' viz.

> This could be a two-part exercise. In so far as it was a matter of determining a pricing policy, say, appropriate for an industry, the Minister of Nationalized Industries would deal with the industry direct. But the stated policies could also contain adjustments required by other Ministers for social obligations and other public interest reasons (page 193, paragraph 893).

A recipe, one might think, for creating confusion!

The only serious support it received for its proposed new ministry came from Mr Aubrey Jones, who wished to abolish the sponsoring ministries altogether and to interpose between the Ministry of Nationalized Industries and the industries themselves 'a large state holding company rather like those that operate in Italy' (page 202, paragraph 931; *Evidence*, pages 682–3 and Q. 2320–1). From the Chief Secretary of the Treasury (whose department, after all, was responsible for promoting the new techniques of which the Committee approved), it heard the following five objections: (1) that it was 'not possible to separate responsibility for securing public interest from the responsibility for seeing that the industries are efficiently run'; (2) that 'Ministers should continue to be responsible for sectors, whether they be in public or in private ownership'; (3) that the proposed Ministry 'would withdraw from the policy-making departments the experience and overall view of the industries that they must have in order to have full regard for the sector of the economy for which they are responsible'; (4) that the proposed Ministry 'would enter into management to such an extent as to deny them (i.e. the industries) the freedom of management which any organization was entitled to demand if it were to function to its best capacity'; and (5) that the proposed Ministry 'would have such a variety of functions, because the industries are varied, that it would be difficult for one Ministry to embrace them' (*Report*, pages 200–2; *Evidence*, Q. 2408–9, 2411, 2410, 2413). Some of these objections, admittedly, are stronger than others; but collectively they constitute a formidable criticism of the Committee's proposal. Its attempt to answer them is one of the weakest passages in the report.

Why has this rather nasty-looking proposal been made? I believe that the Committee has been led astray by a very proper concern for efficiency, combined with a certain *penchant* for making unrealistic distinctions in a manner somewhat reminiscent of the 'Herbert' report. Efficiency and policy cannot be separated in the way suggested; they are the joint responsibility of the industry and the sponsoring ministry, assisted by the Treasury and the DEA. The efficient implementation of policy, as the Committee itself says, is initially the responsibility of management, but the minister is there to see that management does its job in accordance with the agreed socio-economic criteria. The expert assistance he requires for this purpose can and ought to be provided, in the first instance, by the personnel of his department. Any additional assistance, in respect of 'across the board' matters, is surely most suitably located in the Treasury, the DEA, or both; and if departmental resources are insufficient, the universities, independent research agencies and NBPI are ready enough, on request, to mobilize additional expertise. What we need is not a new ministry but a reorganization of the old ministries, whereby the minister has at his disposal people with the requisite skills who enjoy the appropriate status. It is the Fulton Committee, rather than the Select Committee on Nationalized Industries, that seems to have the right answer to this particular problem.

What I believe we also need is an *efficiency audit* agency, advisory in character and independent of ministerial control. Both the results of the policies adopted and the efficiency with which they have been implemented demand objective assessment – and this cannot be done by bodies charged with the formulation of these policies and the supervision of their implementation. Yet it is precisely such an agency, the creation of which was urged in the evidence given by Professor Robson (page 534, paragraph 16) and Mr Thornhill (page 536, paragraph 25) that the Committee firmly rejects. It says that the managers would not like it; that its reports on 'errors and inefficiencies' would increase public and parliamentary pressure for further ministerial intervention; that it would 'distract' ministers, departments and managers from the 'proper and most potentially valuable approach towards securing efficiency in the future, namely the clear definition of policies, and economic obligations and criteria and the development by management itself of the best techniques for operational control'; and that its tendency to concentrate on 'the errors of the past' might inhibit 'wise or brave planning for the future'. This is all very odd; for the Committee must have noticed that these were exactly the objections originally advanced against its own creation. Indeed, it specifically quotes Lord Heyworth's expressions of 'horror' at the prospect of having people 'looking over his shoulder', in the evidence that he gave to the Select Committee of 1952–53, where he and other board chairmen said that a Select Committee on Nationalized Industries would make their lives intolerable (*Report*, pages 170–1).

It is rather difficult to understand the Committee's attitude towards efficiency studies. Their 'proper role', it says, 'is to examine current facts, costs, etc. and the current methods employed for securing efficiency in such matters as pricing policy, demand forecasting, investment appraisal, productivity improvement and cost control, and then drawing on what is now done to make recommendations for the future' (page 171, paragraph 788). This is fine – but what is meant by 'current'? How can one study these things realistically, or indeed at all, without examining the 'out-turn' of past policies and methods – which is just what the Committee wants to avoid? And what does such an examination mean if not 'audit'? Perhaps if the Committee had turned its attention to foreign experience in this field, such as that provided by the French *Commission de Vérification* or the Israeli Comptroller-General, it would have been less inclined to regard 'audit' as a dirty five-letter word.

The pity of it is that the Committee's advocacy of a Ministry of Nationalized Industries and its opposition to an independent efficiency-auditing agency have so far received most of the publicity, with the result that the really fine and constructive recommendations in the report have been comparatively neglected. Having made my criticisms, therefore, I would conclude by repeating my view that, despite all its flaws, this is a very important document, deserving the most careful study. It should inaugurate a new and more constructive stage in our discussions of the affairs of the nationalized industries.

28. THE GOVERNMENT'S RESPONSE[1]

INTRODUCTION

The government welcome this valuable and comprehensive Report, which reviews the developing relationship between Ministers and the Nationalized Industries. They understand the Committee's main thesis to be that Ministers have two quite separate responsibilities giving rise to two distinct functions in this connection. One is their responsibility for the efficiency, in the economic and financial sense, of the industries themselves. The other is their responsibility for the wider public interest.

2. The government accept that these two responsibilities can be conceptually distinguished. For the reasons given in paragraphs 4–10 below, they do not draw the organizational conclusion which the Committee itself draws from this analysis: that the two responsibilities give rise to separable and distinct functions which would be best exercised by different departments. The government do however agree with the Committee that these two responsibilities need to be recognized in order to clarify consideration of the objectives of Ministers and

[1] From White Paper, *Ministerial Control of the Nationalized Industries*, May 1969, Cmnd. 4027, paras. 1–19. Reprinted with permission of the Controller of Her Majesty's Stationery Office.

of the industries. Many of the remaining recommendations of the Committee are designed to secure this clarification, and the government accept them accordingly, as explained below.

3. These recommendations, and the analysis contained in the Report, appear to the government to be as applicable and valid within the present departmental organization as within the alternative structure proposed by the Committee. The government welcome the Committee's recognition of the very considerable progress which has been made in recent years in formulating and publishing statements of government policy towards the nationalized industries. In particular they note that the Committee endorses the general policy contained in the White Paper, Cmnd. 3437, on *Nationalized Industries: A Review of Economic and Financial Objectives*.

A MINISTRY OF NATIONALIZED INDUSTRIES

4. The government have given very careful consideration to the closely argued case in the Select Committee's Report (paragraphs 890–930) for a Ministry of Nationalized Industries. They have, however, concluded that the disadvantage of a major change in the machinery of government on these lines would substantially outweigh the advantages.

5. First, while it is true that the requirements of efficiency in one of the industries and the wider public interest (using both terms in the sense in which they were used by the Committee) may sometimes conflict in particular cases, it does not necessarily follow that the decision-making process would be improved if the two interests were the responsibility of different Ministers. There would inevitably be an initial handicap in that decisions now involving one Minister would commonly involve two, informal consultation within a single department necessarily giving way to more formal exchanges between two. And a polarization of responsibility, under which the Minister responsible for sector policy had no responsibility for efficiency, and the Minister responsible for efficiency no responsibility for the wider national interest, would not of itself be any guarantee that either of these responsibilities would prevail over the other more often than at present. There are of course very many cases in which major conflicts of public interest are resolved within individual departments. This is manifestly true of many large departments, and the application of a principle that in every case of major conflict of public interest the conflicting aspects must be the responsibility of different Ministers would lead to the break-up of the Ministry of Defence, the Department of Education and Science and a good many others.

6.   Secondly, in the government's view the Select Committee's proposal rests on too ready an assumption about the ease with which the sector responsibility and the efficiency responsibility could be separated into self-contained compartments in practice. For example, the government regard responsibility for a rational energy policy and responsibility for the investment programmes of the three nationalized fuel industries, as well as for the efficiency of these industries, as inextricably linked. The same would be true of transport policy and investment in railways and roads.

7.   In neither energy nor transport is it possible to achieve the best investment result in the national interest simply by attention to the profitability of the investment programme of a single industry. It is essential to have regard to the effect of investment in one industry on the return on investment in others. In having regard to these effects, the responsible department is in fact concerning itself with a national energy or national transport policy. If a Ministry for Nationalized Industries took account of these interactions, both this department and the sector departments would find themselves working on energy or transport policy, with resultant duplication and risk of interdepartmental dispute. If it did not, the sector departments would need to concern themselves still more closely with investment programmes, with the same results.

8.   Another implication of separating the sector responsibility and the efficiency responsibility is the division which this would produce between responsibilities for public and private sector undertakings in the same sector. The Committee's proposal assumes a sharp distinction between the type of responsibility exercised in the framework of national energy, transport or civil aviation policy, in relation to the nationalized industries and the sponsorship function in relation to private sector undertakings in the same sector. In practice a lively interest in the performance of, e.g., the privately-owned oil industry, or the private road haulage or civil aviation undertakings, is an important element in sector responsibility; and government policy in relation to these undertakings may affect substantially their investment and their prices. For this reason the sector department must be concerned with all aspects of the economic health of both public and private undertakings in its sector.

9.   Thirdly, the government are in no doubt that the sub-division of responsibilities in relation to each nationalized industry and the creation of a Ministry of Nationalized Industries at arms length from the sector responsibilities would mean more work and more staff in government and in the nationalized industries, which would each be concerned with two government departments. Conflicts of public interest now reconciled within a single department would have to be more formally

debated between two departments and on such issues both departments might want recourse to the industries and to the central departments. The position of the Chairmen of nationalized industries with two departments could become more difficult or equivocal. The burden of information, or consultation and of co-ordination would be greater both in government and in the industries. While there would be two departments instead of one necessarily seeking information from each industry, there would be no single point in government so well informed as at present about each industry and its relationship to sector policy and the wider national interest. It is true that in exchange there would grow up in the Ministry of Nationalized Industries an expertise in dealing with nationalized industries as such. However, there is already in the Ministry of Power a considerable concentration of such expertise, since the business of the department is mainly with nationalized industries. (Reference is made in paragraph 44 below to the development of arrangements for interchange of staff to foster this type of expertise.) In the circumstances the government consider that the exchange which would result from the Select Committee's proposal would not yield a net gain.

10. Fourthly, the government do not believe that the establishment of a Ministry of Nationalized Industries responsible for the efficiency of those industries, but not for sector policy, would reduce intervention in the management of the industries, as the Select Committee hope and expect. It is not enough to say that the powers and responsibilities of the proposed Minister should be no more than those recommended in the Select Committee's Report. The promotion of efficiency could be held to cover a wide range of existing statutory functions as well as new matters. If Parliament were invited to regard the new Minister as having the general efficiency of the industries as his main responsibility, they would tend to expect him to answer on many aspects of the management of the industries, especially in view of the powers recommended. All the pressures of responsibility would be towards greater intervention.

11. The government accept that there would be certain advantages in a horizontal organization, which treated nationalized industry as a function for itself. It is natural and right that the Select Committee on Nationalized Industries should see these advantages very clearly. The government, however, take the view that these gains would be greatly outweighed by losses if the price were the divorce of industry responsibility from sector responsibility. A department responsible for all nationalized industries and all relevant sectors would be too diverse and too large. If the choice between the two methods of organization has therefore to be made, the government consider that organization by sectors is to be preferred.

THE ROLE OF DEPARTMENTS

12.   The government believe that within the existing pattern of responsibilities the tasks of particular departments require further detailed study. They therefore accept the Committee's recommendation (paragraph 541) that discussions should be held between the Treasury, the DEA and the departments to clarify their respective contributions to the control of investment. Because of the importance of investment as a central feature of Ministerial control over the industries, the government believe this to be a most important recommendation.

13.   The government accept the recommendation (paragraph 350) that sponsoring departments should take the initiative in bringing together the industries for discussion of common problems. As the Committee themselves recognize this is already the practice in dealing with some types of problem: but it is intended to extend these contacts with the industries as necessary.

14.   The Committee drew attention to complaints by some industries that they had insufficient access to the Treasury, and recommended (paragraph 822) that in future, in cases where the final decision rested with the Treasury, industries should have the right to state their case to the Treasury; although the Committee also recognized (paragraph 824) that the Treasury was not a court of appeal against decisions of the responsible departments. Government policies towards the industries are of course finally settled by Ministers collectively, not by officials in individual departments. But the government agree that it is right for the industries to have opportunities to meet the central economic departments.

15.   The Committee suggested (paragraph 664) that, in addition to the present statutory powers to issue general directions, and to issue specific directions upon particular subjects specified in the statutes, Ministers should also have a statutory power to issue formal directives upon any specific subject which appears to them to be in the national interest.

16.   As the Committee recognized Ministers have in some cases powers to issue specific directions upon particular subjects defined in the statutes. If circumstances arose in future in which it seemed advisable for a Minister to be able to deal with a particular subject by issuing specific formal directions, for which powers did not exist, the government would seek the necessary powers for the purpose. To this extent, the government accept the Committee's proposal; but they do not propose to take general powers to issue specific directions on any subject to the nationalized industries. Possession of such wide general powers would, in their view, lead to heavier pressure on Ministers to

interfere with the management of the industries than the Committee foresee. It would involve the creation of a new climate in which the industries would be seen to be formally subject to Ministerial control on particular as well as general matters which touched the national interest. This would in the government's view inevitably lead over the years to a gradual encroachment by Ministers on the management responsibilities of the industries, so undermining their efficiency and reducing their capacity to recruit and keep capable top management.

17. The serious problems which arise in defining an elastic concept such as the national interest would be accentuated if it became possible to issue directions on particular as well as general matters. And the fact that Ministers possessed the power of direction would inevitably require substantial additional staff effort over the whole field in which the power could be exercised – even if in a substantial proportion of such cases it was decided not to exercise the power. This would not, in the Government's view, be a worthwhile use of civil service manpower. The government therefore prefer that Ministerial relationships with the industries should be developed within the present statutory framework of control. Within this framework practical conventions and usages have evolved which preserve an acceptable degree of autonomy for the industries while at the same time providing the necessary degree of accountability to Parliament.

18. As the Committee recommended (paragraph 681) the government will re-examine the case for existing Ministerial powers over the research and training programmes of the industries and will propose in due course any amendments to the present statutes that may be found necessary.

19. The Committee recommended (paragraph 867) that Ministers should publish periodic White Papers about the performance and prospects of the industries for which they are responsible; and (paragraph 868) that these should serve as the vehicle for government statements about sectoral policy, on the lines of the 1967 White Papers about Fuel Policy and Railways Policy. This recommendation is noted and will be borne in mind, though the government point out that much information about performance and prospects already appears in the Annual Reports of the Boards which are laid before Parliament each year, and in the occasional White Papers which are laid when Borrowing Bills are before Parliament.

CHAPTER VI

ORGANIZATION

Most of the nationalized industries are very large organizations, and thus offer prime examples of the problems of management on that scale. The first decade of the nationalization saw a great deal of controversy about centralization and decentralization, sometimes of a rather dogmatic kind. Since then there has been a tendency to turn to more complex styles of analysis, and to the employment of professional consultants – McKinsey and Company and other firms were engaged in the 1960s on high-level work for various nationalized industries.

The next series of extracts concern individual industries. The developments in the coal industry, by which production was concentrated in the most efficient pits, needed a simpler system of organization, and the changes of 1967 are described in an article from *Public Administration* by C. A. Roberts, the member for staff on the National Coal Board. A failure of organizational effectiveness with diastrous consequences was shown by the report of the enquiry headed by Lord Justice Davies, into the Aberfan tragedy of 1966, published in August 1967 (H.C. 553, not reprinted here). The report found unequivocally that the disaster, which cost 144 lives, stemmed from the failure of the NCB to initiate any policy in relation to the siting, control, inspection or management of tips.

The next piece is concerned with railways. The White Paper of 1967 (Cmnd. 3439) had been briefly concerned with organization. Printed here is an extract from a paper by the British Railways Board – the *Report on Organization* of 1969. This constitutes the outcome of a thorough review of the railway's management structure carried out after the 1968 transport reforms, and was designed to adjust the industry to changed economic circumstances and a new statutory framework. A similar investigation took place in the new National Freight Corporation, and a report resulted in December 1969 (H.C. 72, not reprinted).

The nationalization of the steel industry coincided with an urgent need to recast the structure of the industry to meet technical progress and requirements for new capacity. There was of course the problem of creating a new structure anyway, out of a variety of established firms. There are in fact three reports on organization which show what was attempted in the early years of the Corporation. The first report, of August 1967 (Cmnd. 3362) recommended a basic division of the industry into four Groups, largely of a regional character – a Midland Group; a Northern and Tubes Group; a Scottish and Northwest Group; and a South Wales Group. These multi-product Groups provided some scope for competition. The second report, of March 1969 (H.C. 163), announced the abandonment of the structure of companies which had up to then survived within the Corporation, and it also declared that the multiproduct Groups would be dropped in favour of a structure based on a small number of product Divisions. The third report, of December 1969 (H.C. 60), elaborates the way in which this system of product Divisions would operate, and it is this report which provides the extract printed in this chapter. These Divisions are held to make for much greater efficiency, by improved rationalization and the optimum use of facilities, each Division acting as a profit centre.

The final paper in this chapter returns to a general theme – that of the salaries of Board members. In 1968–9 the National Board for Prices and Incomes carried out an enquiry into top salaries of Board members and senior executives that ranged over both private industry and the nationalized corporations. The political background of nationalization has always made this a sensitive issue, and the extract from the NBPI report printed here provided a more informed basis for the controversy than was hitherto available.

29. REORGANIZATION OF THE NATIONAL COAL BOARD[1]

C. A. ROBERTS

A FRESH LOOK

In 1964, the Board decided that it would be well to set up an internal committee to review their organization. It was, after all, ten years since the Fleck Report, in which, indeed, it had been envisaged that there would be a further look at the organization after a reasonable number of years. This committee travelled the coalfields and talked to representatives of management at all levels. It reported to the Board in February 1965. The report (which has not been published) made a number of useful recommendations, but those relating to organization at the higher

[1] From C. A. Roberts, 'The Reorganization of the NCB's management structure', *Public Administration*, vol. 44, Autumn 1966, pages 287–93. Reprinted with permission of the author and the editor of *Public Administration*.

levels were to some extent overtaken by the events outlined in the preceding paragraphs.

As the Board's discussions of the committee's recommendations progressed, the fact that the industry was likely to consist of no more than 300–350 collieries by 1970 attained ever greater significance. It was realized that here, at last, was the opportunity to re-shape the organization so as to reduce the number of tiers created in 1946 when there were over 1,000 collieries. Since experience had shown that an Area could control up to twenty collieries, and since the number of separate collieries was expected not to exceed 340 by 1970, a figure of seventeen suggested itself for the number of areas of the future – and the same figure was appropriate for an average annual production of ten million tons per Area, giving a total annual production of 170 million tons. The geographical location of the collieries also suited this number of Areas. Then the question arose whether as many as seventeen Areas could be controlled directly by Headquarters. There was no guide to the answer in the experience of the Board, but modern management theory suggested that this was not only possible but right.[1] Finally, the Board decided that each Area should have direct control over its collieries and that the intermediate level – Groups – should be eliminated.

THE NEW ORGANIZATION

Once the basis of the new organization – Headquarters, Area and Colliery – had been decided, the organization at Area level could be tackled. It was thought right to vest control in one man, to be called the Area Director, who would be personally responsible to the National Board. He would have two Deputies: one, the Deputy Director (Operations) would be responsible to the Director for the control of the colliery operations; the other, the Deputy Director (Administration) would be responsible for the planning of the business of the Area and would be the Director's administrative right-hand man. There would be the following Departmental heads also answerable to the Director:

Chief Mining Engineer
Staff Manager/Secretary
Industrial Relations Officer
Chief Accountant
Marketing Manager
Purchasing and Stores Manager
Scientist
Medical Officer
Estates Manager

[1] cf. J. R. Nelson, 'The Fleck Report and the Area Organization of the National Coal Board', *Public Administration*, vol. 43, Spring 1965, page 53.

Some of these call for special comment:

Chief Mining Engineer. He will, of course, work in close touch with the D.D.(O). His special responsibility will be to provide the technical services required for the efficient running of the pits; and to this end he will have command of the whole range of technical branches. One of the most important of these branches is the *Chief Engineer's*; he will, in fact, have a far bigger role than hitherto because of ever-increasing mechanization, and he will play a major part in the Area's management team.

Marketing Manager. In 1949 the Board created a selling organization in which the whole country was divided into Sales Regions. Each Region, except the London and Southern, contained a Mining Division. The Divisional Marketing Directors and their senior supporting staff combined both Divisional and Regional functions. This organization has amply proved its value. When Divisions cease to be a level of management, the Regional selling organization will continue more or less unchanged. The Area Marketing Manager will be answerable to the Area Director for helping to plan the business of the Area, and for seeing that the coal is despatched from the collieries as required by the Sales organization. He will also be responsible to the Marketing Director of the Sales Region in which his Area is located for helping to foster and to develop the local market for coal.

Purchasing and Stores Manager. The Purchasing and Stores Department was created in 1955 following the recommendation of the Fleck Committee. It soon became apparent that important advantages would accrue from centralized purchasing of a whole range of commodities. Equally, central control of stores-holding could achieve big savings by reducing the number of stock-holding points and the quantity of slow-moving stores held at each. Thus, for some years there has been a steady movement towards the establishment of a unified, centrally controlled system. Under the new organization, the Purchasing and Stores Manager will have a relatively limited function; the main work will be done at Purchasing and Stores Centres which will be under the control of Headquarters direct. There will initially be about eight of these centres; the number will come down to six in a few years. . . .

With the elimination of the Divisional level of management, there will have to be some strengthening both at Area and at Headquarters. An important change at Headquarters is to give the Director-General of Production the support of a very experienced former Area General Manager with the title of Chief Mining Engineer.

Since it is undesirable to increase the number of staff working in central London, a Headquarters office is being set up in Doncaster. It will comprise the whole of Purchasing and Stores Department, the Engineering part of Production Department, and elements of Finance and Staff Departments. Some staff, until recently in Hobart House, have moved to a new office at Harrow, which will also house the Coal Products Division, the London and South Regional Sales Organization, and the Opencast Executive. Eventually, the staff remaining in central London will all be in Hobart House.

Some central services will be provided to Areas from Headquarters outstations. For example, there will be seven offices for the Board's Legal staff in different parts of the country. There will also be seven Computer Centres. Central Workshops and Rescue Stations located in the coalfields will be controlled by Headquarters Production Department. There will be three Pensions and Insurance offices (with Staff Superannuation offices alongside), one each in England, Scotland and Wales. In short, whilst it is the intention to make each Area as far as possible self-supporting, those central services will be provided which it would be uneconomical to provide area by area.

The elimination of the Divisions as a level of management, and the creation of the new-style Areas, will take place at the beginning of April 1967. The period from the beginning of April 1967 to the date, a year or two later, when the new organization is fully established will obviously be a difficult one: the Board's business must be carried on and the reorganization must be completed. To help the Board carry on the business, there will be a Divisional Chairman for each coalfield who will act to all intents and purposes as a member of the National Board with a specific responsibility for his coalfield: he will oversee the Areas' progress towards the objectives set to them and will help to ensure that the Board's policies are carried out. And to progress the work of reorganization during the transitional period, a Controller has been appointed for each coalfield: he is answerable to the National Board for seeing that all the action needed to bring the new organization into being is taken in good time. Some of the present Divisional staff, notably the Staff Directors, will remain in post after April 1967, answering to their parent Departments at Headquarters and helping to bridge the gap between the old and the new organizations.

New structures and complements for the main Departments have been devised for Headquarters and for the Areas. The Area Director will not, for the present, have power to alter the structures or complements for his Area Departments, but the Board will be quick to respond to Directors' recommendations for variations in detail from the pattern laid down which are called for by differing local circumstances and needs.

Job descriptions for the new posts are in preparation and so also is a new General Directive to replace that of 1955.

The filling of appointments in most management grades at Divisions and Areas will be controlled centrally until the redeployment of staff nears completion. Subject to these limitations and to reasonable limitations on powers to spend capital, it is intended to give the Area Directors very wide powers. Areas will be given their objectives and Area Directors will be accountable for their achievement. The computer centres will be available to help them in working out the best of the very many possible ways of achieving the objectives and in assessing the likely consequences of changes in the plans necessitated by changes in circumstances.

IMPLEMENTATION

The Board had decided on the main lines of the reorganization by the late autumn of 1965. The first task was to communicate it to the staff and, to do this, they held two conferences for all the senior staff on succeeding days in the first week of December. Some 250 people attended these conferences. Immediately afterwards, there were meetings with the leaders of the unions representing the various sections of the Board's employees and they were given the same information, oral and written, as had been given to the staff. Meetings were also held at the same time with the less senior staff in all the Divisions and Areas. Within the space of a week, all the non-industrial staff of the industry had been given, or had access to, through their unions, a full account of the Board's plans.

However, the big question in everyone's minds was how the reorganization would affect him personally. Since the process of reorganization and the consequent redeployment of staff were expected to take two to three years to complete, this was not always an easy question to answer. But a good indication could be given to most people. Early in January, all the most senior officials in Divisions and Areas were interviewed in London by members of the Board along with the appropriate Head of Department. They were told what the Board had in mind for them, and there was ample opportunity for objections to be raised and difficulties to be discussed. In the great majority of cases, a good understanding was reached and men went home with a clear idea of what the future was likely to have in store for them – though they knew that changes in some people's prospects might well occur as a result of unforeseen events between the present date and the date when the new appointments took effect. In March and early April, officials in the next tier of management were similarly interviewed in London. By mid-April nearly 800 staff had been seen and people had been earmarked for all the senior posts in the new-style Areas and in the Headquarters Departments. Interviews on the same lines with the less senior staff have since taken place in the coalfields.

The elimination of two tiers of management, the reduction in the number of separate Areas and the fall in the number of separate collieries will obviously lead to a reduction in the total number of staff; this may, at the end of the day, be as much as one quarter of the 47,000 non-industrial staff in employment at the end of March 1965. The Board aim to keep redundancy to a minimum and to achieve the reduction by controlling recruitment, by taking advantage of natural wastage, by offering retirement on reasonable terms to staff aged 60 and above and by transferring and redeploying the remaining staff. Some difficulties can be overcome by having posts 'double-banked' and by allowing complements to be exceeded for a few years. As mentioned earlier, appointments will for some time to come be centrally controlled to ensure that all members of the staff, irrespective of where or at what level they are now working, are treated fairly according to their merits. There will inevitably be a check to promotion for a time; experience suggests that this will not persist for long, and, when the new organization is complete, the proportion of relatively senior posts to the total will be greater than now, so that the promotion prospects of the major junior staff will be improved. A new branch of Headquarters Staff Department is being set up to watch over men's careers and to help to plan them to the best interests of the industry and of the staff themselves.

COLLIERY ORGANIZATION

For the past two years or so the Board have been gradually bringing into effect a strengthened organization for large collieries and this process is now being speeded up. At the same time, preliminary work is in hand directed towards a request to Parliament for a revision of the Mines and Quarries Act 1954, which will bring the statutory provisions more into line with today's needs. Apart from this, the progressive adoption of the system of Area planning and the setting of firm objectives will help the Colliery Manager to do his job better; and the shortening of the line of command may well alleviate the feeling of remoteness from the National Board from which some Colliery Managers have suffered in the past. The reorganization will enable the greatest weight of managerial and engineering talent to be brought to the primary task of getting the coal out of the pit and into the wagon with the maximum efficiency. It will form the right framework for the new technology of coal-mining.

The loyalty and goodwill of the men and women of the coal industry made it possible for the great change of nationalization to be carried through successfully in 1947. The changes that will take place in 1967 are not so drastic, but they too will affect the lives of thousands of men and women in the industry. Once again, they have shown the utmost loyalty and goodwill and this has been reflected in the co-operation and constructive approach of the trades unions representing them. There is therefore good reason to hope and expect that the reorganization will be successfully achieved.

30. ORGANIZATION OF BRITISH RAIL[1]

Part 2 – The Proposed Board and Management Organization

10.   Following the review of the organization of the Board's affairs, we propose that:

10.1 *The British Railways Board should assume a mainly non-executive role* and give greater emphasis to overall corporate planning, policy making and longer term direction of British Rail and each of its other businesses, while ensuring that each business is effectively managed. For each of its subsidiary businesses, other than railways, the Board proposes to continue to set up a subsidiary board chaired by a member of the main Board to direct that business.

10.2 *The Board should delegate responsibility for the management of British Rail and each of its other businesses to a chief executive for each business*, and should assign to him all the functions and activities he needs to carry out his responsibilities effectively. The Chief Executive (Railways) will thus be fully responsible for managing profitably, within Board policies, agreed plans and defined limits of authority, the railway business, and will be held personally accountable for results. Similarly, each of the other chief executives will be held responsible for his business, first by his subsidiary board and, ultimately, jointly with his board, by the main Board. Each chief executive will in turn delegate specific responsibilities within his organization and hold individual managers accountable for their results, again with policy guidelines and limits of authority, while retaining overall responsibility.

10.3 *The organization for British Rail should be restructured under the Chief Executive (Railways)* so that railway activities can be more

---

[1] From British Railways Board, *Report on Organization*, December 1969, H.C. 50, pages 10-19, 23-25, paras. 10-35, 45-58. Reprinted with permission of the Controller of Her Majesty's Stationery Office.

effectively managed to achieve objectives agreed between the Board and the Chief Executive.

The proposed organization structures of the Board and British Rail and the primary responsibilities of each position are illustrated in Exhibits I and II. This chapter of the report explains the proposed organization in detail, and is divided into three sections:

The Board
The Chief Executive (Railways)
The organization under the Chief Executive (Railways).

THE BOARD

This section describes the role of the British Railways Board as a whole, and of the individual full-time and part-time members.

11.   **The Board as a whole.** The Board has a corporate responsibility for discharging the statutory obligations set out in the *Transport Acts 1962 and 1968*. In doing this the Board must direct the affairs of the railways (and other businesses of the British Railways Board) in such a way as to ensure:

11.1 That certain standards of public service and safety are maintained.

11.2 That these standards are achieved within certain financial constraints.

This responsibility cannot be delegated. Each Board member is appointed by the Minister (after consultation with the Chairman) and shares in the corporate responsibility of the whole Board in meeting its obligations.

12. This corporate obligation of the Board can be broken down into more specific responsibilities, of which the most important are:

12.1 *Setting objectives and approving plans.* The Board determines the short and longer term (up to 10 years) objectives and strategies of the British Railways Board as a whole, and of each of its businesses (railways, ships, hotels, etc.). It gains agreement by the Minister that these are consistent with national objectives and government policies, and reviews and approves 5-year plans for each business, ensuring that these are consistent with longer term objectives and strategies.

12.2 *Establishing policies.* The Board establishes explicit policies in all main areas of its activities to guide the management of the businesses, makes these known within the organization and ensures that they are followed.

12.3 *Deciding organization.* The Board determines the best form of management organization for each business within the British Railways Board, and ensures that each business is adequately organized and staffed to achieve its agreed objectives most effectively.

12.4 *Taking major decisions.* The Board makes informed decisions on major matters (e.g., investments, senior appointments, exceptions to existing policy and special issues that do not fall within existing policy) that exceed the authority delegated to the chief executives in charge of each business.

12.5 *Monitoring performance.* The Board monitors the performance of each business by (a) reviewing and agreeing in advance the annual business plans and budgets of each chief executive; (b) reviewing regularly (e.g. quarterly) the actual performance of each chief executive against his agreed annual plans and budgets; (c) ensuring that appropriate and timely action is taken by the chief executive to correct unfavourable deviations from the plan; and (d) taking necessary action to replace any chief executive who fails to meet his plan without good reason.

12.6 *Management development and succession.* The Board establishes policies for the selection, training and development of senior personnel in all its businesses and monitors the application of these policies. It will also itself be directly responsible for all key appointments.

13.   The basic role of the Board as a whole, therefore, is to give continuing leadership and direction to all businesses entrusted to it by the Minister, and to control them effectively, but not itself to 'manage' them. In this role the Board acts as the primary policy maker, planner, decision taker and monitor of results achieved for each business within the British Railways Board.

14.   It is therefore essential that the Board as a whole should be – and should be seen to be – a unified body in agreement on all major policies, issues and decisions. This does not assume that its individual members will always be of the same opinion. On the contrary, their role assumes genuine differences of opinion on many major issues. But it does imply that these issues will be objectively studied and freely discussed by the whole Board (or by relevant Board committees) and that after such full discussion the Board will reach a decision.

15.   **The Chairman.** The Chairman will act as leader and principal spokesman of the Board, ensuring that each member plays his proper part and makes a worthwhile contribution to its deliberations. He will

emphasize the collective responsibility and authority of the Board at all times.

It will be the Chairman's responsibility to see that adequate arrangements are made for achieving and maintaining a close relationship with the Minister and his department.

It will also be his responsibility to ensure that the Board is effectively organized to carry out its responsibilities, both in respect of those matters for which the Minister has a specific statutory responsibility (e.g., the control of investment) and in relation to those other bodies with whom the Board's relations are defined in the statutes.

With the National Freight Corporation, the Chairman has already established, in addition to his personal contacts with the Chairman of that Corporation, a comprehensive structure of joint committees to ensure that both the Board and the Corporation can fulfil their statutory obligations to each other.

He will also maintain effective communication with and among all members on matters of importance by whatever means are most appropriate – memoranda, informal meetings and individual discussions, as well as formal Board meetings. In order to speed the work of the Board, he will establish a Board committee structure to advise or, where appropriate, act on behalf of the Board. He will also, from time to time, discuss with individual members their various duties, making such changes as may be advisable and appropriate to the changing needs of the business.

16. **The Deputy Chairman.** The Deputy Chairman will, in the absence of the Chairman for any reason, exercise the full powers of the Chairman. He will assist the Chairman and act for him as necessary in conducting the business of the Board. He will deal with matters specifically assigned to him by the Chairman and will, on behalf of the latter, co-ordinate as required the various activities of the Board. He may also be assigned special spheres of interest, including the chairmanship of subsidiaries or Board committees.

17. **The Chief Executive (Railways).** The Chief Executive (Railways) will be responsible for managing profitably the major part of the British Railways Board's business. Because of the importance of his task the Chief Executive must be a full-time Board member appointed by the Minister. Thereby, he will participate actively in and contribute to top-level policy making and decision taking for the railway and the Board as a whole.

However, his full-time assignment, which is discussed later in this chapter, will be to manage the railway. Because of this, the Chief Executive position should be separate from that of Deputy Chairman, since the present combined duties of the two posts are clearly too heavy for a single individual.

18.   The Joint Steering Group, whose report was annexed to the government White Paper on *Railway Policy* (Cmnd. 3439), recommended that the responsibility for managing the railway should to some extent be shared. The Board has concluded, however, that the interdependence of the different parts of the railway business makes it essential that the responsibility for the development of business plans, and their execution, as approved by the Board, should rest with a single chief executive.

19.   **Full-time Members.** The principle has been established, and confirmed by the government, that the full-time Board members (other than the Chief Executive (Railways)) should in the main be non-executive. Such members will therefore have no direct-line responsibility for managing any part of the railway system, or with certain exceptions, any headquarters departments.

However, as well as taking part in the affairs of the Board as a whole, Board members will perform a number of important functions that will assist the Board in carrying out its responsibilities. These functions are, briefly, as follows:

> 19.1 *Responsibility for corporate functions.* The Joint Steering Group recommended that because of their importance there should be Board members directly responsible for the functions of planning, finance and personnel. The Board agrees. . . .

> 19.2 *Corporate Planning.* The Board member in charge of this function should be responsible for assisting the Board in developing strategies and corporate plans to achieve the Board's overall financial objectives and for ensuring the quality of planning done within the railway and the Board's other businesses. . . .

20.   *Corporate Finance.* The Board member in charge of this function should be responsible for recommending financial policies and practices for adoption by the Board for all its businesses and for monitoring the application of these and the maintenance of satisfactory professional standards. In addition, he should direct corporate financial activities (e.g., central banking, analysis of business results, internal audit).

21.   *Corporate Personnel.* The Board's personnel activities, which include industrial relations, are dominated by the railway, and dividing these into railway and non-railway is more difficult than in the other functional areas since (1) railway and non-railway businesses have many jobs and graded posts in common, and (2) both railway and non-railway businesses frequently negotiate and consult on pay and conditions with the same trade unions. This calls for a planned approach if undesirable

inconsistencies of pay and conditions between the Board's various businesses are to be avoided.

Hence the Board member for personnel and industrial relations should be responsible for overall personnel and industrial relations policies and practices and for ensuring the quality of these activities within the railway and the Board's other businesses. He must therefore recommend policies and practices to the Board, maintain direct contact with and consequent influence upon trade union leaders and play a positive role in major negotiations with trades unions. In this, the railway Executive Director, Personnel, should work closely with the Board member and place the services and assistance of his department at the member's disposal. The member should also ensure that established policies and practices are adhered to and that non-railway businesses receive satisfactory personnel services from the railway Personnel Department.

22. *Research and Development.* One corporate activity that is different from those listed above is technical research and development. The R & D unit at Derby is almost solely concerned with railway technology; the success or failure of its R & D work will directly affect railway performance and profits; for these reasons it could be argued that it should be under the direct control of the Chief Executive (Railways).

There are, however, good reasons why it should be left where it is now – i.e., reporting to a non-executive member – at least for the present. A long-term need might well develop for research in non-railway areas of importance to the Board. The time scale of R & D is often much longer than that with which the Chief Executive (Railways) is primarily concerned (1–5 years), so it is best kept separate from current railway management. Moreover, the cost of research and development is in many respects a long-term Board investment and could therefore legitimately be excluded from annual railway business plans and budgets. But it is essential that there is a proper link between the research activity and the Chief Executive (Railways) as its principal user, as it is recognized that the rapid adoption of modern technology is necessary for the continuing health of the business. There must also be close relationship between R & D and corporate planning since priorities for all research projects will be set through the Corporate Plan.

23. *Chairmanships of subsidiary boards.* It should be made clear that members appointed as chairmen of subsidiary boards will not normally act as chief executives. In each case there will be a separate manager reporting to the subsidiary board. This will avoid members becoming involved in the current management of the businesses concerned. The terms of reference of a member so appointed can be broadly defined as follows:

23.1 Ensuring that his subsidiary board stays within its proper terms of reference and carries out its tasks effectively

23.2 Helping his subsidiary board to think through and develop its strategies and policies, and to present these to the British Railways Board for approval

23.3 Representing his subsidiary board's interest and point of view at British Railways Board meetings, and answering for it

23.4 Advising the British Railways Board on senior appointments in the subsidiary

23.5 Representing his subsidiary in external relations as appropriate.

24. The Workshops, in particular, represent a major railway activity having a substantial degree of autonomy. The Board sets great value on a degree of separateness and an effective pricing system between the Workshops and the railways as a means of developing financial awareness and reinforcing financial control, both for the providers of a service and those who require a service to be provided for them, and they have, in recent years, steadily developed the supplier/customer relationship between the Workshops Division and the railways.

The Board propose to set up a separate and wholly owned subsidiary company to direct and manage the Workshops, and to operate, so far as the Board's manufacturing powers are concerned, on the lines laid down in the Board's proposals under Section 48 of the 1968 Act (as eventually approved by the Minister). This will of course mean that the results of this company will be separately disclosed.

25. *Chairmanships of Board committees.* One result of the proposed new management organization structure will be a reduction in the number of committees and working parties of all kinds. But a number of major committees will still be retained, chaired by Board members, with terms of reference approved by the Board and in some cases with delegated powers specifically approved by the Board.

The selection of chairmen and members for the main Board committees will reflect the responsibilities of the members concerned. At present, the following main Board committees are proposed:

25.1 Finance

25.2 Investment

25.3 Research and Development

25.4 Supplies

25.5 Technical

25.6 Management Development.

The Board does not propose to set up a separate planning committee, since this is one of the most essential functions of the Board as a whole and cannot be delegated.

From time to time the areas covered by Board committees may change, but they should always be the major areas of Board level responsibility and the areas of major policy or strategic issues. Each committee will advise the Board as a whole on policy and strategic issues falling within its terms of reference and will exercise authority that may be delegated to it to act on behalf of the Board as a whole.

26. *Assignment to areas of special interest or expertise.* It will be helpful to assign individual Board members areas in which they possess or will develop special interest or expertise. They will play a leading role in influencing Board decisions that affect these areas, but will not take any line management responsibility for activities within the areas that are controlled by any of the chief executives. The Chairman will decide the areas of special interest in which full-time Board members should function and he will assign these after discussion with members.

One purpose of such assignments is to ensure that at least one Board member is well informed in each major area of the Board's business so that he can give the Board objective advice (which a chief executive clearly cannot provide) on that particular aspect of the chief executive's plans and performance.

Another purpose is to ensure that the Board has the guidance of an informed member on matters requiring the formulation of new Board policies or the interpretation of existing policies. In this connection a member can and should raise with the Board major issues within his special field of interest that would result in policy or strategy proposals for discussion with chief executives.

To achieve these purposes without eroding the line of authority of the chief executives, Board members must have or be able to obtain all relevant information and must be free to discuss problems with members of the chief executives' management group. For example, within the railways, it will be necessary for the members of the Board to maintain proper contact with the executive directors and regional general managers and their staffs, and to visit the regions as necessary during the course of business.

Members will also be able to call upon the Chief Secretary and his staff for other information they may require, and it will be for the Chief Secretary to keep them advised of all matters of importance with which the Board is concerned and of which they are not advised through other channels.

27. *Responsibility for central administrative and service departments.* There are certain departments that will continue to provide central services to the various Board businesses because it is more economical to do so, or because of the nature of the activity. They will remain within the responsibility of individual Board members. At present these

departments are, for example:

27.1 British Transport Films
27.2 Industrial Design
27.3 Legal
27.4 Medical
27.5 Police
27.6 Public Relations and Publicity
27.7 Supplies.

28. *External representation.* One of the Chairman's major functions is to maintain official or personal relationships within government, industry and other outside bodies, both in the United Kingdom and abroad. Some of these relationships – for example, with the Minister – he must maintain himself, but responsibility for others can be assigned to the Deputy Chairman, the Chief Executive (Railways) and other Board members.

A non-executive member may represent the British Railways Board on the principal trade associations, professional bodies and other external organizations that are relevant to his assigned 'areas of special interest' or the non-railway subsidiaries with which he is concerned.

29. **Part-Time Members.** The description of the role and responsibilities of the Board as a whole, and of its individual full-time members, is generally applicable to the part-time members. Differences are mainly of degree rather than of substance.

The part-time members are appointed by the Minister (after consultation with the Chairman) and have the same degree of shared collective or 'corporate' responsibility to the Minister as full-time members. So in this respect there is virtually no difference between full-time and part-time members.

The main reason for having part-time members is to bring a wider range of experience and judgement, and perhaps a greater degree of objectivity, to bear on the deliberations of the Board, since, by definition, part-time members are also members of other boards or active in other organizations. But for this very reason they clearly cannot spend as much time on Board matters as full-time members. The Chairman will not, therefore, normally assign such specific responsibilities to the part-time members as to the full-time members.

THE CHIEF EXECUTIVE (RAILWAYS)

30. The Joint Steering Group recommended that a single 'Chief General Manager' be appointed with responsibility for controlling and co-ordinating all aspects of the day-to-day running of the railways. This

recommendation was for immediate purposes implemented by appointing a vice chairman (who has since been made Deputy Chairman) specifically to undertake the work of Chief Executive. Since then, the specific responsibilities and authorities to be delegated to the Chief Executive by the Board have been evaluated, and further recommendations about them have been developed.

31.   It is proposed that the Chief Executive's basic terms of reference should be to be responsible to the Board for developing and managing the railway business within the policies laid down by the Board so as to achieve the railway financial objectives and service standards as approved by the Board. This will involve (a) setting out proposed 5-year railway objectives, strategies and policies; (b) developing 5-year and annual railway plans for achieving the railway surplus and other financial objectives and the agreed service and safety standards, within delegated limits of authority and Board policies; and (c) ensuring the effectiveness of the railway organization as a whole.

The Chief Executive will fulfil these terms of reference by:

31.1 *Developing a 5-year plan for railways activities.* Each year he will prepare and submit to the Board a 5-year statement of his proposed railway objectives and his plans for achieving them. . . .

31.2 *Directing the assembly of annual railway plans and budgets.* . . .

31.3 *Ensuring the execution of annual railway plans.* . . .

31.4 *Monitoring performance and reporting on it to the Board.* . . .

31.5 *Taking action within his limits of authority.* . . .

31.6 *Referring to the Board decisions outside his limits of authority.* . . .

31.7 *Providing information to the Board.* . . .

THE ORGANIZATION UNDER THE CHIEF EXECUTIVE (RAILWAYS)

32.   To execute his duties effectively, the Chief Executive will require both headquarters executives to assist him in the central planning and control of the railway business, and regional general managers to represent the 'operating management' of British Rail's geographically dispersed business. Together with the Chief Executive, they will form the Railway Management Group.

33.   Introducing changes in the organization under the Chief Executive will be a 2-phase process. The first phase will be to restructure and strengthen the headquarters departments under executive directors so that they can support the Chief Executive and focus on planning and controlling key elements of the business more effectively.

34.   The second phase will be to review the regional organizations in the light of the revised approach to managing the railways. This phase,

however, cannot be undertaken until the first is at least mostly implemented, because of the risk of possible disruption from making several major changes at the same time.

35. Even though individual approaches to regional organization (e.g. 2-tier structure) are being tried out now, the Board proposes to defer a thorough review of regional organizations until the changes proposed in this report are under way, which will probably be within a year. In due course, however, these organizations must be reviewed to establish new working relationships. Such a review will of itself be a major task and must be based on the proved efficiency of the Board's organization proposals, which are the subject of this report. This does not mean that no organizational improvements will be made in the regions for a year. In making any changes, however, other changes being implemented will be taken into account. . . .

Part 3 – The Planning and Control Process in the New Organization

45. The proposed revisions to Board and railway organizations are designed to define specific responsibilities, for which the Board and senior railway management will be held accountable, to provide a manageable span of control for the Chief Executive (Railways) and to focus top management on the key elements of the railway business. They do not, however, constitute by themselves the fundamental change in approach that is essential if British Rail and the Board's other businesses are to be managed as successful commercial enterprises. The management approach that the Board proposes to adopt as a means of improving its commercial performance requires not only a clearly defined and effectively integrated organization structure, but also systematic planning and control processes based on setting objectives, developing strategies and plans to meet these objectives, and monitoring performance against plan.

SETTING OBJECTIVES

46. Fundamental to the development of sound business plans will be the setting of realistic but stretching objectives for each level of management at the commencement of the planning cycle. Thus, the Board will concentrate on establishing longer term direction of British Rail and its other businesses, and will set each business 1- to 5-year objectives, based on overall Board objectives – derived from corporate plans that will be projected over periods perhaps in excess of 10 years – strategies and policies agreed with the chief executive concerned. Each

chief executive will then establish sub-objectives for individual members of his management group and agree these with them. These objectives will be derived from a systematic review of past business performance and future outlook, and from a realistic evaluation of the performance gap between current trends and long-term objectives set by the Board.

47.   Every executive, down to the lowest level of regional management, will therefore have established objectives, agreed with his superior, for the future planning period, and will in turn establish and agree sub-objectives for each of his direct subordinates. Thus management throughout the organization will be clearly directed and personally committed to achieving results that together meet the objectives for the business as a whole.

DEVELOPING RAILWAY STRATEGIES AND PLANS

48.   Railway plans will thus be developed in the context of established objectives at all levels of management, each executive planning his own activities and directing the formulation of his subordinates' plans to achieve those objectives. In this context, plans will contain not merely a forecast of desired results and a statement of strategy to be adopted, but also a programme of planned action to execute that strategy that includes who is responsible for individual action steps and when each step should be completed. At senior management level these programmes will necessarily be restricted to major action steps; but nevertheless they should be drawn up, and the Chief Executive will hold individual members of his Railway Management Group accountable for carrying them out successfully.

49.   Plans, including specific action programmes, to meet agreed objectives will be developed by the Chief Executive and agreed between him and the Board. Likewise, plans and action programmes for meeting sub-objectives will be agreed between him and individual members of his management group.

50.   Railway plans will cover two separate time scales: longer term (up to 5 years) and annual. The 5-year plan is essential, because major changes to the railway business can only be achieved within this time scale. It then provides a framework within which annual plans can effectively contribute to long-term profitability by establishing the short-term action needed to achieve the required results. The annual plans and budgets also provide an invaluable control tool for regulating the business during the year, as well as accurate means of measuring system-wide management performance.

51.   The overall railway planning and control cycle is illustrated in Exhibit III. The railway's 5-year plan and annual plan and budget are

formulated by integrating and co-ordinating plans developed by both headquarters executives and the regional general managers. Their respective contributions to the planning process and the interactions between them are outlined in Exhibit IV. It should be stressed, however, that planning carried out by the regions will be largely directed by headquarters through objectives and planning guidelines authorized by the Chief Executive. The responsibility for planning the longer term development of the business will centre far more upon headquarters management, who will provide an updated basis on which all levels of railway management can formulate detailed short-term plans within the annual planning cycle.

52. Both short and longer term plans will be developed, reviewed and approved by the Chief Executive for submission to the Board at least 3 months before the financial year commences, allowing time for necessary revisions and integration within the Corporate Plan during October. The Planning Officer (Railways), reporting to the Chief Executive, will do much of the preparatory work in putting this total plan together. But if the regional and headquarters plans conflict on matters of substance, the senior managers concerned, including the Chief Executive himself, will need to resolve the issues in face-to-face discussion.

MONITORING RAILWAY PERFORMANCE

53. Once the agreed railway plan – developed and integrated in the way outlined above – has been accepted by the Board, the Chief Executive will set the execution of the plan in motion. Each of his subordinates will be authorized to proceed with his part of the plan, with the understanding that his performance will be reviewed at regular intervals.

54. Since ultimate accountability for the railway business rests with the Chief Executive, he must retain effective control over the results of its component parts. In order to do so without eroding the authority of his management group members and without becoming involved in the day-to-day details of running the business, he and, in turn, his subordinates, will manage by 'exception'. This implies that the Chief Executive will involve himself in the detailed affairs of his subordinates only when significant deviations from agreed plans occur – i.e., when exceptions to expected standards and performance are identified.

55. Performance will be monitored against plan by regular management reviews. The Board will compare the results of agreed plans at a formal review held at least quarterly, and the Chief Executive will review the performance of individual members of his management group and of

the total business under his control in a similar manner at regular intervals. But effective monitoring will mainly depend upon the quality and efficiency of a management information system geared to allow rapid evaluation of actual results against plan. Such a system will be necessary if the Chief Executive is to challenge, on a factual basis, any shortfall against plan, and not only demand an explanation for the reasons causing the shortfall, but also appraise the specific remedial action proposed by the executive concerned. It is of particular importance in a business that is both geographically dispersed and operationally complex.

56. Because there will always be uncontrollable 'external' factors that affect the execution of a plan, the original planning assumptions and perhaps even its basic objectives may have to change as the year progresses. Planning of this kind is a discipline for putting pressure on all managers to achieve their planned results, but it is unrealistic to suppose that the plans themselves may not have to be altered to meet unplanned events. Such changes should only be made, however, when the Chief Executive is able to satisfy the Board that there is no realistic possibility of achieving the original objectives.

57. It is intended that similar management procedures will be adopted in the Board's other, non-railway businesses. This will enable the Board to delegate the current management of its subsidiaries to chief executives, without losing effective control of the subsidiaries' results.

58. The effort required for developing this complete approach and necessary management information systems and getting them fully operative will be a top management task, which will take at least a year and probably closer to 2 years to achieve in British Rail. However, the considerable investment of management time and effort that it represents will in the end be fully justified by the tighter control that such a system will give the Board over the results of the railway – measured not only in the quality of service provided for its customers, but also in terms of improved profitability.

31. BRITISH STEEL CORPORATION[1]

4. The Corporation's paramount aim in introducing the new system of organization is to further the attainment of its basic objective, which

[1] From British Steel Corporation, *Third Report on Organization*, December 1969, H.C. 60, pages 7–19, paras. 4–52. Reprinted with permission of the Controller of Her Majesty's Stationery Office.

remains as stated in the first Report and is to achieve the maximum long-term return on its capital investment consistent with:

   (i) strengthening its marketing and technological position in the world steel industry;

  (ii) providing British industry with products that are competitive in price, quality and service; and

 (iii) ensuring the efficient and socially responsible utilization of human resources.

The changes in organization now proposed are designed to cure those deficiencies in the existing system which impede the attainment of this objective.

PRODUCT DIVISIONS

5.   The existing Group system has been valuable in a number of ways. First it was an essential instrument in enabling the Corporation to take immediate control of the activities entrusted to it; secondly, substantial progress has been made in integrating the control of operations of the companies brought together in the public sector; thirdly, it has enabled certain measures of rationalization to be taken. In the light of experience gained in operating this system, however, it has become clear that the continued rationalization of the Corporation's activities and the better use of its resources will be advanced by a system which does not divide control of sectors of the business producing and selling identical or very similar products.

6.   Steel products fall into a number of broad categories which are to a large extent sold separately and manufactured in distinct plants. The most economic and efficient utilization of the present production capacity for a particular product or group of products can only be achieved by planning the optimum distribution of the total demand over all the available production facilities. Similarly, the provision of future production capacity in relation to forecast demand must inevitably be planned on a product basis. Both these call for a unified control over the product or group of products concerned. It was recognized in the first Report[1] that the concentration of management expertise and sales and research effort, the rationalization of production and the achievement of the optimum balance of production as between works making the same product were the main advantages that would flow from a grouping on product lines, though at that time this was out-weighed by the need to form the main companies immediately into manageable groupings.

7.   The unification of managerial control over particular products or

---

[1] Report on Organization 1967: paragraph 56(c).

groups of related products could be achieved by a central unification of control over all products. The Corporation decided against this course, partly because of the importance it attaches to preserving a system which incorporates, below the top management of the Corporation, a level of general management to which responsibilities can be delegated for complete sectors of the Corporation's business, and partly because of the time required to implement efficiently the major changes it would involve – and in the meantime these changes would cause too much disturbance for its organization soon after it had already undergone the considerable changes consequent upon nationalization.

8.   The Corporation therefore concluded that the advantage lay with a system of product Divisions and, as noted in the Second Report,[1] it set up in January, 1969, a Committee under one of the Deputy Chairmen to examine in detail the feasibility of a system of this kind and the arrangements for constituting and operating it.

9.   The Corporation has accepted the findings of this Committee that a system consisting of a small number of product Divisions, each operating as a profit centre[2] is feasible and has decided that this system should be introduced as from 29 March 1970. The Minister's consent to this change is required under section 7(3) of the Iron and Steel Act, 1967, and has been sought in presenting this Report.

Principles of System of Product Divisions
10.   The new system of organization must give the Corporation more effective means of:

(a) rationalizing sales where similar products or defined groups of products are involved;
(b) employing its plants to the maximum benefit of the Corporation as a whole;
(c) planning its capital investment programme.

11.   With these broad considerations as a basis, a number of conditions for an effective product Division organization have been established. Each product Division should as far as possible be an identifiable and complete business engaged in making and selling only its own separately defined products. Ideally, each Division should be so constituted that the product range manufactured by works allocated to it does not overlap that of any other Division. This would resolve problems of sales co-ordination, plant loading and determination of capital priorities for projects relating to the same product.

[1] Second Report on Organization: paragraph 55.
[2] See paragraph 13.

12. The Corporation has however adopted the firm principle that individual works should remain undivided for operational purposes: thus works should be allocated to Divisions according to their main product and not split between Divisions (except in a few cases where finishing departments within an existing works are in fact physically distinct). This inevitably results in some overlap in manufacture between Divisions but in practice this is limited and possible conflicts can be avoided by procedural rules, as explained in paragraphs 16 and 17 below.

13. Finally, it is of fundamental importance that each product Division should operate as a profit centre. An undertaking can be regarded as a profit centre when the financial results of the totality of its operation can be measured and when its management has control, within defined constraints, over those results. The authority of the management of the product Divisions will, however, have to be constrained for a number of reasons, and in particular:

(a) to meet the statutory obligations of the Corporation;
(b) to secure the greater good of the Corporation as a whole;
(c) to resolve conflicts of interest between Divisions;
(d) to take into account overall regional considerations.

14. The constraints which have to be imposed have been closely defined; some are mentioned in paragraph 35 below. They will normally take the form of reserving to Head Office the control of specified key matters and the formulation of Corporation policies, programmes and procedures.

Organization of Iron and Steel Activities
15. In the light of the foregoing considerations the Corporation has decided that its iron and steel activities should be organized into four product Divisions to be known as:

> General Steels Division
> Special Steels Division
> Strip Mills Division
> Tubes Division.

In broad terms, the General Steels Division will be responsible for ordinary qualities of plate, heavy and light sections, billets, rods and bars and wire; the Special Steels Division for alloy, stainless and other high-quality steels, forgings, castings and specialized engineering products; the Strip Mills Division for wide and narrow strip, sheet and tinplate; and the Tubes Division for tubes and pipes. Appendix A shows in detail the iron and steel products for which each Division will be responsible. The table on page 11 gives key statistics for the Divisions.

16.   Appendix B lists the works allocated to each Division and the maps in the Appendix show the locations of each Division's works. The Divisions have been so constituted that the extent of overlap between them, i.e. production in one Division of products which are the responsibility of another, is small in comparison to the total output of the Corporation. It relates in particular to certain works in the Special Steels Division: in addition to high-quality steels, these works make non-alloy billets, light sections and bars in grades which are the responsibility of the General Steels Division.

17.   To deal with difficulties arising from this limited overlap a closely defined procedure has been laid down. Briefly, each Division will, as a general rule, be responsible for selling all the products falling within its province whether or not those products are entirely produced by works allocated to that Division. Where, however, a particular works makes a product falling outside the province of the Division to which the works is allocated, the Corporation may arrange for the Division containing that works to continue to conduct the sales to a particular home customer if the works has a well-established and mutually satisfactory sales link with that customer.

18.   Within the product Divisions, works are for the most part to be formed for management purposes into units designated as Groups, comprising a number of separate works. As can be seen from Appendix B, the proposed distribution of works among the new Divisions and Groups will, to a considerable extent, preserve the links between works already established under the present organization. From the viewpoint of many individual works, therefore, this redistribution will entail no great change.

19.   Nor will the proposed recasting of the management framework involve any basic change in the Corporation's management principles. In fact, the principles to which the Corporation has adhered from the start – the line and functional system, the delegation of general management responsibilities to levels below the top management of the Corporation, management by exception, and personal accountability – remain intact. They have however been defined in greater detail supported by new procedures. This is indicated in the later section of the Report describing the proposed management structure.

Organization of Activities other than Iron and Steel Manufacture

20.   A subsidiary, but nevertheless important, part of the Corporation's business is concerned with activities other than the manufacture of the main iron and steel products. Two activities – constructional

engineering and chemicals – are distinct and important businesses in their own right, and should be given every opportunity to develop in their own spheres and not be subordinated to steelworks. The Corporation therefore concluded that separate Constructional Engineering and Chemicals Divisions should be formed. The Minister gave his consent to this, under section 7(3) of the Iron and Steel Act, 1967, in July 1969. Key statistics for these two Divisions are included in the table on page 11; their products are listed in Appendix C, and the works which will be included in the Divisions are shown in Appendix D. The organization of these two Divisions will incorporate the same general principles and management structures as the main iron and steel making Divisions; they will operate as profit centres and are expected to be fully viable.

21.   The remaining non-iron and steel activities will maintain their association with particular iron and steel works. In these cases arrangements will be made by the Head Office to co-ordinate the policies of different Divisions as they affect the same product or activity, e.g. mining and quarrying. Appendix A shows the principal non-iron and steel products and activities that would fall within each iron and steel product Division.

Location of Divisional Headquarters

22.   In addition to its statutory duty to have regard to the desirability of distributing its major commercial and administrative offices throughout Great Britain, the Corporation considered a variety of management factors in determining the location of Divisional headquarters.

23.   The most important criteria are the existence of a nucleus of senior management expertise in the area; the availability of staff and housing; local amenities including social and educational facilities; good transport and other communications with works in the Division and with Head Office; and proximity to main centres of administration and commerce generally. On the basis of these considerations the following locations have been chosen for the headquarters of the six product Divisions, after considering several alternatives:

General Steels Division	Glasgow
Special Steels Division	Sheffield
Strip Mills Division	Cardiff
Tubes Division	Corby
Constructional Engineering Division	Bedford
Chemicals Division	Staveley

24.   For the General Steels Division there will also be a substantial office on Teesside.

MANAGEMENT STRUCTURE

25.   Subject to the statutory provisions of the Iron and Steel Acts, 1967 and 1969, the Board is the ultimate in the Corporation. The Members of the Board, appointed by the Minister after consultation with the Chairman, are collectively responsible under the legislation for the conduct of the activities under the control of the Corporation. It follows that the Board's basic rate is to ensure that the Corporation complies with the requirements of the Acts; to decide the objectives of the Corporation as a whole; to determine the strategies and policies that the Corporation should follow to achieve its objectives; and to see that the strategies and policies are pursued and the objectives achieved.

26.   This role involves the performance of a number of specific tasks by the Board itself, e.g. the setting of financial, commercial, output and technical goals; the review and approval of plans needed to implement its strategies; decisions, subject to any statutory provisions, on entry into new fields, at home and abroad, in which the Corporation can operate with advantage; the review of overall operating plans and results; the approval of major capital investment schemes; the approval of senior appointments; and keeping under review the general policies governing conditions of employment. The Board will also pay particular attention to regional considerations. In advising the Board on the formulation of particular strategies the Chairman will be assisted by a Corporate Strategy unit.

27.   The Chairman of the Board has, in addition to his role as Chairman, a distinct function as Chief Executive of the Corporation. The Board has delegated to the Chairman as Chief Executive defined responsibilities and authorities. In this capacity he is responsible for directing the Corporation's activities within the limits of the policies decided by the Board, and has authority over the entire executive organization of the Corporation. He will have reporting directly to him the Deputy Chairmen, the Managing Directors of the product Divisions and the Managing Directors of six Head Office functional Divisions:

Administration	Operations and Supplies
Commercial	Personnel and Social Policy
Finance	Technical.

This is shown in the organization chart on page 20 which also indicates the Departments of which each functional Division will be comprised.

28.   The Deputy Chairmen, appointed by the Minister after consultation with the Chairman, will not be given executive responsibilities for particular product Divisions or functional Divisions. With a view to promoting the integration of the various functions and product Divisions,

the Chief Executive will delegate to the Deputy Chairmen areas of responsibility that will relate to different aspects of the Corporation's overall activities, each of which embraces several functions and product Divisions. As the chart indicates, one Deputy Chairman will supervise the preparation and monitoring of the Annual Operating Plans of the various parts of the Corporation, and this will require him to be apprised of all aspects of the running of the business of the Corporation within its current pattern. Another Deputy Chairman will be concerned with the Corporation's future pattern of activities, in the broadest sense, and this too will involve all aspects of the Corporation's business. A third Deputy Chairman will be concerned with all international aspects of the Corporation's activities and also with its relations with the United Kingdom government; this again will cover a very wide range of the Corporation's affairs.

29.   Some of the functional Managing Directors may be members of the Corporation's Board, but their roles as Board members, sharing collective responsibility for the Board's decisions, and as functional Managing Directors responsible to the Chief Executive for the activities of their Divisions, are quite distinct. The Divisional Managing Directors, whose undivided attention and effort will be directed towards running their own Divisions efficiently and profitably, would not be members of the Corporation's Board.

30.   The Chief Executive will, however, have an Advisory Committee in which all the Managing Directors, line and functional, will participate, and this will assist his overall control of the Corporation's activities.

31.   The line and functional organization of management will extend throughout the Corporation. The channel of command (or line authority) will be from the Chief Executive through the Divisional Managing Directors to the Directors of Groups or works. At each level similar functions to those listed for Head Office in paragraph 27 will be established, although at some levels more than one functional responsibility may be combined in a single appointment. The heads of these functional departments will be responsible to the appropriate line executive: for example, the Divisional functional Directors will be responsible to the Divisional Managing Directors and the functional Managing Directors at Head Office will be responsible to the Chief Executive.

32.   Managing Directors in charge of functions at Head Office will advise on and recommend policies, programmes and procedures on all matters relating to their functions. In practice they will also exercise, in specific and precisely defined fields, executive responsibilities delegated to them by the Chief Executive – for example the responsibility to control[1] and co-ordinate certain matters on a unified Corporation basis,

[1] For definition of certain of the terms used in this description of the management structure, see Appendix E.

as explained in paragraph 35 below. They will also ensure, through a system of monitoring and consultation, the implementation throughout the Corporation of the policies, programmes and procedures, when approved by the Corporation. Steps will be taken to strengthen in particular the present arrangements for monitoring.

33. The same principles will apply to the role of the functional Directors at Divisional level, but these Directors will be responsible in addition for arranging the necessary flow of information to the functional Divisions at Head Office. These principles will also hold good for functional managers at lower levels.

34. It follows from the above that, within a particular function, a functional manager will not have line authority over functional managers at subordinate management units, except as agreed by the line management of these units.

35. The decision that the product Divisions should operate as profit centres, subject to certain constraints, has been noted in paragraph 13 above. The operation of these constraints will mean that a number of important matters have to be reserved to Head Office either because they fall within the statutory responsibility of the Board itself or because unified control or co-ordination, or the provision of a central service, is in the overall interests of the Corporation. These matters will include, among others, finance (for example the development of standard costing systems, the control of capital expenditure and the financial assessment of plans and capital expenditure proposals, the co-ordination and financial monitoring of annual operating plans, banking, and taxation); development planning; raw materials procurement policy; the acquisition and disposal of interests; the overall determination of personnel and social policy, including industrial relations policy, management development, salary structure and pensions; regional policy, as described later in this Report; overseas interests; and the overall determination of commercial policy, including control of the Corporation's marketing policy and its annual sales plan, and the determination of prices and sales policy in relation to both home and export markets. The above is by no means an exhaustive list but illustrates the wide range of matters that must be controlled or co-ordinated by the Head Office. In any instances of doubt as to where the interest of the Corporation lies, Head Office will, after consultation with the product Divisions concerned, make the final decision.

36. Certain central services will also continue to be provided by Head Office, including legal services, central purchasing of some materials, economic forecasting and other economics services, and certain management services. Research will be conducted both centrally and by the product Divisions and the arrangements are described in Appendix F.

37. The redefinition of the Head Office's responsibilities in relation

to those of the product Divisions will require the strengthening of certain functions at Head Office level, including the creation of new Departments dealing with Operational Standards and Efficiency, Engineering, and Management Services.

38. The respective responsibilities of all managers at Head Office, the Divisions and the Groups of works are being fully and precisely defined as an essential means of ensuring the efficient operation of the management system, and management job descriptions in considerable detail are currently being prepared for each individual concerned.

Management of the Divisions

39. Each Divisional Managing Director will have directly responsible to him the line Directors of Groups of works, the number of which varies according to the size and nature of the particular Division (see Appendices B and D). He will also have reporting to him functional Directors with responsibilities relating to those of their counterparts at Head Office.

40. The Divisional Managing Director will be personally responsible to the Chief Executive of the Corporation for the running of his Division. He will be assisted and advised by a Divisional Board which will consist of the Divisional line and functional Directors, and also part-time, non-executive, Directors including both employee Directors and other persons experienced in such fields as local affairs, education, industry and commerce. The progress of the employee Director scheme, introduced by the Corporation in 1968, is being carefully assessed but the Corporation is confident that the useful role which employee and other non-executive Directors have played, as members of the Boards of the present Groups, can be fully maintained and developed in the new system of organization.

41. The Corporation attaches great importance to the provision of satisfactory opportunities and incentives for its managers and to the development of managerial expertise. The system of product Divisions, with the line and functional organization of management, will continue to place a firm emphasis on individual responsibility, give considerable scope to individual initiative and discretion and provide a succession of levels of responsibility through which managerial experience can be progressively broadened. The Corporation also believes that under the product Division system the incentives for works managements to increase efficiency by reducing costs and improving quality will be as great as hitherto.

Relations with Employees

42. One of the Corporation's main objectives is to ensure the

socially responsible and efficient use of human resources. The new system of organization is designed among other things to further the rationalization of the Corporation's production facilities but the Corporation is determined that the implications of these measures for employees will, as in the past, receive the closest consideration. This will be facilitated by the opportunities which the system presents for strengthening further the role of the Personnel and Social Policy function, including industrial relations, at Divisional and works level. The Head Office will continue to have responsibility for developing and formulating the personnel and social policies of the Corporation as a whole and, when they have been approved by the Board, of monitoring their implementation throughout the organization. But this by no means excludes the initiation of policy by the product Divisions for discussion with and approval by Head Office.

43. A new Social Policy Department at Head Office, responsible for developing policy to meet the problems arising from changes within the industry, will also help to minimize the impact of redeployment and redundancy and help to make alternative jobs available, particularly in isolated communities. This Department will be directly responsible to the Managing Director for Personnel and Social Policy. Individuals within the Personnel and Social Policy function in Divisions will also have specific responsibility for social policy.

44. Higher productivity is crucial to the Corporation's ability to compete internationally. In this context, it is relevant to recall that the Corporation's policy is to encourage productivity bargaining at plant level. This is an area, as with industrial relations generally, where monitoring performance at works is of particular importance and under the new system of organization the monitoring procedures at both Head Office and product Division level will, if necessary, be improved.

Implications for Customers

45. The Corporation is well aware of the overriding need to satisfy its customers. There is no market in which it can ignore competition: for a large number of its products it is by no means the sole United Kingdom manufacturer and in all fields it must face growing competition from imports or from alternative materials. The Corporation nevertheless understands the apprehension felt by some customers that more rationalization might mean less responsiveness to individual customer's requirements.

46. In drawing up its organization proposals, the Corporation has endeavoured to meet various points raised by the Iron and Steel Consumers' Council, mainly in connection with the handling of home sales under the new system of organization. A high proportion of the

Corporation's sales already flow in well-established channels, which will continue to suit both the customer and the Corporation. It is not the intention that the new system of organization should affect these mutually beneficial flows of trade, but in some instances sales by more than one Corporation works can be brought together to give a better service to customers and improvements of this kind can be affected more readily with a product Division organization. Elsewhere, the rationalization of the Corporation's assets may involve changes in the pattern of supply which are desirable from the Corporation's point of view and will yield substantial economies. In these cases, the Corporation will seek the closest consultation with its customers before any proposed changes are put into effect.

47. In short, the Corporation intends that the rationalization of sales and of distribution of orders among its works, which the new system will facilitate should result in an increasingly efficient service to its customers.

PART III – REGIONAL CONSIDERATIONS

48. The maps and lists in Appendix B show the locations of the iron and steelworks of the Corporation and indicate the product Divisions into which each will fall. In most steelmaking areas, including Scotland and Wales, there will be works of more than one product Division. In all such areas it will be necessary to provide, in the context both of their present operations and their future plans, for consultation between the Divisions and also for some common services where justified. Common services could include, for example, certain education and training facilities; accident prevention, health and welfare; recruitment; engineering services; and supply and transport requirements.

49. In addition to these internal matters, provision will be made to continue external liaison and consultation with representative bodies in the regions, including the Regional Economic Planning Councils and Local Authorities. The Corporation will continue to explain to local opinion its plans and policies, in advance of their implementation, and endeavour to secure understanding and acceptance of them within the region concerned. In particular arrangements will be instituted to ensure that the effects of the operations and plans of different product Divisions on the employment, amenities and social capital of an individual region are co-ordinated and can be discussed with outside interests by representatives able to speak for the Corporation as a whole. This will be facilitated by the responsibilities of the new Social Policy function[1] and also by the inclusion of part-time Directors, with local

---

[1] See paragraph 43.

experience and standing, in the Divisional Boards described in paragraph 40.

50. In the Second Report the Corporation affirmed its recognition of the importance of the steel industry to the economies of Scotland and Wales and said that arrangements would be made to ensure that specific attention was given to Scottish, Welsh and regional interests.[1] The Corporation will take steps, through appropriate appointments at senior level and the allocation of specific responsibilities, to secure that it is fully advised on the likely impact on any region of its decisions, particularly those in the planning field. Responsibilities for advising on Scottish and Welsh interests, and for co-ordinating its relations with representative bodies in Scotland and Wales, will be specifically included in the duties undertaken by two Members of the Board. In this capacity these Board Members would not have executive authority over staff in the Head Office or the product Divisions.

PART IV – CONCLUSIONS

51. This Report ends by summarizing the main features of the organization which the Corporation has concluded should be introduced:

(a) To give the Corporation more effective means of rationalizing sales, using its plant to the maximum overall benefit and planning its investment programme, a system of product Divisions should be established in place of the existing Group structure. The new organization as a whole would take effect from 29 March 1970.

(b) This system should comprise four iron and steelmaking Divisions, and two Divisions covering Constructional Engineering and Chemicals. The formation of the two latter Divisions has received the Minister's consent.

(c) The line and functional organization of management should continue to obtain throughout the Corporation.

(d) Each product Division should operate as a profit centre under a Divisional Managing Director responsible to the Chairman as Chief Executive of the Corporation.

(e) The authority of the management of each product Division will, however, have to be constrained to the extent necessary to enable the Corporation to fulfil its responsibilities and to act as a single, commercially successful, business in the competitive and international market in which it must operate. It will accordingly be necessary to reserve to the Head Office responsibility for specified

---

[1] Second Report on Organization: paragraph 56.

key matters, including finance; development planning; raw materials procurement policy; the acquisition and disposal of interests; the overall determination of personnel and social policy and of commercial policy; regional policy; and overseas interests.

(f) The respective responsibilities of management at Head Office, the Divisions and below should be fully and precisely defined.

(g) Organisational arrangements should be made to ensure that the regional implications of the activities and plans of different product Divisions are specifically considered.

52. The Corporation recognizes that there has been a transitional period of disturbance and uncertainty since it was established in 1967. During these initial years it has been welding the previously independent companies into one business and has been gaining the experience to guide it to the best form of organization for the longer term. A period of consolidation is now essential.

32. SALARIES OF BOARD MEMBERS[1]

75. In this chapter we go on to examine the second main question referred to us: this was to make recommendations on the appropriate range of remuneration at senior managerial and Board levels in nationalized industries. The answer requires the application of the principles which we indicated in the previous chapter should in our view apply to top salaries generally. Those principles rested primarily on developing a structure which, above all, rewards the assumption of greater responsibility and individual performance within the job. . . .

The top executives in the nationalized industries who are directly affected by the terms of this reference, as we have interpreted them, number only a few hundreds and although there may be some other consequential adjustments which will flow from the recommendations which we make in this chapter, their effect should not be extensive.

77. It appears to be the case throughout the public sector that at the lower managerial levels salary structures are such that the steps correspond to relative increases in the 'size' of job. But invariably, within every nationalized industry where we have carried out detailed investigations, at some point higher up in the structure a fundamental change occurs. Our evidence shows that in some cases this change is quite dramatic, and the pay differentials between different levels of management,

---

[1] From National Board for Prices and Incomes, report no. 107, *Top Salaries in the Private Sector and Nationalized Industries*, March 1969, Cmnd. 3970, pages 22–31, paras. 75–105. Reprinted with permission of the Controller of Her Majesty's Stationery Office.

which lower down in the range clearly differentiate between degrees of responsibility, suddenly become very much compressed.

78.   One way to illustrate this is by constructing a 'salary line' to show the relationship between size of job and pay level in a nationalized industry. Using the evaluation of a representative sample of jobs and the corresponding pay in four nationalized industries which was carried out for us, all the resulting measurements can be entered on a chart, and it is then found that a characteristic pattern emerges in the form of a sharp break between senior and middle management . . . in each industry studied pay differentials for senior staff are significantly different from those which apply lower down in the structure.

79.   Not only are differentials compressed at the top, but in some cases they become negative – that is to say, a Board member may be paid less than a manager not on the Board. As an example, many of the chief officers below Board level in the two largest industries we investigated, the National Coal Board and British Rail, are paid salaries of £7,500 or £8,000 a year, while Board members themselves have a pay range starting at £7,000. In the gas and electricity supply industries, chief officers of Area Boards, who are not themselves Board members are paid salaries close to that of the Deputy Chairman. In both these cases promotion to the Board to which all these chief officers are responsible cannot be adequately rewarded. We were told of an instance where an area official refused appointment to a deputy chairmanship in another area because the salary difference of £500 a year provided an inadequate incentive to make the necessary move. In the airlines the staff supervising the work of pilots are paid salaries which, in order to maintain a reasonable lead over those of senior captains, must be within the Board members' range. The Atomic Energy Authority, a body which we ourselves did not study in detail, but from which we received evidence, told us that, with Board members receiving £8,000 a year on average, senior management salaries must be fitted into a band between £5,000 and £7,500, which is inadequate for recognizing the number of significantly different levels of responsibility. One consequence of such extreme compression is that it complicates the organization of upper levels of responsibility and of chains of command: the grading of pay bears no relationship to the grading of responsibility.

80.   A second consequence, possibly even more important, is that the existing structure minimizes or even excludes altogether the possibility of using salaries to reward performance. If, as can be the case, the difference in pay between two grades is not much above 5 per cent then there is little scope for setting targets for an executive, or in assessing his performance with a view to some tangible recognition of successful achievement.

81.   A third difficulty arising from the present salary structure concerns recruitment from outside. To a very large extent the nationalized industries, like any other enterprise, rely on filling their senior jobs by promotion from within. The average main Board member or senior executive has served twenty-four and twenty-six years respectively in his industry. But there must be some recruiting from outside, and our evidence points to great difficulties in attracting people of suitable calibre from outside the industry. It is not easy to cite the cases on which this view is based, except in general terms, because to do otherwise would be to violate the confidentiality of the evidence we received. But it can be said that from several of the industries, and all the Departments making appointments to them, we had reports of difficulties in finding suitable people or of refusals by those to whom vacancies were offered on the existing terms. We would not contend that pay is the sole deterrent to recruitment from outside. But it is clear that existing problems of recruitment are such that they must leave considerable doubt about the future prospects in a group of industries in which 70 per cent of Board members and 60 per cent of senior executives are over the age of 55.

82.   To overcome these three difficulties – that of promoting, that of relating reward to performance, and that of recruiting from outside – it follows that the differentials both below the Board and on the Board have to be widened. It does not follow that each step in the salary scale should be equal, still less that the steps should, as often they do in private industry, become proportionately larger as the top is approached. It is true that we have come across cases in the private sector where pay does not always reflect rank, a superior being paid sometimes less than his subordinate. The difference between the private and public sectors, however, is that in the former such cases are infrequent, while in the latter they are very frequent. It may conceivably be that this difference stems in part from the different historical origins of the two sectors. The modern corporation is the lineal descendant of the family concern, the heads of which enjoyed profits; extremely steep increments at the top of the salary structure may reflect this evolution. The public undertaking, on the other hand, reflects the traditional characteristics of the public service, one of which is that financial rewards at the top are not outstandingly high; this is true, for example, of the Civil Service and the Armed Forces.

83.   It certainly is not self-evident that pay in the public sector should entirely match whatever is paid in the private sector. No system of evaluation can provide a fully objective comparison of jobs as between the public and private sectors; subjective judgement must play a large role. One individual might, for example, contend that, because size is larger, responsibility is larger in the public than in the private sector;

another might contend that, since responsibilities in the public sector are shared with Ministers, they are smaller than in the private sector. We cannot rest pay on any such uncertain basis of job comparisons. In any case, save in the most exceptional circumstances when it is considered essential to recruit a particular individual, any attempt in the public sector to match pay in the private sector might push up pay still further in the latter, and thus magnify the problems of the public sector at a later date.

84. The reference requires us to make recommendations about the pay of Chairmen, Deputy Chairmen and Board members. We do not attempt to lay down in detail what the salary structure below Board level should be. That is a job for management. Our recommendations at the Board level are intended to provide the necessary headroom to enable the Board in each case to raise the salary structure below where this is necessary, and to introduce a system of ranges for individuals. These ranges should be used to allow the pay of each manager to be linked with his achievements. The normal expectation should be a progression to the mid-point of the individual's salary range, provided that performance is fully up to the expected standard; progress beyond that point should be exceptional and should recognize outstanding performance. In no case should the progression depend on age or length of service.

85. In enabling each Board to make these changes, we must however again draw attention to the evidence referred to in paragraph 78 above. It follows from the unevenness of the structure demonstrated in our enquiries that the need for adjustment is similarly uneven. In each of the cases illustrated, pay differentials are compressed only at the top end of the scale, and the need for major revisions below Board level is therefore confined to the salaries of a relatively small number of senior executives. It is for each Board to identify the point in its own salary structure at which pay differentials show the change we have described. Some Boards have told us that it broadly coincides with (though it is not necessarily caused by) the limit of negotiated pay scales. It will be in keeping with the spirit of our proposals if, in revising the salaries of posts below Board level, the performance of the individuals holding those posts is brought under review and the level at which their salaries are fixed is influenced accordingly. Where major upward adjustments are required, it would be in keeping with our recommendations for Board levels that these should be staged.

86. The salaries which we recommend for Board members also provide for a range, and we consider that this range should be used in the way we have described above – that is, to reward performance. As things are at present there would appear to be a range, but what little

movement there is through the range is dependent on length of service rather than performance. Decisions about the pay of Board members are statutorily made by Ministers, but we recommend that, in fixing Board members' salaries within their ranges of pay so as to recognize performance, it should be the normal practice for Ministers to be guided by the advice of the Chairmen of the Boards concerned, which they might formulate in consultation with the Deputy Chairmen and, where appropriate, part-time members of the Boards.

87. Not all nationalized industries are equal. We have largely followed present practice in dividing the Boards included in our review into three categories, corresponding broadly with the size of the undertakings; the measurement of individual jobs which was carried out for us in the public sector suggests a correlation between size of undertaking and degree of responsibility, though we would not contend that size of undertaking is the sole indicator of responsibility. Our grouping is as follows:

> Group A – The National Coal Board, British Rail and the Electricity and Gas Councils.
>
> Group B – The two nationalized airlines, the Central Electricity Generating Board, the London Transport Board (so long as it retains its present status as a nationalized industry) and the two main successor organizations of the Transport Holding company, namely the National Freight Corporation and the National Bus Company.
>
> Group C – The Area Electricity and Gas Boards and the two Scottish Electricity Boards.

In Group A the National Coal Board and British Rail are far larger than the other industries in the list, if the value of assets, size of labour force and turnover are taken into account. The British Steel Corporation would also fall into this group for the same reason, but it is not governed by our immediate recommendations, since salaries have only recently been set for it and no question of a general increase in salaries at the top should arise in the case of the Steel Corporation until they are on the same footing as the other major nationalized industries. We would expect the Post Office also to be placed in this group when it becomes a public corporation. The Electricity and Gas Councils also qualify on grounds of size. It has, however, been argued that in their case the devolution of responsibility to Area Boards reduces the task of the central Board, which in electricity supply is primarily a co-ordinating body, though the Gas Council, set up for a similar purpose, is now also responsible for the sale of natural gas. In both cases we consider inclusion in Group A justified by the Chairmen's special position at the head of a Board which includes all the Area Chairmen among its members and by prospective changes in the organization of the industries. The Chairman of the CEGB is also a member of the Electricity Council. The CEGB would qualify for inclusion in Group A in terms of the size of its assets and turnover. On the other hand it is the sole supplier of a single product which it does not have to market. We think its inclusion in Group B appropriate.

88.   BOAC, which is included in Group B, now has a part-time Chairman, and we suggest that his salary should be determined by reference to the proportion of his time given to the Corporation. Similarly, the Chairman of the National Bus Company, which is included in this group, has a part-time appointment; we consider that the question of his remuneration should be decided in the same way.

89.   The following paragraphs show the levels of pay we recommend. They are intended to make good the undue compression of differentials which now occurs at the top and which makes salary policy an ineffective instrument of management. Whether they will succeed in their purpose time alone can tell, and at an appropriate moment a further review will be required. Nor do we recommend that the new levels be attained in one jump. The White Paper states that 'large increases . . . may . . . occur where a much longer interval than twelve months has elapsed since the previous increase or improvement. The need to consider staging in such cases will be particularly important now that the majority of workers will be able to receive only limited increases'. In the present case, where salaries are reviewed rarely and, at Board level, have not been materially altered since 1964, the application of the quoted paragraph of the White Paper (paragraph 44) would appear inescapable. Our detailed recommendations on staging are given in paragraphs 93 to 95 below. We have considered whether, like other Board members, Chairmen and Deputy Chairmen of the main Boards should be given a personal range. Advice to the Minister on where a Chairman should be placed within the range might then rest on analogy with common practice in the private sector, with the part-time members. This would place the latter in a difficult position. We have therefore decided in favour of a single figure for Chairmen and Deputy Chairmen of the main Boards.

90. We recommend the following:

    For Group A Boards:
        Chairman: £20,000
        Deputy Chairman: £16,000
    For Group B Boards:
        Chairman: £17,000
        Deputy Chairman: £13,500 (or exceptionally up to
                           £15,000 – see para. 91 below).

91. For Board members in Groups A and B we recommend the introduction of personal pay ranges, depending on the content and responsibility of each individual job. All the ranges should be contained between the lower and upper limits of £8,000 and £15,000 a year. Each Board member's personal range should allow for a variation of plus or minus about twenty per cent about its midpoint, and as we have explained in paragraph 84 above, progression above the midpoint should be exceptional. We would expect that in Group A Boards the midpoint of members' scales would usually be higher than in Group B Boards; we suggest that the Group A ranges should centre on £12,500 as the most common midpoint, while in Group B Boards the equivalent would be £10,000. But in both cases there will be jobs whose greater or lesser content will make it desirable to use a personal range above or below the normal. If, because of exceptionally heavy responsibility, it is decided to raise the salary of a member of a Group B Board to £13,500 or more, we would expect the same grounds to justify a correspondingly higher salary for the Deputy Chairman if the Board has a full-time appointment at that level.

92. So far as Group C Boards are concerned, the position would be as follows. The Chairmen of the electricity and gas Area Boards, who are also members of Group A Boards, would be paid accordingly, i.e. on a personal range within £8,000–£15,000 limits. The responsibilities of the Chairmen of the Scottish Electricity Boards are wider and include generating as well as selling electricity. We recommend that our proposals for Area Board Chairmen should apply; but it might well be thought appropriate for the Secretary of State for Scotland, who makes these appointments, to make use of the higher end of the recommended range, and in this way to recognize the special responsibilities involved. The following structure for the remaining members of Group C Boards would be appropriate:

Deputy Chairmen: £7,500–£9,500
Other Board Members: £6,000–£8,000.

It is possible that the Scottish Transport Group, which has just been set up to take over the Scottish interests of the Transport Holding Company, should also be in Group C, but we have insufficient information on which to base a firm recommendation.

93. The White Paper permits an exception to the ceiling of $3\frac{1}{2}$ per cent on pay increases for 'Major re-organizations of wage and salary structures which can be justified on productivity and efficiency grounds'. Equally, however, as already indicated, the White Paper prescribes the staging of large increases even when justified – e.g. because the last increase took place some considerable time ago – and in this case we

accordingly recommend that there should be three stages. The first should be put into effect as from the beginning of April this year, and subject to any alterations which further White Papers on the productivity prices and incomes policy make make necessary, should be followed by two further stages at twelve month intervals. The timing of stages 2 and 3 would need to be looked at again should the government substantially modify the present ceiling and the justification for exceptions from it....

104. The proposals we have outlined make possible in the national-ized industries a salary structure which is internally consistent and gives scope for high performance to be recognized. The levels of pay sugges-ted fall below the average level of salaries paid in the private sector. But they appear to be in keeping with the views of the Select Committee on Nationalized Industries, which stated that, while 'the proper rate for the job must be significantly higher than that which is now generally paid', it did not believe 'that the salaries paid to the full-time Chairmen and members of the Boards should necessarily be at the levels ruling in private industry'.[1] We consider that salary structures based on our recommendations, coupled with more flexible pension arrangements, would in the light of recent experience offer pay high enough to attract younger men of ability and ambition into the public sector and ensure that an adequate supply of able senior managers could be found from within the ranks of the nationalized industries themselves or, if neces-sary, recruited from outside. We also consider that to copy the private sector might push the private sector up further. Time alone, however, can tell whether we are right; hence our statement above that at an appropriate time a further review would be required.

105. It is necessary finally to turn to the question of how this review might take place. The Chairmen of the nationalized industries have indicated that they would consider it appropriate for the matter to be remitted to this Board as a standing reference. We would concur with the view that Ministers should have the help of some outside agency with knowledge and experience of pay problems at different levels and not concerned solely with the members of nationalized Boards.

[1] First Report from the Select Committee on Nationalized Industries (Session 1967/68) vol. I, paragraph 306.

CHAPTER VII

EMPLOYEES AND CONSUMERS

This final chapter is concerned with the labour relations and the consumer relations of the industries; but in this concern it may help reflection on the frontiers and the future.

One of the mainsprings of nationalization in Britain has been the need for reorganization, in the search for industrial efficiency. There is, historically speaking, no doubt about that. There has also been, however, a quest for a reformed style of industrial organization in a political and social sense. In these terms the public corporation can be put alongside not only the joint-stock company, but also the consumer co-operative and the co-partnership firm; and, abroad, the co-determination of West Germany, the workers' control of Yugoslavia, and the centrally-planned enterprises of the U.S.S.R. In looking at relations with employees and with consumers, therefore, it must be borne in mind that in other structures these groups claim sovereign powers.

There has not been much attention, in this search for acceptable structures, to the government department itself in recent years: indeed, the latest moves are away from the central machinery of government. However, one long-surviving but little-noticed example of direct administration of public enterprise lies in the State Management Districts scheme in the liquor trade. Since 1916 three Districts – Carlisle in England, and Gretna and Cromarty in Scotland – have had a publicly owned brewery (in Carlisle) and public houses. These are run by general managers under the direct control of government departments, though there is an advisory council. The arrangements are well described in an article 'State Management of the Liquor Trade' by R. M. Punnett, in *Public Administration*, Summer 1966, for which unfortunately there is not space here.

The search away from direct departmental management has led to some concern with mixed enterprise – where control is shared between the government and private capital – and with government ownership of enterprises registered under the Companies Acts. The public corporation is by definition not a company and does not have any shareholders.

It is entirely misleading in this case to regard the Minister, Parliament, the general public or anyone else as shareholders – their concern with a public corporation does not correspond at all to the rights of shareholders under the Companies Acts. But there is now frequently argument that state-shareholding in firms with regular company structures should be widely practised. The example of Italy is often invoked, and is described in M. V. Posner and S. J. Woolf, *Italian Public Enterprise* (Duckworth, 1967). A Fabian Society pamphlet of 1966, *New Public Enterprise*, by M. Posner and R. Pryke advocated more widespread use of the system in Britain.

Consideration of the structure of enterprise must include the role of the labour force, and the extracts reprinted here are concerned with major developments in labour relations in the existing nationalized industries. There have been, of course, a good many changes, reforms and improvements in the decade, as well as some disputes. In the background there was a persistent search by the government for a national incomes policy. One of the main changes was in the coal industry. In June 1966 the National Coal Board signed a national power-loading agreement with the National Union of Mineworkers, after long negotiations. This substituted a new day-wage system for workers on power-loaded coal faces, for the local and traditional piecework arrangements. These old agreements had often been a source of friction and dispute and, in spite of some problems of adjustment, the Coal Board was able to point to a reduction in the number of disputes in the following years.[1] Nevertheless, the difficulty of maintaining a sufficiently high level of remuneration in general inflationary conditions, under the new agreement, was one of the factors contributing to the national coalminers' strike in the winter of 1972.

Another development of wide interest was the status agreement in the electricity industry, which attempted to raise the social status of staff and to reduce overtime working by introducing a system of annual salaries for industrial staff. This is described in the extract printed taken from a pamphlet by Sir Ronald Edwards. Again, the problems arising from the effect of the agreement on total earnings had repercussions after the end of the period, when there was a work-to-rule of power station workers in the autumn of 1970.

An experiment of a different kind but also of great interest was begun in the steel industry. This was an experiment in that form of participation which involves representation of employees on the Board of Directors. In 1967, by agreement with the Trades Union Congress, workers chosen from lists nominated by trade unions began to serve as

[1] National Coal Board, *Annual Reports* for 1966–67 (page 36) and 1967–68 (page 43) (not reprinted).

part-time members of Group (now Divisional) Boards within the steel industry. The arrangements are described in an article by Ken Jones which forms the next item in the chapter. No final verdict on the success of the scheme was available by 1970.

The next contribution turns from the particulars of events in particular industries to a more general theme. In his Hobhouse Memorial Lecture of 1964 Professor H. R. G. Greaves surveyed the possibilities of democratic participation in public enterprise, and while he stressed that '. . . self-government in relation to nationalized industry does not connote absolute, arbitrary and exclusive authority to a junta of workers to impose their will by force', he found that there was much to be done in this direction.

A final extract concerns the consumer consultative machinery in the industries. Since the object of all productive activity must be the satisfaction of consumers, they can scarcely be of minor importance. However, it has always been assumed that the market relationship provides means whereby the customer can exert his power. In the nationalized industries in Britain arrangements were made for an additional approach, in which articulate discussion, instead of fragmented bargaining, could take place. Nevertheless, the apparatus of committees has not made any great impact, few consumers being even aware of its existence. An extract from a report by the Consumer Council (a Government-financed national body, abolished in 1971) which suggests some improvements is printed here. After the end of the decade, further material on this topic appeared in the report of the SCNI on *Relations with the Public* (H.C. 514 of session 1970–71).

33. THE STATUS AGREEMENT IN ELECTRICITY[1]

SIR RONALD EDWARDS, K.B.E.

The Status Agreement was very much concerned with the means to be adopted to raise the social status of our industrial staff and to eliminate overtime working wherever possible. Before referring to the main course of the negotiations I want, therefore, to say a word about these two related matters.

Social Status
Why did the industry decide that the social status of the industrial staff should be improved? This was not a question of pay rates. There are in fact bigger salary differences between the lowest and highest paid

[1] From Sir Ronald Edwards, *An Experiment in Industrial Relations*, n.d. The Electricity Council, pages 3–21. Reprinted with permission of the author.

managerial staffs in the industry than between the more senior industrial staff and the more junior managerial staff. What the supply industry had in mind was that, in various ways, the so-called manual worker was treated as slightly different from and slightly inferior to his colleagues, clerical, administrative and technical. We regarded this as an anachronism. Many so-called manual jobs carry as great a responsibility as office jobs.

In the generating stations most of the industrial staff work either on plant overhaul and maintenance or on operational duties. The plant operators – particularly at the big modern stations – are in direct control of turbo-alternators, boilers and auxiliary equipment worth many millions. Their jobs are to operate this plant with precision, and thereby ensure the continuity of electricity supply in their own area and possibly distant locations. The senior operators are men with years of experience and are well aware of their responsibilities. Should a senior plant operator of a vast turbo alternator have lower status than a girl operating a comptometer or typewriter?

Similarly with plant overhaul and maintenance, the jobs of the skilled men are to keep the plant in operational condition for as much of the time as possible, and to carry out necessary overhauls and repairs in a way which maintains the right balance between speed and quality of work.

On main transmission and on the distribution networks connecting almost every house, factory and office to the supply system, many men have to work on their own or in small groups with a product which may prove lethal if not properly handled. In these circumstances as much depends on personal responsibility as on direct supervision. Socially it is difficult to justify treating such men differently from the technical staff who supervise them or the clerical and administrative staff in the offices.

So we decided to work towards the introduction of annual salaries for all the industrial staff and to get away from the preoccupation with hourly wage rates. It would not have been a mere semantic flight to turn a wage based on hours into an annual salary even if the annual take-home pay had remained the same under the Agreement, which it did not. The annual salary would bring with it the right to a guaranteed income, the right which had for many years been enjoyed by the rest of the staff, of not inevitably having to take a cut in income every time a few hours were taken off – with the supervisor's approval – to cope with a critical domestic problem, to attend a family funeral or to have an interview with a child's headmaster. In these respects our industrial staff were to be treated in the same way as the rest of the staff. We also decided to bring the holiday and sick pay schemes more closely into line with those enjoyed by other staff. Pension schemes were already similar.

One criticism I have heard is that, by calling a labourer a member of the 'staff', by giving him an annual salary and raising his fringe benefits, we would not make him 'socially' different from any other labourer elsewhere. It was suggested that we might have done as some other industries have done; seek to move the dividing line between manual workers and staff down gradually, bringing men on to the staff after they had reached certain levels of responsibility and/or been with the industry for a certain period. We did consider this, but decided against it on the grounds that the dividing line would be extraordinarily difficult to draw in any meaningful way and would cause hard feelings not justified by the balance of gain.

The gap in fringe benefits was to be reduced, not completely closed. In the event the maximum holiday entitlements of the industrial staff are not so large as for most non-industrial staff and the normal working week, which is now 40 hours, is still two hours longer.

The Problems of Overtime

From nationalization in April 1948, down to April 1964, average weekly hours worked by the industry's adult male industrial staff were almost always above the corresponding figure for British industry as a whole and, indeed, in the three years immediately before the Status Agreement was introduced, the figure of average weekly hours worked was always between 49 and 50 hours a week, compared with 47 to 48 hours a week in industry generally. Many men in the industry were, in fact, working 60 hours or more, week in week out. There were many aspects of this practice of heavy overtime that were unsatisfactory. Although I am not particularly impressed with claims for shorter hours in most jobs on health grounds, it is certainly true that, in some cases, the length of actual working hours of some of our men must have risked ill-effects. It is not easy to correlate long hours of overtime with illness and sick-leave but many observers would probably support the view that there has been some association.

More important, the practice and expectation of long, regular overtime results in many bad working practices. Jobs begun in normal hours are spun out to be completed on overtime. Artificial barriers – lines of demarcation – are constructed between occupations so as to provide work for colleagues in other trades. Sickness absence may be increased so that men have to be brought in at premium rates to fill the gaps. Men try to get overtime shared equally among members of a work group irrespective of job needs and individual skills. Men increase their financial commitments in times of heavy overtime and then exert great pressure to maintain this level of overtime in order to meet their financial obligations. Supervisors are under pressure to give way for the sake of maintaining a reasonably happy ship, and also there is the steady temptation to become casual about the use of labour, to lose the habit of counting the cost of extending the working week, and to stop asking whether it is really necessary. Indeed, there is evidence that managers and supervisors, particularly in areas where the demand for labour was strong, had to face irresistible pressures for overtime. It is fair to say in justification of them and of our industrial employees that I do not, for a moment, believe their behaviour was any worse or indeed any different from that of those in other industries. Moreover, the Court of Inquiry[1] which, in April 1964, investigated the breakdown of negotiations in the industry (which I refer to later) stated that it was only overtime that maintained a competitive level of earnings in our industry at that time.

It would be arrant nonsense, however, to suggest that all the overtime in the industry was unnecessary and that it was worked entirely to boost earnings. Some overtime work was inevitable: the fact is that much plant maintenance can only or can most economically be done outside normal Monday to Friday working hours, mainly at week-ends. The then National Agreement provided for day workers to complete their normal 42 weekly working hours (40 now) roughly between 7.30 a.m. and 4.30 p.m. between Monday and Friday. Since week-end work was essential and some evening work too, day workers had to undertake overtime. Similarly with men engaged on consumer services and engineering projects on the distribution network, jobs cannot be organized exactly and economically to fit the pattern 7.30 a.m. to 4.30 p.m. between Monday to Friday. What needed to be done, what could be done, and what we have aimed to do in the Agreement, was to create terms and conditions of employment for different groups of individuals matching as closely as practicable the type of work that they were called upon to do in an industry that works 365 days a year, 24 hours a day.

An Outline of the Negotiations

The most convenient starting point is a memorandum of 4 October 1962, in which the Boards outlined their approach on productivity and status to the trade unions. The section on status reads as follows.

> Boards' Members' approach to the question of the status of manual workers has been prompted by the fact that, while the basic hourly rates of pay compare reasonably with those in other industries, the earnings of manual workers in electricity supply are dependent to a

---

[1] Cmnd. 2361.

considerable degree on premium payments for week-end and over-time working. They have, therefore, considered the possibility of eliminating the bulk of overtime and consolidating earnings into an annual salary based on a normal working week of 42 hours.

Boards' Members recognize that this approach has attractions to all if, without inflating labour costs, and without seriously affecting earnings, the overtime hours can be significantly reduced. They are also aware that it has many inherent difficulties of which the most obvious is that similar grades of employees are at the moment receiving different weekly earnings and working different hours. These differences are so marked that the simple solution of rewarding all at one salary per grade appears to be impracticable.

Some of the other difficulties inherent in this approach might be reduced by:

(i) A staggered five-day week to include Sunday and Saturday working.
(ii) Increased shift working.
(iii) Greater mobility through co-operative maintenance and mobile maintenance teams.
(iv) Acceptance of comprehensive planning, operational research and method study leading to improved utilization of labour.

This is a matter which requires detailed investigation and study which the Boards' Members are ready to undertake with the co-operation of the trade unions and in the belief that if an acceptable solution can be found it will prove to be an important contribution to improving the status of the industrial workers.

The next few months were occupied with the negotiation of a three-year wage agreement and productivity bonus. It was not until April 1963, that a Special (Status) Sub-Committee of the National Joint Industrial Council met to examine, in detail, means of improving the status of industrial staff. Between April and November 1963, they met on nine occasions. The negotiations started with goodwill on both sides, but they ran into increasing difficulty and finally broke down early in 1964. The prospect of serious industrial trouble was averted only by the establishment in April 1964, by the Minister of Labour, of a Court of Inquiry into the dispute under the chairmanship of Sir Colin Pearson. The Report of the Court[1] was published in May 1964. It gives a full account of the negotiations and of the points of view of both sides, together with recommendations on how the immediate problems might be overcome.

---

[1] Cmnd. 2361.

The industry takes the view that any serious dispute affecting the operation of so vital a service as electricity supply which cannot be settled within its own machinery must, in the end, be determined by some form of arbitration or third party review, rather than by resort to force. We therefore made it clear in advance that we sought to honour in both the letter and the spirit the conclusions of the Court. The Court made criticisms, from which neither side escaped, and offered advice on how the negotiations might be resumed. Subsequently the two sides came together again and rapid progress towards an agreement was achieved. The terms of that agreement – which the Court urged should be negotiated 'in stages or phases' – were influenced by the findings of the Court. In particular, the boards, in the light of the Court's report, had to face up to a higher cost than they had envisaged when they began negotiations. I make this point without recrimination and merely because it is relevant when attempting an appraisal of the results of the Agreement.

While the difficulties of the negotiations in their early stages, are well documented, it is not so widely appreciated that, at the beginning of the negotiations and throughout their course, there was full acceptance by the boards and by the trade unions of the aims of the negotiations in principle. The difficulties arose from differences over salary levels and priorities.

THE AGREEMENT IN OPERERATION

. . . Most readers will probably be interested in four aspects of the operation of the Agreement and these are therefore referred to in turn. They are the use of flexible work patterns, employee co-operation, movements in hours of work, rates of pay and earnings, and, finally, changes in manpower.

THE USE OF FLEXIBLE WORK PATTERNS

Stage II of the Agreement, which came into operation from 1 February 1965, improved shift allowances for industrial staff and introduced for dayworkers the staggered work patterns which are described in Appendix III. These patterns of work provide essentially for the normal hours of the work week to be worked at times which fit in with the requirements of the job, while giving employees financial compensation for the disturbance or inconvenience to which this gives rise.

Within the Generating Board the percentage of adult male industrial staff on shift work has increased under the Status Agreement from 40 per cent of the total to 45 per cent (22,902 out of 50,058 in April 1966), over 80 per cent of the shift staff being engaged on continuous three-shift work. In the Area Boards less than 4 per cent of the industrial staff traditionally worked on shift and this percentage has not changed much under the Agreement. But 50 per cent of all Area Board shift workers (1,578 out of 3,147) were in April, 1966, working on the intermediate shift arrangement specifically provided under the Status Agreement. The figures for the Scottish Boards are similar.

The staggered work patterns have proved to be well suited to two sets of conditions: the first where there is a fair amount of regular and predictable work which can only be done out of normal hours or which can be done more economically at that time; and the second where the size of job units is such that the work fits more satisfactorily into days of a different length from those found on normal daywork.

The first of these conditions exists extensively within the Generating Board and by April 1965, just a few months after Stage II was agreed, about 70 per cent of the dayworkers were engaged on staggered work patterns and, by April 1966, about 92 per cent (24,932 out of 27,156). The work pattern most commonly used is the seven-day stagger pattern with week-end work (within the normal 5 day, 40 hour week) occurring on from one week-end in four to three in four. These arrangements are meeting the needs of the Generating Board and the generation sides of the two Scottish Boards.

The two conditions for using stagger work patterns are not so commonly found on the distribution side of the industry and while, since February 1965, there has been a steady increase in their use, only 26.5 per cent (21,434 out of 80,934) of all Area Board day employees were engaged on staggered work patterns by April 1966. Most of these are engaged on the staggered hours pattern of work, which has a particular value in that hours of work can be varied at seven days' notice to meet particular work needs. This staggered hours pattern of work is quite widely used by linesmen, jointers and meter readers and collectors.

Employee Co-operation
The staggered work patterns gave Boards an increased measure of flexibility over the times of the day and week in which they employed their industrial staff. But there was another type of flexibility which was also required in greater measure and that was flexibility in the use of labour skills – inter-occupational flexibility, as it is often called.

Under Stage I of the Agreement the Joint Statement on Employee Co-operation provided specifically for this inter-occupational flexibility. No restrictions were to be placed on the form or extent of employee co-operation so long as the rate for the job was paid and men were not temporarily upgraded to craft duties. Where the definitions of duties of grades of employees, as set out in the NJIC Agreement, appeared to limit co-operation, such definitions should be deemed to be superseded by this co-operation agreement.

The issue of this statement was followed by what was probably the most extensive and detailed exercise in consultation that this industry has undertaken – consultation which began with senior managers and trade union officers, continued down the line and finally involved many hundreds of informal meetings between departmental heads and working groups of employees. At these meetings specific proposals for revising working practices were presented, discussed and, in many cases, agreed.

The results are impossible to measure with precision because conditions and levels of co-operation have always varied considerably from place to place and because many other influences were at work. Lists of improvements in employee co-operation have been provided by local management, but in the end one has to form one's own judgement of their value. The industry has certainly benefited from the use of the co-operation agreement, but the extent has varied considerably in different parts of the industry. There is still room and justification for further improvements under the terms of the co-operation agreement.

Hours, Rates, Earnings

The impact of the Agreement on the industry is nowhere more apparent than in changes in hours worked. One of the aims was 'the elimination of overtime working wherever possible' and the boards, supported by the trade unions, set about working to this end. They were assisted by the co-operation agreement and by January 1965, average weekly hours of adult industrial staff had already begun to fall from the pre-status level – from 49.3 hours in April 1964, to 47.9 in January 1965. Then came Stage II with its provisions for staggered patterns of work and the reduction in hours of work was accelerated. By April 1965, the average weekly hours worked were down to 45.1, by October 1965, to 41.8, and they have remained at about that level ever since. In the course of 18 months or so there had been a reduction in average weekly hours worked of about 15 per cent and the industry, instead of being one of the heaviest overtime industries in this country, was actually working less overtime than all but two out of 130 industries whose hours of work are published in the Ministry of Labour Gazette. As would be expected, some Boards have achieved bigger reductions than others, but the Generating Board and a number of Area Boards have now virtually eliminated the regular use of overtime and employ it for emergency work only.

Salary rates for industrial staff were increased under Stage I as described in Appendix III. They were further increased in February

1965, the last instalment under the terms of the three-year wage agreement negotiated in 1963, and again in February 1966. Before the Status Agreement and since it has been in operation the weekly wage (salary) rates of electricity supply craftsmen and labourers have, like their fringe benefits, always compared favourably with rates prevailing generally in British industry and with rates in industries employing similar skills.

In many industries, however, wage rates are enhanced by bonuses, piece rates and other enhancements of various kinds, so that weekly wage rates are no longer a reliable guide to weekly earnings or take-home pay. The combined effect of Status and other changes (not least the fall in hours) has been substantially to increase the hourly earnings of the industrial staff and more modestly to increase their weekly earnings. Between April 1964, and April 1966, the average hourly earnings of adult male industrial staff in electricity supply increased from 82.6d. to 108.7d. (an increase of 31 per cent) and weekly earnings from 339s. 4d. to 378s. 5d., an increase of 11 per cent. The hourly earnings increased much more than in industry generally, but the weekly earnings by less. Weekly earnings in April 1966, were somewhat below the average for industry generally, but on the other hand electricity supply industrial staff enjoyed shorter hours than most and a higher level of fringe benefits, especially sick pay and pensions.

Manpower and the Growth of the Industry
It would be neat and satisfying if it were possible to eliminate the effect of other changes which have taken place in the industry since July 1964, and present a simple piece of cost/saving arithmetic on the impact of the Agreement in that time. But in fact many unrelated changes have taken place in the last 30 months, not least the continued growth of the industry and the introduction, from July 1965, of the 40-hour week.

In March 1966, there were 155,000 industrial employees in the industry in Great Britain, about 8 per cent more than in March 1964. This annual growth rate of 4 per cent compared with a figure of about 1.5 per cent in the previous ten years.

The increase in industrial staff manpower in the Area Boards in these two years was small, in spite of an annual growth in sales of electricity which averaged 6.7 per cent per annum and a fall of about 6 hours in average weekly hours worked. The heavier growth in manpower took place on the generating side of the industry. Plant capacity in the Generating Board had, in the years before the Status Agreement, been increasing at an annual rate of 1,700 MW, but in the two-year period up to March 1966, the corresponding annual increase was over 2,700 MW. Nearly one-third of the Generating Board's manpower increase arose from the need to man this new capacity and a similar amount from the need to augment shift rotas under the 40-hour week. In this period the average weekly hours worked by the Generating Board's industrial staff fell by over 11 hours or 25 per cent. The experience of the two Scottish Boards was similar.

One complaint that the union's have had from their members is the assertion that this shortening of hours of work has caused the industry to put out to contractors work that would otherwise be done by the industry's own staff. And the contractors, it is argued, pay high bonuses and give long hours of overtime. Certainly it would be idle to deny that it is very uncomfortable to carry through the operation on which we have been engaged in a period of over-full employment, when other employers will give almost any terms in order to keep and get men. Nevertheless, the extent to which the industry was forced to employ contractors because of the operation of the new Agreement has been grossly exaggerated. All cases are looked at with great care and the unions can take complaints to Area Board Chairmen and CEGB Regional Directors. Such problem as there was is now well under control.

THE AGREEMENT IN PERSPECTIVE

The Agreement is complex and could not be expected to bring its full results immediately or even over a period of a few years. In many of its aspects it is quite specific in character, but it also prescribes in more general terms the lines on which the industry might advance in the future.

For these reasons it is simply not possible to attempt any final judgements at this stage. On the other hand, we have a clear obligation to make periodical appraisals on the facts and experience as these accumulate and it is an appraisal of this nature which I now wish to make.

PREVAILING CONDITIONS IN THE INDUSTRY

The terms of the Agreement were much influenced by conditions which prevailed at the time that it was negotiated and of these conditions I would select three which were of special importance.

First, the industry was, in the early sixties, extremely short of generating plant and was also short of network capacity. The priority was therefore that the industry's plant and equipment should be used to the maximum degree possible and in these circumstances overtime had tended to get out of hand and any attempt at reduction without a major agreement might have led to disaffection and loss of men to the extent of jeopardizing the security and adequacy of the system.

Secondly, in the prevailing conditions of a tight labour market, the industry was in a difficult position since (in common with power industries in the rest of the world) it has never offered piece-rates or bonuses which would have enabled it to compete with wage drift generally. Without excessively high hourly wage rates, overtime represented practically the only way in which the industry could match earnings elsewhere.

Thirdly, the industry, as a responsible employer, has always done its best to comply with government incomes policies. This in itself severely limited the scope of experiments in industrial relations and indeed led to some of our most serious disputes with the unions. Against the background of the prevailing incomes policy the Board's members of the NJIC, in negotiations, were attempting to get agreement on major changes in work practices without committing themselves in advance to substantial changes in the industry's labour costs. For a long period the main promise which they were able to make to the trade union side was that the industrial staff would benefit from the Agreement mainly in terms of increased leisure. It became clear however that to have maintained this standpoint to the end would have destroyed the possibility of introducing the scheme. The Pearson Court of Inquiry itself expressed the view that the industry was unrealistic in thinking that the scheme could be put through without some addition to its wages bill, although it was added that, in the long run, the scheme should begin to pay for itself.

Costs and Benefits

We have of course undertaken some studies of the cost of the scheme in the industry so far. In making these studies we have had to identify and measure costs which cannot be attributed to the introduction of the scheme itself. Such costs include (a) the growth of the industry, including labour costs to man the new capacity; (b) the salary increases attributable to the existing three-year salary agreement; and (c) the reduction of the normal work week from 42 to 40 hours in July 1965. This reduction in the length of the normal working week was made at the same time as the Stage II settlement, but it was not part of the status proposals. In any case it is difficult to appraise the economics of the scheme without knowing what would have happened to wages had we not introduced it. Personally I think our labour costs are higher than they would otherwise have been – but not appreciably so. I would not, in any case, want to base my judgements on the value of the scheme on whether or not it has so far added to our labour costs. I would prefer to accept that there has been some additional costs and develop the argument, in which I have some confidence, that those additional costs were worth while, taking the long view. The argument is based on four main propositions.

The first is that, in an industry such as electricity supply, it made no sense that the contracts of employment for industrial staff assumed Monday to Friday working (except for shift workers) and that all work done outside normal hours rested on voluntary *ad hoc* decisions of the employee and his supervisor. Where the work to be done falls into quite a different pattern then the contract of employment should recognize this. For that reason I regard the stagger work patterns principle which has been built into the Agreement as a major step forward. It is true that, so far, these patterns have been more extensively used on the generation than on the distribution side of the industry, but in the power stations the need was self-evident whereas, in distribution, the full scope for staggered working can only be recognized through lengthy and varied experience. It may be that we shall wish to add to the present patterns of work available so as to meet more precisely the changing needs of the Boards. But the principle is right for this industry and, for that matter, may well have extensive application elsewhere.

The second proposition is that, through the terms of the Joint Statement on Employee Co-operation (the co-operation agreement), we have made a valuable start on the job of making more flexible, and therefore more effective, use of the skills of our employees. Some people take the view that we should have made a list of work practices which could be eliminated and that we should have 'bought' this list in negotiations item by item so that the Boards would know exactly what they were paying for. Looking back on the negotiations I believe that, in the circumstances at the time, we were right to proceed as we did.

The third proposition is that the Agreement has enabled the industry to make a break with a tradition of heavy, regular overtime work. I have already expressed the view that this is often inefficient, and not merely in the narrow sense of men wasting time by working slowly. It has a more corrosive effect than that. If management, because of loosely controlled overtime, are able to look to an open-ended labour supply they may become slovenly in planning their use of labour and careless in its supervision. Slovenliness and carelessness do not stay restricted to one activity in an undertaking; they are weeds that grow and spread rapidly. The electricity supply industry does not compare unfavourably in labour control with other industries, but I am certain that the time had come to face up to the overtime problem. The movement of hours since the Agreement was made shows that it gave the necessary support and provided some of the means necessary to the achievement of this end. We have reached the point for the first time since the thirties at which the axing of a standard working week means more than simply determining the point at which men begin to work at an enhanced rate.

This is not without its social price. The young and vigorous industrial worker may well say 'I have nothing to give in order to increase my income other than my leisure time. In your industry you now deny me this possibility'. There is some truth in this. The justification is that on balance the hard case of the good worker willing frequently or continuously to work a longer day is outweighed by the sum of disadvantages. Some overtime may be necessary but the rules must buttress the authority of the manager who has to say 'no' when overtime is not really necessary.

Fourthly, the Status Agreement has been justified as a big step forward in assimilating the general conditions of industrial staff to those of the rest of the industry's employees. The trade unions representing the clerical, administrative and technical staff did not object to this principle. Indeed they supported it. Nevertheless it would be disingenuous to state that what was done for the industrial staff had no repercussions.

Attitudes to the Agreement

The technical staff argued that, as they were required to supervise the industrial staff, they were greatly affected by the change in conditions of employment of the latter. In the end an agreement was reached with the technical staff trade union which, for an annual payment to every technical employee, 'bought out' the voluntary nature of technical staff overtime. I will not go into the pros and cons of the agreement except to say that it certainly had merits in its own right and the cost cannot therefore all be loaded on to the status scheme from which it stemmed.

In some ways the reaction of the clerical and administrative staff was more significant. They already believed that, in the race for higher pay, they were being outpaced by the technical staff. The co-operation payments to industrial staff caused the clerical and administrative staff, who considered that they had co-operated over the years, to ask with increasing persistence why one group of employees should be paid for what another group had given voluntarily. The employers sought, by certain structural changes and offers, to meet the case as far as they thought they should. But they could not go as far as the unions demanded. In the end, with a serious industrial dispute at hand, the matter was referred by the Government to the NBPI whose recommendations[1] were broadly in line with the employers' own proposals. Since then these proposals have been put into effect with, one hopes, the removal of much of the feeling of resentment.

The three lessons which can be learned from this experience are firstly that, when one group of workers in an undertaking has its lot

[1] Cmnd. 2801.

bettered the others will argue for comparable treatment; secondly, they will still argue this way even when they are doing as well as similar workers are doing elsewhere; and thirdly that when one group is paid for greater flexibility others, who think they have already co-operated to the full, will demand equivalent treatment. Long-standing relativities within an industry are important.

It would not be accurate to say that the Board's negotiators had not realized beforehand that the proposed changes in the status and pay of the industrial staff would have repercussions on the rest of the staff, but they may have underestimated their extent. The lesson is an important one for the future of industrial relations generally and it was not lost on the NBPI. They stated in their report[1] that where greater changes in practice are required for some sections of staff than from others, with considerable accompanying changes in earnings, 'there can be left a sense of disturbance which should be reduced if the harmony of the enterprise is to be restored'.

I have so far said little about the trade unions. The Status Agreement involved radical changes in the working lives of many men and it was inevitable that some employees should have resented them and expressed this resentment against their union officers. But the great majority of these officers, at every level in the industry, met their members, faced their criticisms, and explained to them the long-term benefits which would accrue from this Agreement. Within the negotiating machinery itself they and the Boards' members established a speedy and effective method of dealing with the difficulties which arose from time to time. Without such loyalty to the agreement, and the courage which it often demanded, the industry might not have overcome so readily the early difficulties that it encountered.

As to the industrial staff themselves, it is difficult to form any general opinion of their reactions. As I have said, many who had been used to working long hours of overtime strongly resented the loss of overtime earnings and, in the early stages at least, found the increased leisure a poor compensation. But there is evidence that this resentment is now diminishing and that many employees are coming to terms with the new work arrangements.

Conclusion

My final word is this. Negotiations on the Agreement were begun in 1962 and were completed in stages in 1964 and 1965. It remains true even now that there is no other agreement of this type which has been negotiated and applied for a whole industry. In this sense we were pioneers and like all pioneers we had to learn as we went along. As

[1] Cmnd. 2801.

Stage II of the Agreement, in particular, shows, we learnt a great deal about the importance, as far as practicable, of relating increased payments to improved working practices or patterns. In due course we shall, with the co-operation of the trade unions, doubtless make further advances. We have made a start, but none of us would claim that our labour productivity is yet as good as we are jointly capable of making it.

Acknowledgement

I am extremely grateful to Mr R. D. V. Roberts, Member of the Electricity Council responsible for industrial relations, and to his colleagues in the department for their help in the preparation of this paper.

34. EMPLOYEE DIRECTORS IN STEEL[1]

KEN JONES

Like all other nationalized industries the British Steel Corporation has a statutory duty to develop machinery which will result in employees being involved through their trade union representatives in reaching decisions that affect them. However, the Corporation made it clear, even before it officially came into existence, that it firmly believed that, in addition to fulfilling its obligations under the Iron and Steel Act 1967 to establish consultative and negotiating machinery, additional efforts should be made to develop ways which would ensure effective trade union involvement and employee participation in the management of the industry. For instance, the proposal made by the Corporation to the TUC for employee directors is not a requirement of the Act.

BROADEST SENSE

Early in its deliberations the Organizing Committee of the Corporation faced up to the problem of defining what it considered was meant by participation. Eventually participation was defined as including '. . . being asked to give advice before a decision is taken (i.e. *consultation*) or being a party to a joint management/trade union decision (i.e. *negotiation*) or, in the case of employees serving on Group Boards as part-time Directors, sharing responsibility for a management decision.' Thus from the very beginning participation was envisaged in the broadest sense possible to include consultation and negotiation but in addition intro-

---

[1] From K. Jones, 'From shopfloor to boardroom', *Industrial Society*, October 1970, pages 7–8. Reprinted with permission of the author and the editor of *Industrial Society*.

ducing to a nationalized industry the idea of part-time employee directors.

The second problem was, what grades should be covered by the formal provisions for participation? It was decided that all grades in the industry up to and including the level of Assistant Departmental Head (this meant that only 2,000 in the whole industry of almost 270,000 were to be left out of the arrangements) should be encouraged to belong to representative organizations which in turn should negotiate wages and working conditions with the Corporation. Similarly, employees up to the level of Assistant Departmental Managers should participate in the consultative/advisory committees and also these employees should be represented among the employee directors.

A considerable amount of public attention has been focussed on the proposals made by the British Steel Corporation to increase the participation of its employees in shaping the policies of the industry through becoming part-time directors of the original four Group Boards, now reorganized into six Product Divisions.

It should be explained that these Group Boards were not statutory bodies and all appointments to them were made by the Chairman of the Corporation. The Group Managing Director was directly responsible to the Chairman for the performance of the Group and, following the 'line executive' basis of organization, was the undisputed commander of the Group, advised by the members of his Board. The same basic principles apply in the new divisional structure: managerial authority at divisional level is vested in the Divisional Managing Director, subject only to responsibility to the Chief Executive of the Corporation, who delegates this authority. However, the Divisional Board has a crucial advisory role in the region of management decisions and consists of full-time line and functional directors as well as part-time directors.

The initial proposals regarding the employee-directors were made by the British Steel Corporation to the Trades Union Congress in May 1967. The main points in the proposals were:

- They would be appointed for a period of three years by the Chairman of the Corporation after consultation with the Trades Union Congress.
- That the employee directors should become part-time members of the Group Boards but when they were not functioning as directors they would continue in their normal jobs.
- While functioning as part-time directors they would enjoy the same status and conditions as other part-time directors.
- During the period when they were employee directors they would be expected to resign any trade union offices held.

- They would serve on the Group Boards of Groups other than those in which they worked. (This particular clause was eventually changed after discussions with the Trades Union Congress so that the employee directors in fact served on Group Boards which were responsible for the works in which they were employed.)
- Towards the end of the three year period there would be a joint assessment by the Trades Union Congress and the British Steel Corporation of the value and the experience of the employee director experiment.

The Trades Union Congress and the individual trade unions in the steel industry co-operated fully in the experiment and eventually the TUC received approximately 120 nominations for the twelve employee director posts from the majority of the trade unions who were members of the TUC Steel Committee, which is composed of the nationally recognized unions who are affiliated to the TUC. The TUC then produced for the British Steel Corporation a short list of approximately thirty and the Chairman consulted widely within the corporation before making his selection. The individual unions used a variety of selection procedures but in nearly all cases the individuals were nominated by their branch, which in the steel industry is usually workshop based.

CONSIDERABLE EXPERIENCE

The twelve men were drawn from a wide range of occupational grades: operators, maintenance men, clerical grades, supervisors, technicians and one assistant departmental manager. They were representative of the major trade unions in the industry and were also chosen to give a rough geographical representation among the major works in the British Steel Corporation. The individual characteristics of these twelve men were diverse but they all had one thing in common: they had very considerable experience as part-time trade union officers and over half of them had either been members of the executive councils of their unions or had sat on other national committees of their organizations. In addition many had considerable experience of local community activities; one, for example, had been mayor of a borough and several had been county councillors or town councillors.

It was recognized both by the TUC and the BSC that these men would require some preparation before taking up their duties. Consequently a joint TUC/BSC Training Course was held for a period of five weeks. This was an extremely intensive exercise and the object was to make these experienced men aware of the problems and policies of the British Steel Corporation as a whole, and also to give them an appreciation of general economic problems and the role of the TUC, to make them familiar with certain of the management techniques and procedures with which they would come into contact.

PRELIMINARY ASSESSMENT

After a period of approximately nine months it was felt that there was a need to make some preliminary assessment of the way in which the experiment was developing. The people who could best make this assessment were the employee directors themselves, so arrangements were made for them to hold a week's seminar, at the end of which they produced a document summarizing their feelings about the experiment. The outcome of the seminar was a series of meetings between the employee directors, the Chairman of the Corporation, the Board Member for Personnel and Social Policy, the old Group Managing Directors and the newly designated Divisional Managing Directors.

Eventually it was decided that there was a need to produce a job description. This was done in very close consultation with the employee directors and was also discussed with the Steel Committee of the TUC. This job description makes it clear that the employee directors should be involved in working parties, advisory committees, and other *ad hoc* committees plus formal and informal meetings of functional and line managers as well as attending Divisional Board Meetings. Also, in addition to attending their own trade union meetings, they were, by invitation, to attend the meetings of other trade unions and joint consultation meetings. This new job description formally came into operation with the formation of the new Divisional Boards on 29 March 1970.

At national level over two-thirds of the employee directors are now sitting or have sat on advisory committees or working parties on a wide range of topics and at the Divisional level the employee directors are becoming involved formally and informally in commercial, planning and other functions in addition to the type of activities concerned with the Personnel and Social Policy function in which they were involved prior to the reorganization of the Corporation. Furthermore a number of the trade unions concerned have advised their branches that they should make a point of inviting the employee directors, who might well belong to different trade unions, to attend their branch and other meetings.

At the time of the reorganization it also became necessary to appoint two additional employee directors in the iron and steel sector and to appoint one employee director in each of the Chemicals and Constructional Engineering Divisions. These additional appointments, plus the fact that the role of the employee directors is now more precisely defined, has given rise to the question as to whether or not it is possible to attempt to assess the employee director experiment on what will really be only one year's experience within the new situation. The Corporation and the Steel Committee of the TUC have therefore decided that it would be advisable to continue the experimental period for one additional year.

DIFFERENT VIEWPOINT

It would be quite wrong to attempt to state categorically that the employee director experiment has, or has not, been a success. It is clear that employee directors have made a useful contribution to the discussions held in the first Group and now the Divisional Boards, where they are able to bring a different viewpoint to the problems which are being discussed. This viewpoint is valuable because although these men are not representatives of the employees in the sense that they are not elected by them nor do they formally have to report back to them, it is felt that the employee directors are representative of the feelings, attitudes and opinions of the mass of our labour force.

The Corporation recognized some time ago that it would be difficult for it to assess objectively the effectiveness of this experiment in employee participation in management. Consequently it decided to co-operate with the International Institute of Labour Studies in Geneva in promoting an academic study of the whole employee director experiment. This is being conducted quite independently of the BSC and the TUC by research fellows at four British universities and their only obligation to the BSC and the TUC is to provide a report of their findings.

This report should be invaluable in helping the BSC and the TUC to decide whether or not the employee director experiment should continue in its present or modified form, or whether it should be abandoned in favour of some alternative approach. The Corporation is prepared to look at this experiment with the TUC with a very critical eye to determine how best to further employee participation in the management of the British Steel Corporation.

35. DEMOCRATIC PARTICIPATION AND PUBLIC ENTERPRISE[1]

H. R. G. GREAVES

IV

One view – which seems to accept a technocratic *status quo* – is that the

[1] From H. R. G. Greaves, *Democratic Participation and Public Enterprise*, Hobhouse Memorial Trust Lecture, May 1964, Athlone Press, pages 14–27. Reprinted with permission of the author, the London School of Economics and Political Science and the publishers.

proper way to regard the organization of workers is as a permanent opposition, an opposition that can never be a government. Indeed, industrial democracy is to be given that interpretation. There is need for an opposition in industry, for otherwise it would be autocratic. 'Industrial dictatorship has gradually been modified in the democracies by the growth of the unions, but the fundamental basis of industrial management is still totalitarian in design.'[1] 'We must remember that industrial units are not voluntary associations and autocracy therefore becomes all the more dangerous',[2] the men being in fact tied pretty closely to their jobs. It is this need for an opposition that makes it necessary for the workers' organization to be strong; strength requires unity and justifies the authoritarian discipline which often characterizes trade union organization. 'The defence of the second-grade democracy of the trade unions is, then, that they must present a united front to the employers; that if their internal democracy were more perfect, industry would be less democratic, since its opposition would be too weak.'[3] This view would in fact seem to be the official one of the unions themselves. For their justification of not sharing in the control and direction of public corporations has been the essential need for them to maintain their independence; their right, that is, to be free to oppose.

Another view, however, which corresponds to earlier aspirations, is that the workers need a voice in the control and management of their industry. It is this to which the idea of consultation most nearly corresponds. 'It is fundamental to any plan for the organization of a public service', said the TUC in 1944,[4] 'that the workpeople have the right to a voice in the determination of its policy. . . . The right . . . must, therefore, find a formal place in its organization and operation.' While this claim has been recognized in principle in the nationalization Acts, and in many of the procedures established under them, it has often not been fully honoured in the spirit by management. Often enough, too, 'the Union organization has been insufficiently staffed and specialized to participate with full effect at "higher" levels of consultation'.[5]

The TUC assertion continued: 'There must further be some guarantee that this expression [of the voice of the workpeople in the industry] shall be effective in the formulation of its policy.' But when, to such practical insufficiencies in the unions' contribution, is added their declared policy of maintaining independence of management responsi-

---

[1] B. C. Roberts: *Trade Unions in a Free Society*, 1962, p. 181.
[2] H. A. Clegg: *Industrial Democracy and Nationalization*, 1951, p. 22.
[3] Ibid., page 23.
[4] *T.U.C. Interim Report on Post-War Reconstruction*.
[5] *A Plan for the Mines*, issued by the Derbyshire Area of the National Union of Mineworkers, May 1964, page 23.

bility, the meaning to be attached to giving them an effective voice must remain ambiguous. It is surely significant that they did not define more clearly. Within the scope of this ambiguity – or should one not rather say, ambivalence ? – lies much of the difference between the concepts of consultation and workers' control.

For it is in quite other terms that the older aims of workers' control were put forward. Thus Tawney said that 'they must choose whether to assume the responsibility for industrial discipline and become free or to repudiate it and continue to be serfs'.[1] This means power; they cannot be responsible unless they have it; they cannot be blamed for repudiating it unless they have it or can have it. Besides, the contrast is with the lot of the serf or the unfree. It resembles G. D. H. Cole's assertion[2] that the fundamental evil to abolish is not poverty but slavery, poverty being the symptom, slavery the disease. It is like this rather later statement:

> Any scheme of socialized industry must provide the beginnings of a 'new status' for the workers in that industry. The bondage of servitude must be exchanged for the freedom of citizenship. A mere transfer from private to public ownership . . . is insufficient.
>
> The workers demand power: power to share the government of the industry in which they are engaged. They will accept the responsibilities and obligations imposed by the acquisition of that power. This has been demonstrated in the movements which have been built by the workers, such as their trade unions and labour organizations; their friendly societies; the Co-operative Movement, and the part they have played in international labour organization, and the local and national government.[3]

However, when we look behind this last bald demand for power, put forward as a criticism of official Labour Party and trade union policy, at what seem to be its practical implications, they appear less uncompromising than at first they sound. Indeed, 'power to share the government of the industry' can easily be interpreted to mean much of the same thing as 'having the right to a voice in the determination of its policy.' Thus the difference between the second and third views, consultation and workers' control, seems to have been narrowed, or even to have become more apparent than real in more recent parlance. They both remain, nevertheless, distinct from the first view where labour is regarded as a sectional interest concerned only to press its claims against all, and against the public owner just as against the private.

---

[1] *The Acquisitive Society.*
[2] *Self-Government in Industry*, 1917.
[3] John Cliff: *The Worker's Status in Industry*, 1933.

This aspect of the case can best be cleared away at the start. The negotiating procedures, the collective bargaining, on such matters as wages and hours, are of course one way in which the workers make their voice heard, in which they influence important decisions affecting the running of their industry. They represent one element, and one not to be discounted, in industrial self-government. But labour treated as a permanent opposition is not to be confused with labour as a responsible participant in the exercise of authority. And it is with joint consultation as a means of implementing this that we are here concerned.

We have now perhaps had enough experience of this to consider whether it does in fact mean giving the workpeople in an industry any real voice in its management. There are bodies dealing with it at national, divisional and works level. It is a general instruction of the nationalization Acts that they shall be set up: every worker is entitled to be represented on them. Much has been written upon what seems to have become an established part of the administrative system of the public sector. There are reports from the industries themselves and accounts and criticisms by participants and outside commentators. Out of all this it should now be possible to draw some tentative conclusions.

There is no evidence that, given the actual organization of nationalized industry, more than a minority of the workers in it are in fact straining at the leash to enter into all the problems of management, to develop their own policy for it in an objective way and in the national interest.[1] Official trade union policy has been on the contrary to eschew such responsibility in order to retain full freedom to pursue their traditional function of fighting for their members' interests. To explain the trade unions' unwillingness to accept the responsibility which is the corollary of their greater power is not, however, to justify it. But it must be added that their behaviour often reveals a sense of responsibility of a negative kind, of preventing complete breakdown. Anyway, the State seems to have endorsed their attitude. And on the basis of this fact we must admit that, not having been given responsibility, the workers can scarcely be blamed for failing to exercise it. The question has hardly been allowed to arise. Nor have experiments in the sharing of management in the private sector, of which the well-known Glacier Metal case is an example,[2] justified the proposition that the great majority of those engaged in an industry seek to devote their energies to thought about direction and management: they are content to leave such matters to others. There should be nothing, let it be repeated, surprising in such a

---

[1] Cf. W. A. Robson: *Nationalized Industry and Public Ownership*, 1960, page 357.

[2] Cf. Elliott Jaques: *The Changing Culture of a Factory*, 1951; J. A. Mack, *Political Quarterly*, vol. 27, No. 3.

discovery: how many citizens in a modern democracy have the same attitude to the complex, and some even of the simpler, problems of its government and administration? Anyone is mistaken, then, who believed in a general desire by the workers to run their industry, or who based the demand for workers' control on the desire of most workers to charge themselves with the responsibilities of management.

So the evidence can hardly be said to support the assumption of the syndicalist or guild socialist that the workers in an industry had in general – without preparation, education or training – either the wish or the inborn ability to manage it themselves. The naive belief must be modified. Where they have been brought into consultation the pattern of their behaviour has shown some uniformity. Initially, and as might be expected, their main interest has been in their own immediate conditions of work. It has extended from this – which belongs to the sphere of negotiation rather than consultation – into matters of welfare, amenities and so on. Only thereafter has it reached out to problems of policy, such as the efficiency and improvement of production, marketing, etc. But it surely is significant that in many cases it has in fact done so. Indeed, one can discern a pattern of growth from the narrower concern with matters of their immediate needs, through a more generalized interest in welfare, up to a real sharing in responsibility for providing a satisfactory service. This last has not been an easy or automatic growth, but it is impossible to examine the record without concluding that there has been a gradual education in this direction – however uneven as between one industry and another – of being aware of a sharing in responsibility, and even of taking pride in the rendering of a national service. Questions of efficiency and even of general industrial policy, from being at first excluded, have begun to come on to the agenda.

It is difficult to give a generalized view of the subjects brought before the Consultative Committee for consideration without grossly over-simplifying the position. It would, however, be true to say that questions of welfare, safety, amenities, education and training have loomed very large on the agenda of most committees and that questions of efficiency and productivity have occupied a much less prominent place. Yet in studying the annual reports of the public corporations one gets the impression that increasing attention is being paid by the advisory councils to matters of technical or administrative efficiency.[1]

While this development has been a general one, it has varied markedly from one industry to another. Two factors seem to have most influenced it. One would be tempted to say that where the previous relations

[1] W. A. Robson, op. cit., page 350.

between owners and men were bad, and nationalization had more lee-way to make up, the development had been slower. This has been said, and there is truth in it. But the coal industry, which had one of the worst records before, has had one of the best in recent years. The terms of reference given by the National Coal Board to the National, and to Colliery, Consultative Committees have included such questions as use of manpower and equipment, development projects, training and education, use of foreign labour.[1] On the other hand, the railways, which also had a poor record, have not improved nearly as much. The second factor is the success of the industry itself. The sense of being in a declining sector of the economy is not conducive to the taking of responsibility, or to pride in participating in it. Obviously it is harder to be proud of British Railways than of the electricity service. (Whether it need have been is another matter beyond the scope of the railwaymen, and of this paper.) In this latter case, of electricity, there has been a remarkable change of emphasis from 'fringe interests and activities to the main problems affecting the industry's efficiency'.[2] And it offers one of the most successful examples of workers' participation.

V

But certain fundamental weaknesses underlie the system and make it fall short of effective participation. For these weaknesses the blame belongs to the trade unions and to the State.

The trade union policy of avoiding contamination by management-responsibility has gravely weakened the impetus to workers' participation. It has deeply affected the whole administrative set-up of public enterprise. Two consequences may be specially noticed. One is the tendency to cut them off from the channels, whether called joint consultation or anything else, through which workers are or might be represented in the flow of management and policy decision. Perhaps it is better, as Cole thought, that the two functions of negotiation with management and representation in it should be separately organized, that all employed in the workshop should be the basic unit for any pur-poses connected with self-government. But there is also much to be said for the contrary view that workers' representation should not be thus complicated and confused. Persons thinking so are apt to point to Yugoslavia.[3] A second consequence has been a certain betrayal of the

[1] But see the interesting comments on shortcomings in the Derbyshire Area of the N.U.M. pamphlet already cited.

[2] See R. D. V. Roberts and H. Sallis: 'Joint Consultation in the Electricity Supply Industry 1949–59', *Public Administration*, vol. 37.

[3] Cf. F. Singleton and A. Topham: *Workers' Control in Yugoslavia*, 1963.

moral case which, as we have seen, lay at the centre of the claim for democratic participation in industrial government. It has meant that the psychological importance has been too much lost sight of, both of the recognition of human dignity and of the conferring of social significance upon work, which is given by sharing in its direction and control, a sharing which requires representation and accountability. This psychological importance is not lessened even where the work involved is monotonous or mechanical.[1]

There are also relevant defects in trade union organization. Such are the low pay of officials and the unsatisfactoriness of their career except as an avenue to management. From this culmination of promotion trade union policy cuts them off; or rather, it ensures that the best men, when promoted, are thus lost to the movement and aloof from any process that can be called participation. Again, other charges can be brought. The trade unions have not been nearly aware enough of the need for research and training. They have often been rightly criticized for their unadaptability to technical advance, for clinging to restrictive practices, for failure to face the problems of redundancy. Apathy on the part of the members has been often matched by the unrepresentativeness of officials and their remoteness from the body of trade unionists. The problem here of course is partly one of size; and the remedy may at least partly lie in concentrating effort more on organization at workshop level. The failures, we can suspect, may have much to do with the restricting effects of the trade union policy of unconcern or irresponsibility in relation to the problems of policy facing the management of their industry. They seem as unlikely to be remedied as the divorce of authority from the mass, of management from workpeople, of 'we' from 'they' until some sense of self-government is achieved.

If these weaknesses, so far as democratic participation is concerned, must be recorded as a criticism of the history of public enterprise, nevertheless, as an acute American observer has said:

> Nationalization has unquestionably been a powerful instrument for 'modernizing' labour relations in the affected industries. The amount of attention now being paid to the training of new recruits, to providing opportunities for higher education, to systematic promotion policies, to job evaluation and work study, to the improvement of methods of wage payment, to personnel records and to personnel research – the attention that management is giving to these subjects is immeasurably greater than it was before nationalization . . . the nationalized industries, which once included some of the most back-

---

[1] I agree with Denis Butt: 'Workers' Control', *New Left Review*, July, 1961, page 33.

ward on this score, must now be counted as among the most advanced. Where labour relations only recently exercised a residual claim on management's attention and energies . . . today it constitutes an 'overhead' claim that is constant, specialized, and formalized.[1]

Although there has been such direct improvement, it has not been consistent. If the generality of workers do not feel that they have a voice in the control or a share in responsibility, and this has something to do with the defects of trade union policy, it also has much to do with the manner in which the State has failed to organize the administrative system in this public sector. By comparison with that other, much longer established, branch of the public service, the Civil Service, there has been nothing like the attention paid to the problems raised. For much more than half of the last century or so there has been public inquiry directed into one part or another of Civil Service organization. Royal Commissions, Parliamentary, Treasury, Departmental and other committees have been in almost constant session. The Treasury has kept a continuous vigilance. The Whitley System has been in operation for close on half a century. Not much of the lessons of all this has been considered relevant to these newer problems. Nor has the need for official thought upon them been recognized. It seems to have been regarded as enough to lay down general requirements – for negotiation with the unions and for joint consultation – and to provide simply that the governing bodies should be appointed by the Crown instead of shareholders. Merely to reproduce the pre-nationalization order with these variations, and then sit back hopefully expecting the growth of a truly public service, informed throughout by a spirit of responsible participation, is surely improvident and over-sanguine.

VI

We need to ask what are the conditions for the development of a public service. Some essential ones can be suggested. The first is that its members shall be conscious of it as a *service*, with a character and structure of its own – as in some sense the profession of Tawney's ideal. Here the parallel of the civil service is not irrelevant. Nor is it an accident that the aim of developing this into a profession, with its own standards, pride and self-respect, and its own institutions of self-government, coincided with its unification and its conversion into a career service in the late nineteenth century. When any public economic service can be seen in the same light, with its top posts as the possible climax of a career in it, when all its posts are part of a structure integrated by

---

[1] G. R. Baldwin: 'Nationalisation in Britain: a Sobering Decade', *Annals of Political Science*, 310, 1957, page 45.

309

principles that are accepted because they are just, give fair opportunity to all, are objectively worked out and publicly proclaimed, then and only then can it be expected to develop the sense of being a profession. As long as it continues to be divided along the present lines, which do not belong to the pattern of service at all, but to that of owners or directors on the one hand and their servants on the other, the idea must necessarily be denied of that co-operative participation which is characteristic of a profession. It must also mean that a psychology different from that prevailing in private industry is unlikely to emerge.

The second essential condition to a public economic service is that those engaged in it shall be able to see it as *their* service. The problem here is one of how 'to democratize industry by finding ways and means of allowing ordinary workers to exercise a more creative role than they occupy as lever pullers and button pushers . . . one of raising the dignity of man in his capacity as an industrial worker'.[1] For it to be *their* service the members of it must have, within a federal structure, a voice in its concerns. This democratic participation, whether it be called joint consultation, having an effective voice in policy, or even workers' control, must mean that all shall have the opportunity to contribute an informed judgement, and shall see activity directed to conform with it. This does not imply the impossible result that everyone's view shall prevail, nor even decision by the counting of heads, expert and skilled along with unskilled. Dignity is not so much lessened by defeat in reasoned argument as by being disregarded. Contributing informed judgement does carry with it, however, the immediate implication that information shall be fully available, and available before decisions are taken, that all the cards shall be on the table. It also carries the longer-term implication of the widest opportunity for education and training in the ability to understand and use such information, a course to which help should come from the university and the technical and staff-training college.

That the service shall be consciously a *public* service is the third essential condition of its success. We are concerned not merely with self-government in nationalized industry. Democratic participation and public enterprise is both wider and more forward-looking. Enterprise means what it says. In the private sector we rely, or are supposed to rely, on the profit motive to supply it. What are the substitutes in the public sector? Professional pride and vocational responsibility are only part of the answer. Each needs, too, to have the power creatively to develop its own service in accordance with a national plan in which it effectively shares; and at this level there is at present a striking lack of

[1] B. C. Roberts, op. cit., page 179.

provision for its effective and public contribution. To be effective it must be represented as of right at the top level where some attempt is made to bring order and co-ordination into national policy on investment, productivity, wages, prices, etc. For its contribution to be public it must be able to speak publicly for itself, and we must put an end to the false belief that all this pertains to some illusory apolitical business-world and not to the polis. The attempt to insulate the board from politics has removed the pride of status, surely itself conducive to enterprise and responsibility. It has greatly weakened the capacity of every such public enterprise to speak for itself, to contribute to the making of national economic policy, and to put across its image to the public with authority. Each one needs powerful and forceful spokesmen denied it by this hypercautious system. And making the public aware also requires much more attention to publicity and public relations than has so far been given.[1] They should be brought into the picture of problems, achievements, plans. How many of us are even aware of what we owe as citizens, let alone of what is being done with it on our behalf – for example, the considerable research successes in the coal industry ?

Democratic participation has to do with the outside, as well as the inside, of the service, with the social whole as well as the industrial, fraction. Here its classic articulation is through elections, party, Parliament and ministerial responsibility – through the nationalized industries' subjection to ministerial directives and supervision – through their annual reports to Parliament, and the activities of the standing Select Committee on Nationalized Industries upon them.

To these must be added the attempt to find a specific public served, by way of consumers', and consultative advisory, councils. But this last endeavour surely leaves much to be desired. It must be doubted whether a vertical division of the public into consumers of coal, gas, electricity, rail services and so on can ever succeed in contributing enough to solving the problem, which is one of finding a real public, a real community unit in some degree conscious of itself as such. For what is needed is to foster public consciousness of ownership, and the public service consciousness of serving an identifiable public. This means not the separation of the several services but their co-ordination – in terms at least of relations with the public. Those relations are of course two-way relations – explanation of policy to the public is one direction, obtaining an expression of the needs of the public and their criciticism of service is the other. When an area public is seen as the joint consumer and producer of fuel, electricity, gas, rail and road transport, postal, health, local authority services, and such central government services as

---

[1] Cf. M. Shanks, (ed.) *The Lessons of Public Enterprise*, 1963, p. 210.

town and country planning, public enterprise may more readily enter into the consciousness of a community that co-operates in conducting its own services. But this calls for regional institutions, and carries us into the vexed question of local government areas which it is impossible to pursue here. It may be doubted, however, whether until it is answered we shall be able to avoid that kind of madness whereby an overspill town is planted and factories and houses built by one authority, power supplied by another, its rail services removed by a third, no alternative road transport provided by a fourth, and no road improvements made by a fifth.

To conclude, then, the concept of self-government in relation to nationalized industry does not connote absolute, arbitrary and exclusive authority to a junta of workers to impose their will by force. There are important elements of it already present in the nationalization Acts and in the procedures for joint consultation developed under them; and some signs are visible of the men becoming educated into responsible participation, and management learning to recognize the desirability of this; both need much strengthening. Having an effective voice in decision means the provision of regular opportunity for informed judgement to be brought to bear, with all that this implies. Shortcomings lie both in the weakness and remoteness of trade union organization and in failures on the part of the State. The State has not treated seriously enough the administration and staffing structure of this branch of the public service, over its whole range from the members of its boards downwards. And much needs to be done in central and regional government to relate more closely both the larger community served and the smaller community performing the service, to what is, after all, a joint enterprise, a co-operative undertaking. Nor has sufficient attention been paid to the difference between the negative implications of a policy of nationalizing industry and the positive requirements of a policy of developing public enterprise. The words of the French Commissaire Général du Plan are relevant here: 'Rationality and democracy are linked. For the first without the second would be powerless to create the required ardent adhesion to the goals of the Plan. And the second without the first would deprive the expansion of the economomy of its full fruits.'[1]

36. CONSUMER CONSULTATION[2]

Having studied in some detail the consultative machinery in the four

---

[1] Preface to J. and A.-M. Hackett, *Ecconomic Planning in France*, 1963.

[2] From Consumer Council, *Consumer Consultative Machinery in the Nationalized Industries*, HMSO, 1968, pages 59–64. Reprinted with permission of the Controller of Her Majesty's Stationery Office.

industries of electricity, gas, solid fuel and transport, and advanced in the course of the text a number of suggestions as to how we think its effectiveness might perhaps be enhanced, it now remains to look at the machinery as a whole in more fundamental terms and to attempt to distill from the more detailed descriptions and analyses of previous chapters the salient principles which govern both its purposes and its system of operation.

THE NATURE OF THE CONSUMER CONSULTATIVE ROLE

The purpose underlying the setting up of the consultative machinery in these four industries – as it was stated at the outset and has been developed in the course of the study – is essentially a simple one. In its basic terms, it is to meet the need of the consumers concerned for a means of bringing their influence to bear upon the industries and also, if necessary, of securing redress against them. That there should exist this need of the consumers, however, derives, in turn, from the existence of limitations on their freedom of choice – the consumer's most compelling sanction against a supplier. For them, this freedom is all but unavailable, or at most only partially available. And this for three reasons – one of them associated with the consumers themselves, one with the nature of the products or services and one with the position of the suppliers.

There is, first of all, little freedom of choice for these consumers between whether to buy or not to buy, because the products and services in question – electricity, gas, coal and transport – have become virtual necessities in the modern world. Secondly, choice between one product or service and another is restricted by the fact that they are mostly only partial substitutes or substitutes only over a period of time. And, thirdly, choice between one supplier and another for most of the particular products or services was eliminated when the industries themselves became nationalized, leaving the state as the only supplier. Thus, each of the industries is in a position in relation to its consumers that is to a greater or lesser degree 'monopolistic', depending on the extent and 'mix' of its threefold insulation from the competitive forces of the market. It was to arm these consumers with a countervailing sanction with which to oppose an undue exercise of such monopolistic – or imperfectly competitive – power against them that the consultative machinery was originally devised. Its value to the consumer, therefore, must hinge on the degree to which in each industry there is such a monopolistic position (in the threefold sense of above) to be met and, in so far as there is, its effectiveness in meeting it.

So far as the supply position is concerned, the three nationalized fuel industries have each a complete or nearly complete monopoly over the generation or production of their own particular fuels. (The electricity industry has to compete with a certain amount of generation by private plants and the coal industry with gas coke and manufactured solid fuels.) But, whereas the electricity and the gas industries also have monopolies over the distribution of their respective fuels to the consumer, the distribution of solid fuels is almost wholly in the hands of private merchants in competition with one another. Furthermore, the retailing of electricity and gas appliances and equipment is to a large extent undertaken by the electricity and gas industries themselves through their local boards, though against growing competition from private retailers. Of the three fuels, electricity now has a virtual monopoly so far as use for lighting is concerned; on the other hand, for heating purposes, there is strong competition between electricity and gas and, to a lesser, and decreasing, extent, coal. But the competition for heating purposes is effective, so far as the individual consumer is concerned, only at the time of installation or purchase, since a heating system or an appliance is not likely to be changed, once it has been installed or purchased, until some years, probably many years, have elapsed. By contrast, public transport is, as we have seen, in a rather different position. For, apart from the several separately provided forms of public transport, each competing with the other and no one of them, except the railways, a monopoly in its own field, there is strong – and growing – competition from private road and also air transport. But what is more important, however, is that the various forms of transport are much more readily substitutable one for the other than are different systems of heating. A journey is usually at most a matter of hours and not, like a heating system, a commitment for years. Consumer decisions have therefore to be taken much more frequently, giving consumers that much more scope for exercising their sanction of choice.

It becomes evident, therefore, that the electricity and gas industries are, overall, each in strongly monopolistic positions in relation to their consumers, notwithstanding the keen competition between them; that the solid fuel industry is less so; and that public transport is becoming increasingly competitive as between its various forms and with private transport (though this may soon be qualified in some degree by new developments in the field of co-ordination). On this assessment, there would seem to be a more clearly delineated and needful task to be performed by the electricity and gas consultative organizations than by those in the solid fuel and, still more so, in the transport industries. This no doubt goes far to account for the more elaborate and more active machinery to be found in the two former industries, as also (apart from the special matter of railway closures) for what appears to be the insufficient use, and the much curtailed role, of the transport users' consultative committees since 1962.

If, however, the purpose of the consultative machinery is to provide the consumers, in default of the option of being able to withhold or transfer their custom, with a substitute means of influencing the operation of monopolistic power, how does the machinery enable this consumer influence to be exerted? Although the answer to this question will have emerged piecemeal and by implication from the more detailed approaches of earlier chapters, it is desirable to develop it explicitly here in more general terms.

THREE SIGNIFICANT FEATURES OF CONSULTATIVE ORGANIZATION

There are, we suggest, three features of the machinery we have been studying which are of especial significance for its effective use on the consumers' behalf. One of these is the degree to which the consultative bodies are representative of cross-sections of relevant and informed consumer opinion, thus enabling them each to speak with a collective voice, whether about matters arising out of individual complaints or in connection with more general matters, and be equipped to enter responsibly into consultation with the appropriate decision making authorities. A second is the extent to which the bodies are organized at levels which correspond to those of the decision-making authorities with whose policies and practices they are most directly concerned, so that consultation with such authorities can be on a basis of relative equality. The third concerns the right of the consultative bodies to pursue the consumers' case, in default of response to representations at their own level, by means of representations to *higher* level decision-making authorities (e.g. the Minister), thus invoking the sanction that, in effect, lies in reserve behind all of their efforts on the consumers' behalf.

It is these three features of organization which seem to us to be the key factors in determining the scope for effective action by the consultative machinery. How the four separate structures of that machinery fare in these three respects – which must to a large degree categorize their usefulness to their consumers – will have emerged in the course of the previous three chapters and not need to be dwelt upon here. Notably, however, in regard to the second of them, the electricity and gas consultative councils would seem to be in the best position, being organized on the same decentralized basis, and at the same level, as their respective area boards, even though, as we have seen, there seems to be something of a consultative vacuum at the national level in both industries. By contrast, the local transport users' committees bear no relation, at least in their boundaries, to the regional railway boards, although the Central Committee, being a national body, is at the same level as the four national boards with which it deals.

Quite apart, however, from the existing position of the consultative bodies in regard to these three features of organization, there are two general questions, stemming from the second and third of the features, that need to be raised. One of these is whether the hierarchical patterns of the consultative structures are now losing some of their former correspondence to the decision-making patterns of their industries, as these latter change, and need, in consequence, to be made more adaptable so as to respond to such changes. The other is whether there are any further, largely untapped, reserves of 'higher' reference to which the consultative bodies can – and should – turn, if the need arises, to uphold the interests of the consumers they represent. These are both questions which seem to us to have important bearings on the future development and effectiveness of the consultative machinery and need to be looked at, if only briefly, at this final stage of the present study.

RESPONSIVENESS OF THE CONSULTATIVE MACHINERY TO CHANGE

In raising the first of these questions, relating to the responsiveness of the whole machinery to change, we are doing so rather in order to open it up to future discussion than to attempt ourselves to provide answers, at least other than those we have been led to suggest in earlier chapters. For it is a question that, in our view, now needs to be discussed and in the most comprehensive and authoritative way.

Except to a limited – and not very helpful – extent in the case of the transport committees, the consultative arrangements in the four industries concerned have remained virtually unchanged for twenty years. Yet these twenty years have been years of substantial and far-reaching change – in the scale and pattern of consumer demand, in technological development in the industries themselves and in the financial and other policies of successive governments. And the prospects ahead is of still more change. If the coming of nuclear power and the discoveries of natural gas are likely to prove the most dramatic and transformative in impact of the new developments, they are not the only ones that will leave their mark. Less dramatic but little, if at all, less transformative are the new management techniques and systems of control that the nationalized industries, like other large industries striving for greater efficiency and productivity, are going to need to introduce to an ever-increasing extent. Perhaps, too, the present, or future, governments will turn to different financing concepts for these industries, shifting – it may be either way – the balance of the cost burden as between consumers and taxpayers or between current consumers. And, moreover, the prospect of changes is likely to be a continuing one and not limited to the next five or ten years. For the very character of the now emerging milieu of cumulative innovation is such as must be inseparable from a tempo of change which is more likely to increase than to slow down.

Inevitably, this has led, and is leading to, a re-patterning in the various industries of their centres and levels of decision-making – including some of the decision-making which most directly affects the interests of their consumers. It is because of this that we consider it timely to raise the question as to whether the consultative machinery in these industries is not now to some extent being passed by, leaving it in danger of becoming less and less geared to bring pressure to bear on the consumers' behalf where it is needed most. Quite apart from certain aspects of this problem that have been drawn attention to earlier (e.g. the lack of adequate *national* consultative facilities in the electricity and gas industries), it seems not unlikely that, if a thoroughgoing official review of the machinery in the light of changes that have taken, and are taking place in the structures of the industries concerned were to be undertaken, it would disclose a need for some substantial organizational adaptations.

As the machinery exists and functions by statute, any such adaptations, if to be made, would, of course, require further legislation. In this event, we suggest that, having regard to the now more fluid and faster-changing environment in which the machinery must work, any new enactments which merely provided for such adaptations as were shown to be necessary would not be enough, since this would only serve to 'freeze' the machinery in a new form and thus lead to the whole problem coming up against later. What, additionally, it seems to us such enactments must provide is for a degree of *self*-adaptation, not present in the existing structures, to be built into the revised machinery. This way, the purely machinery would acquire a measure of organizational, as well as operational, autonomy, which, we suggest, it is now time for it to acquire, if it is to function to full effect in circumstances so very different from those obtaining when it was first set up. Though it would be inappropriate to attempt to pursue this suggestion further here, we have raised it as a principle of approach which we consider ought to enter into any review that may be undertaken of the existing legislation governing the consultative machinery.

TWO WAYS TO GREATER CONSUMER INFLUENCE

The second of the general questions which we have to raise concerns the right of the consultative bodies to represent the consumers' case to higher authority. As this right is a key component in the bargaining armoury of these bodies, it is important that, should the need arise, it should be made use of to the full.

The various representational procedures statutorily open to the consultative bodies in the four industries have already been described and discussed and a number of suggestions made as to how we think that some of the existing arrangements might perhaps be improved. As laid down, however, the highest level to which these bodies can formally take their representations is to the Minister of Power (or to the Secretary of State for Scotland) in the case of the fuel industries and to the Minister of Transport in the case of the transport industry. If, therefore, support is withheld at this level, then there remains no further official move open to them, should they still consider they have any case to pursue.

Quite apart, however, from our suggestion in chapter three that there was need for an independent tribunal to which complaints requiring reference beyond the minister concerned might be taken for final settlement, there are, we suggest, two further *informal* ways in which the consultative bodies could – and, if need be, should – exercise pressure on behalf of their consumers, when more formal procedures no longer avail. One of these is by winning the support of public opinion through publicity specifically directed to this end; the other, by winning the support of members of parliament.

Through the Support of Public Opinion
It does seem to us that the consultative bodies generally do not seem fully to recognize how potent an instrument they have available to them for winning public support, when they have a case of substance to fight, in the form of appropriate publicity. In this present age of mass communications, publicity is peculiarly adapted to press for what, in effect, is the essentially mass character of at least the major consumer requirements. It is true that certain chairmen of consultative councils have appeared on television to protest against increases in electricity or gas charges and others have been reported in the press after making speeches criticizing the financial conditions under which their industries have to operate. By and large, however, the kind of publicity which the councils and committees normally seek is, as we have already seen, primarily descriptive in character, dealing with what they can do and what they are doing to serve the consumer, so that they themselves may become better known and thus be able to provide better service. Only rarely, so far as we have been able to discover, do they use publicity that is overtly persuasive with the object of harnessing public support to a

specific or general consumer interest. As a result, the image of themselves that they tend to put over is one that is largely judicial and only occasionally partisan. And there is, of course, good reason for this. A great deal, perhaps in volume the bulk, of their work does involve a judicial attitude in dealing with complaints and in balancing the arguments as between consumers and boards. Moreover, in pursuing matters of policy with the boards, it is quite natural for the consultative bodies to wish to do what can be done in a climate of co-operation, assisted by a mutuality of confidence, rather than by resorting to a mobilization of outside pressures. Generally, too, it is likely to be the more rewarding way.

From time to time, however, problems do arise which call for a recourse to more combative and publicly proclaimed pressures than can be brought to bear in private around a conference table. Quite often, these are problems in connection with which the boards themselves have relatively little scope for the exercise of independent discretion, being themselves circumscribed by other pressures from outside. Demands for increased wages, financial obligations to be met, increased prices for essential supplies or equipment – these and other such externally imposed conditions necessarily have the effect of narrowing a board's room for manoeuvre. This is often evidently the case with the electricity and gas area boards, when they have to raise their tariffs. They would no doubt prefer not to raise them, but find that they have little option open to them. In this sense, they are, in effect, 'on the same side' as their consultative councils. It would seem, therefore, that it is more often – though by no means always – when boards are *unable*, rather than unwilling, to meet the consumers' case that the consultative bodies have need of some further recourse, over and above their formal right of approach to higher authority, if they are to become more effectively combative on the consumers' behalf. And they may also need one when they feel they have good grounds for opposing, or seeking a modification of, government policies which they judge to be inimical to their consumers. The harnessing of public support by means of publicity is just such a recourse and one which, we consider, the consultative bodies should not hesitate to resort to when, in their view, they have a case of sufficient merit to pursue. For them to do this would, we believe, not only give greater weight to the representations they make to higher authority but would add greatly to their public reputation and to their meaningfulness to consumers in general.

Through Support in Parliament
The other informal way open to consultative bodies for increasing the consumer pressure which they can bring to bear, when they feel it to be called for, is through efforts to win support among members of

parliament. Effective publicity, leading to the support of public opinion, will certainly help in this; but it is only through close and co-operative contact with members of parliament, and, when necessary, through the active canvassing of their help, that this support is likely to be won. Moreover, as consumer interests are apt to be specific (e.g., fuel, transport, etc.) rather than general, members of parliament supporting a particular case need the backing of adequate and authoritative briefings. And it is here that the consultative bodies are uniquely equipped to help with cases affecting their own consumers.

The main initiative for gaining consumer support in this quarter must, so far as the nationalized industries are concerned, come from the consultative bodies themselves. By building up better liaison with members of parliament and providing them with authoritative briefings when required, by more publicity for representations made on important matters and by the development of collective attitudes on national issues affecting their consumers, these bodies can themselves do much towards winning support in parliament, when the occasion for doing so arises. And the fact that they were prepared to do so, and were known to be prepared to do so, would, we suggest, have the effect of enhancing their influence with the government, with their industry and with the consuming public.

THE STATUTORY FRAMEWORK

To implement many, if not most, of the suggestions we have put forward in the course of this study must involve changes of one sort or another in the statutory provisions governing the organization and functioning of the consultative machinery in the four industries. Since, however, the provisions have for the most part remained substantially, and in the case of gas and coal completely, unchanged over twenty years, it seems to us that the time is now ripe for a comprehensive official review of the machinery to be carried out, leading to a revision of the framework in the light of present and foreseeable future conditions.

Should this be done, there are two general respects in which the framework needs, in our view, most to be changed. One of these is in the direction of greater independence of organization and action for the consultative bodies than some of them appear to have under present arrangements, especially in connection with matters of national policy. (That some of the more progressive bodies, notably in the electricity and gas industries, appear in fact to have developed their functioning beyond what a literal interpretation of the statutes would indicate is in itself a sign of healthy growth, yet one that calls, none the less, for the statutes to be revised to suit the changed conditions of today.) The other, which we have discussed earlier in this chapter, is in the direction of greater self-adaptability for the machinery in each industry, so that it may itself adapt to changing requirements, without need for the laborious and, in the nature of things, infrequent remedy of new legislation.

THE CONSULTATIVE MACHINERY AS A FACTOR IN PRODUCTIVITY

As a concluding point, we think it important to refer, very briefly, to an aspect of the consultative machinery that is apt to be overlooked, yet one without which the overall picture cannot be complete. This is its significance for the national economy in the connection of being a contributory factor making for increased productivity in the industries in which it operates.

So far, we have been looking at the machinery solely in terms of its service to consumers, since this was our principal purpose in undertaking the study. In the present chapter, however, we have come to see it, distilled to its essentials, as a means for providing a countervailing mobilization of consumer influence with which to confront the exercise of monopolistic or near-monopolistic power by the boards of the nationalized industries concerned: as in effect, the counterpart, in sustaining the consumers' influence under monopolistic conditions, of the consumers' freedom of choice in the market, in doing the same thing under competitive conditions. To the extent that the machinery can succeed in doing this, it not only serves the consumers themselves but, by the fact of 'strengthening' them in relation to the industries in question, creates a situation which tends to leave the industries with little option, but to make themselves more productive. Pressed, as these nationalized industries are, by demands, on the one hand, from their workers for increases in wages and, on the other, by the Government for a minimum return on investment, they can meet these two sets of demands, each apt to be unyielding, only either at the expense of the consumers or by becoming more productive. So long as the consumers themselves are 'weak', then to make them pay in one way or another, whether by higher charges or poorer service, is generally the easier way out. If, however, through the mediation of consultative machinery, the consumers can acquire some of the 'strength' enjoyed by consumers in a competitive market, then the only recourse remaining to the industries is that of greater efficiency and greater productivity.

It can be seen, therefore, that the consultative machinery in the industries we have been examining – and indeed, for the same reasons, appropriate variants of the machinery, if they were to be devised and set up, in other monopolistic or near-monopolistic industries, whether public or private – has an important part to play in helping the consumers to exercise a *positive* influence upon these industries in the direction of greater productivity. And, in doing this, it must serve also to underline the fact that these consumers, being integral elements of economic processes, are not just passive recipients of the goods produced or services provided, needing only to be protected or given redress, but, like consumers making their choices in a competitive market, active participants in shaping the future of their industries, with all the attendant responsibilities that this entails.

INDEX

Major references are in bold type